Foundations of Social Inequality

FUNDAMENTAL ISSUES IN ARCHAEOLOGY

FOUNDATIONS OF SOCIAL INEQUALITY
Edited by T. Douglas Price and Gary M. Feinman

Foundations of Social Inequality

Edited by

T. DOUGLAS PRICE
AND
GARY M. FEINMAN

*University of Wisconsin–Madison
Madison, Wisconsin*

PLENUM PRESS • NEW YORK AND LONDON

Library of Congress Cataloging-in-Publication Data

On file

ISBN 0-306-44979-X

© 1995 Plenum Press, New York
A Division of Plenum Publishing Corporation
233 Spring Street, New York, N. Y. 10013

10 9 8 7 6 5 4 3 2 1

Printed in the United States of America

To Leslie J. Price, Theron D. Price,
Ester Buchholz, and Stephen E. Feinman,
for the many years of love, support, and care

Contributors

Kenneth M. Ames • Department of Anthropology, Portland State University, Portland, Oregon 97207

Jeanne E. Arnold • Department of Anthropology and Institute of Archaeology, University of California, Los Angeles, California 90024-1510

Richard E. Blanton • Department of Sociology and Anthropology, Purdue University, West Lafayette, Indiana 47907

Robert D. Drennan • Department of Anthropology, University of Pittsburgh, Pittsburgh, Pennsylvania 15260

Gary M. Feinman • Department of Anthropology, University of Wisconsin–Madison, Madison, Wisconsin 53706-1393

Antonio Gilman • Department of Anthropology, California State University, Northridge, California 91330-8244

Brian Hayden • Department of Archaeology, Simon Fraser University, Burnaby, British Columbia, Canada V5A 1S6

Stephen Plog • Department of Anthropology, University of Virginia, Charlottesville, Virginia 22903

T. Douglas Price • Department of Anthropology, University of Wisconsin–Madison, Madison, Wisconsin 53706-1393

Dale W. Quattrin • Department of Anthropology, University of Pittsburgh, Pittsburgh, Pennsylvania 15260

Preface to the Series

The concept for this publication series on critical issues in archaeological thought and research originates in a growing awareness and concern that archaeology must actively pursue the development of theories of human society. Our discipline has for years begged and borrowed from many fields a variety of useful and appropriate ideas and theories concerning the social, political, economic, and ideological aspects of human society. Much of the theory for our archaeological perspectives has come directly from social and cultural anthropology and its foundation in ethnography. The description of the enormous variety of human society from all parts of the world and comparison of commonalities and contrasts in the first three-quarters of this century fostered an explosion of questions and answers in ethnology about the variability and nature of human society. However, the age of discovery and exploration of the surface of the earth is coming to an end. To a large degree, cultural anthropology is turning to other areas of human behavior. Ethnography, especially among nonindustrialized peoples, is much less a focus than in previous decades.

On the other hand, archaeological information is growing rapidly, and our questions need to be informed by a larger body of theory on the operation of past and present human societies. As illustrated in this volume, all sources for ideas are legitimate. Theory can be woven together and constructed from diverse domains in the social and historical sciences as well as generated directly by archaeologists. In fact, archaeology is becoming a wellspring of thinking on change in human society. It draws on reexaminations of ethnographic accounts, documentary histories, architectural analysis, information theory, ecology, and the comparative analysis of archaeological materials. We see this comparative and global investigation of human diversity to represent one logical outgrowth from the traditional foundation and aims of holistic anthropology as defined by Franz Boas and others at the beginning of this century.

Fundamental Issues in Archaeology, then, is a new series of publications focusing on current, critical issues of broad relevance in anthropological archaeology. The thrust of the volumes will be topical and comparative, rather than areal or methodological; we will concentrate on issues, rather than techniques or regional syntheses. We will consider both monographs and edited volumes that are concerned with basic questions of research and theory. The series will publish both fully authored monographs and integrated edited works that fit its theme and goals. We welcome manuscripts and suggestions for the evolution of *Fundamental Issues.*

GARY M. FEINMAN
T. DOUGLAS PRICE

Preface to the Volume

The concept for this first volume in the *Fundamental Issues* series grew originally out of conversations between the two editors. We began with a common concern that many of the symposia that take place at national meetings of archaeologists tend to be rather hurried presentations of short papers with very little opportunity for digestion, discussion, or debate. We decided that one way to influence the nature of such all-too-rote symposia might be to provide an example of what we would like to see happen. For our symposium topic we chose one of mutual interest—the emergence of social inequality. This transformation in human social organization lies at the base of our societies today and is closely related to many important questions about the human past, including the transition to agriculture and the rise of hierarchical society. There are few more fundamental concerns in any discussion of societal evolution. As evident in this volume, it is a topic that requires an archaeological perspective and profits from the thoughtful consideration of ethnographic data.

The symposium, which took place at the Society for American Archaeology annual meeting in St. Louis in 1993, was well attended. There was a great deal of communication and interchange on this controversial subject, along with a variety of views expressed. In sum, the symposium fulfilled our goal of increasing dialogue and debate in an open forum on a subject of very broad and general concern. Because of the interest and discussion generated by the papers presented, we decided that the papers—expanded and elaborated for the present volume—would be of use and benefit to a larger audience. That decision, and the abilities, interests, and knowledge of the participants in the symposium, led to the volume before you.

We carefully selected the participants in the symposium, seeking individuals with an established record of involvement in the study of social inequality, who are in pursuit of both ideas and information. We have tried to incorporate both in this volume, and its organization reflects that decision. The main body of this book is divided into chapters that emphasize theoretical questions regarding social inequality and those that examine archaeological evidence from various times and places. The interplay between new ideas and information is at the creative forefront of any science, and that is certainly the case here.

Another decision that we made was to try to incorporate information from a variety of time periods and areas. Too often the focus of enquiry regarding social inequality has turned to a particular time period, area, or level of organizational complexity. Perspectives of social inequality have frequently insisted on a rigid dichotomy between egalitarian and hierarchical. Such black-and-white distinctions rarely characterize human society. As Brian Hayden argues in his seminal paper in this volume, the pathways to power and inequality are varied and follow a stepwise, rather than a uniform, threshold. Our decision to include different areas and periods of time has meant that the nature of social complexity among hunter-gatherers has also been a focus in the volume. We would argue, in fact, that foundations of inequality among prehistoric human societies cannot be understood without reference to hunter-gatherers.

Our thanks go to all of the participants and the audience in the symposium, who made it an exciting place to be. We also thank the contributors to this volume for the care and speed with which they finalized their written contributions and their ready response to requests for revisions, artwork, and the like. Working with this group has made the preparation of a volume, always an onerous task, practically pleasant. Finally, our editor at Plenum, Eliot Werner, has been a continuing source of help and advice.

T. DOUGLAS PRICE
GARY M. FEINMAN

Contents

Chapter 3 • Social Inequality, Marginalization, and Economic Process

Jeanne E. Arnold

Chapter 4 • The Cultural Foundations of Inequality in Households

Richard E. Blanton

Chapter 8 • Social Inequality and Agricultural Resources in the Valle de la Plata, Colombia   207

Robert D. Drennan and Dale W. Quattrin

Chapter 9 • Prehistoric European Chiefdoms: Rethinking "Germanic" Societies   235

Antonio Gilman

PART IV. CONCLUSION

Chapter 10 • The Emergence of Inequality: A Focus on Strategies and Processes   255

Gary M. Feinman

Part I

Introduction

Chapter 1

Foundations of Prehistoric Social Inequality

T. DOUGLAS PRICE AND GARY M. FEINMAN

Over the course of our human past there is no more fundamental transition than the emergence of inequality. In many regions of the world, this critical shift occurred long before the advent of written history and "civilization." The investigation of this subject thus falls squarely in the realm of prehistoric archaeology. Yet, surprisingly, this critical transition has received less analytical attention to date than other key evolutionary episodes such as the origins of agriculture or the rise of the state.

For many years, anthropologists and archaeologists have used a rather stark and simplistic model to contrast egalitarian and nonegalitarian societies. Hunter-gatherer groups and some small-scale agricultural societies were thought to be largely egalitarian, with essentially equivalent roles, rights, and privileges for all members. These egalitarian groups were viewed as having as many positions of status available as there were individuals to fill them. Theoretically, the number of positions of status should be unlimited since there was no competition for them. In contrast, nonegalitarian societies were described as large and hierarchical. Mechanisms such as ranking or stratification served to define each individual's position in society by birth. In such societies, there were far fewer positions of status, power, and authority available than there were individuals to fill them and competition was common.

T. DOUGLAS PRICE and GARY M. FEINMAN • Department of Anthropology, University of Wisconsin–Madison, Madison, Wisconsin 53706-1393.

Foundations of Social Inequality, edited by T. Douglas Price and Gary M. Feinman. Plenum Press, New York, 1995.

This rigid dichotomy promoted an exacting perspective on how the concepts of egalitarian and nonegalitarian were understood and, consequentially, on how behavior was represented and contrasted in human societies (e.g., Flanagan 1989). This strict dichotomy also forced models to explain how inequality emerged *de novo* from egalitarian conditions. This was, as can be seen, a very narrow and incomplete view.

Studies in various fields in recent years have greatly modified this perspective and pointed to the fact that forms of inequality are ubiquitous to human society (Flanagan 1989; Gardner 1991; Leacock and Lee 1982). More specifically, ethnographers have documented the presence of nonegalitarian relations among a variety of hunter-gatherer groups studied in the 1960s and 1970s (e.g., Cashdan 1980; Collier and Rosaldo 1981). Distinct inequalities along the lines of age and sex were noted among these groups. These reports served as basic and essential reminders of the presence of inequality in all human societies. Every human population that we know exhibits aspects of egalitarian and nonegalitarian relations. Characteristics such as inequality, power, wealth, and others vary in degree along a continuum among societies (e.g., Feinman and Neitzel 1984). Inequality has a number of different dimensions—political, economic, ideological—and these are not necessarily coterminous.

This recognition has admitted a new perspective on the rise of social inequality, forcing archaeologists and others to reexamine many previous ideas and models. The important question for archaeologists considering the emergence of inequality becomes not when and how status differentiation emerged, but rather when and how it became formalized or institutionalized in society. By institutionalized, we mean that these differences become inherited and socially reproduced. The appearance of institutionalized inequality provided the foundation for the development of larger, more complex hierarchical forms of social and political organization. At the same time it is equally important to remember that the institutionalization of inequality was not a simple binary transformation.

THE CHAPTERS IN THIS VOLUME

It is in this light of new perspectives on society and inequality that the chapters in this volume address the major factors involved in the emergence of nonegalitarian relationships. In the next chapter, Brian Hayden, in a wide-ranging and, no doubt, controversial essay on what he calls transegalitarian societies, considers the transition to social inequality in a series of alternative steps or pathways. Exclusive control of food opens the door to social and economic inequalities. In Hayden's perspective this control is obtained by the use of debt that is created by various methods, including warfare, communal feasting, bridewealth payments, and the formation of corporate kinship groups.

Within transegalitarian societies, individuals known as aggrandizers are categorized by Hayden as Despots, Reciprocators, or Entrepreneurs; inequality and surplus production increase through these categories. The archaeological correlates of these stages in transegalitarian societies are discussed and the distinctive characteristics of each stage described.

Hayden's model is materialistic in the sense that aggrandizing behavior and social changes are assumed to be functional and adaptive. He distinguishes between independent and group resource families as one important dichotomy in transegalitarian societies. Hayden's concern is with the means to power in terms of control of resources, control of labor, and control of trade. This control of power arises only in situations of surplus and often involves an intensification of agricultural production to support more activities.

In Chapter 3, Jeanne Arnold considers the role of marginalization in the rise of social inequality, especially in the context of labor. In this situation, aggrandizers (or opportunists in her terminology) emerge with greater control and power through control of labor. Arnold elaborates a definition of marginalization and offers three elements of this process through which labor is shifted from the household or the kin group to an elite: (1) household labor is appropriated by suprakin forces, (2) some members of households contribute to projects that benefit aspiring elites, or (3) individuals are brought into core activities of economic development but marginalized from control. These strategies can occur at different organizational and spatial scales, thus the institutionalization of inequality is not necessarily or strictly a household or community-based process.

In Chapter 4, Richard Blanton considers the role of the household in the rise of inequality and makes several important distinctions. Drawing on a cross-cultural sample of peasant households, Blanton contrasts a "household continuity" strategy with a "neolocal" strategy. These strategies have different implications for the way that labor is amassed and recruited within households. They also tend to employ different means of social integration and control. As in Feinman's chapter, these household and architectural differences are argued to engender more than one pathway toward the constitution of factions, the manipulation of symbols, and so the bases of inequality and power.

Strong empirical support for the theoretical themes developed in the first four chapters can be found in each of the subsequent chapters. In Chapter 5, Doug Price returns to questions about the origins of agriculture and the emergence of social inequality. Price makes the argument that the beginnings of hereditary status differentiation are in fact associated with the spread of agriculture. Using a case study from the prehistory of southern Scandinavia, Price examines the transition from foragers to farmers in this area. The earliest evidence for the appearance of domesticated plants and animals is directly associated with the first monumental tombs for a limited number of individuals and extensive trade networks in both exotic and utilitarian materials. Such a pattern suggests that social inequality arrives with the first agriculture and may be part and parcel of the neolithic revolution. Examination of the archaeological record of prehistoric hunter-gatherers reveals no unequivocal examples of institutionalized social inequality prior to the origins of agriculture. Although there are well-known ethnographic examples of hierarchically organized hunter-gatherers, they are relatively limited in time and space. For these reasons, Price suggests that complexity among hunter-gatherers expands along horizontal dimensions, as seen in the intensification of existing components of technology, subsistence, exchange, and the like. On the other hand, dramatic changes in settlement size and organization, trade, ritual, and social organization are found among early farming populations.

In Chapter 6, Ken Ames writes on chiefly power and household production on the Northwest Coast of North America. He evaluates two theories for the rise of elites, as managers or as thugs. The central question of his contribution concerns the circumstances under which inequality becomes institutionalized and persists irrespective of production levels and other social and economic changes. Ames examines the relationship between production, consumption, and power on the Northwest Coast where elites have been present for 3,000 years. He concludes that power is basically a difference in the wealth of households. Elite individuals control the resources of their own households but can only influence those outside their immediate relations.

In Chapter 7, Steve Plog examines the ethnographic and archaeological evidence concerned with the question of egalitarian and nonegalitarian relations in the prehistoric Southwest. Plog, like Drennan and Quattrin in Chapter 8, argues that a direct correlation between productivity and aggregation or surplus cannot be assumed. Social relations must be considered in addition to environment in any complete explanation for the origins of inequality in the American Southwest.

Plog focuses on Chaco Canyon in New Mexico to examine the role of wealth and staple production in the rise of aggregated societies of later prehistory. Wealth as items of symbolic value is contrasted with the staple production of food and technological goods. His central question has to do with how social inequality is financed. Plog notes that social inequality does not emerge in the Southwest until there were sedentary groups with agricultural economies. Plog sees a pattern in which mobility declined and control of individual resources increased, leading to social conflict within and among villages. At the same time, Plog argues, limits on sharing in times of risk resulted in a change in the food-sharing ethic and new relations between people. The formation of lineages may have reduced sharing obligations within a group and at the same time provided a structure for status differentiation.

Plog concludes that staple production was a necessary, but not sufficient, condition for social inequality. In ways very similar to those discussed by Hayden, Plog sees agricultural intensification as a development that goes hand in hand with the growth of leadership and the recruitment of followers. Feasting and gift-giving demonstrate success and attract others. Nonlocal goods are correlated with long-distance exchange and appear to be important in the development of political authority. The use of exotic materials by local aggrandizers in an effort to attract followers and power is a common theme in this volume.

In Chapter 8, Dick Drennan and Dale Quattrin examine the relationship between social inequality and agricultural resources in the Valle de la Plata, Colombia, during the first millennium A.D. The concern of the authors is with the formation of chiefdoms but their conclusions are of significant import for all questions regarding the foundations of inequality. Regional settlement pattern data are used to compare the location of sites and site clusters to prime agricultural land. Settlement clusters are associated with large tomb sites, but cannot be shown to map on modern land use patterns or on the best agricultural soils. The conclusion of the study is an important one—that site location and settlement distribution are apparently more closely related to social and political factors than to agricultural or environmental ones. Agricultural productivity does not appear to be the sole or principal base of chiefdom formation. This information has broad relevance to the foundations of social inequality, especially when considered at the scale of regions or populations. Continuing this theme from an earlier paper, Drennan and Quattrin view the importance of social and political relations as essential in the investigation of the institutionalization of social inequality.

In Chapter 9, Antonio Gilman emphasizes the importance of achieved versus ascribed status in human society. The institutionalization of inequality is a turning point in social evolution. Gilman examines this premise at the other end of prehistory, in the context of the Iron Age and Middle Ages in Europe, and focuses on the chiefdoms of Germanic Europe. Gilman points out that most adaptational accounts of redistribution as a function of chiefdoms are unrealistic in assuming that elites will redistribute wealth in bad times. Gilman uses data from his survey of the Copper and Bronze Ages in La Mancha, Spain, to document increasing social and political complexity. It is clear, for example, that in this area the development of intensive agriculture was associated with incipient class stratification. Gilman further examines the question of managerial versus exploitative mechanisms in the intensification of social complexity. The evidence from La Mancha supports the premise that inequalities emerge in the competition over areas suitable for intensive farming (in contrast to the results of Drennan and Quattrin in Chapter 8).

In the concluding chapter, Gary Feinman examines the historical context of questions about social inequality in the consideration of recent theoretical developments and archaeological perspectives. He focuses on the decoupling of agriculture and inequality that has taken place in the last 10 years or so. This distinction necessitated archaeologists to consider the emergence of inequality apart from considerations of food production and forced attention to factors other than subsistence and environment in a search for causality. Feinman contrasts two paths in this search for causality—one that regards resource abundance and substantial population as necessary and the other that seeks conditions of food stress and population pressure. Feinman argues for an intermediate position focusing on the dynamics of both internal (societal) and external factors (climate, environment, demography) in order to best understand the emergence of social inequality.

Feinman examines other important concepts in the study of inequality. With regard to population, Feinman argues that there are many aspects of demography that must be considered. The concept of population is a catchall of variation, rather than a variable itself, in formulas for societal change. In order to invoke population in our discussions of the emergence of inequality it is necessary to isolate the specific components of relevance. The concept of egalitarian also requires consideration. Anthropology has begun to recognize that inequality is present in all societies, from hunter-gatherers to intensive farmers, often along lines of age, sex, authority, skills, and prestige. The important question then becomes not when did inequality appear but, rather, why does inequality intensify and become institutionalized. This change in perspective permits us to track the emergence of certain previously existing characteristics as they evolve into the diagnostics of social inequality. Such recognition has also brought increasing focus on the individual as entrepreneur, accumulator, or aggrandizer in society and his or her role in accelerating the growth of inequality.

Finally, Feinman proposes alternate pathways toward social inequality in terms of two general, coextant strategies, one corporate based and one network based. Network-based strategies are those in which leaders' prestige and support depend largely on linkages to individuals in other societies and places. Exotic items and the production of portable wealth and personal adornment play an important role in these contexts, serving to display and legitimize individual authority and success. In corporate-based contexts, inequality emerges from the manipulation of relations between various societal segments, for example, kin groups. Variation in the sizes of different kin factions and the resultant inequalities in production often lie behind these ideological manipulations, which allow the leaders of specific corporate factions to amass power. Less emphasis is placed on specific individuals in corporate-based contexts. These different strategies are viewed as organizational modes that crosscut a range of hierarchical variation in human societies.

THE THEMES OF THIS VOLUME

As editors of this volume we have been struck by the remarkable congruities among these chapters. Without elaborate instruction or direction, the individual authors often touch on the same themes and logic and follow a similar trajectory in their contributions. These common themes, we believe, document a clear line of thought on the development of social inequality currently emerging in archaeology and mark exciting new trends in the study of social change. These themes are elaborated below.

The chapters in this volume revolve around fundamental questions concerning the rise of institutionalized social inequality. Previous discussions of this topic have often focused on the relationship between social inequality and factors viewed as external to society, such as population, climate, environment, or other forces (e.g., Johnson and Earle 1987; Matson 1985). Such studies, however, have become increasingly frustrated since no direct cross-cultural correlation can be found to link such exogenous forces and internal change in society. Certainly, climate and environment define the geographic field of play and in part provide the conditions under which social transformations occur, but the specific behavioral changes that take place are a selection from a larger repertoire of choices available to human societies. It is no longer sufficient to expect that human socioeconomic strategies simply emerge or were prompted by particular external conditions. Increasing attention is being given to internal decisions within societies that bring about change. It is these internal developments, often closely related to changes in social and ideological behaviors, that appear to be the immediate mechanisms of change in society and the forces that we need to understand in order to explain transitions such as the emergence of social inequality. A focus on such internal developments puts humans in control of their destiny, within the context of their environment of resources, climate, and other neighboring groups.

Another of the themes that emerges in this volume concerns the social context of change. Virtually all of the authors argue that social inequality develops in areas of abundant resources and in environments of little risk. As Hayden (Chapter 2, this volume) puts it, "resource abundance and the ability to consistently produce surpluses were key factors in the emergence of socioeconomic inequalities, economically based hierarchies, and economically based complexity." Within a context of abundant resources, it is difficult to imagine that too many people or too little food causes the emergence of hierarchical organization.

Another path that threads its way through the volume relates to shifting scales of focus in the analysis of social change. Archaeologists in previous decades focused on prehistoric cultures or traditions, defined by artifact types, often lasting hundreds of years. Research questions were oriented toward that very general scale and often dealt with issues such as the origins or first occurrence of observed characteristics and the spread of new traits or peoples. There was little concern with societies per se or with the resolution of different organizational levels or scales within those societies.

Resolution has improved in archaeology with the growth of knowledge and analytical techniques. Today we endeavor to examine changes in society, corporate groups, households, and individuals as our units of analysis and as different foci of change. Throughout the volume there are discussions of mechanisms of inequality that operate at local corporate group or regional network levels. Such distinctions are important in categorizing different pathways to the accumulation of wealth and power. In the case of the emergence of institutionalized equality, interest moves to the individual in prehistory and the importance of aggrandizing or opportunistic behavior by a few. Anthropological terms such as head man or big man as accumulator are common to the discussion. These individuals have been reported in the ethnographic record and are clearly the focus of status differentiation in emerging hierarchical societies.

There are many interesting questions and many interesting answers posed in this volume. It is clear that social forces are regarded as most immediate in the formalization of social inequality. It is clear that environment and population are of relevance but more indirectly involved in discussions of causality. It is also clear that inequality operates in all societies and along a number of different dimensions. There is agreement that the institutionalization of status, i.e., the inheritance of wealth and position, represents a major threshold in the evolution of inequality. The question of course remains as to why such behavior was acceptable in the first place and under what conditions relatively autonomous individuals in human societies gave up aspects of wealth, power, and decision-making to a small component of their number. It is our hope that the directions indicated in this volume will encourage new research oriented toward resolution of that question.

REFERENCES

Cashdan, E., 1980, Egalitarianism among Hunters and Gatherers, *American Anthropologist* 82:116–120.

Collier, J. F., and M. Z. Rosaldo, 1981, Politics and Gender in Simple Societies, in: *Sexual Meanings: The Cultural Construction of Gender and Sexuality* (S. B. Ortner and H. Whitehead, eds.), Cambridge University Press, Cambridge, pp. 275–329.

Feinman, G., and J. Neitzel, 1984, Too Many Types: An Overview of Sedentary Prestate Societies in the Americas, *Advances in Archaeological Method and Theory* 7:39–102.

Flanagan, J. G., 1989, Hierarchy in Simple "Egalitarian" Societies, *Annual Review of Anthropology* 18:245–266.

Gardner, P. M., 1991, Foragers' Pursuit of Individual Autonomy, *Current Anthropology* 32:543–572.

Johnson, A., and T. Earle, 1987, *The Evolution of Human Societies from Foraging Groups to Agrarian States,* Stanford University Press, Stanford.

Leacock, E., and R. Lee, 1982, *Politics and History in Band Societies,* Cambridge University Press, Cambridge.

Matson, R. G., 1985, The Relationship between Sedentism and Status Inequalities among Hunters and Gatherers, in: *Status, Structure, and Stratification* (M. Thompson, M. T. Garcia, and F. Kense, eds.), Archaeological Association of the University of Calgary, Calgary, pp. 245–252.

Part II

Theoretical Perspectives

The first chapter in this section of the volume is an extensive examination of the various trajectories through which one or a few individuals rise to power in human society. These pathways in essence describe the fundamental mechanisms through which egalitarian societies give way to social inequality. To this task, Brian Hayden brings a consuming interest in prehistoric hunter-gatherers and social evolution. Hayden has studied foragers in Australia and on the Northwest Coast of North America as part of his interest in the emergence of social complexity. This important chapter charts the various pathways through which leaders emerge in egalitarian contexts.

Jeanne Arnold has investigated the emergence of social complexity among the prehistoric native coastal peoples of California. Her work has led to the recognition of currency and elaborate exchange systems in this area. In her chapter she emphasizes the control of labor in the rise of inequality, as that control shifted from the household or kin group to an elite.

Richard Blanton's archaeological foundations have been concerned with the rise of hierarchical society in highland Mexico, first in the Valley of Mexico and later in the Valley of Oaxaca. More recently, Blanton's interests have concerned economic anthropology and are reflected in his contribution here. Using ethnographic data from Highland New Guinea, Blanton examines the role of household structure and organization in a search for the beginnings of social inequality. Household strategies for survival and success influence the way labor is organized and how social integration and control are structured. This theme is elaborated in Blanton's book *Houses and Households: A Comparative Study,* from Plenum Press.

Douglas Price has focused largely on hunter-gatherers and the emergence of social complexity among foragers. Turning in this volume to the transition from foraging to farming, he argues that the beginnings of social inequality occur in a critical period during the early Holocene at the same time domestication and extensive exchange systems are developing. Information from his investigations of the transition to agriculture in southern Scandinavia provides evidence for this discussion. A more detailed consideration of the prehistoric transition to agriculture appears in Price and A. B. Gebauer's new volume entitled *Last Hunters—First Farmers,* from the School of American Research.

Chapter 2

Pathways to Power

Principles for Creating Socioeconomic Inequalities

BRIAN HAYDEN

INTRODUCTION

It has been commonplace to describe relatively simple forms of nonegalitarian societies as "tribal" or "ranked." However, these terms were formulated without reference to causal models and they are vague. My goal is to establish a better understanding of how nonegalitarian societies emerged from an egalitarian hunter gatherer base. This topic has captured the attention of a wide range of scholars over the past several decades, and there exist a number of excellent syntheses of the endeavors directed toward understanding the emergence of complexity (Arnold 1993; Coupland 1988; Earle 1987, 1989; Feinman and Neitzel 1984; Johnson and Earle 1987; Tolstoy 1989). The principal contending schools of interpretation in archaeology view complexity as developing due to population pressure, needs for more efficient management of risk or information; economic efficiency (redistribution), the monopoly of long-distance trade routes; manipulation of social or ideological factors; the simple hiving off of daughter communities resulting in community hierarchies; circumscription (social or geographic), coercive exploitation, ritual values, external threats, labor-intensive investment in productive facilities, other

BRIAN HAYDEN • Department of Archaeology, Simon Fraser University, Burnaby, British Columbia, Canada V5A 1S6.

Foundations of Social Inequality, edited by T. Douglas Price and Gary M. Feinman. Plenum Press, New York, 1995.

means of controlling resources including irrigation; scalar effects related to increasing community sizes or population densities; storage. There are structuralist and cognitive explanations as well. Rather than review these earlier contributions, I will proceed directly to a discussion of some other questions and data that I have gleaned from both archaeological and ethnographic data. I would like to acknowledge the great debt that everyone currently wrestling with the problem of the origin of complex societies owes to the many scholars that have previously dealt with the problem. I will refer to many of them in the following discussions. I have decided to limit the present discussion to hunter-gatherers and agriculturalists, recognizing that pastoralists may exhibit somewhat different developmental trajectories (per Johnson and Earle 1987).

Complexity on the Northwest Plateau

My involvement in the issue of complexity stems from a long-standing interest in complex hunter gatherers as well as from the excavations that I am undertaking at an unusually large prehistoric housepit village in the interior of British Columbia near the town of Lillooet on the Fraser River. From my own work in the region as well as the work of others (e.g., Pokotylo et al. 1987; Styrd 1973), it is clear that the large prehistoric communities around Lillooet were occupied by complex hunter-gatherers: the communities are semisedentary; have high population densities; used status items including coastal shells, copper ornaments, and nephrite tools; and there are pronounced status differences in grave goods. My research goal has been to understand the social and economic organization of these communities. However, I found that the existing models and classifications of culture types provided little guidance in terms of understanding how the socioeconomic system operated, how socioeconomic inequality was generated or maintained, and more importantly whether to view the prehistoric Lillooet communities as representing powerful chiefdoms, moderately powerful Big Men, or relatively weak leaders with little political power. Much of my archaeological data did not seem to fit traditional characterizations of power and status distinctions. The most bothersome discrepancy was the expectation that high-status burial goods in children's graves should only occur in chiefdom types of communities, whereas there seemed to be a number of archaeological and ethnographic instances of high-status burial goods accompanying children in communities that lacked clear chieftainships (e.g., Mainfort 1985:576; O'Shea 1984:251; Rothschild 1979; Shennan 1982:30).

Definitions

Before turning to these issues, the question of terminology should be addressed. I view the use of cultural types as useful not only heuristically, but also as a conceptual tool that assists in the manipulation of complex abstractions. In the best situations, types correspond to real nonrandom constellations of characteristics related to each other in a meaningful causal fashion. At the same time, it is clear that all the cultural characteristics to be considered (power, ownership, stratification, class mobility, sedentism, wealth, surpluses, warfare, bridewealth, corporate groups, and others) exist as a continuum (per Feinman and Neitzel 1984). Nevertheless, without global abstract categories it is nearly impossible to discuss or deal with special constellations of these different variables that our intuitive sense tells us constitute a recurrent cultural pattern.

Thus, there have been many attempts at defining and characterizing the range of societies between egalitarian and chiefdoms (see Figure 1). The terms "tribe" and "rank," formulated by cultural anthropologists, are the most commonplace and are based on social or political characteristics. Neither is very satisfactory for dealing with the archaeological issues that I am concerned with (see also Renfrew 1982:2–3). Both include such a wide range of societies that their utility is diminished, especially since neither is concerned with

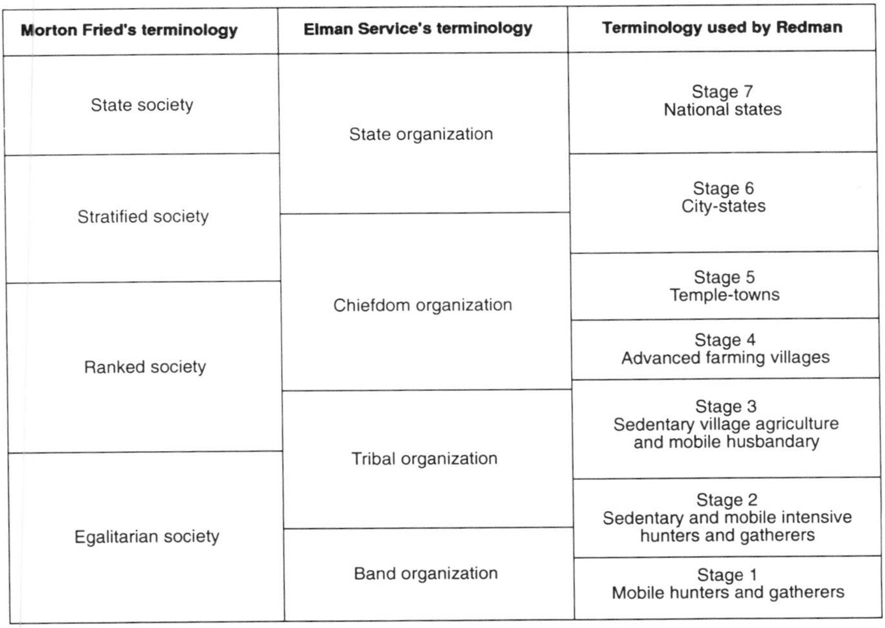

Morton Fried's terminology	Elman Service's terminology	Terminology used by Redman
State society	State organization	Stage 7 National states
Stratified society		Stage 6 City-states
	Chiefdom organization	Stage 5 Temple-towns
Ranked society		Stage 4 Advanced farming villages
	Tribal organization	Stage 3 Sedentary village agriculture and mobile husbandary
Egalitarian society		Stage 2 Sedentary and mobile intensive hunters and gatherers
	Band organization	Stage 1 Mobile hunters and gatherers

Figure 1. A schematic representation of various typologies of cultural complexity (from Redman 1978:203).

attaching its concepts to archaeological indicators. How, for example, can it be established that there were not enough social positions for everyone, or that kinship was the criterion for social integration, or that prestige and status were restricted, or that reciprocal versus redistributive exchange occurred? And what is the justification for the claim that high status was void of economic or political power (Fried 1960:721, 728)? Neither "tribe" nor "rank" involves causal models that are widely used in archaeology. Fried's (1960:719–720; 1967) concept of rank assumes that community fissioning and "random social mutations" were prime agents and that unexplained forces limit the number of status positions available. I view prestige and the number of status positions available as essentially epiphenomena to the more fundamental issue of power.

Service's notion of tribe implies a political unity or connection between communities that often does not exist among groups classified as tribes and the term carries mainly agricultural or pastoral implications. At best, it appears to be the equivalent of a linguistic group. Service also maintains that how people thought of themselves was the key variable in explaining stratification, whereas economics were viewed as unimportant (Service 1962:148–149).

Rather than attempt to revive these encumbered terms, I prefer to use Clark and Blake's (1989) term "transegalitarian" to refer to societies that are neither egalitarian nor politically stratified ("politically stratified" societies include chiefdoms with relatively fixed classes and a hierarchical settlement pattern). The term transegalitarian, too, is very broad and involves much variability including simple horticulturists and complex hunter-gatherers. Thus, within the general class of transegalitarian societies, I will attempt to make several further critical distinctions. I will not deal in any great detail with egalitarian (generalized) hunter-gatherers since I have discussed them at length elsewhere (Hayden 1981, 1990, 1992a). Nor will I deal with chiefdoms in any detail since there are excellent discussions of their characteristics and probable socioeconomic mechanics (Clark and Blake 1994; Earle 1987, 1989).

Following Clark and Blake (1994), I shall use the term "aggrandizer" to denote any ambitious, enterprising, aggressive, accumulative individual (elsewhere referred to as accumulators, or "triple A" personalities) who strives to become dominant in a community, especially by economic means. The term subsumes Great Men, Head Men, Big Men, elites, and chiefs.

I will also make a distinction between two idealized community extremes: communities in which subsistence activities can and are largely carried out by independent families (as in New Guinea) versus communities in which key subsistence resources require cooperative labor to exploit or where limited key subsistence resources are controlled by corporate groups within the community, as on the Northwest Coast (Figure 2). Due to the awkwardness of descriptive labels for these concepts, I shall refer to them simply as "in-

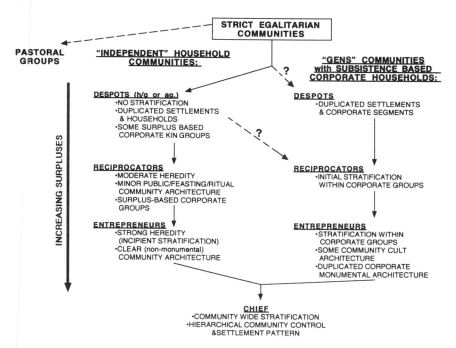

Figure 2. A schematic depiction of the proposed evolutionary sequence among communities with independent family households and communities based on group control of subsistence resources. In the present overview, it is not clear whether Despot communities ever establish subsistence-based corporate groups (group control) or whether these corporate groups initially emerge at the Reciprocator level.

dependent" family communities and GENS (group exploitation of nucleated subsistence) communities, that is, communities with resource-owning corporate groups. I apologize to social anthropologists for the acronymic misuse of one of their terms, but it does convey the general group versus individual distinctions that are critical here. The term "*corporate* groups" refers to lineages, clans, or other residential associations that may have exclusive control over subsistence resources, but may also exist for other reasons such as accumulation of bridewealth. Obviously, independent and GENS community types are extreme forms in what must be a continuum, but they are valuable heuristic models. Moreover, they are probably causally related to two of the three major means aggrandizers use to obtain power: control of labor (in independent communities) and control of subsistence resources (in GENS communities), versus control of trade (attributed to pastoral communities by

Johnson and Earle [1987:193], but also a prominent feature in other community types).

Assumptions

As a result of the problems in using rank or tribe to understand my archaeological data, I decided to examine in closer detail ethnographic accounts of communities that ranged from barely nonegalitarian societies to chiefdoms. I concentrated on the New Guinea Highlands and northwestern North America because these areas exhibited nearly the full range of development that I was interested in and because of the considerable work that had been conducted in these areas. My inquiry was guided by several key questions and assumptions:

1. Any human population numbering more than 50–100 will include some ambitious individuals who will aggressively strive to enhance their own self-interest over those of other community members. This is a simple given of variability in human psychology. This is not construed as a genetic imperative that deterministically affects all humans, but as a simple aspect of human genetic and developmental variability. Such individuals have always been a force to be reckoned with, in some cases being repressed, in some cases being channeled into noneconomic domains such as ritual competition, and in some cases being given greater freedom to compete. This is equivalent to the assumptions of others (Beteille 1981; Sahlins 1958:1; Voytek and Tringham 1989:496) that a tendency toward inequality is inherent in all societies, and is only restrained or permitted free reign by a system of checks and balances reflecting economic conditions and the self-interest of other community members. As Cashdan (1980:119–120) concluded: "Inequality . . . can therefore be explained best not as the development of any formal organization of 'ranking' or 'stratification,' but, rather, as the inevitable result of the *lifting* of the constraints that produce strict egalitarianism."

2. Some forms of inequality based on sex, age, ritual knowledge, and other skills have always existed among generalized hunter-gatherers (Beteille 1981; Sahlins 1958:1), but where these inequalities do not have an economic base, their effects on overall community complexity are limited to ephemeral.

3. The kinds of pronounced inequalities and cultural complexity in communities that archaeologists and ethnologists usually refer to when they discuss complexity are directly related to economic production and control of economic surpluses.

4. The most critical question to be asked is how some individuals manage to convert economic surpluses into power or other benefits and how they induce other community members not only to produce surpluses but also to surrender control over those surpluses.

5. Any explanation must entail behavior and decisions that are perceived to be in the self-interest of community members at large, especially the supporters of aggrandizers. This also recognizes that self-interest often leads to conflicts of interest between individuals and subgroups within the community.

6. Models that are useful must have real evolutionary consequences of importance. This means that for long-term phenomena and general trends, explanations based on the pursuit of prestige, esteem, status seeking, or other psychological motives without practical consequences (per Lemonnier 1990a:47, 49; Young 1971:211) are unsatisfactory.

7. A critical element in the establishment of power and other benefits is the development of private (or corporate) property, binding contracts, and especially debts—a central aspect of traditional gift exchange that Mauss (1967) recognized. As Wohlt (1978:100) has stated it: "A bigman prospers by indebting others." Walens (1981:13) makes the same point: "The nobleman's success was achieved only through careful deployment of his food resources to create reciprocal obligations from those people whom he fed" (see also Lightfoot and Feinman 1982:66). Gosden (1989) has recently restated the observation that debt constitutes the central principle of social organization, political centralization, and power—a point that cannot be emphasized enough. In fact, cross-cultural analyses have shown that private possession of food and debt relations are highly correlated (Rudmin 1992), and that ownership is related to resource density and reliability (Dyson-Hudson and Smith 1978; see also Matson 1985). Thus, one of the most critical questions to ask is how are binding, or "contractual," debts created in transegalitarian communities.

Justifications of Assumptions

Before proceeding with the presentation of ethnographic data, I want to address the validity of some of the assumptions listed above. From my previous work dealing with complex hunter-gatherers and simple horticulturists (Hayden 1981, 1990, 1992a,b; Hayden and Gargett 1990), it seemed apparent that resource abundance and the ability to consistently produce surpluses were key factors in the emergence of socioeconomic inequalities, economically based hierarchies, and economically based complexity. I realize that there are many functional models for these developments; however, field research did not indicate there was any community "need" behind the emergence of inequality, whereas that was the model I expected to be validated when I went into the field.

In the *initial* stages of emerging socioeconomic inequality, resource stress results in the annulment of both the advantages and the surpluses that incipient elites manage to acquire for themselves. This is due to the power and self-interest of the majority of the community. I discuss these matters in more detail elsewhere and provide several ethnographic examples from the Lillooet region and the Maya Highlands (Hayden 1992b, in press; Hayden and Gargett 1990). My research led to the realization that individual or small group claims of special access to resources as well as rights to hoard food must be negotiated with the rest of the community. Moreover, recognition of these rights varied as resource conditions changed. If this is generally the case, it follows that the only condition under which the majority of people in a community will tolerate priviledged access to resources (whether at the source or in processed form) is when the majority is assured of enough resources to survive in normal times. Ownership is only tolerated when it has no adverse effect on most others or when it actually provides some advantage.

As further support for this assumption, numerous archaeologists and ethnographers have noted a strong positive relationship between resource richness and abundance, on the one hand, and social complexity involving socioeconomic inequalities and resource ownership, on the other hand (e.g., Andel and Runnels 1988:241; Arnold 1992:63, 1993:85; Barth 1961; Carlson 1993; Clarke et al. 1985; Cowgill 1975:514–517; Donald and Mitchell 1975; Dyson-Hudson and Smith 1978; Feil 1987:5–9; Gould 1982; Hames and Vickers 1983:10; Hunn 1990:214; Kirch 1984:120; Matson 1985:245–252; Ruyle 1973; Sahlins 1958; Watanabe 1983:217). Other authors have limited themselves to the position that rich resources are required for the development of complexity (e.g., Blake and Clark 1989:9; Carlson 1976, 1991:121; Hildebrandt and Jones 1992:389; Lightfoot and Feinman 1982:66; Matson 1985; Modjeska 1982:86, 101; Price and Brown 1985). In all cases, it is evident that rich resources result in high population densities that are strongly correlated with socioeconomic complexity (Cordy 1981).

Moreover, it follows as a corollary of this assumption that feasts involved in acquiring power should not be predicated on need but on surpluses. This is amply supported in the ethnographies. Feasting only occurs in good times and is elaborated as a function of the food available (Young 1971:190). It was aggrandizers who organized these food exchanges (Young 1971:78, 173). In contrast, poor ecological areas with low production had less feasting, while starvation resulted in the abandonment of villages rather than feasting behavior (Wohlt 1978:110; Young 1971:174, 260). Moreover, numerous authors have noted the essentially nonutilitarian, or surplus, nature of feasting transactions (Feil 1987:59; Mauss 1967:70; Modjeska 1982:102), together with the fact that intensified food production was due to *social* demands rather than subsistence demands (Feil 1987:245; Young 1971:255, 264). As Modjeska (1982:92) phrases it, with the surplus represented by pigs, one could obtain wives, children, and allies, placate enemies, and perhaps influence the spirit world. Put more bluntly, wealth was used to win followers and control others (Mauss 1967:73), or even more succinctly: abundance equals power (Young 1971:155). This is similar to Cowgill's (1975:517) arguments that latent entrepreneurs are stimulated by the prospect of something to be entrepreneurial about (new opportunities), not by hardships. Heavy feasting and social demands may have strained household or environmental resources and led to malnutrition for some ambitious people in transegalitarian societies, but it is highly unlikely that environmental stresses or poor nutrition led to feasting or political centralization.

In the case of the Northwest Interior communities, it is clear that the most complex, hierarchical, and nonegalitarian groups were associated with the most productive salmon fishing locations on the Fraser and Columbia rivers, namely, in the Lillooet region and the Dalles region. The same was true on the coast (Donald and Mitchell 1975). The interpretive positions that emphasize the importance of surpluses and abundance for the development of socioeconomic inequalities contrast with interpretations that argue that initial inequalities and complexity emerge from conditions of episodic resource stress or population pressure (e.g., Arnold 1991, 1992; Binford 1983:221; Burley 1979, 1980; Halstead and O'Shea 1989; Johnson and Earle 1987:14; Keeley 1988; Kirch 1984:150 versus critiques in Netting 1990) or from the need to manage risk (e.g., Ames 1985; Coupland 1988; Earle 1987:293, 1989:85; Kirch 1984:150; Schalk 1981; Suttles 1960, 1968).

The assumption of self-interest (or perceived self-interest) being the ultimate determining force behind human behavior and change is a widespread, but not always acknowledged, assumption. It is at the base of all evolutionary ecological models, sociobiological models, Marxian models, and has even been claimed as a new perspective by postprocessualists. It has been emphasized by Cowgill (1975:507, 514–516), Wells (1984:36–37), Burch (1988:106, 109), Mead (1961:497), and more recently has even been recognized by the award of a Nobel prize to James Buchanan for his proposal of self-interest as a major model in political theory (Lewin 1986). Numerous ethnologists comment on the ambitious, self-serving motivations of transegalitarian aggrandizers (Feil 1987:234; Mauss 1967; Modjeska 1982:64–65; Strathern 1971:215–216; Young 1971:187).

Other support for the above assumptions will be cited during the following discussions.

A NEW MODEL

While generalized hunter-gatherers exhibit little if any expression of economically based inequalities, these distinctions are much more pronounced among complex hunter-gatherers and simple horticulturists. From an evolutionary perspective, it therefore makes most sense to look to complex hunter-gatherers for the mechanics of inequality. Like Cashdan (1980), I have argued that generalized hunter-gatherers suppress economically based competition over resources because competition is destructive of their limited resource base and results in decreased chances of survival. Competitive behavior is therefore channeled into other arenas such as ritual and mate acquisition. Only when subsistence surpluses become available on a regular basis can economically based competition emerge, and this is precisely the condition that characterizes complex hunter-gatherers. As a result, individuals or small groups within complex hunter-gatherer communities develop exclusive control over some resources; they use surpluses in competitive ways to establish inequalities in power; they generate prestige technologies[1] and regional systems of exchange to obtain prestige commodities; they establish lineages to consolidate control over resources and surpluses; and they eventually establish class systems involving owners of resources, commoners, and slaves (Hayden 1981). This basic approach is similar to the type of Head Man dynamics that Harris (1988) has discussed for a number of years. Horticulturists basically continue and elaborate this pattern (Carlson 1993; Shnirelman 1992; Testart 1982).

In order to answer the question of how ambitious individuals starting off in egalitarian societies could transform excess production into personal power under normal conditions when everyone had adequate food for their own subsistence needs, I realized that ethnographic accounts of competitive feasts involving contractual debts provided an important key that had been largely neglected by archaeologists and ethnologists. The key features that I saw as important did *not* involve redistribution as a central mechanism, but rather debt. The attractiveness of the competitive feasting model consisted of (1) the generation and use of surpluses as a central feature, (2) a new evolutionary phenomenon (economically based competition over surpluses and labor) rather than the ubiquitous stresses and circumscriptions that must have always characterized human populations, and (3) an appeal to the immediate material self-interest of all participants. As we shall see, it also had important evolutionary consequences.

Subsequent research into emergent cultural complexity and feasting behavior has indicated that competitive feasts occur in several forms (including competitive Mesoamerican cargo feasts) and that as a whole, they probably occur only under a fairly limited range of circumstances, representing brief

---

[1]Prestige technology refers to the production of goods that maximizes available labor inputs and that only loosely meets performance requirements, as opposed to practical technology that maximizes efficient manufacturing and tool performance.

periods in the evolution of socioeconomic inequalities in many regions. Other kinds of feasting behavior precede and succeed competitive feasting; these will be the focus of the following discussions, as will the associated strategies for concentrating power involving warfare, bridewealth, child growth payments, corporate lineages, and claims to supernatural power. As I view the situation at present, the feast, although still an important central element in the strategies of aggrandizive individuals to acquire power, is more appropriately seen as one of several related strategies forming different types of constellations as resources and the possibilities of effective power inequalities increase.

The key elements in the evolutionary scheme to follow are (1) the relative amounts of surplus that can be produced on a consistent basis by families or larger economic groups (or perhaps more accurately, the degree to which increased labor inputs will generate food surpluses) and (2) the changing strategies used by aggrandizers to control and increase that surplus. I will suggest that as the potential for surplus production increases, inequalities also progressively increases through Despot, Reciprocator, and finally Entrepreneur types of organization, a model strongly advocated by Feil (1987) and congruent in many respects with models developed by Johnson and Earle (1987). These are roughly equivalent to the social anthropological terms of Great Men (Despots), Head Men (Reciprocators), and Big Men (Entrepreneurs), although definitions have shifted from structural ones to materialist ones. It should be noted that the term "Big Man" has often been used to include all three of these types of leaders; however, I would use Big Man in the much more restricted sense that Lemonnier (1990a) has proposed. Various kinds of public feasts constitute one of the most critical strategies at all three of these levels and have direct archaeological consequences.

It is relatively clear how competitive feasts (versus other feast types) can generate power and how they appeal to the self-interest of supporters. The Entrepreneur/Big Man organizers benefit by establishing a wide network of contractual debt relationships that motivate people to produce and surrender surpluses that Entrepreneurs can disproportionately control. If successful, Entrepreneurs therefore exert more control over labor and also obtain direct material profits in the form of increases in wealth. The supporters hope to profit from their investments in feasts by promises from Entrepreneurs of repayments *with interest* for their contributions, as well as increased influence in the affairs of the community through their close association with the aggrandizers of the community.

Competitive feasts only seem to emerge under unusually abundant resource conditions preceding the development of true chiefdoms. It is now apparent that there is a prior type of feasting that appears under conditions where resources are more limited, but not so limited as to make strictly egalitarian communities essential for survival. In contrast, under even more severe conditions where resources are very limited and vulnerable to over-exploitation, egalitarian economic behavior and ethics are the only ones that the majority of the community tolerates because sharing of resources is critical for survival (Cashdan 1980:119–20; Winterhalder 1986).

Before discussing the various forms of transegalitarian communities, it is important to emphasize that the community types I describe are based on strategies used to create or extend control. As Johnson and Earle (1987:59, 61) have noted, *integration* (related to the strategies of extending control over people) is a separate phenomenon from *stratification* (related to control over resources). Specifically, ownership of highly localized resources or resource procurement/processing facilities (prime fishing rocks, prime migration ford-ings, boats, weirs, game fences, drying houses) appears to lead to stratification and GENS communities even where modest surpluses are produced. This has led some researchers to propose that localized resources are essential for the development of socioeconomic complexity (e.g., Matson 1985:246); however, consideration of the New Guinea data indicates that localized resources or facilities may be a special (albeit common) case and not necessarily a critical factor. An important similarity between the GENS communities of the North-west and the independent family communities of New Guinea is that ag-grandizers in both community types used the same strategies to consolidate power within their respective group of supporters and to extend control beyond that group—depending on the magnitude of surpluses capable of being produced and co-opted in each case. However, only in the Northwest could aggrandizers also effectively control access to *spatially restricted* re-source locations or productive facilities (fishing rocks, weirs, boats, deer fences, drying sheds) and thus create a distinctive hereditary class *within* each corporate group. This class had managerial rights over the resource locations and facilities of the group. As Ames (Chapter 6, this volume) notes, even here (as in New Guinea) house chiefs could exert little direct power over free household members, although chiefs did have life and death power over their slaves. In New Guinea, the more ubiquitous access to productive land prob-ably limited the development of social stratification within support groups.

EGALITARIAN COMMUNITIES

Among hunter-gatherers, population densities of less than 0.1 people per square kilometer are generally associated with egalitarian behavior and ethics. Among simple horticulturists, the population density associated with full eco-nomic egalitarianism (lacking private ownership) may be somewhat higher. Some forms of feasting occur among egalitarian groups, but as strictly celeb-

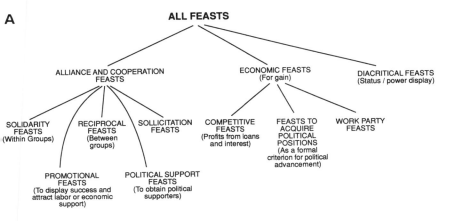

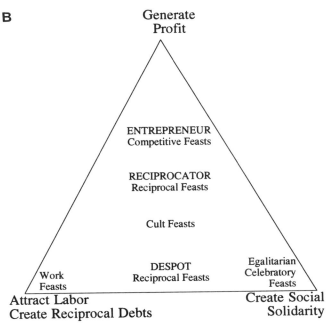

Figure 3. Types of feasts (A) suggested for egalitarian and transegalitarian communities. The major purposes of these feasts (B) can often be combined in various ways.

ratory events with the conscious or unconscious goal of reinforcing solidarity between people and groups (Figure 3). Warfare also occurs between egalitarian communities, but is not very intensive or frequent and makes most sense as a potential strategy to be activated if resources and help from allies should fail completely (Hayden 1992:175–177). Where marriage is organized, there is a direct exchange of personnel or the establishment of inviolable alliance relationships. Economic surpluses are limited or inconsequential or unreliable. The uncertainties of success in hunting and gathering render sharing necessary for survival (Winterhalder 1986). For similar reasons, there is no restricted access to resources, no competition over resources, and no accumulation of wealth. A number of people have suggested that until the introduction of metal tools and/or new high-yielding domesticates, the people of the eastern Highlands of New Guinea (Feil 1987:9) and the central Amazonian rainforest (i.e., the Yanomamo and other groups; Good 1993; B. Ferguson, personal communication, January 1991) were generalized hunter-gatherers similar to Australian Western Desert or Tasmanian hunter-gatherers.

TRANSEGALITARIAN COMMUNITIES

Despot Communities

Under conditions where resources become significantly more abundant, more dependable, and less vulnerable to overexploitation than in generalized hunter-gatherer communities (due to new extractive and/or storage technology combined with favorable productive environments), it is no longer critical to share all resources since most domestic groups can be assured of adequate food under normal conditions. In contrast to egalitarian hunter-gatherer communities where even the most determined efforts to procure food could often meet with limited success, resources in transegalitarian communities could be had easily enough in normal times so that lack of food was due more to laziness than bad luck. Under these conditions, families began to produce food exclusively for themselves and claim ownership rights over the foods that they procured and stored (Gould 1982). Direct ownership over procured food became especially important where extra effort was required to properly prepare foods for long-term storage and where there was a need to conserve stored foods for use during lean seasons. One's self-interest dictated that effort spent to obtain food (where everyone could satisfy their own needs) should primarily benefit oneself. Direct ownership was essential to prevent excessive "mooching," a pervasive emic theme in many transegalitarian ethnographies. Once people began keeping and, where necessary, storing produce for themselves, it would have been natural to produce surpluses as hedges against periodic shortages or even to produce surpluses for minor exchange or gifts as had always been the practice among hunter-gatherers at a small scale to create alliances.

Exclusive control over the food produced by oneself or one's family opened the door to the development of socioeconomic inequities. As Rudmin (n.d.) concludes from his exhaustive cross-cultural survey, "egalitarianism and private property do have trouble coexisting." However, during periods of shortage, despite attempts to maintain exclusive control over the food that one procured and stored, the old behavioral patterns of mandatory sharing were clearly invoked again to ensure survival of the group (see Hayden 1992b). Thus in communities with somewhat precarious surpluses even in normal years, there is a continuing emphasis on community solidarity or well-being versus individual benefit; selfishness is not tolerated (e.g., Modjeska 1982:90).

Moreover, because surpluses are uncertain and minimal, only limited economic "contracts" are agreed to, involving reciprocal exchange of equivalent items (one pig for one pig) or corporate responsibility for exchanges involving significant amounts of surplus. It is under these conditions that the first strategies are developed by ambitious individuals to enhance their own power. Once the egalitarian fetters (that were developed to deal with highly variable individual foraging success and recurring shortages) were relaxed under improved resource conditions, ambitious individuals must have realized that there were surpluses, or potential surpluses, capable of being generated within their communities that were going to waste. If they could but devise a means to manipulate community interests, these ambitious, accumulative aggrandizers could control some of the surplus and derive considerable benefit for themselves. The best and most highly motivated minds of an epoch began to scheme.

What I suggest is that these first unfettered (or less fettered), ambitious aggrandizers frequently created what Godelier (1982) and others (Lemonnier 1990a:28, 144–145) have called "Great Man" societies and what I refer to as Despot societies. Lemonnier (1990a) has acknowledged that his examples can be viewed as one end of an evolutionary sequence. Feil (1987) has stated this more explicitly. Originating with Godelier, the term Great Man society is a structuralist construct based on "equal exchange." In contrast, the term Despot society is a more archaeologically useful definition that emphasizes the limited amounts of surplus and prestige exchange, a high incidence of warfare, the existence of reciprocal feasting to obtain military allies, and the use of compensation payments to allies for injuries and deaths that they suffer in battles for hosts.

The Despot type of community characterizes the eastern New Guinea Highlands and other select locations in the world. In New Guinea, enough surpluses are produced to sustain the production of occasional pigs in domestic groups as well as to obtain some shells, feathers, salt, and ground stone axes via exchange. Pigs are the main embodiment of surplus food and labor (Lemonnier 1990a:59–63; Modjeska 1982:57, 62, 105). Despot communities do not have competitive feasts, but feasts of solidarity and alliance; Great Man Despots are not necessarily wealthy as a result of their own *productive* efforts, but they typically play prominent roles in warfare, and, more importantly, they play central roles in peacemaking and in arranging death compensation payments that provide access to benefits unavailable to others, such as choice foods, prestige goods, coercive power in demanding surpluses, and power in negotiations. Other leadership roles, especially involving rituals, may be dispersed among different people in the community. Both Lemonnier (1990a:119) and Godelier (1982) state that only exchange of equivalent items occurs in Great Man societies; however, they state elsewhere that death compensation payments are used to establish peace *everywhere* in New Guinea (Lemonnier 1990a:114), and that death compensation payment is a key factor in changing the practice of "equivalent exchange." Thus, equivalent exchange and egalitarianism may be community ideals, but may not always be adhered to in practice. In the eastern New Guinea Highlands where Despot communities were concentrated, the environment is poorest for horticulture and surpluses are minimal (Feil 1987:9, 22, 60–63). The area was unsuitable for taro production, the main prehistoric plant domesticate. Population densities ranged at European contact from one to six people per square kilometer (Modjeska 1982:53; Lemonnier 1990a:22)—comparable to many complex hunter-gatherer densities—while the pig population (representing surplus production) varied essentially from zero to about 8 per square kilometer.

The most striking social feature of the eastern Highlands is the high incidence and intensity of warfare, a feature that also characterizes the Yanomamo area—an area that may have also recently emerged from low hunter gatherer levels of production (Good 1993; B. Ferguson, personal communication, January 1991). Feil (1987:231) explicitly links the expansion of the resource base to an increase in warfare, as does Cowgill (1975:517) in a more general fashion. This pattern appears to be far from coincidental and suggests that warfare was one of the most common, and perhaps one of the first, strategies used by ambitious men to manipulate community resources and affairs for their own interests. Other strategies that appear to have been used include bridewealth payments, the formation of corporate kinship groups, and communal feasts (Figure 4). These strategies will now be discussed in more detail.

Simple Extortion

How, precisely, can warfare advance the interests of ambitious men? There are several suggestions in the ethnographic literature. There have been

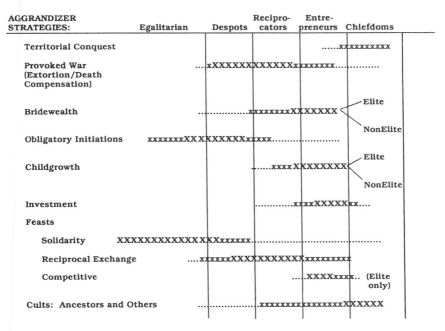

Figure 4. Proposed major strategies used by different types of transegalitarian aggrandizers to increase their control in communities.

occasional suggestions that ambitious men and groups might benefit from subjugating weaker communities. However, as Keeley (in press) points out, there are no ethnographic examples of such subjugation prior to chiefdoms. Less complex groups simply lack the infrastructure to administer and maintain such undertakings.

More congruent with the data is Lemonnier's (1990a:38) suggestion that Great Men Despots essentially extract support, services, and food from other community members by providing military protection for them while they work in their gardens as well as by the judicious use of threats and raw force. This is similar to Gilman's (1981) extortion scenario for developing complexity. Given a relatively unpredictable surplus production at the family household level, producers may have been reluctant to agree to any contractual loans or debts for fear of having to default and suffer reprisals. In such circumstances, the extortion and threat strategy may be relatively more effective in motivating people to produce and surrender surpluses. It seems likely that incipient Despots may have intentionally provoked and promulgated confrontations between communities in order to motivate others in their own communities to seek protection from Despots. By generating a climate of danger, Despots could make strong demands on the rest of their communities for power and goods. In some instances this strategy (and others) clearly led to the concentration of considerable power in the hands of Despots who married up to 20 wives and who killed members of their own community at whim (Feil 1987:104–105). These individuals were supported by the community because their fearsome reputations provided increased security from attack.

Although the organizational talents of some Despots may have been limited to extortion, others with deeper insights into social dynamics must have realized that force by itself was very costly and ineffective in the long run for acquiring power and increasing benefits to themselves (Blau 1964:199–229; Earle 1989:85; Godelier 1978; McGuire and Paynter 1991:8; Modjeska 1982:92). Oppressors who did not provide any positive benefits could easily be deposed in relatively egalitarian communities. In order to provide positive motivation for producing surpluses, some Despots appear to have initiated a system of death compensation payments. This practice provided important benefits in terms of laying the foundations for military alliances as well as stopping conflict between groups when costs of war became too great. Such a system must have benefited many families faced with escalating losses from war, and must have quickly spread to other communities, even those with socially inept Despots.

The War Payments Strategy

It is essential to realize that in addition to "protection" payments, what makes warfare a useful tool for ambitious aggrandizers is not necessarily the conflict itself, but the creation of debts that can be partly managed or manipulated by those with ambition. This is what differentiates transegalitarian warfare from warfare in egalitarian communities. Debt is created in three ways: (1) when individuals are killed in battle, retaliatory killings can be avoided by paying for the initial death with economic surpluses; (2) in order to secure allies for battles, surpluses can be used to pay potential or actual allies for their support; (3) when allies suffer losses in battles, they must be compensated by wealth payments for those losses. All of these situations are predicated on the practice of substituting the value of economic surplus for a human life—a practice that does not appear to occur to any great extent among strictly egalitarian societies where a human life must be paid for with a human life (i.e., strict equivalent exchange or revenge). Lemonnier (1990a:105ff., 119, 136) and Modjeska (1982:56) have stressed the importance of this substitution step in establishing nonegalitarian societies and in promoting the intensification of production. The result of these factors was that the initiation of fights became a costly affair that could only be contemplated when there was adequate surplus to pay allies (Wiessner and Tumu n.d.).

I suggest that it was the ambitious aggrandizers (rather than the "social logic" that Lemonnier (1990a:25) invokes) of the community that orchestrated this change in values. Ambitious men may have argued publicly that it was to the interest of the community to use its surplus wealth to sue for peace, but privately they must have hoped to use the resultant situation to their own benefit. As Sillitoe (1978:254) puts it:

> A big man must manipulate the opinions of his fellows so that their actions will further his political ambitions . . . he may encourage violent redress if he thinks the time is ripe for a war in which he can extend his field of influence or . . . if he does not think war is a good idea he will press for a peaceful settlement. . . . Big men do not therefore directly control or initiate wars but they do use their influence . . . to further their own ends.

And as Wohlt (1978:99) observes:

> The bigman manipulates . . . interpersonal relationships and the ambiguities surrounding who proper receivers are for his own and his group's advantage. He is nothing if he is not a genius at devising intricate plans which seem to benefit everyone, including the persons who do not receive pigs, and then convincing people to implement them. . . . By the time he is fifty he has several wives, much land, a pig herd, a network of helpers . . .

Wiessner and Tumu (n.d.) make similar points, stating that a Big Man had to convince supporters that he acted in their interests even though he was really acting in his own self-interest.

The above suggestions concerning the manipulation of war to expropriate surpluses and increase power by Despots may seem somewhat Machiavellian. However, many ethnographers have commented that aggrandizers frequently appear to stir up and manipulate conflict between communities in order to further their own interests (Lemonnier 1990a:95, 98, 126; Sillitoe 1978:254, 260, 265; Strathern 1971:54, 76–77, 98, 183). As Modjeska (1982:92) observes, warfare was often "a subterfuge . . . for the mobilisation of men and finances by *wei tse* in the pursuit of power and domination," while Sillitoe (1978:269) categorically states that, "it is not a distortion to see big men as Machiavellian in their disguised attempts to use war for their own political ends" and Wiessner and Tumu (n.d.) report that flimsy excuses, such as Peeping Toms, or the theft of a single stalk of sugar cane, were resorted to in order to start wars. Where excuses could not be found, some men bribed individuals to kill others in order to start wars. Ethnographers also note that war reparations were so central to Big Man careers that wars were sometimes started for the benefits of war reparations and subsequent exchanges. Young men were even willing to die fighting if they knew that their family would benefit through death payments (Wiessner and Tumu n.d.).

Of importance for the present discussion is the fact that transegalitarian warfare required both military and economic strength. It is as the organizer of the compensation payments, generally entailing subsequent exchanges, that ambitious individuals could acquire additional advantages for themselves (Modjeska 1982:87). They could motivate community members in a positive fashion to produce and surrender surpluses rather than obtaining these through extortion and protection racketeering that was unstable at best. As organizers of compensation payments, Despots had access to advantages and resources that others did not have. In fact, Wohlt (1978:98) even states that aggrandizers organized fights *because* they could organize compensation and exchange, and that if the Big Man was killed, his supporters would stop fighting because they could not underwrite the requisite exchanges and payments on their own. Organizers of death compensation payments could skim off surpluses for themselves, they could consume or receive the best surpluses that their own community and other communities had to offer, they could create networks of indebtedness and mutual aid, and they could put strong pressures on individuals within their kinship group to produce surpluses or face the consequences of adversely affecting the group's ability to defend itself. Under these conditions, even women, who were the most exploited and oppressed members in the Despot communities, readily recognized the need to produce surplus pigs to be used in lineage war compensations for peace. Thus, women acquiesced to having their pig production expropriated (Modjeska 1982:81).

Typically, the amount of wealth deemed to equal the value of a human life for compensation payments was far more than normal individuals or families could amass (Wiessner and Tumu n.d.; Wohlt 1978:86). Among the Duna, one death had to be compensated for by the payment of 30 pigs and leaders tended to appropriate the pigs of lesser men for war payments (Modjeska 1982:91, 105). I feel that this appropriation of surplus for peacemaking was a key strategy of economically ambitious individuals. It was the need to involve the productive surplus of large numbers of people that enabled Despots to become involved in the generation and management of wealth without necessarily producing it themselves and without appearing to amass wealth in an unacceptably selfish fashion. Appearing to profit too much from these situations could be too blatant a contravention of egalitarian ideals, could attract envy, and could be dangerous, necessitating the subterfuge of "feigning poverty" and acting for the good of the group (Sillitoe 1978:253; Young 1971:112, 155). But in all aggrandizer strategies, whether based on labor, resources, or trade, the key objective is restricting access and concentrating control in the hands of aggrandizers.

Typically, too, Despots organized people closest to them (those most easily manipulated) into corporate kinship groups. Sometimes there was no apparent reason for these groups to exist other than to produce surplus wealth that could be pooled in order to pay compensation for warfare deaths, to pay allies, or, in more complex communities, to pay bridewealth to obtain brides (Modjeska 1982:83, 97, 107). I will refer to these as *surplus*-based corporate groups. Many African lineage systems typify surplus-based lineage systems according to Modjeska, while Meillassoux (1981) elaborates the argument in an extreme form. Such corporate groups were clearly present in some eastern Highland New Guinea communities where the same quality land was available to everyone. Significantly, Feil (1987:226) observed that the formation of lineages was a function of resource surplus and the price of brides. As noted earlier, in other environments, corporate kinship groups cooperated in order to control important localized economic resources that were critical for basic subsistence needs, although they also frequently produced surplus wealth. These resources include fishing locations (Spier and Sapir 1930), unusually rich agricultural land, weirs, game fences (Smith 1978), or other labor-intensive facilities. I will refer to these as *subsistence*-based corporate groups. Johnson and Earle (1987:59, 61) suggest that these cases represent a slightly different evolutionary trajectory involving stratification earlier in development phases than communities with equal access to all economically important resources.

Despite Despots' attempts to bind kin together as corporate supporters, because the ability to produce surpluses was limited, so were the demands that other members would tolerate; calls for too frequent wars or payments to allies could lead to corporate kin shifting their residences to other communities (Modjeska 1982:92). Nevertheless (contra Johnson and Earle 1987:157–158), the intense endemic warfare that characterized many emergent transegalitarian societies does not appear related to resource or land scarcity, or to population density (Feil 1987:66), but to a significant or sudden increase in resource availability (Feil 1987:231) and the resultant scramble by ambitious aggrandizers to find ways to control those surpluses. This is undoubtedly why warfare persisted along the Northwest Coast with European trade despite substantial population reductions from epidemics creating major increases in resources per capita. Codere (1950:68) emphatically states that Northwest Coast warfare was not due to scarcity, while Cowgill (1975:517) makes a more general case for warfare stemming from surpluses. As Lemonnier (1990a:96) and others note, discontented exchange partners can often precipitate war, while aggressive aggrandizers often use accusations of sorcery, backed by the threat of war, as ways of demanding overdue payments (Modjeska 1982:100). Mauss (1967:11), too, noted in his classic study that defaulting on exchanges or on expected (contractual) return payments was tantamount to a declaration of enmity and must surely have been a major motive for warfare. Sillitoe (1978:260) and Keeley (in press) are even more categorical. Such defaults would inevitably occur where communities were pushing the limits of their productive and investment capacities, and defaults clearly did lead to fighting in extreme cases (Strathern 1971:159, 168, 171).

Bridewealth

Although many authors state that Despot/Great Men societies practiced a direct, equivalent exchange of women in marriage (one wife given for one received; Feil 1987:139, 143; Godelier 1982:31; Lemonnier 1990a:72, 119; Modjeska 1982), and although this may have often been the case, there are nevertheless other indications cited by these same authors that something else was beginning to transpire in Despot communities. For instance, Feil indicates that this was more of an ideal rather than a practice and that bride service was widespread. The bride service expected of men could be substantial, amounting to three pigs and three cuscus (marsupials) in one case (Feil 1987:142). Undoubtedly, the strong emphasis on warfare as a strategy for the manipulation of power and wealth undermined the importance of bridewealth since women were strongly devalued where war was intensive. Where warfare was endemic, communities emphasized endogamy. Thus, while bridewealth may not have been prominent, there are some signs of initial manipulation. Because it only becomes notable in Reciprocator types of communities (to be discussed next), I will deal with the bridewealth strategy in more detail there.

Corporate Kin Groups

In New Guinea, where each family has access to productive resources and where little cooperative labor is required for exploitation of resources, families operate as relatively independent subsistence units. Under these conditions, it is evident that the formation of lineages or other forms of corporate kinship groups is primarily to pool and use surpluses and wealth in the pursuit of peace through death compensation payments or to acquire allies, and in more complex communities to obtain wives (Modjeska 1982:83). As Burch (1975:293–294) indicates, corporate kinship groups are not significant in most hunter-gatherer societies (aside from complex hunter-gatherers), nor are they important in industrial societies. Corporate kinship appears to be significant only in transegalitarian and nonindustrial stratified societies. As I suggested above, the emergence of corporate kinship groups, like warfare, was probably promoted by ambitious aggrandizers as a key strategy to enable them to manipulate resources and surpluses within their own communities. Although Johnson and Earle (1987:157–158) relate the development of corporate kin groups to population pressure, there is little data from New Guinea or the Northwest to support their position. Rather, the data indicate that where individual households are relatively self-sufficient in terms of subsistence, corporate kin groups develop under conditions of surpluses (Feil 1971:226; Modjeska 1982:83, 107). At the Despot level, these surplus-based corporate kinship groups would have appealed to the self-interest of all corporate members in terms of increasing their security from attack.

In other environments, such as the Northwest Coast and the Northwest Interior, cooperative labor involving several families was important for the effective procurement or processing of basic subsistence resources, including the building of structures to dry and store surplus foods, the construction of weirs, and the labor required to take and process the maximum number of salmon at peak migration times (see, e.g., Hayden 1992b). Under these conditions, individuals or families that supplied capital and labor to enhance (intensify) the productivity of specific resource locations could claim not only exclusive control of that produce, but also priviledged use of the resource locations (e.g., weir sites) that they had developed or enhanced. Other community members recognized these claims in normal times because the investments of some families in more intensified production probably brought benefits to the entire community in terms of exchange goods, increased stored surpluses that could be used for feasts or famine relief, and access to the improved resource procurement facilities when not being used by the "owners." Such facilities tended to be managed by a closely related group of families that resided together as a residential subsistence-based corporate group with one family recognized as titular owner (Hayden and Cannon 1982). Tenant families often resided in the same house as the managerial families. These conditions seem to have promoted much greater socioeconomic inequalities within these GENS communities and concentrated much more power in the hands of the "owning" families (the hereditary chiefs and elites) than was the case with the New Guinea Despot societies where all families could be self-sufficient in subsistence foods.

Despite the differences in power that existed *within* groups as a consequence of corporate versus autonomous family control of subsistence resources, many of the strategies employed to consolidate and extend power appear to have been the same in both the GENS communities of Northwest North America and the "independent" family communities of New Guinea. These strategies include the emphasis on warfare and the use of feasts for communal functions. Other characteristics that they have in common involve the emphasis on the community or group rather than the individual and the direct exchange of wives in some places.

In the Northwest, the closest analogue to the New Guinea Despots was probably the upstream or peripheral areas of the Interior Plateau where salmon runs were less abundant and less reliable than in central or lower drainage areas. Groups such as the Chilcotin, Carrier, Lakes Shuswap, and Nicola occupied areas of low surpluses (Bussey and Alexander 1992:40–43). Surpluses were more limited and erratic than the major salmon streams of the Plateau and Coast; population densities were lower; exchange was less significant although some prestige items were present; and these groups were most noted on the Plateau for their raiding and warfare, which Dawson (1892:25) describes as being constant throughout the Plateau, but especially in the north (see also Cannon 1992; Teit 1909:540, 550)—descriptions reminiscent of the New Guinea Highlands. Oral histories from the Plateau groups often feature descriptions of warrior Despots (e.g., Teit 1909:557–559, 561–563). Bussey and Alexander (1992) have recently synthesized much of these data. The Tutchone should probably also be included since they are characterized by Despot rulers with only limited surpluses in the community (although European trade goods and firearms may have increased the power of Despots [Coupland 1988, 1994; LeGros 1982, 1985]). It is important to emphasize that Bussey and Alexander as well as Cannon clearly relate the differences between the peripheral and core river Plateau groups to resource and production differences. All of these characteristics closely parallel differences in New Guinea between Despots and other aggrandizers.

Feasting

The final strategy that I suggest was used by intelligent, ambitious aggrandizers to promote the production of surpluses in their communities and to control those surpluses and community labor was the feast. There are many types of feasts (Figure 3). In Despot communities, few people could meet demands for high levels of surplus production and would probably rarely enter into contractual debts requiring the future production and repayment of surpluses. Therefore, most contractual agreements could not be fulfilled on a reliable basis and Despots had to be content with more vague promissory agreements to provide limited surpluses used for the most important of community affairs. Moreover, because surpluses were limited, they had to be pooled from many families in order to be significant. Despot community feasts were corporate displays without any markings of individual contributions, where all food was massed in one central area. The main form of wealth was food, especially plant foods and game in the poorest areas (Lemonnier 1990a:32). Producers of these hard-won surpluses were generally loath to surrender their wealth entirely to another community with very uncertain prospects of the other communities being able to return the debt. This meant that feasting foods were consumed primarily within the community where they were produced (Feil 1987:246) and that surpluses were used mainly to enhance solidarity within the community (and to attract more labor and manpower to it), or to host allies or potential allies and pay them for battle losses. In short, feasting exchanges that occurred within communities may precede feasting exchanges between communities (Lemonnier 1990a:129). I suggest that Despots promoted the importance of feasts according to the most compelling pretexts that they could find and urged other community members to produce extra food—and perhaps foods with special qualities— so that the group would appear successful and wealthy and powerful to allies invited as guests and to their own membership (Feil 1987:238, 252–253). Despots must have argued that success in impressing hosted groups was critical to success in war and in obtaining desirable mates. These displays were in essence advertising costs for attracting desirable people into important relationships—a topic discussed in more detail in subsequent sections.

The ostensible reason for holding these feasts and dances from the community's point of view was to attract and consolidate labor in the form of productive workers in the community, good mates, and good military allies— all essential for survival in the Despot community environment. Large communities were critical for success in warfare (Strathern 1971:16). In fact, feasts did function in all these ways and provided important survival and evolutionary benefits to those that were most successful in hosting feasts. Thus, this type of feast continued to be used in all types of transegalitarian communities, often becoming the largest feasting events of communities (P. Wiessner, personal communication, October 1991).

However, from the Despot's point of view, the actual pretext that was used for holding such success-display feasts was probably more or less irrelevant. The important element was motivating other community members to support feasts and limited exchanges thereby marshaling community or kinship labor. This labor was used to produce a surplus of food and to acquire prestige goods used for display in dancing or rituals, all of which Despots could manipulate much in the same fashion as they manipulated death compensation payments. In Big Men (Entrepreneurial) communities, Strathern (1971:215–216, 219) explicitly states that self-interest and contractual obligations were the basis of exchange and that exchange feasts enhanced the total control of Big Men in community affairs. It seems reasonable to view Despot organizers of community feasts as motivated by the same factors.

The importance of the feast as a strategy probably lies in inherent human emotional reactions to giving and receiving satisfying foods as well as special gifts. Dietler (1990:366) maintains that feasts are universally used for mobilizing labor in subsistence agricultural communities. Friedman and Rowlands (1978) have argued that feasting is the key to understanding the emergence of hierarchies. I largely agree, although I would replace their structuralist causality with a materialist one. In the case of Despot communities, the exchange of surplus production between two groups (or even within a group in the simplest case) is the critical feature. If a group could be persuaded to hold a feast for whatever reason, members implicitly accepted the responsibility of producing surpluses and surrendering some control of those surpluses. All feasts were also public displays with public accounting or recognition of any surpluses given by one group to another. They were opportunities to exhibit the relative success and membership benefits of a group.

Critical to displaying wealth and success was the ability of the host or hosts to procure, display, and give away difficult-to-obtain or specialized labor-intensive items. Obtaining such objects via regional trade networks and/or by supporting local craft specialists therefore eventually became absolutely essential features of reciprocal and competitive feasting in most cases although this development appears to have been minimal at the Despot level. Another important feature of the feast was the public reckoning of the receiving group's or individual's obligation to return an equal or better amount of food and gifts received, thus establishing contractual, jurally validated debts (Wohlt 1978:104–105). If feasts given to other groups were not reciprocated within a reasonable length of time, if the surpluses expended were not returned by allies, or if gifts were refused, this was a sign of social and economic rupture and could be interpreted as a declaration of war (Mauss 1967:11; Strathern 1971:154, 168, 171). In the more complex groups, return payments that only equaled the original amount given indicated that one party wanted to terminate an exchange relation (Wohlt 1978:96).

The obligations and bonds incurred at feasts could be strengthened even further by carrying them out in ritual or sacred contexts. This is undoubtedly one reason why ritual performances are integral parts of almost all transegalitarian feasts (Mauss 1967:70). The more impressive and powerful such rituals were, the stronger the moral contract could be construed to be, besides which obtaining ritual paraphernalia through exchange could be used as yet another pretext for promoting the production and surrender of surpluses often involving debts. Dancing and lavish costuming are recurring themes in all transegalitarian feasts, becoming more elaborate and complex as surpluses increase (Strathern 1971:119). In the more complex transegalitarian societies dance and ritual participation become an indication of support for the organizers and their power as well as a means of attracting supporters and wives (Wiessner and Tumu n.d.). As Wiessner (1989:60) notes:

> The fact that all of the dancers could co-ordinate their dress, and that each individual was well-connected enough to obtain the valued shell and feather decorations for the dance, conveyed an impression of group strength, unity and wealth. Each individual stood to benefit from showing identity with a wealthy and unified group, in terms of promoting exchange and discouraging warfare, as groups from other valleys were potential enemies.

Support within Despot communities for feasts could have been facilitated by agreements that producers would consume large portions of their contributions within their own communities (at least initially), in addition to promises that they would be feasted by other groups in return. Finally, feasting as a strategy of control had the advantage that it could be combined with other strategies such as warfare payments and bridewealth payments to create more effective manipulation of surpluses. Thus, by making death compensation and feasts essential aspects of warfare, Despots succeeded in making warfare an economic, as well as a military, community endeavor that could be manipulated by Despots for their own benefit (Modjeska 1982:91).

Archaeological Implications

The archaeological correlates of the Despot type of community organization and inequality include relatively small communities (frequently defended where they were sedentary) and relatively low population densities compared to more developed transegalitarian communities; pronounced evidence of warfare; very limited amounts of prestige goods or regional exchange; limited evidence for feasting including communal eating, cooking, and dancing areas; relatively egalitarian residences and wealth indicators; and limited differences in grave goods, with the most wealthy grave goods restricted almost entirely to adults (acquired status). Because of limited surpluses and the minimal competitive use of foods in Despot communities, I would not necessarily expect initial domestication to emerge at this level, although this is not entirely inconceivable. On the other hand, imported, genetically enhanced domesticates that were more productive than wild forms could be more cost effective to use than wild foods. Such varieties might be adopted by Despot communities (or any other community type), as was the case with the sweet potato in the eastern New Guinea Highlands.

A number of complex hunter-gatherers and simple horticulturists exhibited Despot types of organization and inequality. Among prehistoric hunter-gatherers, Mesolithic or early Neolithic types of communities with pronounced evidence of conflict and limited prestige goods constitute the best archaeological candidates for this type of community organization, for example, the Nubian Mesolithic at Sahaba (Wendorf 1968), the early Middle period Chumash in California (Lambert 1992; Lamber and Walker 1991; Walker 1989), the early and middle phases on the Northwest Coast (beginning ca. 2500 b.p.) with the increasing skeletal evidence for violence (Coupland 1988:238–239; Beattie 1980; Cybulski 1992:158; in press), and Linear Bandkeramik plus some Middle Neolithic settlements in Europe with fortifications, violent deaths, low population densities, and limited prestige goods all occurring in achieved status contexts (Keeley 1992; Sherratt 1982:23–24). Interestingly, the upper range of violent death is very similar for both the ethnographic cases, such as the Yanomamo or similar South American groups (30–45%; Ferguson 1989; Keeley, in press), and the archaeological cases such as the Chumash and Northwest Coast cultures (20–32%; Lambert and Walker 1991; Cybulski 1992).

Reciprocator Communities

While many authors have noted the extreme ends of the power continuum in the New Guinea Highlands (Great Men Despots versus Big Men Entrepreneurs), Lemonnier (1990a) has introduced the term "Leader" to refer to intermediate types of inequalities and power centralization associated with other distinctive characteristics. This appears to be generally consistent with Johnson and Earle's (1987) use of the term "Head Man." Instead of these terms, I will use the term "Reciprocator" in this discussion because it is specifically formulated for archaeological modeling. Lemonnier repeatedly stresses that there really is a continuum of change and that it is difficult to find completely qualitative differences between the varying types of aggrandizers and communities. The distinguishing characteristics of Leaders for Lemonnier (1990a:123ff.) are that the communities are overtly nonegalitarian, that Leaders openly compete with each other within their communities, that there is more emphasis on their organizing and financial role (combined with their ongoing role as warrior leaders) although still nominally for the benefit of the group, and that they initiate exchange with ex-enemies for their own benefit. Leaders are also described as being wealthier, having more wives, having larger social networks and followers, and as participating in many marriage exchanges. For Lemonnier, they are clearly an evolutionary step toward the Big Man Entrepreneurs, and differ only in degree.

Thus, although Lemonnier does not make clear statements on the issue, one can expect Reciprocators (Leaders) to employ all of the same strategies used by Despots for creating debts, power, and surpluses. However several strategies achieve new emphasis and importance. These include bridewealth, exchange investments, more diverse and elaborate feasts, and possibly child growth payments. Each merits some explanation.

Bridewealth

Lemonnier (1990a:100, 111) observes that communities without Big Men (i.e., Despot or Reciprocator communities) often give wives or pigs to allies that have sustained battle losses on their behalf, and that substitution of wealth (primarily pigs) for human lives is fairly common in societies without Big Men. By extending this principle to marriage, that is, by transforming the egalitarian ethic of exchanging a woman for a woman into the transegalitarian ethic of exchanging wealth for a woman, Reciprocators could achieve several self-serving goals.

First, bridewealth enabled Reciprocators with economic advantages to obtain more desirable (generally more productive) wives by simply paying more than other men in their community. Bridewealth may easily have begun as a supplemental payment to bride service or other more egalitarian wife exchange arrangements.

Second, the substitution of wealth for wives enabled wealthy Reciprocators to obtain more wives than they might otherwise be able to acquire, thereby acquiring more productive labor to increase their economic advantages (Lightfoot and Feinman 1982:67). In essence, this could create a positive feedback situation.

Third, bridewealth was an extremely powerful and effective mechanism for creating and enhancing wealth and power inequalities between families in the same community.

Fourth, bridewealth could eventually obligate everyone who wished to marry to produce substantial amounts of surplus as well as going into debt (Lemonnier 1990a:78, 80).

Fifth, as in most of tribal Africa (Modjeska 1982:56–58, 67–68), bridewealth payments exceeded the net worth of most junior members of the community, thus placing junior men who wished to marry firmly under the control of, and in contractual debt to, aggrandizers with wealth. Men that wanted to marry had to attach themselves to corporate kinship groups or unrelated aggrandizers. Marriage could thus become largely a contract (and alliance) between corporate kin groups (Rosman and Rubel 1971:13; Wiessner and Tumu n.d.).

Sixth, bridewealth payments, like death compensation payments, could be promoted by aggrandizers as "loans" of wealth rather than payments (or a combination of the two). Reciprocators from different corporate groups could agree between themselves to reciprocally pay back these loans in a never-ending cycle of exchange that not only could be portrayed to the community as solidifying relations between the groups (and ensuring the flow of mates for the future), but would also continually create a demand for the production of surpluses and of debts both between groups and within groups. As more people were married, more surpluses were required, and more debts were created. Naturally, it was the Reciprocator who organized these debts, and perhaps only minimally engaged in active production. It appears that marriages involving bridewealth were usually contracted between groups in different communities, presumably in the attempt to widen the network of surplus and power potentially available. The earliest period described in the oral traditions that Wiessner and Tumu (n.d.) recorded in New Guinea indicates that marriages were purposefully arranged to channel, access, and extend the flow of goods. This tendency is certainly strong in the more complex Entrepreneurial communities (Lemonnier 1990a:136; Rosman and Rubel 1971:13) and must have begun earlier. In Reciprocator communities, bridewealth and the subsequent exchanges appear to be of equal importance to warfare-related strategies for increasing production and concentrating power. In fact, since warfare could inhibit marriages and wealth exchanges between groups, some ethnologists argue that warfare tends to progressively diminish in importance as the material benefits to be gained from marriage (and other) exchanges increase (Feil 1987:83; Lemonnier 1990a:129). However, the progressive replacement of warfare by exchange as the principal strategy used by aggrandizers to acquire power and wealth may not become significant until Entrepreneur levels of exchange are achieved. In fact, it is possible that the increased surpluses and competition that characterize Reciprocator communities might actually increase warfare to maximum levels in these communities. The issue is unclear from ethnographic data and there is disagreement on the subject among ethnographers. Leaving aside the potentially disruptive effect of warfare, in other culture areas the relation between marriage, bridewealth, and the concentration of wealth and power has often been noted (e.g., Modjeska 1982:56–58, 67–68; Saenz 1991; Yanagisako 1979). Thus, the strategy of using bridewealth to create inequalities, debt, and surplus production appears very widespread at certain levels of surplus production in transegalitarian societies, although variants such as the use of marriage to establish trading partnerships (Wood 1980:105) also occur in some instances.

Child Growth Payments

Unfortunately, most of the comparative ethnographies from New Guinea provide little detail on child growth payments in Reciprocator communities, although Mauss (1967:6, 26) indicated their importance elsewhere in Melanesia. Child growth payments are certainly strongly developed in New Guinea Entrepreneur communities as well as in equivalent communities on the Northwest Coast (Rosman and Rubel 1971:174, 187, 195, 198). I suspect the initial expression of this strategy is to be found in Reciprocator communities, and thus I will outline the strategy here. Child growth payments are simply the logical extension of bridewealth where surpluses are abundant enough to warrant still higher marriage payments. In fact, Wohlt (1978:81) states that when a wife dies, her clan has to be compensated for the costs of raising her. Her funeral payments are, in essence, belated child growth payments. By investing wealth in children at specified life events (birth, namings, first menstruation, initiations, tatooings, piercings) and in costly training for specific roles, the parents (or corporate group) successively raises a child's value, especially as a marriage partner. Anyone wishing to marry such a child would therefore have to provide a marriage payment (and/or funeral payment) comparable to or exceeding the amount invested in the child in order to compensate the investing group for the loss of their investments in an explicitly valued corporate member. Among the Tlingit, Oberg (1973:33, 35, 81, 121) clearly links the brideprice to feasts and potlatches held for elite children's stages of maturation. Clearly advantageous for aggrandizers, such practices would increase the volume of exchange, stimulate expropriateable wealth production even further (both to underwrite the growth payments and to return the higher marriage exchange payments), and create larger, more binding debts between groups as well as within groups. The short-term advantage to the corporate or support group paying for the child growth events would be a strong claim on the child and the expectation of eventually receiving large amounts of wealth in marriage payments. This investment of labor and resources in children for exchange purposes is not fundamentally different from the investment of labor and resources in the raising and fattening of pigs or cattle for exchange. Both are means of converting, concentrating, and storing food surpluses in highly valued and desired forms. As we shall see, child growth strategies have a number of profound implications for understanding the archaeological record and the development of hereditary elites.

Investments

Lemonnier (1990a:35, 123) clearly states that the power of Reciprocators (Leaders) is largely based on the manipulation of wealth and that they use investments and intervillage exchange networks, but not on as large a scale as Entrepreneurial Big Men. The enhanced control that this exchange provided and the motivating self-interest of Reciprocators was undoubtedly the same in nature as Entrepreneurs (Strathern 1971:215–216, 219). In the Entrepreneur communities of New Guinea, investments are returned with an increment, or interest (the "moka"), in addition to the original loan. Thus, profit is involved. In Reciprocator communities, it does not appear that increments are mandatory or even expected, although to be able to do so is a sign of economic success and power. The simple loaning out of wealth (generally pigs in New Guinea) and its simple return in the future is often all that is involved. While this may not seem to represent economically rational behavior, it involves several advantages.

First, it enables producers to continue to amass wealth without having to store it or care for it (or in the case of pigs, feed it). This circumvents the severe limitations that begin to develop in the accumulation of subsistence surpluses after one's immediate subsistence needs are fulfilled.

Second, it continues to create debts and contractual relationships, which are the real core of aggrandizers' power and what they probably seek most. Debts and investments can be increased simply by increasing one's investment relationships.

Third, there is always the hope that an increment may be returned with the original loan, thus creating a profit, but also increasing the exchange amount in the next cycle. In Reciprocator societies, it seems clear that surplus production is not reliable or abundant enough for most people to feel confident that they will be able to pay back any increases on loans. Rather than risk reprisals for defaulting if interest payments were mandatory, they would probably avoid accepting loans, thus forcing Reciprocators to accept less advantageous exchanges such as simple return in kind for investments.

Investment can take place as a private loan between individuals; however, this has a very limited effect. An important point in the ethnographies is that exchange takes place primarily between the wealthy members of communities—those who have proved that they can return payments of surplus. According to Wiessner and Tumu (n.d.), successful aggrandizers and clans are sought for investments. Community members lacking surpluses are viewed as high-risk loan prospects, and typically the interest on loans to poor individuals is considerably higher than the lower-risk loans to the wealthy (Lemonnier 1990a:36; Rosman and Rubel 1971:30). The same principle still helps determine loan rates in contemporary industrial societies. Investments with successful corporate groups (versus individuals) must have been viewed as even more secure. This partly explains the emphasis on corporate death compensation payments, corporate marriage payments, corporate funeral payments, corporate housebuilding payments, or other major events as pretexts for establishing investment exchanges in Reciprocator communities. Such corporate exchanges generally occur at formal feasts that require the support of the corporate kin members (Rosman and Rubel 1971:27).

Feasts

Reciprocator communities had a range of feasts. In some of these feasts, like the previously described Despot communal feasts, a portion of surplus (wealth) was used in consumptive displays of success meant to impress and to attract desirable members (labor). In fact, food was generally given even to nonsupporters of feasts (Oberg 1973:123; Young 1971:225), who in some cases could constitute up to 50% of a community or corporate kin group (Strathern 1971:138, 143). Such "generosity" must have helped dissipate open envy, discontentment, and clandestine mischief of nonparticipants that could sabotage aggrandizers' plans.

In other types of feasts, such as reciprocal exchange feasts (Figure 3), conspicuous consumption displays of success and wealth could take many forms, including competition between Reciprocators to produce the largest yams (sometimes up to 100 kg; Clark and Parry 1990:296, 333), competition to produce other foods that were given to the hosted rival Leaders or allies or left to rot in public displays (Feil 1987:246; Young 1971:162), or the competitive use of valuable fish oil that was burned rather than eaten. I will discuss the destruction of property used as displays of success in greater detail in the concluding comments. The portion of the feasting surplus that remained after such displays was given away as a contractual investment with the stipulation that at least the equivalent be returned within a reasonable amount of time (typically five to ten or more years for big feasts) together with a comparable meal. Lemonnier (1990a:135) has argued that Reciprocators used these feasts as competitive arenas between individuals and groups, but that the rivalry was not as pronounced as in the more complex Entrepreneur "competitive" feasts, and that rivalry did not always take the form of production increments. Rivalry could also be expressed in terms of control over human resources by the sophistication and paraphernalia of dancers, ritual ceremonial displays, and military displays. The main core of these reciprocal exchange feasts, especially when combined with bridewealth and death compensation payments, seems clearly related to the generation of surpluses, debts, and power. However, the fragility of this power is emphasized by Chowning (1979:73):

> Eventually they [followers] will receive their rewards—shared prestige, return gifts of food and valuables, the pleasures of the accompanying ceremonies, and aid from the big man when they need it—but only if the big man is successful, and he will only be successful if he has persuaded his followers that he is likely to be.

Commensurate with the increased role and frequency of reciprocal exchange feasting in Reciprocator communities must have been increases in the size of feasting facilities, the amounts of prepared surpluses, and the volume of prestige goods, both local and imported. The bottom line of using feasts in the quest for wealth and power is (1) that people commit themselves to producing a surplus, (2) that the surplus is loaned out, (3) that lenders expect to benefit, and (4) that feast organizers expect to benefit even more. The specific benefits or other details may vary, but these core features are probably constant.

It is at the Reciprocator level that individual household economic production and exchange becomes the lynchpin for acquiring wealth and power. Like contemporary small capitalists starting businesses, Reciprocators work especially hard to amass the capital necessary to begin the somewhat risky investment cycle and to enhance their subsequent relative position. As Young (1971:89, 108) observed, in order to be a successful aggrandizer, it was necessary to be a *good* gardener. Leading Reciprocators vigorously promoted a strong work ethic among all their community coresidents to pay off debts. It is also at the Reciprocator level that the manipulation of ideology to consolidate positions of power can first be discerned. In Young's (1971:80) study, for example, success at gardening and especially in producing large yams was largely attributed to the personal magical abilities of the male gardeners. Promoting themselves in this role, Reciprocators would often do garden magic for others much as aggrandizers in more complex communities claim intercession abilities with powerful supernatural forces.

Examples

Modjeska (1982) clearly identifies the Duna as typical of the intermediate types of societies that Lemonnier refers to as Leadership (Reciprocator) communities. In addition, the lowland New Guinea communities described by Young (1971), with their corporate feasts, the intervillage rivalry and attempts to outproduce each other, and their relatively limited potential for surplus production, seem to exemplify the lower end of the Reciprocator category.

In the North American Northwest, the best ethnographic examples of Reciprocator GENS communities can be found around the moderately productive fisheries on the Plateau, that is, the Interior "core riverine" area where salmon surpluses were moderately abundant compared to coastal or more peripheral Interior regions. The Thompson "chiefs" in particular resemble the Reciprocator head men of New Guinea in many respects. Thompson "chiefs" were not hereditary, although sons often succeeded their fathers. A chief's rank was determined by his wealth and personal characteristics, especially his oratory and warrior abilities, but the wealthy held the most important positions and exercised influence by giving feasts and presents. There were no women chiefs and they had no voice in councils or matters of public importance (Teit 1900:289–290, 1906:255; compare Burch 1975:225–228). These characteristics are almost identical to Reciprocators in New Guinea, and as in New Guinea, cultural beliefs and values, such as the killing of a stranger after a death in the family (Teit 1900:355), ensured that there would always be good reasons for raids or warfare if it served individual interests. Other characteristics of Plateau Reciprocators include elaborate training and maturation celebrations for elite children, largely reciprocal feasting with little competitive feasting, extensive regional exchange, reduced warfare (compared to the Despot communities in the peripheral regions), wealth exchanges at marriage, and the holding of some slaves. The work ethic was still relatively strong among these elite groups as well (Teit 1900, 1906, 1909). The Owens Valley Paiute (Bettinger 1978, 1983) provide another good example, although their position in the regional trade network seems to have enhanced their complexity beyond what might be expected on the basis of local resources alone.

The most important function of these "chiefs" was to organize feasts at which extensive trading took place. Some coastal groups of northwest Alaska also appear to be typical Reciprocator groups, combining warfare, fear, and exchange of surpluses to gain political and economic control (Burch 1975, 1980).

Archaeological Expectations

As previously discussed, compared to Despot communities, indications of warfare may decrease or increase or remain constant in most Reciprocator communities, while exchange feasting associated with marriages and other events acquires a greater importance. Thus, it could be expected that the first elaboration of feasting facilities or public architecture in communities with "independent" family households would occur with the first significant concentration of power and wealth and with the first substantial production of surpluses (e.g., the building of men's houses by Reciprocators; Lemonnier 1990a:123). These specialized structures are often viewed by archaeologists as "temples" or other ritual buildings used to create group bonds (Earle 1989:86), but I would suggest that they are more appropriately interpreted as feasting or related structures built at the instigation of Reciprocators to enhance the importance of feasting and to display the power and wealth of the community that Reciprocators could control. As we shall see with Entrepreneurs, ancestors, too, were often involved in successful feasting, and structures emphasizing their importance also emerged at early stages of transegalitarian complexity. In GENS communities, large corporate group residential structures usually serve as feasting facilities. Commensurate with these developments would be the enlargement of the exchange sphere over a large region for obtaining prestige goods, as well as a greater production and circulation of prestige goods and possibly the first noticeable differentiation of domestic structures according to socioeconomic inequalities (Lightfoot and Feinman 1982:67). In the early transegalitarian communities in the Oaxaca Valley, Feinman (1991) notes that high-status households had regional contacts, whereas others had only local contacts.

Perhaps most importantly of all, however, are consequences in terms of grave goods. If I am correct in assuming that child growth payments are first expressed in Reciprocator communities, then it is logical to expect children (mainly of Reciprocators) who have had investments of wealth made in them at some of their life stages to be accompanied by lavish displays of their worth when they die prematurely. Standard archaeological interpretations of ascribed status lead archaeologists to expect lavish grave goods accompanying children to occur only in stratified class societies, that is, chiefdoms and states. However, on the basis of archaeological and ethnographic examples, it seems clear that this practice of ascribing status to children begins in many typical transegalitarian societies without socioeconomic stratification or settlement hierarchies (Mainfort 1985:576; O'Shea 1984:251; Rothschild 1979; Schulting 1994:62; Shennan 1982:30).

Reciprocator communities should also exhibit moderate levels of population density, depending on whether their subsistence base is hunting and gathering or horticultural. Given the more overt economically competitive nature of Reciprocator societies and the enhanced role of feasting and specialty foods, plus the competitive nature of food exchanges and debts at feasts (involving not only production of large food quantities but also the competitive production of prestige foods of large size, high value, and high labor costs; Lightfoot and Feinman 1982:66; Rosman and Rubel 1971:179; Young 1971:167, 241), I expect the first evidence of domestication to appear in complex hunter gatherer societies organized at the Reciprocator level. It is interesting to note that in the Near East, Cauvin (1978:77, 116–117) has argued that domestication was not a function of ecological pressures, but of social changes. He notes, for example, that the bull became an important symbolic animal before it was domesticated. Both of these observations fit well with the model of feasting that is being proposed here since feasting is expected to develop under conditions of surplus and involve difficult-to-procure animals like bulls that could be used as symbols of bravery, power, and prowess.

The likelihood of domestication taking place probably increased substantially as Reciprocator communities emerged in ecological niches conducive to domestication (as opposed to cold climates). Given the increased importance of feasting, serving vessels for feasting or public rituals should also exhibit competitive prestige elaborations in most Reciprocator communities, whether of wood, special gourds, elaborate baskets, pottery, or stone. Thus, part-time specialized craft production should become apparent for the first time and continue to increase in intensity and sophistication as social complexity, stratification, and the size of transegalitarian communities increase (Clark and Parry 1990:298, 307, 323).

GENS communities with corporate group control over resources should exhibit some pronounced differences between constituent corporate groups in terms of wealth and power and size. Feasting and performance areas within the larger corporate group residences may become evident. Within these residences, distinctions between owner or elite domestic areas and common supporters or slaves should be evident. I view the prehistoric Keatley Creek housepit village near Lillooet as a good representative of a very advanced Reciprocator community or more probably a simple Entrepreneur community featuring subsistence-based corporate groups. Members of this community were involved in a very widespread regional exchange network in prestige goods (especially coastal shells and obsidian); they produced labor-intensive prestige goods (copper tubular beads, nephrite adzes, bone and stone sculptures); there are clear distinctions between owner and nonowner domestic areas within the large corporate residences; there are pronounced differences in grave goods including rich child burials; there may be community cult structures; warfare (ethnographically) was not as intensive as in other areas; and domesticates occur in the form of dogs.

Other archaeological examples that I would propose include the Natufian in the Levant with rich child burials (Henry 1985), Early and Middle Jomon communities in Japan, the Indian Knoll community with wealthy child burials (Rothschild 1979), the Late period Chumash with their abundance of regionally exchanged beads and still-elevated levels of violent death (King 1978, 1990; Lambert 1992; Lambert and Walker 1991), the late prehistoric Iroquois, some Basketmaker and early Pueblo villages (Lightfoot and Feinman 1982), some European Upper Paleolithic groups, and the European Neolithic causewayed enclosure communities where feasting, ritual, and sometimes violent conflict were prominent (Clarke et al. 1985:134). Also of importance is the explicit link between these developments and an increase in resource production (Clarke et al. 1985:134; King 1990:117–118).

Entrepreneur Communities

The potlatch and moka systems described by Codere (1950) and Strathern (1971) constitute the classic Entrepreneur competitive feasts. In these cases, environment and technology created favorable conditions for the reliable production of substantial surpluses especially with the intensification of labor. Whereas New Guinea Despot feasts involved at most 10–20 pigs, Entrepreneur competitive feasts involved thousands of pigs with individual Entrepreneurs contributing 100–500 by themselves (Feil 1987:238–239; Lemonnier 1990a:139–140). Population densities are unusually high: for hunter gatherers up to 10 or more people per square kilometer, and for horticulturists up to 100 or more people per square kilometer. Under normal conditions in Entrepreneur communities, those who want to produce surpluses can, and it is in this situation where increment payments on loans are regularly expected and agreed to even between close individual exchange partners who do not compete with each other (Wiessner and Tumu n.d.; Wohlt 1978:96). Besides the intensive food production efforts of the immediate family, loans and investments become *the* major avenue to wealth, success, and power. Entrepreneurs therefore use all previous pretexts for establishing exchange relationships (especially death compensation and marriage payments), they initiate more individual exchange relationships, they organize larger and more elaborate feasts of many types with blatant competition between participating corporate groups and individuals, and they invest considerable amounts of wealth in child growth payments (Modjeska 1982:108; Rosman and Rubel 1971:132, 174, 87, 195, 198). The self-interest behind these strategies is fundamentally the same as previously documented. There are two significant changes, however.

The first change involves the use of profit as a means of attracting supporters. The greater the return profit that Entrepreneurs could offer their supporters for contributions to competitive feasts, the stronger would be the motivation of supporters to produce surpluses and to permit Entrepreneurs to influence the use of surpluses. This would also indirectly increase the total contractual debt in the community. Thus, in addition to the competitive display of wealth and success in order to attract desirable labor (supporters, laborers, mates, exchange partners), competitive feasters compete with each other to generate as large interest payments as possible in order to attract exchange partners and feasting supporters. Gifts from Entrepreneurs to supporters are important *public* parts of feasts (Wohlt 1978:29). Surpluses are used overtly to control others and win supporters (Mauss 1967:73; Strathern 1971:219). Self-interest together with contractual debts motivate and make this feasible through competitive wealth exchange feasting (Strathern 1971:215–216).

Contractual debts involving interest payments are the underlying economic logic behind the frenzy to give away (to invest) as much as possible— even to the point of temporary impoverishment—and to consume food and wealth in the most lavish fashion possible. On the Northwest Coast, Boas (1966:77) identified the underlying principle of the potlatch as the "interest bearing investment of property." Oberg (1973:98), too, clearly viewed the main purpose of the feast as economic, saying that it "is really an investment of surplus food in the community at large which will later bring in certain returns to the house that makes the original investment." A potlatch "cancels not only old debts but creates new credits" (Oberg 1973:127). Failure to meet contractual debts could result in the equivalent of foreclosure—enslavement or military reprisals (Mauss 1967:3, 40; Oberg 1973:118–119). Ritual performances, dances, costuming, and serving bowls all become more important arenas for competitive display than in Reciprocator communities. Obviously, the rates of interest that are typically cited in the literature (30–100% per year; Codere 1950:70; Mauss 1967:30; Strathern 1971:98) cannot be sustained for long by any environment or economy. Thus, supporters must have often received considerably less than they were promised, much as modern stock investors are led to believe they will reap large returns on their investments but generally are disappointed. The important aspect of these feasts was the public contractual exchange of wealth. In the western Highlands of New Guinea, where Entrepreneur communities flourished, there was an unparalleled diversity of occasions on which wealth exchanges were considered appropriate. While the actual pretext may not have been critical, some pretexts were obviously more compelling than others.

The second major change from Reciprocator to Entrepreneur systems was in the importance of warfare. While warfare was still important (perhaps in large part due to defaulting or other disputes about loans; Feil 1987:268; Keeley, in press; Mauss 1967:3; Strathern 1971:154, 168, 171) and was avowedly manipulated by Entrepreneurs for their own economic interests (Strathern 1971:54, 76–77, 98, 183), warfare could also be viewed as interfering with profitable exchange (Feil 1987:68–73; Lemonnier 1990a:129, 134). Feil and Lemonnier argue that there was a significant reduction in the frequency and intensity of warfare among Entrepreneur communities from the high peaks reached in Despot or Reciprocator communities. This is supported by archaeological data from the Northwest Coast and California showing a decline in violent deaths in the late prehistoric periods (Figure 5; also see Cybulski 1992). Moreover, on the Northest Plateau, it is clear that the communities producing the largest surpluses and engaging in the most trade (e.g., Fraser River Lillooet and Canyon Shuswap) were the least warlike (Teit 1906:236). Teit (1909:541) even explicitly states that peace "was requisite for their valuable trading interests." Ports of trade exemplify the most extreme expression of this principle, and several places on the Plateau (e.g., the Dalles) seem to have functioned in this capacity.

The New Guinea ethnographers also suggest that it was more difficult to gather large numbers of warriors together for raids in Entrepreneur communities because increasing numbers of people viewed fighting as being contrary to their own marital and exchange interests. When conquests were successful, victors often took over land outright, but I suspect that sometimes victors may have imposed exchanges at exorbitant rates of interest on the vanquished since high rates (up to 300%) were signs of superiority (Lemonnier 1990a:152) and might even set the stage for chiefdom types of settlement hierarchies. In Entrepreneur communities, individuals could often produce surpluses on a reliable basis and engage in profitable economic investment on their own. As a result, surplus-based corporate kinship groups such as lineages may have begun to weaken.

As a variation on these trends in warfare, Wiessner and Tumu (n.d.) have documented an historic instance of an elaboration of New Guinea fighting into "great wars" at the Entrepreneur levels *to generate exchange* via payments to allies and death compensations. That is, instead of using marriage payment or feasting strategies to create debts and exchange, huge confrontations were organized where the beginnings and endings were highly orchestrated; where intense socializing involving courtship, feasting, and dancing continued for months or even years; where warriors fought in their most lavish costumes; where fighting was prohibited outside of formal battles; where territorial gain

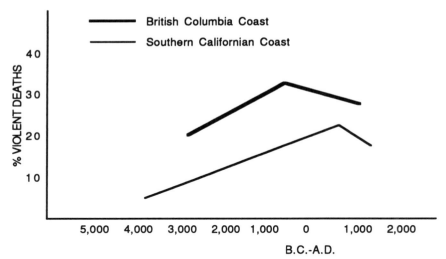

Figure 5. The percentage of violent deaths (attributed to warfare by the analysts) gradually rises in both the Northwest Coast (Cybulski, in press) and the California Chumash (Walker 1989) areas during the period of initial indicators of complexity. After reaching maximum values of 32% and 21%, respectively, these levels subsequently decline. This decline appears to support suggestions by authors who suggest that the increasing importance of marriage and competitive feasting strategies act to limit warfare to some extent in Big Man communities. Using the terminology of the present chapter, the initial increases in violence and prestige items would represent Despot societies, maximum occurrences of violence accompanied by increasing indicators of a prestige economy probably represent Reciprocator societies, while decreases of violence with maximum development of prestige economies represent Entrepreneur societies.

was prohibited; but where people were killed and success or failure carried real consequences involving the ability to recruit allies or the initiation of more "serious" battles after the great wars. While the intensification of this kind of warfare was an alternate strategy for generating exchange and wealth, in the long run it was not as effective as competitive feasting (the moka and tee) and was replaced by competitive feasting. However, this example does indicate that some variability in emphasis on different strategies was possible at the Entrepreneur level, although some strategies were clearly more common and more effective than others.

In addition to death compensation payments and competitive feasts, marriage became a primary sphere of exchange and for acquiring wealth. Not only were child growth payments elaborate, but children of elite families underwent prolonged and costly training for various roles: elite wives, political leaders, warriors, hunters, runners, ritualists. In some cases, menstrual seclusion or boys' initiatory vision quests could be very costly and last many years (e.g., Kan 1989:88, 91–92; Wiessner and Tumu n.d.). The apparent motive behind this functionally unnecessary and costly elaboration of training was to increase the value of children in terms of marriage payments and subsequent exchanges. Thus, bridewealth increased considerably in Entrepreneur communities, and affinal relationships were sought for their economic value while establishing a biological family was often of only secondary importance (Boas 1966:55–56; Feil 1987:72; Rosman and Rubel 1971:76, 117–118, 156). Wealthy families naturally sought out equally or more wealthy families for marriage alliances. To broaden the exchange network these marriage alliances were generally between wealthy families of different communities (Lightfoot and Feinman 1982:67; Schulting 1994:84–85; Sproat 1987:72). Numbers of polygynous marriages also increasingly extended "chains" of investment, debt, and credit over wide areas (Feil 1987:250; Lemonnier 1990a:136; Rosman and Rubel 1971:13; Strathern 1971:115–121). When marriage became the main pretext for exchange and profit, women's status increased significantly (although still well below that of men; Feil 1987:72, 215ff.; Modjeska 1982), warfare may have decreased, and matrilineal kinship groups probably emerged in many groups together with origin myths and major cults focused on women (Feil 1987:221).

This emphasis on the exchange role of marriage may be one important reason why matrilineal organization tends to occur in many communities with relatively elaborate transegalitarian political organizations (Allen 1984; Feil 1987:121), for example, the Tlingit. Typically, elite women in Entrepreneur communities maintained close ties with their families of orientation and because of their great value often ranked much higher than commoner men. There were even occasional Big Women who participated in moka exchanges and had their own exchange partners, although this was rare and did not involve public roles, or at best involved minor participatory ones (Feil 1987:222, 226–227). Similar characteristics were found among some of the Northwest Coast groups, such as the Bella Coola and Kwakiutl (Rosman and Rubel 1971:119, 135, 164), where women could even be chiefs of corporate groups; however, in both New Guinea and the Northwest Coast, men clearly dominated the most important economic and political arenas and were even the *exclusive* members of important matrifocal cults (Feil 1987:221, 231; Modjeska 1982; Rosman and Rubel 1971:58). That marriage was simply a pretext for exchange is demonstrated by the fact that in Entrepreneur communities of the Northwest Coast such as the Bella Coola and the Kwakiutl, fictitious marriages were arranged if no suitable mates were available. In these cases, exchange marriage contracts were drawn up between an individual and another individual's body part (a foot, or leg) or with a dog belonging to the family (Boas 1966:54–56; Rosman and Rubel 1971:117–118, 156, 198). This was explicitly done to enable one family to exchange wealth with another, and it is interesting that it only occurred in societies with competitive feasts and profit-driven exchanges.

Several other characteristics of Entrepreneurs are worthy of note. Like Reciprocators, Entrepreneurs are ambitious individuals (Young 1971:187) who frequently try to concentrate all important roles of power in their own hands, including financial, political, military, and ritual roles (Lemonnier 1990a:144–145). Their role in ritual and feasting spheres is of particular interest for archaeologists.

Beginning in Reciprocator communities, supernatural claims to power constitute one strategy that aggrandizers in most areas of the world attempted to use in order to bolster their influence and power (e.g., Kan 1989). Supernatural claims could also be used as important validation or legitimization for Reciprocator, Entrepreneur, and chiefly privileges. Validation is important for retaining power (Blau 1964:199ff.). Reciprocators and Entrepreneurs therefore took credit for some natural misfortunes to enhance their reputations as powerful agents of supernatural forces (Young 1971:185)—a strategy that often backfired when general misfortune occurred, Entrepreneurs being blamed for all misfortunes (Jewitt 1974:98). Entrepreneurs and Reciprocators also promoted their ancestors as powerful supernatural beings that channeled supernatural forces directly through aggrandizive descendants (Kan 1989:82; Shnirelman 1990; Wiessner and Tumu n.d.), while the living aggrandizers promoted themselves as possessing powerful magic (stemming in part from powerful ancestors) that could influence reproduction and subsistence success (Young 1971:80). As a consequence, these aggrandizers competed with each other to produce the largest yams (Clark and Parry 1990:296, 333; Young 1971), implying the greatest supernatural power, and they promoted death cults for their ancestors, who were portrayed as supernaturally powerful (often involving the reverence of preserved heads or bodies). Aggrandizers therefore frequently devised the construction of ancestral "ritual" structures, including burial grounds and shrines that made manifest the power and importance of their ancestors. These and other ritual structures that were directly or indirectly associated with feasting events were administered by aggrandizers, their families, or their supporters. Such structures included death cult structures; men's houses used by the Entrepreneur and his ceremonial support group as residences, sacrificial huts, feasting and cooking shelters; wealth display huts; ceremonial grounds; and "temples" (Strathern 1971:8, 38–39, 195; Young 1971:80, 190–193). These types of facilities should be much more prominent in Entrepreneur than Reciprocator communities.

As ritual leaders, aggrandizers also appear to use community (or secret society) cult rituals as a continuing pretext for holding exchange and competitive feasts, for these are recurring elements in Reciprocator and Entrepreneur societies (Feil 1987; Rosman and Rubel 1971; Wiessner and Tumu n.d.; Young 1971:230). These structures and features as well as those mentioned in the preceding paragraph are probably some of the first specialized community structures to appear in the archaeological record and have almost universally been interpreted as ritual structures. Whether used directly for feasting or in less direct means of ritual control, their occurrence is puzzling unless explanatory frameworks are provided that link them to other important changes in these early communities, especially strategies used to promote the production and control of surpluses. In all transegalitarian societies, aggrandizers have probably attempted to promote and manipulate belief in their own supernatural powers and in the power of their ancestors for their own benefit. But it is only as the economic power of aggrandizers increases that they can convince other community members to accept these claims, and can appropriate more overtly the prerogative of being the primary communicator with, and spokesman for the will of, powerful ancestors or other spirits. Their special status was sometimes reinforced by using a special language, the requirement that commoners address them through intermediaries, and by the reduced menial work that Entrepreneurs performed (Wiessner and Tumu n.d.; Desmond Peters, personal communication, April 1992).

At the Entrepreneur level, aggrandizers were still viewed as representing the community or the corporate kinship group and were expected to provide some benefits to their constituents (Feil 1987:255; Lemonnier 1990a:81; Rosman and Rubel 1971:132). Nevertheless, their own self-interest was also clearly evident. Following Mauss (1967:72), both Lemonnier (1990a:33) and Modjeska (1982:93) even state that they had "capitalist" characteristics. Entrepreneurs had a great deal of wealth and many wives and engaged in a great deal of transactional, investment, and administrative work. They sought wives and children that were hardworking and productive. Entrepreneurs tended to establish crafted prestige goods as substitutes for food production in order to enhance their investment schemes, and they tended to control access to both imported and locally crafted prestige goods (through their regional connections to other Entrepreneurs or their control over high labor investments; Clark and Blake 1994) to further increase their control over the finance system (e.g., the control of the coastal shell trade necessary for marriage in Highland New Guinea or the dentalium shells necessary for marriage among many groups of the Northwest; Feil 1987:117, 160; Schulting 1994:92–93). Like Feil, Clark and Parry (1990:323) suggest that this control over important prestige items may have been critical in the emergence of chiefdoms. Similarly, Brunton (1975), Bishop (1987), and others have argued that both natural access constraints, such as those imposed by long distances, and artificial access constraints, such as control over exchange imposed by aggrandizers, result in increased socioeconomic and political complexity. Lemonnier (1990a:73) explicitly states that effort investment is the primary criterion for items used in economic competition, while Clark and Parry (1990:297) add that prestige goods in transegalitarian societies not only involve high labor costs to procure or produce but also have conspicuous display characteristics. In addition to controlling exchange, wherever possible, aggrandizers attempted to extend their control over basic subsistence resources to the point of even charging fees for passage through owned territories (Irimoto 1990; Wheeler 1990). However, this appears to be an alternate or reinforcing strategy rather than an absolutely critical one for socioeconomic inequality to develop in many cases, even in some chiefdoms (see Helms [1979] versus Earle and Preucel [1987:511] and Matson [1985:246]).

Finally, although there is some tendency for roles to be inherited even in Despot communities, the tendency is stronger in Reciprocator communities, and much stronger in Entrepreneur communities. About 75% of New Guinea Entrepreneur Big Men had fathers that were also Big Men. During their lifetimes, these Entrepreneurs tried to establish their sons with one or two wives and a number of moka partners, even transferring moka partnerships at death, practices similar to Kwakiutl transfers of trade and privileges to sons (Feil 1987:120; Lemonnier 1990a:44–45; Rosman and Rubel 1971:132; Strathern 1971:120, 171, 210–212; Young 1971:77). Some aggrandizers even made advance death payments that would be returned to their children like a transegalitarian version of life insurance (Wohlt 1978:83).

In Entrepreneur communities there is a substantial division into elite families and nonelites, with slavery appearing among the more elaborate Entrepreneur societies where independent family households constitute the basic subsistence unit (Feil 1987:118, Strathern 1971:204–205; Watanabe 1983:217), and in virtually all GENS Entrepreneur communities. Competition between rival Entrepreneur contenders both within their own communities and between communities is often very pronounced, even though these are frequently the same individuals with which they exchange investments and whose children they accept as in-laws.

Charlie Nairn and Andrew Strathern's 1974 film *Kawelka* shows many of the above characteristics in a most graphic form.

On the basis of descriptions of ancestor worship, slaves, "chiefs," exclusive territorial ownership, and charges for resource use by nonowners, some Ainu may represent Entrepreneur-type communities (see Irimoto 1990; Ohnuki-Tierney 1974:74–79; Watanabe 1983).

Resource-Based Corporate Groups

Competitive feasting involving interest payments is clearly one of the most common strategies used for extending personal power and wealth both within and between communities in the Entrepreneur societies of New Guinea and the Northwest Coast. This strategy reflects a common ability to produce surpluses, and results in many other behavioral similarities (especially in marriage exchanges, and child growth investments) as Mauss (1967) and others have noted. The only major difference in comparing the New Guinea and Northwest Coast examples involves the independent family versus the corporate group control over subsistence resources and the differences in individual power that these imply *within* corporate groups.

The amount of power concentrated in the person of the subsistence-based corporate Entrepreneur (often referred to as a house "chief") and his associated elite families appears to be much greater than among Entrepreneurs in communities with independent families. The elite corporate families constitute the legitimate owners or managers of key resources inherited from ancestors that originally developed extraction facilities or otherwise established privileged access to the resource locations. The resultant difference in power and stratification within corporate groups, between owners and tenants, seems to have had substantial effects on the expression of power within these corporate groups. Successful and wealthy groups capable of controlling large surpluses had hereditary elites who performed little or no menial work and whose daughters were kept in seclusion so that they never performed menial work and even had difficulty walking properly (Barnett 1955:180). These groups owned considerable numbers of slaves and conducted raids with the sole aim of obtaining more. In fact, the apparently exceptional level of violence among some GENS-type Entrepreneur communities such as the Kwakiutl and Haida may be the product of the importance of slave raiding by corporate elites for prestige, production, and profit. Coastal corporate group elites also supported a level of craft specialization unusual for other independent household Entrepreneur communities.

In many respects, each successful resource-owning corporate group was like a mini-chiefdom, and if one's definition of a chiefdom was based simply on interpersonal power or craft specialization, these corporate groups would constitute chiefdoms. However, if one approaches the definition of community types from the perspective of strategies used to acquire power and wealth, and the degree of extension of power, it is clear that the successful coastal corporate groups were using exactly the same strategies to generate surpluses as those used in New Guinea Entrepreneur societies, that is, marriage wealth exchanges and competitive or reciprocal feasting. Elite owners of resource locations may have used their control over these resources and people to produce initial (and limited) surpluses employing tenant labor. But effectively expanding that initial surplus beyond the corporate household was dependent on investment and marriage wealth exchanges. And this is why elite power in the Northwest Coast never extended to the control of more than one, or even an entire, community. From these perspectives, the Northwest

Coast cultures were Entrepreneur organizations, not chiefdoms (Miller and Boxberger 1994). They had socioeconomic stratification within corporate groups, but lacked chiefdom level political "integration," to use Earle's terms. This special, power-enhanced type of Entrepreneur organization might be called a "GENS Entrepreneur community" and its administrative head, a "GENS Entrepreneur."

Almost all the major groups on the Northwest Coast as well as the Plateau Wishram, Lillooet, and Canyon Shuswap appear to have had these Entrepreneur types of communities. On the coast, the Salish, the Bella Coola, the Kwakiutl, the Haida, the Tlingit and the Tsimshian all had some potlatches where increased returns were expected (Barnett 1955; Boas 1966; Dawson 1880; Garfield 1966; Krause 1956; Oberg 1973; Spier and Sapir 1930; Stott 1975; Swanton 1975; Teit 1906). These potlatches were generally associated with important events such as housebuilding, funerals, elite puberty or maturation rites, carved pole raisings, or simply potlatches whenever they could be afforded (Oberg 1973:33). Intervals between large potlatches were of the same order of magnitude as in New Guinea, 5–10 years. As previously noted, wealth exchanges dominated marriages in all groups, and child growth payments appear to have been quite elaborate for elite children; anyone lacking nose or ear ornaments looked "like a slave" (Schulting 1994:62). There was copious production and use of prestige goods in transactions, elite women had relatively high status, and aggrandizer advantages were passed on to offspring. Political power was limited to the corporate group or village (see Rosman and Rubel 1971). Moreover, as among New Guinea Entrepreneur communities, war was frequently not for conquest of land or for resources (Rosman and Rubel 1971:124, 139). The seemingly high incidence of warfare on the Northwest Coast (compared to the Interior groups, or even other Entrepreneur groups) may be related to the use of slaves for both prestige and practical purposes in economically powerful resource-based corporate groups. Slaves were predominantly captured in raids (Dawson 1880:132; Garfield 1966:29; Krause 1956:84) and were even viewed as one of the primary benefits of war, as well as being a primary constituent in amassing property (Swanton 1975:54). Defaulting on debts must have also contributed significantly to the motivations for war. War was ended among the Lillooet—as well as in New Guinea—by holding a major feast (potlatch).

Archaeological Indicators

In both hunting–gathering and horticultural Entrepreneur communities, I suspect that population densities approach the upper limits possible for these respective systems of production since the ethnographically recorded densities are among the highest for hunter-gatherers or horticulturists. Clearly, people were being motivated to extract as many resources from their environments as possible, and Entrepreneurs used every strategy in their repertory to increase people's willingness to enter into contractual debts necessitating the production of surpluses. However, it was primarily agricultural communities that provided a potential "bottomless pit of labor intensification and production surplus" (Blake and Clark 1989) fueled by debt creation. It was among these more productive food-producing communities that further evolution of complexity took place. True chiefdoms must have been exceedingly rare among hunter-gatherers, and may not have existed at all prehistorically.

Grave goods were lavish for Entrepreneur elites, including elite children. Shnirelman (1990:130) observes that bones of aggrandizers were considered to have potent magic. Entrepreneur graves might include ritual paraphernalia such as the elaborate spoons for feeding ancestors (ca. 4000–3000 b.p.) found at Pender Island on the Northwest Coast (Carlson 1991) or the ritual objects in Russian Upper Paleolithic graves (Soffer 1985:472). Elite women's graves might sometimes contain wealth on a par value or even occasionally greater value than that associated with elite males. In the case of more mobile, hunter-based Entrepreneur or Reciprocator communities such as those of the Upper Paleolithic, probably fewer permanent structures were built (Binford 1990:134; Soffer 1985:473) and proportionately more wealth might be interred with aggrandizers due to the problems their less powerful surviving kin might have in transporting wealth. That is, without the control over others' labor that rich or powerful men would have (many wives, children, slaves, or retainers to carry wealth and possessions), excessive possessions could become encumbrances for highly mobile subsistence-oriented families.

Specialized feasting and ritual structures, cooking facilities, prestige serving vessels, and open-air gathering areas should be present in communities with independent subsistence households, while GENS Entrepreneurs could probably command enough resources and labor within their own corporate groups to create some monumental structures such as the Northwest Coast longhouses and totem poles, or European megaliths. Ritual structures can exhibit a variety of poses (sacrificial structures for ancestors or feasting, wealth display structures for feasts, ancestral shrines, men's houses, feasting grounds, and others). Houses and communities of powerful Entrepreneurs can be expected to be larger, more lavish, and associated with more prestige goods and foods (Lightfoot and Feinman 1982:66–67; Shnirelman 1990:128). The competitive production and consumption by Entrepreneurs of special, labor-intensive foods for feasts (Rosman and Rubel 1971:179; Young 1971:167, 241) should constitute very strong pressures to domesticate feasting foods where the ecology is also conducive. Prestige food-serving containers for feasts should occur in many households throughout Entrepreneur communities since ritual feasting paraphernalia must have frequently been used in all investment transactions, whether between individual partners or between communities. Similarly, efforts of Entrepreneurs to involve as many people as possible in elaborately costumed dances performed at feasts could result in the relatively widespread occurrence of exotic shells, birds' wings, and other ornaments in many households of Entrepreneur communities.

Given the high levels of surplus food production and prestige item production that characterize Entrepreneur communities, plus the need to display success, it can be expected that destruction of wealth might occur as well as some evidence for slavery or human sacrifice. Destruction of wealth probably does not occur in other transegalitarian communities or is much more limited. Evidence for warfare in Entrepreneur societies may be comparatively less developed than in Reciprocator or advanced Despot societies although it often stays at high absolute levels due to the effectiveness of warfare in motivating people to produce surpluses for obtaining allies and for establishing peace. Regional exchange networks should be the largest of all transegalitarian networks and involve generalized elite styles and values forming "interaction spheres" that could extend out to include more peripheral Reciprocators and even Despot communities in the area. Interaction spheres involving prestige items probably begin to emerge at the Reciprocator level, but to a more limited degree. Significant craft specialization should be present as a corollary of the transformation of food surplus into wealth (Clark and Parry 1990).

In GENS communities, corporate residences should attain even larger dimensions than in Reciprocator communities and exhibit even more internal socioeconomic differentiation. At all levels of transegalitarian communities, resource-based corporate groups should display ownership of key resources; however, as the power of elites increases, control over more and different types of resources can be expected to spread, including for example, shell-collecting areas, hunting areas, and lithic sources. Similarly, in all transegalitarian communities, the power of aggrandizers is largely limited to their own community, and there is little evidence of settlement hierarchies with unusual monumental architecture at central places such as typifies chiefdoms.

Archaeological examples of Entrepreneur communities probably include a number of early Neolithic "Old European" cultures in the Balkan area, early Megalithic communities in western Europe (Sjögren 1986), European Battle Axe and Beaker cultures (Sherrat 1982:24), Late and Terminal Jomon, the Neolithic Liangzhu culture of China with its rich burials and wealth destruction (Xuanpei 1992), Late period Chumash (Arnold 1991, 1992), Near Eastern

Neolithic communities such as Çayönü (Davis 1991), Barra phase communities in coastal Chiapas with abundant prestige serving vessels (Blake 1994:44; Blake and Clark 1989; Clark and Blake 1989), protohistoric Huron villages, Marpole and later communities on the Northwest Coast, and at a simple Entrepreneur level the large prehistoric communities in the Lillooet region of the British Columbia Plateau, such as Keatley Creek, at the height of their development. The most wealthy Upper Paleolithic communities in Europe may have had Entrepreneurs, very possibly owning reindeer migration fordings and forming resource-based corporate groups.

Chiefdoms

I have been following Johnson (1973:2) in defining chiefdoms as a polity with two- or three-tiered hierarchy of communities. Arnold (1993:77) would add two other criteria to this definition: hereditary inequality, and some elite control over domestic labor. In chiefdom communities, the chief's position tends to be strongly hereditary, slavery is common, the competitive feast no longer appears to serve as a primary means of organizing the community or extending general control, and warfare involving the conquest of new land and the incorporation of more communities into the bottom of the settlement hierarchy are prominent. It is not my purpose to explore these later developments in detail; however, several observations are worth making on the basis of previous discussions.

First, chiefdoms occur in environments that lend themselves to even greater surplus production and intensification than Entrepreneur communities, often involving intensive agricultural practices and irrigation.

Second, by successfully manipulating strategies used at the transegalitarian levels, Entrepreneurs could eventually maneuver themselves into positions where they could invest so much wealth in the growth payments for their children that only the families of other chiefs (or elites) could provide the requisite bridewealth. Even at the Entrepreneur level, the tendency for children of Entrepreneurs to marry the children of other Entrepreneurs is pronounced (e.g., Wiessner and Tumu n.d.). On the Northwest Coast, elite offspring married other elite offspring, and families that could afford the luxury of raising girls with no productive abilities were deemed to be the most powerful and desirable marriage allies. The immediate purpose of increasing child growth value would be to increase the amount that supporters were supposed to produce and invest, as well as increasing the volume of debt owed to the chief by other groups for giving a valuable child in marriage. This practice would have excluded a large number of people from being able to compete with the chief for the ultimate control of the debt system, resulting in an almost closed class system in which strict heredity of resources, wealth, and power became established. Thus, the hereditary aspect of chiefdoms may be incidental and not central to the emergence or functioning of chiefdoms, despite (or in addition to) its ultimate sociobiological self-interest value. Interestingly, child growth investments continued to grow in importance in early states as did elite ownership of resources.

Third, because of this development, profit-based Entrepreneur competitive feasts (used primarily by the general populace as a means to select aggrandizers or corporate groups for support when succession was not fixed; Rosman and Rubel 1971:112, 203) were emptied of their function and disappeared. Other authors, including Mauss (1967:91) and Gregory (1982:201) have pointed out that gift exchanges like the Kula flourished most where chiefdoms were the weakest, and where power hierarchies were unstable, while Randsborg (1982:135) and Cannon (1989) have both argued that ostentatious material displays became most pronounced when there was uncertainty in reckoning relative status (i.e., positions of power), resulting in competition for succession. Some forms of competitive feasts probably continued to be used among the lower-level elites in chiefdoms as criteria for promotion to positions of power and to increase the value of elite children, but they do not appear to be broadly based feasts with obligatory interest payments geared to attract supporters such as are found in transegalitarian communities. Nevertheless, the chief is still expected to "give" considerable quantities of goods to community members and especially to other elites, which, as was previously noted, is a ubiquitous trait among transegalitarian aggrandizers. Interestingly, the chief often collects surplus support payments from other community members on the pretext of financing community wars, investments in elite children, harvest festivals, or important feasts (Kirch 1984:263, 1991). However, power and support no longer appear to be predicated on providing direct investment profits to supporters in return for their feast contributions. Rather, benefits to contributors seem to be of a more indirect nature.

A fourth observation in relation to chiefdoms is the extension, intensification, and elaboration of the importance and use of ancestors to validate claims to power. Chiefs become the direct descendants of the most powerful ancestors and the main priests of the ancestral cult. Communities are organized into real and fictitious lines of descendants from founding ancestors (clans). Chiefs, like transegalitarian corporate heads, erect monumental ritual structures to promote their ancestors as powerful supernatural agents.

The special residences, funerals, specialized craftsmanship, territorial conquests, and other well-known features of chiefdoms need not be documented here.

Of all the Northwest Coast groups, the best argument for a chiefdom type organization can be made for the nineteenth-century Nuuchalnulth Ahousaht of Clayoquot Sound, who had established a political and military confederacy dominated by one group, a large central administrative community, and an active program of territorial conquest (Marshall 1992). In addition, there was strict inheritance of the chief's position (Rosman and Rubel 1971:80) and no interest payment was expected for gifted loans (Rosman and Rubel 1971:90). Moreover, as in Polynesia, Nootkan chiefs collected food quotas before feasts. Garfield (1966:33) suggested that the Tsimshian might have been chiefdoms before the nineteenth century. In New Guinea, Feil (1987:117–118) and others argue that chiefdoms may have existed in the Mount Hagen area before the introduction of the sweet potato, and that chiefs controlled access to shells from the coast by controlling trade, thus creating a monopoly on the wealth necessary to marry. They also had slaves.

I need not go into the archaeological indicators of chiefdoms since this subject has been more than adequately covered by others (Arnold 1993; Earle 1987, 1989; Johnson and Earle 1987; Peebles and Kus 1977), and is beyond my immediate goal of dealing with transegalitarian societies.

CONCLUDING COMMENTS

Before closing, there are a number of general points that I would like to make. Although I have outlined what I perceive to be the most important community elements for understanding the remarkable changes that take place from egalitarian to chiefdom levels of organization, there are numerous other elements that can also be understood in terms of the strategies of aggrandizers and supporters, for example, increasingly egocentric and ostentatious displays, the blurring of political boundaries, changes in corporate group strength, the importance of genealogies, the overtness of competition, and unrestricted versus restricted warfare. Other topics warranting some comment are funerals, recruitment, and general models of causality.

Funerals

Funerals figure prominently as major events requiring reciprocal feasts, even in some of the simplest transegalitarian communities. This may appear puzzling, and can be accounted for by a number of different theoretical models. However, I would suggest that aggrandizers at all levels feel that the death of prominent men in the exchange networks threatens to extinguish the debt structure and the pressures for exchange that such individuals helped to establish. To keep these debt structures operating after the death of principal players, funeral feasts are held in which debts are reaffirmed, or if necessary, regenerated. The important point is not whether the kin of the deceased gives the funeral feast or whether an affiliated kin group gives the feast (which is Rosman and Rubel's main concern). The important point is that a feast be given by *one* of the traditional exchange groups and that it entails a future obligation of exchange even if it is only a reciprocal funeral feast when someone in the other group dies. Thus, funeral feasts involving wealth exchanges or reciprocal obligations to expend surpluses are ubiquitous on the Northwest Coast and New Guinea and in most transegalitarian societies. Funerals can also be used by the corporate groups to which the deceased belonged as public displays of their wealth and power through lavish feasting and destruction of wealth through burying it in the form of grave goods. It is pertinent to note that funerals are not the only venues for these public displays, and some cultures may use alternate contexts for their displays. The advertising message of all display behavior is clear: high-quality and successful corporate members are rewarded by successful corporate kin groups—both in this life and in the afterlife, and in the most powerful transegalitarian communities are even given companions or servants.

Attracting Labor and "The Give-Away"

This observation leads to another important feature of transegalitarian communities: the central importance of attracting energetic, productive, competent, skilled, and successful labor (supporter-producers, military allies, wives, administrators, craft specialists, corporate members, and tenant workers). It is upon the ability to attract such labor that the success of the aggrandizers, as well as their supporting or corporate groups, depends. In the words of one of Drucker's (1951:273) informants: "If his 'tenants' are good . . . then . . . he can do much (i.e., potlatching). If they are no good . . . he can do nothing." Corporate administrators need good labor to exploit the resources they own. At a more general level, Gosden (1989) and Webster (1990) have emphasized the critical role that control over high-quality labor plays in the emergence of nonegalitarian communities. Many ethnographies stress the strong, almost puritan work ethic promoted by aggrandizers at all levels of transegalitarian communities and the work-oriented values sought by aggrandizers in recruiting supporters and tenants (see also Nairn and Strathern's film *Kawelka*). However, in all these societies, there are also clear statements about supporters and tenants maintaining their residence options open so as to be able to affiliate with Entrepreneurs or corporate groups that provide the most benefits and fewest excessive demands. As Rosman and Rubel (1971:173) state, corporate residence "choices are made on the basis of a type of strategy involving rank of seat obtainable, rank of group involved, and its size and power." Especially desired positions might be acquired by purchase or even by killing the occupant (Rosman and Rubel 1971:131). Similar strategies operate in New Guinea (Modjeska 1982:92), and when aggrandizers became overbearing, then envy, accusations of sorcery, desertion, and even assassination resulted (Jewitt 1974:98; Lemonnier 1990a:125; Young 1971:111, 155; also see Blake and Clark 1989 for a discussion of transegalitarian checks and balances). These constitute powerful checks on aggrandizers' power in transegalitarian communities.

These negotiated affiliations between administrative aggrandizers and potential participating members of kinship and resource corporate groups frequently resulted in a very heterogeneous group of corporate residents. Aggrandizers probably found it easiest to use kinship ties for recruitment, but they also used other means including marriage (especially motivated by possibilities to acquire resources), the bestowing of titles on desirable potential members thereby increasing the value of the individual, and providing other material enticements (Feil 1987:130–131; Rosman and Rubel 1971:76, 83, 159). Actual recruitment appears to have been far more flexible than the emic ideologies recorded by social anthropologists generally suggest. For instance, while patrilineal norms were used to promote corporate solidarity in New Guinea, 18–51% of the actual corporate group members were not blood relatives or wives' relatives (Feil 1971:130–131; Strathern 1971:37). Similar observations have been made for a wide range of transegalitarian and chiefdom societies (Allen and Richardson 1971:49; Deetz 1968:47; Kirch 1984; Leach 1961; Sahlins 1958, 1965:105). Clearly, relying on cognitive-based ethnographies and strictly emic descriptions will not advance our understanding of how transegalitarian communities actually operated—a conclusion that has been evident for scores of years (Malefijt 1968:96; Radin 1920). McGuire and Paynter (1991:11) discuss the issue in more general terms.

It seems evident that the main goal of aggrandizers was to attract, control, and manipulate labor. To do this, aggrandizers had to provide tangible benefits (some share in the feasting, exchange profits, use of corporate resources and facilities, rights to membership in other groups, security, acquisition of desirable and valuable mates, and positions of power especially for the most talented; Lemonnier 1990a:42; Rosman and Rubel 1971:79). However, the expenditure of surpluses or profits for conspicuous displays of wealth also constituted essential advertising and self-promotion to indicate which groups were the most successful, the most wealthy, and the most powerful, thereby enabling them to attract the best labor. Many types of artifacts and features were created with no apparent purpose other than to advertise success.

While practical technologies served to produce food or solve material requirements of life, and while prestige technologies had inherent value that could be traded or invested, "promotional" technologies had neither. They could not be used in a practical sense, nor could they be exchanged as valuables. Promotional (advertising) technologies included objects specifically made for grave offerings or ritual offerings (and never used in other contexts); many luxury feasting foods; monumental ancestral poles, megalithic tombs, and burial mounds. Obviously, prestige objects sometimes were also used as promotional objects, especially when they were destroyed (e.g., consumption of exchangeable foods; killing of slaves, dogs, horses; dropping swords or other wealth into rivers or oceans). However, other objects and features were purely promotional, an important aspect of human behavior and the archaeological record that has not heretofore been generally recognized.

Large quantities of food and special delicacies were consumed at group-sponsored feasts and valuable goods were interred at funerals without expectation of direct return. Burial of wealth with the dead constituted a form of destroying wealth, as if to say that a family or group was wealthy enough that they did not have to take goods from the dead. Such burial offerings and displays could become very elaborate, as in the Neolithic Chinese Liangzu culture (Xuanpei 1992). However, aggrandizers also used other more flamboyant techniques of destroying wealth, such as burning valuable oils, throwing coppers into the sea, killing slaves, or slaughtering valuable animals for consumption (Gregory 1982:61). In some Northwest Coast ethnographic accounts, it appears that corporate group members also viewed the ability to support highly trained and lavishly equipped corporate Entrepreneurs as another means of advertising the success or wealth of the group.

According to Clark and Blake (1989), the terms "prestige," "status," and "rank" are emic euphemisms for "success" used by community members to advertise the relative benefits involved in making affiliation or exchange choices—a view that I share totally. In addition, Renfrew (1982:3) finds prestige and similar concepts too vague to be useful archaeologically. In addition to the importance of giving to create debts (and to acquire allies or in-laws), conspicuous consumption to advertise success constitutes the basis for the nearly universal emphasis in transegalitarian communities on the need for aggrandizers to give some food, wealth, and assistance to supporters or to others and to avoid appearing selfish (Burch 1988:106, 109; Feil 1987:112, 117; Gosden 1989:359; Mauss 1967:36; Modjeska 1982:90; Rosman and Rubel 1971:79, 90). Moreover, in the investment sphere, if they do not loan out wealth, it adversely affects other people's ability to exchange, invest, and get ahead. People with wealth who do not promote exchange by loaning wealth to others are reviled as incompetent managers of wealth who thwart the aspirations of kinsmen and others. In many groups, generosity is explicitly used to attract followers (Rosman and Rubel 1971:79). Ultimately, the generosity of aggrandizers is a calculated economic strategy meant to centralize control in their own hands and increase production (Mauss 1967:72). They operate much like contemporary businessmen with recruitment expense accounts or job benefits calculated to attract skilled, productive employees and administrators. In biology, animal behaviorists have also recently emphasized the importance of costly "advertising" displays such as antlers in reproductive success (Beardsley 1993). In all transegalitarian societies, most people are guided by their own self-interest, and aggrandizers will only be successful to the extent that they can appeal to the self-interest of others and manipulate it for their own benefit. The high costs required to promote the self-interest of others, including dissipating envy and attracting desirable personnel through success displays, probably constitute the single most important reason for the inability of aggrandizers in all types of transegalitarian communities to establish a permanent social, corporate, or settlement hierarchy. The surpluses remaining after these expenditures were simply not sufficient to sustain more complex types of relationships.

Rosman and Rubel (1971:90) and other social anthropologists express the view that the altruistic cultural imperative to be generous (in exchange for esteem) is so overpowering that it leads people to contravene their own material self-interest and become destitute (the traditional foil for economic rationalism and cultural materialism in traditional societies). Such claims are simply untenable in terms of ethnographic reality. As Mauss (1967:1, 73) clearly recognized: "In theory gifts are voluntary, but in fact they are given and repaid under obligation. . . . Prestations which are in theory voluntary, disinterested and spontaneous, but are in fact obligatory and interested." For him, transegalitarian gift-giving constituted an archaic form of contract, and wealth was primarily a means of controlling others. It is evident from all the previous ethnographic accounts that giving and feasting are indirect techniques of control and generating more wealth (see Burch [1988:106, 109] for a similar observation among complex Eskimo communities). Contrary to the statements of some social anthropologists, *the mere act of giving wealth away by itself does not result in increased power for the giver. To be effective, wealth must be given away in contexts that generate recognized and binding obligations* or other expected practical benefits (see Lightfoot and Feinman 1982:66).

These techniques do not work all the time any more than capitalist techniques of investment produce wealth in every business venture. Many modern businessmen experience repeated failures and bankruptcies. In both transegalitarian and capitalist societies, it is the promise, potential, and prospect of substantial increases in wealth and power that motivate people to spend and borrow. And transegalitarian aggrandizers and contemporary land or stock investors frequently live in reduced circumstances in order to reinvest all possible surpluses in wealth creation projects. To become established in such a system, it was first necessary to amass wealth and credits, which required considerable work (Connolly and Anderson 1987:124). However, transegalitarian aggrandizers were no more assured of success than enterprising capitalists and many must have lost all their investments due to adverse circumstances or incompetence. Similarly, not everyone who invests in the stockmarket today can be said to understand the logic of the market; it would seem by some accounts, such as Rosman and Rubel's, that not every individual who made investments in transegalitarian communities understood how aggrandizive strategies worked either. Thus, anecdotal examples of individuals who lost their wealth in giving potlatches hardly makes a convincing case for a cultural norm of generosity acting to override common sense and economical self-interest. The important thing is that there was some chance of increasing wealth and power if one was able to play the socioeconomic gambit successfully. It may even be a lawlike generalization that the greater the potential gain, the greater the risks people were willing to take. To complicate matters even further, the logic of some traditional strategies was clearly upset by the sudden wealth made available to all members of communities in contact with Europeans, and by the massive native depopulations that accompanied epidemics of European origin.

Variability

This raises another issue in terms of the goodness of fit of the model that I have proposed here and the wide variety of ethnographic cases that are documented. Many social anthropologists have focused on the great diversity of cultures recorded ethnographically to argue that cultural tradition by itself is a factor that frequently overpowers common practical good sense and even natural selection (Lemonnier 1989, 1990a,b). Other social anthropologists note that European contact, even indirectly, profoundly transformed indigenous cultures before ethnographers arrived, and that the rate of change has been unusually rapid since this contact. Some of these ethnologists express the suspicion that features such as residence and descent were formerly much more in sync with each other and that economic changes have led to rapid changes in one sphere (e.g., residence) and lagged changes in other spheres (e.g., descent ideology; Leach 1961). Clearly, times of rapid change must involve learning and adaptation curves of different durations for different aspects of behavior and belief.

All of the major synthetic models attempting to explain variability in the New Guinea Highlands have been accompanied by disclaimers concerning the many cases that do not fit general patterns. I suggest that a great deal of the nonconforming variability here and elsewhere is due precisely to the rapid changes accompanying the introduction of new crops, new diseases, large-scale population movements, new desirable goods, items such as firearms or the horse that became essential for survival, and new trade patterns of the last few centuries. All of these factors tend to disrupt the long-term adaptations of cultures to their natural and human environments that could only have been more highly patterned prehistorically.

However, even given these disruptions, some general patterns are still discernible, such as the difference between the strategies used in communities composed of independent subsistence households of New Guinea versus the strategies based on corporate control of resources on the Northwest Coast. Generalized hunter-gatherer versus complex hunter-gatherer adaptations provide another example of highly patterned cultural traits that appear to have persisted despite European influences. Because of these and other factors (such as observer biases or omissions), it should not come as a surprise that Feinman and Neitzel (1984) found considerable variability in the roles of transegalitarian and chiefdom-level leaders. However, I feel that the greatest source of variability in their specific results stems from the lumping of all transegalitarian and chiefdom societies together, thereby failing to make important distinctions concerning the different types of strategies used by Despots, Reciprocators, Entrepreneurs, and chiefs. In fact, the most pronounced trends that they derived from their ethnographic survey support the three-stage model that I have presented. Notably, the most common functions of leaders were related to warfare and leading "ceremonies." As the number of functions increased, there was a much stronger emphasis on leading feasts, controlling trade, and negotiating alliances (Feinman and Neitzel 1984:53) similar to the strategies adopted by Entrepreneurs.

In this exploratory excursion into the evolutionary stages of transegalitarian communities, a number of very basic patterns reoccur and seem to make good sense. Limited and unreliable surpluses are associated with low population densities, an emphasis on community-wide (or corporate) transactions involving surpluses, feasts held to acquire allies and bolster group solidarity, limited integration of exchange or political networks, limited prestige goods or wealth, and promotion of compelling community interests (especially defense and offense or raids to acquire food or wealth) by aggrandizers to force coresidents to produce and surrender surpluses. Much higher levels of surpluses are associated with higher population densities; strategies of investing surpluses via marriage, exchange partners, or competitive feasts; more individualization of exchange; and much wider integration of exchange and political networks.

These are the most basic elements involved in using potential surpluses to generate wealth and power that can be concentrated in the hands of aggrandizers for their own benefit. However, just as there are many ways of making prestige serving containers meant to impress guests at feasts (they can be made of wood, ceramic, stone, basketry, gourds, or other materials), so the goal of motivating people to produce and surrender surpluses can be achieved by a number of strategies, including the fabrication of external threats, war compensations to allies, promotion of raiding or aggressive warfare for material gain, acquiring more desirable mates, child growth payments and bridewealth, reciprocal feasting for allies, material gains from competitive feasting, pumping up the supernatural power of ancestors, group advertising to attract desirable resident workers, and probably other strategies.

While some of these strategies clearly appear to be more common at the Despot, Reciprocator, or Entrepreneur level (see Figure 4) it is certainly possible that the specific mix of strategies could have varied from one group or area to another even though they exhibit the same surplus conditions and the same levels of integration. As an extreme example, manipulation of warfare appears to have been a common initial and continuing strategy of prehistoric aggrandizers all along the West Coast of North America and in other Mesolithic/early Neolithic communities (Keeley, in press). However, in the Levant, there is no skeletal evidence of warfare from the Paleolithic through the Neolithic (A. Belfer-Cohen, personal communication, April 1992; Bar-Yosef, personal communication, July 1993), even though prestige items and socioeconomic inequalities are well attested. If this almost unique interpretation of peaceful transegalitarian communities is sustained by future analyses, these societies would represent a very different mix of strategies than characterizes most other transegalitarian societies.

Thus, although there may be some strong patterning of basic strategies associated with the different levels of surplus among Despot, Reciprocator, and Entrepreneur societies, there may be alternative evolutionary trajectories in terms of the specific strategies or mixture of strategies used at each level. Hence, it may be most realistic to use polythetic rather than monothetic definitions when dealing with the various levels of complexity in transegalitarian communities. In polythetic classifications, not all defining characteristics need be present in all cases, but only some majority of characteristics. At this point, we do not have a detailed understanding of why levels of warfare vary within levels of transegalitarian societies. There are a number of factors that could affect the reliance on warfare as well as other aspects of transegalitarian communities, such as the degree of social stratification, slavery, development of prestige technologies, and development of wealth exchanges. These factors may include:

1. Independent family subsistence organization versus GENS communities (affecting power inequalities within groups and slave-raiding frequencies).
2. Surplus-based versus resource-based corporate groups, with more

emphasis on the control of trade and marriages (via bridewealth) in surplus-based corporate groups.
3. Local traditions, historical accidents, and cultural or individual idiosyncrasies.

These factors may have secondary overlaying effects on the *basic* transegalitarian nature of a community, but the basic nature of the community organization is probably determined by the amount and reliability of surplus production. Thus, greater localization and labor-intensive requirements of some resources (e.g., very productive fishing weirs in highly seasonal environments) may favor the formation of resource-based corporate groups that are highly stratified internally (see Schalk 1981), even though the absolute amount of surplus might not be any greater than in communities where resources are more easily accessible to all independent families and where social stratification is lacking, such as in New Guinea. How much of this secondary variability can be attributed to specific resource or environmental conditions and how much can be attributed to historical factors will only be determined by much more intensive research on transegalitarian communities.

At this point, it seems that variability in some decisions, such as whether to destroy wealth by burying it with individuals, burning it at funerals, giving it away with *no* return required, destroying it at marriages or feasts, or simply by eating it in the form of expensive foods, is largely culturally determined. The essential element is the public destruction or consumption of wealth, and there is a wide range of public contexts equally conducive to creating the intended effect. This is similar to the choice of materials to make (or the art motifs to decorate) prestige food containers. As long as these containers serve their main function of impressing guests, it makes little difference what they are made of or how they are decorated. In contrast, the choice of strategies for controlling surpluses can have major, direct effects on the successful accumulation of wealth and acquisition of power. Since these have direct consequences for survival, we can expect them to be much more highly constrained over the long term. Just how constrained probably cannot be resolved using existing ethnographic information. It will be up to future generations of archaeologists to determine their coherency or lability in the developmental trajectories of transegalitarian communities throughout the world.

Causality

A few final notes on implications for other models of inequality are warranted. It is clear from the New Guinea, Yanomamo, Calusa (Widmer

1988:268), Mokaya (Clark and Blake 1994:21), Ainu (Watanabe 1983:217), and many other cases that food storage is not a necessary element in the emergence of transegalitarian societies at any level (contra Ingold 1983; Keeley 1988; Testart 1982). In the examples just mentioned, staples are left in the environment until needed for consumption. Storage may have had an accelerating effect on the development of inequality, but other factors appear to have been much more fundamental to the process. From previous discussions concerning warfare and lineage formation, it should be apparent that neither population pressure nor circumscription appears to have played a significant role in creating inequality or complexity. It is interesting that Feinman (1991) examined the early transegalitarian archaeological data from Oaxaca with the question of population pressure in mind and found little hard evidence for population pressure or agricultural risk, but considerable support for the notion that residents of transegalitarian communities were attracted to these centers by wealth. At a slightly higher level of complexity, Andel and Runnels (1988:241) similarly found that complexity evolved under conditions of rich resources and surpluses, rather than agricultural risk. Wenke (1989:143), too, observed that early Egyptian agricultural communities were self-sufficient with duplicated and redundant functions and resources. Given such situations, it is difficult to explain the emergence of complexity in traditional functionalist or stress-model terms (see also Netting 1990 contra population pressure) or to explain the strong ubiquitous emphasis on ritual.

While my discussion of transegalitarian pathways to power has touched on the practical evolutionary advantages, it is important to spell these out explicitly. The success of groups in displaying their wealth and power directly affected their ability to attract high-quality mates, allies, and other supporting labor. Individual and group ability to attract such people was directly related to survival, human reproduction, and health. As a result, seemingly nonutilitarian "ritual" and feasting activities played critical roles in biological and cultural evolution. Those who did not participate in these activities (or proved inadequate in them) were increasingly marginalized and divested of power within their own communities, or at the regional level they were overrun by other communities. The size of military forces, which was the main criterion for success in warfare (Strathern 1971:16), was directly dependent on the ability to produce surpluses and marshal them for use in acquiring and compensating allies. Within Entrepreneur communities, 25–30% of the population became poor and marginalized (including denigrated servants and slaves), while 13% of the household heads were recognized as Entrepreneurs of varying degrees (Strathern 1971:201). Even in Reciprocator communities, individuals not participating fully in exchanges suffered social and economic disadvantages (Modjeska 1982:90). Thus, the evolutionary and practical consequences of feasting and wealth exchanges combined with marriage and death compensations were of vital importance for individuals and communities (see also Kosse 1994).

In closing, I would like to suggest that the assumptions of materialist practicality and self-interest, combined with basic resource constraints and characteristics, as well as genetically variable human predispositions such as aggressive dominance tendencies among some individuals, provide more insights into the development and variability of transegalitarian communities than do appeals to cultural norms, social logic, or cognition. It is important to emphasize that it only takes a few aggrandizers in any community to create widespread and profound socioeconomic changes if they are given free reign and if the resource base is conducive. As already noted, residence decisions are clearly governed by practical self-interest considerations rather than norms. Another example of self-interest overriding authority, norms, and values is the refusal of younger brothers to accept older brothers' self-serving ideology of domination despite their elders' greater authority in ritual matters (Modjeska 1982:64–65, 83, 107). These examples support the view that ideology is a relatively transparent artifice used primarily to legitimize rather than create socioeconomic power (Earle 1989:85; Fried 1987; Matson 1985; Wolf 1982). Even Rosman and Rubel (1971:108) view myths as serving to justify social structure.

Thus, the proposition that cultural values and cognitive ideas determine behavior appears to be minimally useful for understanding the important transformations that occurred in transegalitarian communities, especially since ideal values often persist long after actual behavior has changed for economic or other practical reasons (e.g., Turner 1985:217). From a structuralist or cognitive perspective, the size of groups and their control over resources should be of little consequence, whereas these are critical variables in materialist models such as the one I have proposed. It is therefore of considerable importance that cross-cultural studies have demonstrated strong relationships between maximum community size, total population, the number of elite functions, status markers, and political complexity (Feinman and Neitzel 1984) or that there are strong correlations between the largest community size, cultural complexity, and the number of craft specialists (Clark and Parry 1990:307). Similarly, Blau (1977:241) found that the consolidation of administrative and economic power is a function of the size and resources of an organization. That aggrandizers everywhere understood this relationship seems clearly evident in their persistent and innovative attempts to find ways to increase the productivity of their respective support groups as well as the size of the network of support that they could muster.

In the preceding pages, I have tried to begin the process of reformulating ethnographic accounts so that they will be more useful to archaeologists and so that they will represent a more finely honed evolutionary sequence. I have made concerted efforts to tie the various strategies discussed, and the various levels of transegalitarian societies, to specific archaeological manifestations. These are summarized in Table 1 and Figure 6. In brief, emphasis on death compensations and the management of warfare should be reflected in fortifications, armor, violent deaths, parry fractures, and settlement patterns. Emphasis on the control of brideprice payments can lead to the formation of residential corporate groups in extreme cases, possible female-oriented cults and figurines, and richly endowed adult female burials in cultures where wealth is buried with the dead. Use of child growth payments can generally be expected to lead to rich child burials in cultures where wealth is interred with the dead. Use of surpluses to obtain political power and some control of others' products will involve the development of prestige technologies. Reliance on reciprocal and competitive feasts can result in the development of prestige food vessels, initial forms of public architecture, regional trade, and domesticated feasting foods. Investment strategies with interest payments can be expected to lead to wider regional trade networks, higher volumes of prestige goods, increased craft specialization, and, frequently, systems of numeration in physical form. Finally, the auxiliary emphasis on ancestral power to justify claims to supernatural abilities should affect burial practices, evidence for cults (e.g., the keeping of skulls), and the occurrence of special burial or cult structures.

Table 1. Archaeological Consequences of Transegalitarian Aggrandizer Strategies

Strategies	Archaeological manifestations
Provoked war	Fortifications Trauma and violent deaths Armor
Bridewealth	Surplus-based residential corporate groups Rich female burials Female cult figurines
Child growth	Rich child burials
Investment exchange	Regional exchange High volume of prestige goods Craft specialization
Ancestor and other cults	Shrines and public ritual architecture Burial shrines
Reciprocal and competitive feasts	Feasting-related facilities and structures Domesticates Prestige food vessels

Most Common Changes in Archaeological Traits in Transegalitarian Communities

X - maximal expression

• - minimum expression

- absent or not detectable

	Egalitarian	Despots	Reciprocators	Entrepreneurs	Chiefs
Resource Abundance and Resources Invulnerable to Overexploitation or Degradation	....	•••••••xxxxxxx		XXXXX**XXXX**	
Usual Hunter/gatherer population densities (people/km^2)	.01-<.1	.1-.2	.2-1.0	1.0-10.0	
Warfare	.... ••	xxXXXXXXXXXXXX	Xxxxxxxx	xx**XXXX**	
Rich Burials:					
Adult Males	........•••••	•••• xxxxxxx	XXXXxx **XXXX**		
Adult Females	................••.	.xxxxxXX	x**XX**		
Children	.........••	xxxxXXX	**XXX**		
Regional Exchange					
(Interaction Spheres)	XXXXXXxx ••	•• •xxxxx	XXXXX	**XXX**	
Craft Specialization	....	•••xxxxx	XXXXX	**XXX**	
Feasting Facilities					
Non-corporate	....	.xxxxx	XXXXX	**XXX**	
Corporate (internal)		xxxx	XXXXX	???	
Cult Facilities (esp. ancestral)					
Non-corporate	....	••••xxx	XXXXX	**XXX**	
Corporate		........•••	xxxxxXX	**XXX**	
Female Cult Figurines			...x**XXXXX**?		
Domesticates		....••••xxx	XXXXXX	**XXX**	
Prestige Food Vessels, (quality)		... ••••xxx	XXXXX	**XXX**	
Prestige Food Vessels, (frequency)		...••••XXX	**XXXX**xxxxx		
Wealth-based corporate groups (lineages)		...•• .xxxX**XXX**xxxx		....	
Socioeconomically Distinct (High Status) Households		....••••x	XXXXX	**XXX**	
Community Hierarchies		.... ••x	**XXX**		

Figure 6. Comparisons of material and other cultural trait trends proposed for egalitarian to chiefdom societies.

These distinctions and other indicators of strategies and resources in the archaeological record have led to the conclusion that the prehistoric inhabitants at the Keatley Creek site in British Columbia were probably organized at the initial Entrepreneur level amidst the panoply of transegalitarian communities.

ACKNOWLEDGMENTS

I am extremely grateful to T. Douglas Price and Gary Feinman for the opportunity to present this research. I have benefited greatly from the work of, and exchanges with, Polly Wiessner, Pierre Lemonnier, John Clark, and Michael Blake, who have shared many of the same questions that I have dealt with. I also appreciate the very helpful suggestions and input from Antonio Gilman, Ofer Bar-Yosef, Alan MacMillan, Ernest Burch Jr., Rick Schulting, and D'Ann Owens-Baird, who helped as well with the ethnographic survey. Anita Mahoney and Jim Spafford capably navigated the various versions of this chapter through numerous text and figure changes, for which I am very thankful.

REFERENCES

Allen, M., 1984, Elders, Chiefs, and Big Men: Authority, Legitimation and Political Evolution in Melanesia, *American Ethnologist* 11:20–41.
Allen, W., and J. Richardson III, 1971, The Reconstruction of Kinship from Archaeological Data: The Concepts, the Methods and the Feasibility, *American Antiquity* 36:41–53.
Ames, K., 1985, Hierarchies, Stress, and Logistical Strategies among Hunter-Gatherers in Northwestern North America, in: *Prehistoric Hunter-Gatherers* (D. Price and J. Brown, eds.), Academic Press, Orlando, pp. 155–180.
Andel, T. van, and C. Runnels, 1988, An Essay on the "Emergence of Civilization" in the Aegean World, *Antiquity* 62:234–247.
Arnold, J., 1991, Transformation of a Regional Economy: Sociopolitical Evolution and the Production of Valuables in Southern California, *Antiquity* 65:953–962.
Arnold, J., 1992, Complex Hunter-Gatherer-Fishers of Prehistoric California: Chiefs, Specialists, and Maritime Adaptations of the Channel Islands, *American Antiquity* 57:60–84.
Arnold, J., 1993, Labor and the Rise of Complex Hunter-Gatherers, *Journal of Anthropological Archaeology* 12:75–119.
Barbeau, M., and W. Beynon, 1987, *Tsimshian Narratives 2: Trade and Warfare,* Canadian Museum of Civilization, Ottawa.
Barnett, H. G., 1955, *The Coast Salish of British Columbia,* Greenwood Press, Westport.
Barth, F., 1961, *Nomads of South Persia,* Waveland Press, Prospect Heights, Illinois.
Beardsley, T., 1993, Honest Advertising, *Scientific American* 268(5):24–27.
Beattie, O., 1980, *An Analysis of Prehistoric Human Skeletal Material from the Gulf of Georgia, British Columbia,* Unpublished Ph.D. dissertation, Archaeology Department, Simon Fraser University, Burnaby, B.C.

Beteille, A., 1981, The Idea of Natural Inequality, in: *Social Inequality* (G. Berreman, ed.), Academic Press, New York, pp. 59–80.

Bettinger, R., 1978, Alternative Adaptive Strategies in the Prehistoric Great Basin, *Journal of Anthropological Research* 34:27–46.

Bettinger, R., 1983, Aboriginal Sociopolitical Organization in Owens Valley: Beyond the Family Band, in: *The Development of Political Organization in Native North America* (E. Tooker and M. Fried, eds.), American Ethnological Society, Washington, D.C., pp. 45–58.

Binford, L., 1983, *In Pursuit of the Past,* Thames and Hudson, New York.

Binford, L., 1990, Mobility, Housing, and Environment: A Comparative Study, *Journal of Anthropological Research* 46:119–152.

Bishop, C., 1987, Coast–Interior Exchange: The Origins of Stratification in Northwestern North America, *Arctic Anthropology* 24:72–83.

Blake, M., 1991, An Emerging Early Formative Chiefdom at Paso de la Amada, Chiapas, Mexico, in: *The Formation of Complex Societies in South-East Mesoamerica* (W. Fowler, Jr., ed.), CRC Press, Bota Raton, pp. 27–46.

Blake, M., and J. Clark, 1989, *The Emergence of Hereditary Inequality: The Case of Pacific Coastal Chiapas, Mexico,* Paper presented at the Circum-Pacific Prehistory Conference, Seattle, Washington.

Blau, P., 1964, *Exchange and Power in Social Life,* John Wiley, New York.

Boas, F., 1966, *Kwakiutl Ethnography,* University of Chicago Press, Chicago.

Brunton, R., 1975, Why Do the Trobriands Have Chiefs? *Man* 10:544–558.

Burch, E., Jr., 1975, *Eskimo Kinsmen,* American Ethnological Society Monograph 59, West Publishing, St. Paul.

Burch, E., Jr., 1980, Traditional Eskimo Societies in Northwest Alaska, *Senri Ethnological Studies* 4:253–304.

Burch, E., Jr., 1988, Nodes of Exchange in North-West Alaska, in: *Hunters and Gatherers 2: Property, Power, and Ideology* (T. Ingold, D. Riches, and J. Woodburn, eds.), Berg Publishers, New York, pp. 95–109.

Burley, D., 1979, Specialization and the Evolution of Complex Society in the Gulf of Georgia Region, *Canadian Journal of Archaology* 3:131–144.

Burley, D., 1980, *Marpole: Anthropological Reconstructions of a Prehistoric Northwest Coast Culture Type,* Department of Archaeology, Simon Fraser University Publication No. 8, Burnaby, B.C.

Bussey, J., and D. Alexander, 1992, *Archaeological Assessment of the Cariboo Forest Region,* Report prepared by Points West Heritage Consulting, on file with the British Columbia Provincial Archaeology Branch, Victoria.

Cannon, A., 1989, The Historical Dimension in Mortuary Expressions of Status and Sentiment, *Current Anthropology* 30:437–458.

Cannon, A., 1992, Conflict and Salmon on the Interior Plateau of British Columbia, in *A Complex Culture of the British Columbia Plateau* (B. Hayden, ed.), University of British Columbia Press, Vancouver, B.C., pp. 506–524.

Carlson, R., 1976, Prehistory of the Northwest Coast, in *Indian Art Traditions of the Northwest Coast* (R. Carlson, ed.), Archaeology Press, Simon Fraser University, Burnaby, British Columbia, pp. 13–32.

Carlson, R., 1991, The Northwest Coast before A.D. 1600, *Proceedings of the Great Ocean Conferences* 1:109–136.

Carlson, R., 1993, *Evolution of the Northwest Coast Cultural System,* Paper presented at the annual meeting of the Society for American Archaeology, St. Louis.

Cashdan, E., 1980, Egalitarianism among Hunters and Gatherers, *American Anthropologist* 82:116–120.

Cauvin, J., 1978, *Les premiers villages de Dyrie-Palestine du IX^{eme}au VII^{eme}millenaires avant J.C.,* Maison de l'Orient, Lyon.

Chowning, A., 1979, Leadership in Melanesia, *Journal of Pacific History* 14:66–84.

Clark, J., and M. Blake, 1989, *The Emergence of Rank Societies on the Pacific Coasts of Chiapas, Mexico,* Paper presented at the Circum-Pacific Prehistory Conference, Seattle, Washington.

Clark, J., and M. Blake, 1994, The Power of Prestige: Competitive Generosity and the Emergence of Rank Societies in Lowland Mesoamerica, in: *Factional Competition and Political Development in the New World* (E. Brumfiel and J. Fox, eds.), Cambridge University Press, Cambridge, pp. 17–30.

Clark, J., and W. Parry, 1990, Craft Specialization and Cultural Complexity, *Research in Economic Anthropology* 12:289–346.

Clarke, D. V., T. Cowie, and A. Foxon, 1985, *Symbols of Power at the Time of Stonehenge,* National Museum of Antiquities of Scotland, Edinburgh.

Codere, H., 1950, *Fighting with Property,* University of Washington Press, Seattle.

Connolly, B., and R. Anderson, 1987, *First Contact,* Penguin Books, New York.

Cordy, R., 1981, *A Study of Prehistoric Social Change: The Development of Complex Societies in the Hawaiian Islands,* Academic Press, New York.

Coupland, G., 1988, Prehistoric Economic and Social Change in the Tsimshian Area, in: *Prehistoric Economies of the Pacific Northwest Coast, Research in Economic Anthropology, Supplement 3* (B. Isaac, ed.), JAI Press, Greenwich, Connecticut, pp. 211–244.

Coupland, G., 1994, Review of *Salmon and Storage, Canadian Journal of Archaeology* 18:150–152.

Cowgill, G., 1975, On Causes and Consequences of Ancient and Modern Population Changes, *American Anthropologist* 77:505–525.

Cybulski, J., 1992, *A Greenville Burial Ground,* Canadian Museum of Civilization, Ottawa.

Cybulski, J., in press, Culture Change, Demographic History, and Health and Disease on the Northwest Coast, in: *In the Wake of Contact: Biological Responses to Conquest* (G. Milner and C. Larsen, eds.), Wiley-Liss, New York.

Davis, M., 1991, *Social Differentiation at the Early Village of ·Cayönü, Turkey,* Paper presented at the annual meeting of the American Anthropological Association, Chicago.

Dawson, G., 1880, *Haida Indians of the Queen Charlotte Islands,* Appendix A, Geological Survey of Canada, Report of Surveys and Explorations.

Dawson, G., 1892, Notes on the Shuswap People of British Columbia, *Proceedings and Transactions of the Royal Society of Canada* 9(2):3–44.

Deetz, J., 1968, Hunters in Archaeological Perspective, in: *Man the Hunter* (R. Lee and L. Devore, eds.), Aldine, Chicago, pp. 281–285.

Dietler, M., 1990, Driven by Drink: The Role of Drinking in the Political Economy and the Case of Early Iron Age France, *Journal of Anthropological Archaeology* 9:352–406.

Donald, L., and D. Mitchell, 1975, Some Correlates of Local Group Rank among the Southern Kwakiutl, *Ethnology* 14:325–346.

Drucker, P., 1951, *The Northern and Central Nootkan Tribes,* Smithsonian Institution, Bureau of American Ethnology, Bulletin 144, Washington, D.C.

Dyson-Hudson, R., and E. Smith, 1978, Human Territoriality: An Ecological Reassessment, *American Anthropologist* 80:21–41.

Earle, T., 1987, Chiefdoms in Archaeological and Ethnohistorical Perspective, *Annual Review of Anthropology* 16:279–308.

Earle, T., 1989, The Evolution of Chiefdoms, *Current Anthropology* 30:84–88.

Earle, T. (ed.), 1991, *Chiefdoms: Power, Economy, and Ideology,* Cambridge University Press, Cambridge.

Earle, T., and R. Preucel, 1987, Processual Archaeology and the Radical Critique, *Current Anthropology* 28:501–538.

Feil, D., 1987, *The Evolution of Highland Papua New Guinea Societies,* Cambridge University Press, Cambridge.

Feinman, G., 1991, Demography, Surplus, and Inequality: Early Political Formations in Highland Mesoamerica, in: *Chiefdoms: Power, Economy, and Ideology* (T. Earle, ed.), Cambridge University Press, Cambridge, pp. 229–262.

Feinman, G., and J. Neitzel, 1984, Too Many Types: An Overview of Sedentary Prestate Societies in the Americas, *Advances in Archaeological Method and Theory* 7:39–102.

Ferguson, R. B., 1989, Ecological Consequences of Amazonian Warfare, *Ethnology* 28:249–264.

Fried, M., 1960, On the Evolution of Social Stratification and the State, in: *Culture in History* (S. Diamond, ed.), Columbia University Press, New York.

Fried, M., 1967, *The Evolution of Political Society,* Random House, New York.

Friedman, J., and M. Rowlands, 1978, *The Evolution of Social Systems,* Duckworth, London.

Garfield, V., 1966, The Tsimshian and Their Neighbors, in: *The Tsimshian Indians and Their Arts* (V. Garfield and P. Wingert, eds.), University of Washington Press, Seattle.

Gilman, A., 1981, The Development of Social Stratification in Bronze Age Europe, *Current Anthropology* 22:1–24.

Godelier, M., 1978, Infrastructures, Societies, and History, *Current Anthropology* 19:763–771.

Godelier, M., 1982, *La production des grands hommes. Pouvoir et domination masculine chez les Baruya de Nouvelle-Guinee,* Fayard, Paris.

Good, K., 1993, *Yanomami: Hunters and Gatherers or Horticulturists, Which Came First?* Paper presented at the 7th International Conference on Hunting and Gathering Societies, Moscow.

Gosden, C., 1989, Debt, Production, and Prehistory, *Journal of Anthropological Archaeology* 8:355–387.

Gould, R., 1982, To Have and Have Not: The Ecology of Sharing among Hunter-Gatherers, in: *Resource Managers* (N. Williams and E. Hunn, eds.), Australian Institute of Aboriginal Studies, Canberra, pp. 69–92.

Gregory, C. A., 1982, *Gifts and Commodities,* Academic Press, London.

Halstead, P., and J. O'Shea, 1989, *Bad Year Economics,* Cambridge University Press, Cambridge.

Hames, R., and W. Vickers, 1983, Introduction, in: *Adaptive Responses of Native Amazonians* (R. Hames and W. Vickers, eds.), Academic Press, New York, pp. 1–28.

Harris, M., 1988, *Culture, People, Nature* (5th ed.), Harper and Row, New York.

Hayden, B., 1981, Research and Development in the Stone Age: Technological Transitions among Hunter/Gatherers, *Current Anthropology* 22:519–548.

Hayden, B., 1990, Nimrods, Piscators, Pluckers, and Planters: The Emergence of Food Production, *Journal of Anthropological Archaeology* 9:31–69.

Hayden, B., 1992a, Introduction: Ecology and Culture, in: *A Complex Culture of the British Columbia Plateau: Stl'atl'imx Resource use* (B. Hayden, ed.), University of British Columbia Press, Vancouver, pp. 3–46.

Hayden, B., 1992b, Conclusions: Ecology and Complex Hunter/Gatherers, in: *A Complex Culture of the British Columbia Plateau: Stl'atl'imx Resource Use* (B. Hayden, ed.), University of British Columbia Press, Vancouver, pp. 525–564.

Hayden, B., 1993, *Archaeology: The Science of Once and Future Things,* Freeman, New York.

Hayden, B., in press, Thresholds of Power in Emergent Complex Societies, in: *Emergent Social Complexity* (J. Arnold, ed.), International Monographs in Prehistory, Ann Arbor.

Hayden, B., and A. Cannon, 1982, The Corporate Group as an Archaeological Unit, *Journal of Anthropological Archaeology* 1:132–158.

Hayden, B., and R. Gargett, 1990, Big Man, Big Heart? A Mesoamerican view of the Emergence of Complex Society, *Ancient Mesoamerica* 1:3–20.

Helms, M., 1979, *Ancient Panama*, University of Texas Press, Austin.

Henry, D., 1985, Preagricultural Sedentism: The Natufian Example, in: *Prehistoric Hunter-Gatherers* (T. D. Price and J. Brown, eds.), Academic Press, Orlando, pp. 364–384.

Hildebrandt, W., and T. Jones, 1992, Evolution of Marine Mammal Hunting: A View from the California and Oregon Coasts, *Journal of Anthropological Archaeology* 11:360–401.

Hunn, E., 1990, *Nch'i-Wana, "The Big River:" Mid-Columbia Indians and Their Land*, University of Washington Press, Seattle.

Ingold, T., 1983, The Significance of Storage in Hunting Societies, *Man* (n.s.) 18:553–571.

Irimoto, T., 1990, *Changing Patterns of Ainu Land Use and Land Rights in a Historical Context*, Paper presented at the 6th International Conference on Hunting and Gathering Societies, University of Alaska, Fairbanks.

Jewitt, J. R. (D. Smith, ed.), 1974, *The Adventures and Sufferings of John R. Jewitt, Captive among the Nootka, 1803–1805*, McClelland and Stewart Ltd., Toronto.

Johnson, A., and T. Earle, 1987, *The Evolution of Human Societies*, Stanford University Press, Stanford.

Johnson, G., 1973, *Local Exchange and Early State Development in Southwestern Iran*, University of Michigan Museum of Anthropology, Anthropology Papers, No. 51, Ann Arbor.

Kan, S., 1989, Why the Aristocrats were "Heavy" or How Ethnopsychology Legitimized Inequality among the Tlingit, *Dialectical Anthropology* 14:81–94.

Keeley, L., 1988, Hunter-Gatherer Economic Complexity and 'Population Pressure': A Cross-Cultural Analysis, *Journal of Anthropological Archaeology* 7:373–411.

Keeley, L., 1992, The Introduction of Agriculture to the Western North European Plain, in: *Transitions to Agriculture in Prehistory* (A. Gebauer and T. D. Price, eds.), Prehistory Press, Madison, Wisconsin, pp. 81–96.

Keeley, L., in press, *War before Civilization*, Oxford University Press, New York.

King, T., 1978, Don't That Beat the Band? Nonegalitarian Political Organization in Prehistoric Central California, in: *Social Archaeology* (C. Redman, M. Berman, E. Curtin, W. Langhorne, N. Versaggi, and J. Wanser, eds.), Academic Press, New York, pp. 225–248.

King, T., 1990, *Evolution of Chumash Society*, Garland Publishing, New York.

Kirch, P., 1984, *The Evolution of the Polynesian Chiefdoms*, Cambridge University Press, Cambridge.

Kirch, P., 1991, Chiefship and Competitive Involution: The Marquesas Islands of Eastern Polynesia, in: *Chiefdoms: Power, Economy, and Ideology* (T. Earle, ed.), Cambridge University Press, Cambridge, pp. 119–145.

Kosse, K., 1994, The Evolution of Large, Complex Groups: A Hypothesis, *Journal of Anthropological Archaeology* 13:35–50.

Krause, A., 1956, *The Tlingit Indians*, University of Washington Press, Seattle.

Lambert, P., 1992, *Warfare and Violence in Prehistoric Societies of Coastal Southern California*, Paper presented at the 26th annual meeting of the Society for California Archaeology, Pasadena, California.

Lambert, P., and P. Walker, 1991, Physical Anthropological Evidence for the Evolution of Social Complexity in Coastal Southern California, *Antiquity* 65:963–973.

Leach, E., 1961, *Pul Eliya: A Study of Land Tenure and Kinship*, Cambridge University Press, Cambridge.

LeGros, D., 1982, Reflections sur l'origine des inégalités sociales à partir du cas de Athapaskan Tutchone, *Culture* 2:65–84.

LeGros, D., 1985, Wealth, Poverty and Slavery among the 19th-Century Tutchone Athapaskans, *Research in Economic Anthropology* 7:37–64.

Lemonnier, P., 1989, Bark Capes, Arrowheads and Concorde: On Social Representations of Technology, in: *The Meatning of Things* (I. Hodder, ed.), Unwin Hyman, London, pp. 156–171.

Lemonnier, P., 1990a, *Guerres et Festins,* Editions de la Maison des Sciences de l'Homme, Paris.

Lemonnier, P., 1990b, Topsy Turvy Techniques: Remarks on the Social Representation of Techniques, *Archaeological Review from Cambridge* 9(1):27–37.

Lewin, R., 1986, Self-Interest in Politics Earns a Nobel Prize, *Science* 234:941–942.

Lightfoot, K., and G. Feinman, 1982, Social Differentiation and Leadership Development in Early Pithouse Villages in the Mogollon Region of the American Southwest, *American Antiquity* 47:64–85.

MacDonald, G., 1989, *Kitwanga Fort Report,* Canadian Museum of Civilization, Ottawa.

Mainfort, R., Jr., 1985, Wealth, Space, and Status in a Historic Indian Cemetery, *American Antiquity* 50:555–579.

Malefijt, A. de W., 1968, *Religion and Culture,* Macmillan, New York.

Marshall, Y., 1992, *A Political History of the Nuu-chah-nulth People,* Unpublished Ph.D. dissertation, Archaeology Department, Simon Fraser University, Burnaby, British Columbia.

Matson, R. G., 1985, The Relationship between Sedentism and Status Inequalities among Hunters and Gatherers, in: *Status, Structure and Stratification* (M. Thompson, M. T. Garcia, and F. Kense, eds.), Archaeological Association of the University of Calgary, Calgary, pp. 245–252.

Mauss, M., 1967 [orig. 1925], *The Gift: Forms and Functions of Exchange in Archaic Societies,* Norton, New York.

McGuire, R., and R. Paynter, 1991, *The Archaeology of Inequality,* Blackwell, Oxford.

Mead, M., 1961 [orig. 1937], *Cooperation and Competition among Primitive Peoples,* Beacon Press, Boston.

Meillassoux, C., 1981, *Maidens, Meal and Money,* Cambridge University Press, Cambridge.

Miller, B., and D. Boxberger, 1994, Creating Chiefdoms, *Ethnohistory* 41:267–293.

Modjeska, N., 1982, Production and Inequality: Perspectives from Central New Guinea, in: *Inequality in New Guinea Highlands Societies* (A. Strathern, ed.), Cambridge University Press, Cambridge, pp. 50–108.

Nairn, C., and A. Strathern, 1974, *Kawelka* (also: *Onka's Big Moka*), Grenada Television International, London.

Netting, R., 1990, Population, Permanent Agriculture, and Politics: Unpacking the Evolutionary Portmanteau, in: *The Evolution of Political Systems* (S. Upham, ed.), Cambridge University Press, Cambridge, pp. 21–61.

Oberg, K., 1973, *The Social Organization of the Tlingit Indians,* University of Washington Press, Seattle.

Ohnuki-Tierney, E., 1974, *The Ainu of the Northwest Coast of Southern Sakhalin,* Waveland Press, Prospect Heights, Illinois.

O'Shea, J., 1984, *Mortuary Variability,* Academic Press, Orlando.

Peebles, C., and S. Kus, 1977, Some Archaeological Correlates of Ranked Societies, *American Antiquity* 42:421–448.

Pokotylo, D., M. Binkley, and J. Curtin, 1987, The Cache Creek Burial Site (EeRh1), British Columbia, *British Columbia Provincial Museum Contributions to Human History* No. 1.

Price, T. D., and J. Brown, 1985, Aspects of Hunter/Gatherer Complexity, in: *Prehistoric Hunter-Gatherers* (T. D. Price and J. Brown, eds.), Academic Press, Orlando, Florida, pp. 3–20.

Radin, P., 1920, The Autobiography of a Winnebago Indian, *University of California Publications in American Archaeology and Ethnology* 16:381–437.

Randsborg, K., 1982, Rank, Rights and Resources: An Archaeological Perspective from Denmark, in: *Ranking, Resource and Exchange* (C. Renfrew and S. Shennan, eds.), Cambridge University Press, Cambridge, pp. 132–140.

Redman, C. (ed.), 1978, *The Rise of Civilization,* Freeman, San Francisco.

Renfrew, C., 1982, Socio-economic Change in Ranked Societies, in: *Ranking, Resource and Exchange* (C. Renfrew and S. Shennan, eds.), Cambridge University Press, Cambridge, pp. 1–8.

Richards, J., 1990, *The Stonehenge Environs Project,* Historic Buildings & Monuments Commission for England, London.

Richards, J., 1991, *English Heritage Book of Stonehenge,* Batsford/English Heritage, London.

Rosman, A., and P. Rubel, 1971, *Feasting with Mine Enemy,* Waveland Press, Prospect Heights, Illinois.

Rothschild, N., 1979, Mortuary Behavior and Social Organization at Indian Knoll and Dickson Mounds, *American Antiquity* 44:658–675.

Rudmin, F., 1992, Cross-Cultural Correlates of the Ownership of Private Property, *Social Science Research* 21:57–83.

Rudmin, F., n.d., Cross-Cultural Correlates of the Ownership of Private Property, Ms. under review.

Ruyle, E., 1973, Slavery, Surplus, and Stratification on the Northwest Coast: The Ethnoenergetics of an Incipient Stratification System, *Current Anthropology* 14:603–617.

Saenz, C., 1991, Lords of the Waste: Predation, Pastoral Production, and the Process of Stratification among the Eastern Twaregs, in: *Chiefdoms: Power, Economy, and Ideology* (T. Earle, ed.), Cambridge University Press, Cambridge, pp. 100–118.

Sahlins, M., 1958, *Social Stratification in Polynesia,* University of Washington Press, Seattle.

Sahlins, M., 1965, On the Ideology and Composition of Descent Groups, *Man* 97:104–107.

Schalk, R., 1981, Land Use and Organizational Complexity among Foragers of Northwestern North America, in: *Affluent Foragers* (S. Koyama and D. Thomas, eds.), National Museum of Ethnology, Senri Ethnological Studies 9, Osaka, pp. 53–75.

Schulting, R., 1994, *Mortuary Variability and Socioeconomic Status Differentiation on the Northwest Plateau,* Archaeology Department, Simon Fraser University, Burnaby, British Columbia.

Service, E., 1962, *Primitive Social Organization: An Evolutionary Perspective,* Random House, New York.

Shennan, S., 1982, From Minimal to Moderate Ranking, in: *Ranking, Resource, and Exchange* (C. Renfrew and S. Shennan, eds.), Cambridge University Press, Cambridge, pp. 27–32.

Sherratt, A., 1982, Mobile Resources: Settlement and Exchange in Early Agricultural Europe, in: *Ranking, Resource and Exchange* (C. Renfrew and S. Shennan, eds.), Cambridge University Press, Cambridge, pp. 13–26.

Shnirelman, V., 1990, Class and Social Differentiation in Oceania, in: *Culture and History in the Pacific* (J. Siikala, ed.), Finnish Anthropological Society Transactions no. 27, Helsinki, pp. 125–138.

Shnirelman, V., 1992, Complex Hunter-Gatherers: Exception or Common Phenomenon? *Dialectical Anthropology* 17:183–196.

Sillitoe, P., 1978, Bit Men and War in New Guinea, *Man* 13:252–271.

Sjogren, K.-G., 1986, Kinship, Labor, and Land in Neolithic Southwest Sweden: Social Aspects of Megalithic Graves, *Journal of Anthropological Archaeology* 5:229–265.

Smith, J., 1978, Economic Uncertainty in an "Original Affluent Society": Caribou and Caribou Eater Chipewyan Adaptive Strategies, *Arctic Anthropology* 15(1):68–88.

Soffer, O., 1985, *The Upper Paleolithic of the Central Russian Plain,* Academic Press, Orlando.

Spier, L., and E. Sapir, 1930, Wishram Ethnography, *University of Washington Publications in Anthropology* 3.

Sproat, G., 1987, *The Nootka,* Sono Nis Press, Victoria, B.C.

Stott, M., 1975, *Bella Coola Ceremony and Art,* National Museum of Man Mercurey Series, No. 21, Ottawa.

Strathern, A., 1971, *The Rope of Moka,* Cambridge University Press, Cambridge.

Stryd, A., 1973, *The Later Prehistory of the Lillooet Area, British Columbia,* Unpublished Ph.D. dissertation, Department of Archaeology, University of Calgary, Calgary.

Suttles, W., 1960, *Variation in Habitat and Culture on the Northwest Coast,* Proceedings of the 34th International Congress of Americanists. (Reprinted in Y. Cohen, 1968, *Man in Adaptation,* Aldine, Chicago, pp. 93–106.

Suttles, W., 1968, Coping with Abundance: Subsistence on the Northwest Coast, in: *Man the Hunter* (R. Lee and I. Devore, eds.), Aldine, Chicago, pp. 56–68.

Swanton, J., 1975 (1909), *Contributions to the Ethnology of the Haida,* American Museum of Natural History, Memoir, vol. 5.

Teit, J., 1900, *The Jesup North Pacific Expedition, IV: The Thompson Indians of British Columbia,* Memoirs, American Museum of Natural History, 2.

Teit, J., 1906, *The Lillooet Indians,* Memoirs, American Museum of Natural History 2(5):193–300.

Teit, J., 1909, The Shuswap, *American Museum of Natural History Memoirs* 2(7):447–789.

Testart, A., 1982, The Significance of Food Storage among Hunter-Gatherers, *Current Anthropology* 23f:523–537.

Tolstoy, P., 1989, Chiefdoms, States and Scales of Analysis, *The Review of Archaeology* 10(1):72–78.

Turner, E. R., 1985, Socio-political Organization within the Powhatan Chiefdom and the Effects of European Contact, A.D. 1607–1646, in: *Cultures in Contact* (W. Fitzhugh, ed.), Smithsonian Institution Press, Washington, D.C., pp. 193–224.

Voytek, B., and R. Tringham, 1989, Rethinking the Mesolithic: The Case of South-East Europe, in: *The Mesolithic in Europe* (C. Bonsall, ed.), John Donald Publishers, Edinburgh, pp. 492–499.

Walens, S., 1981, *Feasting with Cannibals,* Princeton University Press, Princeton.

Walker, P., 1989, Cranial Injuries as Evidence of Violence in Prehistoric Southern California, *American Journal of Physical Anthropology* 80:313–323.

Watanabe, H., 1983, Occupational Differentiation and Social Stratification: The Case of Northern Pacific Maritine Food-Gatherers, *Current Anthropology* 24:217–219.

Webster, G., 1990, Labor Control and Emergent Stratification in Prehistory Europe, *Current Anthropology* 31:337–355.

Wells, P., 1984, *Farms, Villages, and Cities,* Cornell University Press, Ithaca, New York.

Wendorf, F., 1968, Site 177: A Nubian Final Paleolithic Graveyard near Jebel Sahaba, Sudan, in: *The Prehistory of Nubia,* vol. 2 (F. Wendorf, ed.), Fort Burgwin Research Center and Southern Methodist University Press, pp. 954–995.

Wenke, R., 1989, Egypt: Origins of Complex Societies, *Annual Review of Anthropology* 18:29–55.

Wheeler, P., 1990, *Land and Property Ownership: Changing Perspectives,* Paper Presented at the 6th International Conference on Hunting and Gathering Societies, Fairbanks, Alaska.

Widmer, R., 1988, *The Evolution of the Calusa: A Nonagricultural Chiefdom on the Southwest Florida Coast,* Tuscaloosa, University of Alabama Press.

Wiessner, P., 1989, Style and Changing Relations between the Individual and Society, in: *The Meaning of Things* (I. Hodder, ed.), Unwin Hyman, London, pp. 56–63.

Wiessner, P., and A. Tumu, n.d., *An Oral History of Enga,* Book ms. in preparation at Max Planck Institute, Andechs, Germany.

Winterhalder, B., 1986, Diet Choice, Risk, and Food Sharing in a Stochastic Environment, *Journal of Anthropological Archaeology* 5:369–392.

Wohlt, P., 1978, *Ecology, Agriculture and Social Organization: The Dynamics of Group Compo-*

sition in the Highlands of Papua New Guinea, Unpublished Ph.D. dissertation, University of Minnesota, Minneapolis.

Wolf, E., 1982, *Europe and the People without History,* University of California Press, Berkeley.

Wood, W. R., 1980, Plains Trade in Prehistoric Intertribal Relations, in: *Anthropology on the Great Plains* (W. R. Wood and M. Liberty, eds.), University of Nebraska Press, Lincoln.

Xuanpei, H., 1992, Liangzhu Culture, in: *Gems of Liangzhu Culture.* Shanghai Museum, Shanghai, pp. 27–33.

Yanagisako, S., 1979, Family and Household: The Analysis of Domestic Groups, *Annual Review of Anthropology* 8:161–205.

Young, M., 1971, *Fighting with Food,* Cambridge University Press, Cambridge.

Chapter 3

Social Inequality, Marginalization, and Economic Process

JEANNE E. ARNOLD

INTRODUCTION

A select roster of very complex hunter-gatherer societies, many on the western coastal fringe of North America, were sedentary or semisedentary and developed wealth-based exchange systems and hereditary inequality (e.g., Ames 1991; Arnold 1992a,b, 1993; Coupland 1988; Hayden et al. 1985; see also Marquardt 1988). Indeed, because many of these societies were still in existence at the time of colonial and frontier contact in the American West, and descendants were still living during the birth of anthropology as a discipline, ethnographic and archaeological records of these cultures are comparatively rich. As a result, opportunities to study the foundations of social inequality are in few places in the world more favorable than they are among these societies, which include the Chumash and other groups of California, many of the peoples of the Northwest Coast and Alaska, and societies of the British Columbia Plateau.

Despite the positive impact of the Price and Brown (1985) volume and

JEANNE E. ARNOLD • Department of Anthropology and Institute of Archaeology, University of California, Los Angeles, California 90024-1510.

Foundations of Social Inequality, edited by T. Douglas Price and Gary M. Feinman. Plenum Press, New York, 1995.

other recent contributions, many scholarly works examining developmental paths toward complexity still begin by excluding complex hunter-gatherers, signaling the long-standing view that social inequality is a phenomenon linked only to agricultural societies. Yet the more complex nonfarming societies clearly belong in any comprehensive discussion of the foundations of social inequality; indeed, study of these societies (and their immediate predecessors) is undoubtedly critical to the further refinement of theory on emergent complexity (Arnold 1993; Hayden, Chapter 2, this volume).

This chapter evaluates the process of marginalization as a force in the rise and reinforcement of socioeconomic inequality in a range of societies, including agriculturalists and complex-hunter gatherers. My interest stems from studies of the role of marginalization in cases of emergent and frontier-area inequality. *Marginalization* is the process by which established or emerging elites create socioeconomic relations of superior versus subordinate/dependent through manipulations of labor and distributions of social resources. This chapter will show that emerging elites in both hunter-gatherer and farming societies promote their own advancement and initiate various economic changes at the community and regional levels that effectively marginalize people in several important ways. For instance, as rising elites begin to accrue power, privilege, and status, they draw increasingly economically dependent sectors of the population (budding craft specialists are one example among many) into important production roles or labor-intensive group activities. If rising elites learn to control the information or technology critical to economic success and thus orchestrate networks of interdependencies that limit power outside their small circle, then nonelites become marginalized from positions of substantial political or economic influence. This process establishes the foundation for permanent social inequality. Important potential sources of emerging elite power include, most fundamentally, control over human labor, but also over information (see also Kelly 1991) and/or transportation (Arnold 1996). Emerging leaders become, in essence, labor brokers for lineages, moieties, villages, or regions, depending on the scale of activity and type of societal interaction. In this chapter, we explore the process of social and economic marginalization, drawing from the histories of complex hunter-gatherers, craft specialists, and early agriculturalists.

MARGINALIZATION: THEORETICAL UNDERPINNINGS

In this analysis, the term marginalization is used to refocus attention on important socioeconomic changes and processes that accompany and define developing social inequality in a range of prestate contexts. Marginalizing behavior occurs at different nodes of social interaction and in societies of various scales; it may, for example, be observed between households, between elites and commoners, between communities, and between societies of any type or size (hunter-gatherer, agricultural, colonial) at borders and frontiers. This definition of marginalization indicates that rising leaders devise and accelerate socioeconomic changes and explicitly counters the position that leaders and followers (and, thus, marginal positions in prestate society) are created by large-scale social processes beyond their control. Political models such as this, centered on the role of human agency in social change, obviate teleological, vitalistic explanations.

In short, opportunists create marginality in society. The process of marginalization itself revolves around elite strategies to develop control over labor and the products of labor, broadly speaking (Arnold 1992a, 1993; Brumfiel 1992; Gilman 1981; Gosden 1989; Hayden 1993; Roscoe 1993), thereby creating dependencies, obligations, and debts among members of a population. The ability of aspiring elites to orchestrate labor organization and related factors such as transportation, crafts, information, or resources, in ways that limit individual power and create more or less benign-appearing interdependencies, will determine the degree to which they succeed in building power.

To paraphrase Binford's (1983:231) expression of one extreme of the political model, power doesn't come from being nice. While the realities of social positioning may well correspond with this idea that power-building is rather unambiguously exploitative, it is also probably true, as Brumfiel (1994) and others imply, that the appearance of consultation and negotiation with those who are being marginalized is an essential part of elite success in the emergence of social hierarchy. That is, while the process of marginalization does involve increasing power disparities because elites are largely shaping the contexts in which they will operate, nonelites can and do take action of various kinds and may insist on some level of rewards and benefits, whether they be ideological or material. In any case, the dynamics of commoner resistance to (or cooperation with) hierarchization, frontier expansion, or the imposition of new ideologies should be considered together with the activities of the elites in the analysis of emerging inequality (Brumfiel 1992; Paynter 1985:172).

The point here is that marginality is not a passive result of other developments; it is a socioeconomic or political divisiveness created and shaped largely by ambitious leaders or entrepreneurs. But equally important, we must evaluate in what context marginalization occurs. As has been emphasized recently, the opportunity to initiate these kinds of changes often arises under conditions of stress or other significant change (Arnold 1992b, 1993; Binford 1983:221–222). Any number of stimuli may create resource imbalances, promote ideological changes, or alter subsistence potentials (positively or negatively); such opportunities are natural windows for accelerated aggrandizive activity. These opportunistic moments include, but are not limited to, times of environmental decline or unusual bounty, population pressure, population movements, epidemics, large-scale conflicts, and the like (see Arnold 1993).

The alternative explanation is that aggrandizive self-starters possessed the vision and ability to shape their own success with no change in their surroundings—that is, with no alterations of the potential to initiate labor or resource control, management of exchange, or the acquisition of wealth. This might be labeled the "bootstrap elites" model, in which elites are "self-made" successes during calm, normal social and economic conditions. The model is problematical and seems implausible, particularly from the standpoint of the commoners who would be marginalized by the onset of bouts of entrepreneurial elite activity. There would seem to be little reason for them to tolerate marked breaches of social rules regarding sharing of resources and information. Systematic reneging "on social relationships with impunity," as Binford (1983:220) describes the power struggle, and bald establishments of private ownership claims over communal resources, would seem to be acceptable only during stresses or changed circumstances, rather than during normal conditions. This is a narrow but important point that serves to distinguish two kinds of political models. The one perspective assumes that aspiring elites act within windows of opportunity that facilitate their objectives; the second claims that elites have the ability to create hierarchy at will from largely egalitarian conditions.

Hayden (1993, Chapter 2, this volume) argues that only environments providing impressive quantities of consistently reliable (essentially inexhaustible) food resources will facilitate elite emergence. While many of Hayden's data from British Columbia and other regions are intriguing, it may be worth considering that new plateaus of resource availability, innovations in transportation or procurement technology, and/or ideological shifts perhaps played roles in addition to ambitious activities of aggrandizive individuals within the favorable environments of the various regions he discusses. A broad array of social, technological, and environmental data would of course need to be investigated to fully address these kinds of questions. Meanwhile, in the current literature there is some consensus that increasing marginalization of sectors of society by rising elites is an animated, proactive process, not a vitalistic, inevitable one (e.g., Brumfiel 1992, 1994).

Placing a greater emphasis on purely economic transactions, Gosden (1989), following Sahlins (1974), argues that debts incurred in cycles of exchange create social differentiation. Importantly, it is not the mere act of giving and receiving that forms the basis of inequality, but the ability of certain individuals to restrict access to particular kinds of gifts or products. If some parties can consistently bestow classes of objects that cannot be repaid, they invest the exchange process with a level of indebtedness that cannot be overcome. This fact is quite relevant to the current discussion because it represents a clearly calculated process of economic marginalization, devised by persons able to accumulate information and wealth at the expense of ordinary members of a community through increasing control over the production and/or distribution of specialized or imported goods.

Operationalizing the Concepts

The importance of social change in spatially marginal locales such as frontier and boundary areas has been addressed by Green and Perlman (1985). Socially and economically marginal communities may or may not correspond to spatially marginal communities. Indeed, the concept of spatial marginality itself depends on our definition of margin; is a coast, for instance, at land's end and therefore marginal, or should perhaps some coasts—and some communities along them—be viewed as "gateway" communities central to a water-based exchange network and well-positioned to capture both aquatic and terrestrial resources (Arnold 1996)? Either way, relative spatial isolation does not necessarily result in low social or economic rank; quite the contrary may be true. Margins from one point of view may be from another perspective natural corridors of communication, and thus "strategic locales for controlling the flow of merchandise" (Hirth 1978:37). Certainly frontier areas may witness marked social change, where people and ideas move frequently and the potential may be substantial for unequal wealth accumulations and enhanced social positions to develop for aspiring elites.

To address the issue of marginalization and the rise of socioeconomic inequality, I discuss several points regarding cultural marginality. Most fundamentally, the process of marginalization may occur within or between societies. In the examples to follow, I examine the marginalization of (1) craft specialists, (2) classes of landless laborers, such as slaves in native Northwest Coast societies, (3) whole communities, and (4) one ethnic group at the expense of another. These are several scales of social, political, and economic separation of the powerful from the disenfranchised. I also examine the degree to which anthropologists recognize marginalization as an active or passive process, and I consider whether scholars are conceptualizing this process in terms of members of society who become geographically or socioeconomically marginal.

A *margin* is a border, boundary, or edge, as opposed to the center, middle, or interior. *Marginal,* as an adjective, refers to along an edge or border, or in a second sense of the term, something that is barely useful or profitable, as in "he owns a marginal business" (Stein and Flexner 1984). *Marginalization,* then, when applied to cultural evolution, refers most broadly to a process by which persons or positions are separated from central operations of a society. It implies, as well, instability, expendability, lack of power, and an absence of full integration with centralized decision-making. We may examine ethnographic and archaeological cases whereby this is expressed in a variety of ways, including marginalization through unequal access to labor and possibly to information, resources, or transportation and distribution of goods. Separations from the power of decision-making and from control over returns on labor investments are perhaps the most important factors to investigate. I focus on inequality over and above what exists based on age and gender.

While this concept also shares foundations with well-established social theory regarding in-groups and out-groups, "us" and "the other," and "the marginal man" (Park 1969), my use of marginality is more closely linked to economic issues. It describes the actions of a few to create and then occupy central, controlling positions for themselves, simultaneously creating a group with a large membership that does not have comparable access to resources and information. This mirrors Max Weber's argument that the creation of new social structures and positions depends on a "push" supplied by charismatic individuals. Such people develop new offices, new symbols, and new dependencies among commoners. Most fundamentally, power is the capacity to get things done "through the agency of others" (Roscoe 1993). That is, through the development of control over other people, or through control over structures that dominate others, emerging leaders place demands on labor to further their own goals (Brumfiel 1992; Roscoe 1993). Marginality is often reinforced by patterns of conspicuous consumption of wealth, status, and prestige (Veblen 1953).

In the following case studies selected to highlight concepts that have shaped recent research on these social processes, I contrast Dean Arnold's (1985) notion of the marginality of ceramic craft specialization, Meillassoux's (1981) views on the rise of differential control over social reproduction, slavery in the societies of the American Northwest Coast (Donald 1985; Mitchell 1985; Ruyle 1973), and the clash of Euro-American and Native American cultures during the frontier period of California (Hurtado 1988). These examples allow us to examine the course of marginalization and increasing social inequality on several different levels and center on marginalization as a *process*.

The particular social, economic, or political tactics used by individuals to marginalize others, the specific objectives of the participants, and the outcomes will vary substantially from case to case. I suggest, however, that the process of marginalization has three common elements: (1) household labor begins to be appropriated by suprakin forces rather than autonomously managed by traditional family leadership (Arnold 1993; Brumfiel 1992:555); (2) basic costs of reproduction remain in the household and the domestic mode of production continues in some form, but some persons must also contribute regularly to projects that benefit aspiring or established elites; and (3) persons are brought into core activities of new economic development, but they are systematically limited in their ability to influence society's operations because they are separated from information and the ability to direct their labor and its products as they choose. That is, marginalized persons are incorporated into primary economic activities through the appropriation of their labor, but they are shifted farther from various spheres of control (Roscoe 1993). Sahlins (1958:7) and others recognized decades ago that the regulation of labor, of which craft specialization is but one example, is a mechanism by which rising elites may build or extend economic power. This often is initiated as elder males begin to control the labor of women and related, dependent men, but a major ideological breach may be essential to stimulate the first appearance of permanent control over the labor of nonkin (Arnold 1993; Barnard and Woodburn 1988:28).

The marginalizing process can be most effectively seen as a mechanism by which social inequality may develop; that is, it is a process fundamental to the way emerging elites achieve (or reinforce) economic leadership. It is neither a cause, per se, nor a consequence of social inequality, although arguments might be made for either. In contexts of social evolution within a single society, for instance, aggrandizive individuals may use strategies to economically marginalize others as a tool (a mechanism) to build influence and wealth. I do not wish to ignore the process of ideological marginalization in this discussion, because it is undoubtedly an important product of the processes I describe, but in my view the economic processes of marginalization are the more fundamental ones. Ideology may play a role of extraordinary importance in reinforcing domination once inequality of some form is in place, but exploration of this topic would fill another chapter. Let us now turn to the examples.

Craft Specialists and Marginality

In his influential discussion of ceramic production and specialization, Dean Arnold (1985) has argued that the practice of ceramic craft specialization should be seen as a poor cousin to traditional farming in most contexts worldwide. He believes that only individuals or families who become separated from land tenancy or ownership turn to specializations such as pottery-making. Drawing upon a wide array of ethnographic examples, primarily Third World peasant societies, Arnold demonstrates that in many such cases ceramic specialists are situated on marginal agricultural lands and are unable to support their families by relying on farming alone; hence, they develop ceramic crafts to stabilize domestic income. Farmers on rich agricultural land, in contrast, are affluent and enjoy higher status and the direct returns of a subsistence income; they do not turn to crafts.

This is an argument that spatial or geographical marginality characterizes craft specialists. Specialists reside at or beyond the border of productive farming lands, and as a consequence, they suffer socioeconomically as they are forced to turn to crafts. But the model is also driven by considerations of population pressure. Arnold shows that crafts arise as populations swell (or the land is degraded) to a point where the land cannot sustain all families or all communities. If no strategy or technology is sufficient to improve yields enough to support the population, "movement into crafts" is common and occurs "sooner in marginal land than in more fertile areas" (Arnold 1985:192). It is further argued (Arnold 1985:193) that crafts require "additional labor and greater risks than agriculture," although the data do not necessarily substantiate the claim that craftspersons must expend more labor. It appears that Arnold would equate the sale or exchange of ceramics to obtain food with a greater investment of labor than farming requires, but this is not always the case.

Nonetheless, it does seem true that for many contemporary Third World societies, pottery-making is an undesirable occupation, one that failing farmers may adopt out of economic necessity (see also Binford 1983), although when demand for pottery involves more complex factors, including display of ritual and social symbols, potters enjoy high social position (Arnold 1985:198). Marginality for many ceramic specialists may be simultaneously geographic (in that specialists are on lands peripheral to the greatest potential concentration of wealth) and economic (in that specialists are of lower rank or status than farmers) (Arnold 1985:226).

The process of the emergence of specialists and the development of inequality, as Dean Arnold describes it, is extremely passive. These changes occur as population pressure builds, and unfortunately situated individuals who occupy the poorer land become specialists who descend by default into a lower echelon of society. Arnold does not incorporate motivation or human manipulation of economic circumstances into this model. Moreover, it is obvious that no one would *choose* a craft as an occupation; therefore, those who became specialists and thus socioeconomically marginalized were in a sense victims of an acephalous process. From this perspective, the rise of social differentiation is unrelated to ambition, power, or politics; there is no role for human agency, socioeconomic negotiation, factional competition, and the like.

I find quite different processes at work in an analysis of the rise of craft specialization in the Channel Islands of California. In this context, the emergence of intensive prehistoric specializations was the apparent result of a reorganization of labor negotiated by a rising elite group (Arnold 1992a,b,

1993). This kind of role for political motivation in the rise of social inequality, based on leadership involvement in the control of labor, resources, exchange, and the like, has its parallels elsewhere and is emphasized by numerous other scholars (e.g., Brumfiel 1992, 1994; Cowgill 1981; Hayden, Chapter 2, this volume).

While many ceramic craft specialists are geographically marginal, Late period Channel Islands Chumash bead makers resided in some of the richest coastal zones in North America. Under normal, cool-water conditions, these areas provided an exceptional bounty of marine resources (Arnold 1992b). Nonetheless, craft specializations such as intensive shell-bead making first developed during a stressful warm-water period when these villages were temporarily rather marginal from a subsistence standpoint, lending some support to Dean Arnold's marginality argument. Interestingly, shell-working (and other) specializations continued and indeed thrived for several centuries after the ocean reverted to very favorable cool-water conditions (Arnold 1992b). This suggests that the relationship between marginality and specialization may be very complex.

It is important to note that major innovations that tie crafts to ideology or wealth may stimulate demand and raise the importance of the craft. This in turn elevates the status of its practitioners. Shell beads were of extraordinary importance in Chumash social negotiation, ceremonies, exchange, and external relations. Both ethnohistorical and archaeological data suggest that Chumash bead makers were likely in the upper-middle ranks of Chumash society, neither at the very top nor the bottom. They do not appear in the top echelon because those who orchestrated intensive cross-channel canoe trade separated specialists from the ability to manipulate distributions of their products (Arnold 1996). Thus, specialists, even relatively important ones, in many cases become marginalized by elites from information and central decision-making processes (Roscoe 1993).

Inequality and Marginalization on the Community Level

Claude Meillassoux (1981) writes in *Maidens, Meal and Money* that because human reproduction is the same as the production of labor power, the family in more complex societies often continues to supply labor power through its reproductive activities, even though it may be deprived of control over its productive ones. Meillassoux (1981:41–45) argues that the need to ensure an adequate work force to carry out farming tasks historically necessitated for the first time among agriculturalists a cultural concern about numbers of children (size of the work force), lateral ties, social relations through the generations and seasons, and kinship. Elders assumed managerial roles and began to assert themselves in the arena of marriage arrangements. Repro-

duction became an intensely political process and elders increasingly manipulated women by arranging marriages. However, it was only when elders
began to systematically skim from bridewealth payments, or refused to dis-
pose of bridewealth in the normal fashion, that social inequality began to
emerge (Meillassoux 1981:73). The productive and reproductive cycles became dissociated, and the movement of women or children was replaced by
the movement of (former) bridewealth items as aspiring leaders strengthened
their control over matrimonial arrangements. Yet true class relations and thus
true inequality developed only when a whole agricultural community came to
dominate another entire farming community (Meillassoux 1981:79–83).

Meillassoux fails to allow for increased social complexity among complex
hunter-gatherers in this model, since his discussion exclusively relates to the
agricultural economy (Meillassoux 1981:40). However, let us set this problem
aside in order to evaluate internal contradictions in the argument. Meillassoux
(1981:73) claims that "the will to dominate" by one faction may prompt
bridewealth-hoarding behavior and result in the elevation of that faction's
status, yet he also argues that social control always derives not from possession of wealth but from management of reproduction (Meillassoux 1981:72).
At the same time, he contends that elders never fully exploit juniors within
their own community; indeed, no form of class relations arises within a
community, because whole communities must exploit others (Meillassoux
1981:81) for inequality to occur. He asserts, but does not effectively substantiate, that each community acts in solidarity as a whole, producing bridewealth as a single unit (Meillassoux 1981:69), farming as a unit (Meillassoux
1981:40), producing surpluses and caring for older and younger nonpro-
ducers as a unit (Meillassoux 1981:50–60), and the like. In this view, the only
way to marginalize one facet of society is to pit one community against
another. This position appears to be largely indefensible when confronted by
ethnographic examples.

For instance, studies of emerging inequality in Northwest Coast hunter-
gatherer societies indicate that among a number of groups who were intermediate between egalitarian societies and chiefdoms, much like Meillassoux's
sedentary farming societies, households were distinctly self-interested units
that controlled resources, produced goods for potlatches, and took on debts
and obligations (e.g., Hayden, Chapter 2, this volume). Entire communities
did not share these tasks and rights (Coupland 1985). Furthermore, slaves
existed within communities and within households, and thus the appearance
of social stratification in this kind of society appears to lie not in the relative
power of one community over another, but in class relations within and
between households (Donald 1985). Residential corporate groups, which
included two or more nuclear families, large cooperative households, and
shared extractive activities (such as fish harvests), were unranked initially

(Coupland 1985:221), but through time may have been managed by a Big Man into a more surplus-oriented, wealthy group, spurred by his desire for prestige and material goods. Such leaders could further expand their labor force—and thus the residential corporate group's productive potential and relative standing—through slavery and arranged marriages. According to Donald (1985:238–240), Chilkat Tlingit and Kwakiutl economic units were centered around property-owning, resource-controlling house-groups or descent groups that were also clearly ranked relative to one another.

While the residential corporate group superficially may resemble Meillassoux's "domestic agricultural economy" in its potential for inequality to develop from incipient control over various activities by elders and in its small-group self-sufficiency, it in fact operated quite differently. The Northwest Coast residential corporate group exhibited unambiguous household ownership of resources and economic self-interest, and marginalization of people occurred both within the corporate group (slavery) and between ranked corporate groups, which developed comparatively more or less wealth and prestige, based largely on their production and harvesting capabilities (Coupland 1985; Hayden, Chapter 2, this volume). Most Northwest Coast leaders openly competed within communities (Hayden 1993:28, 45) and bridewealth in particular was used to enhance wealth inequities between families in the same community. This contrasts sharply with Meillassoux's view of the communally oriented, internally egalitarian, benignly cooperative, small agricultural society. In short, these are incompatible models of emergent inequality. Ethnographic data from a range of complex hunter-gatherer societies seem to more effectively support a model of aspiring elites prompting marginalization among factions within households and/or within communities. We shall see another example of this in our next case.

Slavery as Marginalization

Slavery represents the extreme marginalization of one sector of a society and its labor and reproductive power. Slavery was a common way of systematically marginalizing people in Northwest Coast societies; slaves generally were the losers in interethnic conflicts. Indeed, the institution of slavery created a second level of society fully subservient to the core leadership. Mitchell (1985) shows that all of the Northwest Coast groups had slaves, constituting as much as 25% of the population of some groups in the historic era, although more typically the percentage of slaves ranged from 5% to 15%. Northwest Coast peoples may well have had three social strata: what Donald (1985) characterizes as titleholders, commoners, and slaves. The appearance of the institution of slavery in hunting–gathering society, with all its implications for control over human labor and the economy, is a cause for considerable consternation among some cultural evolutionists who are reluctant to acknowledge the development of legitimate power or ranking in nonfarming societies.

Yet there is little doubt that unmitigated control by household chiefs over the labor of as much as 15–25% of the adult population represented an extraordinary source of social and economic power. Labor manipulation clearly played some rather significant role in the formulation of social inequalities in this region. Ethnographers have debated at length whether slavery was a major prehistoric phenomenon that continued into the historic era in the Northwest or was a minor institution that expanded substantially during disruptive, intense conflicts over wealth and trade during the historic era. Donald (1994) and others have recently summarized some of the data to substantiate a prehistoric origin for slavery. Space is inadequate to consider this issue at greater length, but this does lead us to consider yet another scale at which marginalization occurs.

Marginality, Labor, and Frontierism

The process of assimilating California Indians into American frontier life during the nineteenth century was violent, oppressive, and divisive, even more so than most historians concede. This process in part parallels the process of emergent inequality through intercommunity or interethnic conflict because of the central role of changing control over labor, although writ on a grander scale. The events and policies of the 1830s to the 1860s that were forced on Indian peoples systematically marginalized them in all ways. They were forced into social and economic dependence, partitioned from power and information, separated from any kind of self-sufficiency, and compelled to accommodate the work patterns, religion, and sexual demands of American frontier life (Hurtado 1988). This process, played out between more and less powerful cultures, is discussed as well by Paynter (1985). Paynter demonstrates that labor in many kinds of frontier settings was often brought into highly exploitative positions, ranging from tenancy to slavery. What is germane here is that the ability of the dominant group to bring more and more labor under its control resulted rather quickly in exaggerated wealth inequities and higher social positions for some (Paynter 1985:177–178). Although Euro-Americans approached the western frontiers with considerably more power, wealth, and influence than the native groups they encountered, thus bringing with them *de facto* higher status, the way they brought native labor under control to further consolidate socioeconomic standing also has broad parallels in simpler, internal transformations within native Californian societies, as we will see.

In the Gold Rush regions of California during the mid-1800s, native labor became essential for white frontiersmen who needed to develop pastoral, agricultural, and metal resources (Hurtado 1988:7). The Indian household became the biological source of the work force serving the frontier, yet it was forced to continue to sustain Indian workers at home with food, clothing, and shelter. Men began to work for wages (although a few decades earlier, most natives at the California Missions were not compensated for their labor; Hornbeck 1989:425) and Indian households became increasingly stratified. Women continued to provide subsistence in traditional ways and thus supported the men, who provided the labor to the dominant economy (see also Wallerstein 1984). Indian labor thus "subsidize[d] incipient capitalism even as the native economy [was] being displaced" (Hurtado 1988:9).

Although the forces exerting themselves on frontier Sierran native Californians were violent and without consent, the role of some household members in supporting an increasingly wage-based (and less subsistence-oriented) household economy, as males pursued income from the outside, may have a counterpart in internal changes within native societies. I turn again briefly to the Chumash to illustrate this point. During the rapid transformations toward economic specialization that occurred ca. A.D. 1200–1300 in Chumash territory (Arnold 1991, 1992b), some Chumash household members (of unknown gender) expended increasing amounts of labor and energy on specialized tasks such as bead making for external consumption, while others within that unit must have supported normal household activities to a greater extent. Returns came to specialist households in exchange for surplus products, but a percentage of goods or foods was expropriated by those who manipulated the trade and/or transportation. In this case, the households ultimately expended more total labor and yet were alienated from some of the fruits of that labor by traders (Arnold 1992b, 1993, 1996). Increasingly wealthy trader-elites, with new powers beyond the reach of commoner households, managed the distributions of island-made shell bead exports. Commoners became dependent on distribution networks they could not control and were consequently economically marginalized by this process.

It appears likely that elite boat owners were the persons who controlled transportation through exclusive management of plank canoes and thus regulated exchanges of goods between the Channel Islands and the mainland (Arnold 1992b, 1996). The Island Chumash specialist household was marginalized to the extent that it was no longer self-sufficient, it did not directly gather information pertaining to long-distance social and economic matters (see Kelly 1991), and it was in a poor position to garner power. As long as others managed distributions of goods, specialized producers were unable to fully control their own economic fortunes. Similarly, during the Gold Rush, among the first things native commoner households lost were (1) their ability to control labor and its products and (2) their ability to gather and assess critical social and economic information (Hurtado 1988). These are essentially the same components of *economic* and *informational* marginalization seen in the Chumash example, although of course important differences remain in the degree of force used to assure power inequities in the two cases.

SUMMARY

This chapter uses the concept of marginalization in an attempt to refocus and clarify our thinking regarding emergent social inequality. We have explored different scales of patterning: people economically marginalized others within households and communities, between communities, and in border and frontier situations, using persuasion, intimidation, coercion, and the like (see Cowgill 1981). Some scholars have seen rising inequality as a completely passive process; such interpretations seem particularly inconsistent with the data we have reviewed from complex hunting and gathering societies. Meillassoux rests his argument for inequality on social controls (elder control over marriage, with an element of political motivation), largely ignoring the impact of both technological innovation and ambition, while others view the foundations of inequality from vantage points such as the Northwest Coast, where competition, aspirations toward wealth and influence, and control over the labor power of some sectors of society (via slavery) were the most powerful agents of change (Donald 1985; Ruyle 1973). This latter position generally holds that opportunists devise strategies for social change, but success may depend upon making these strategies seem attractive, important, and/or legitimate to the majority. Elite actions may be made palatable, for instance, by frequent feasting and other celebrations during which commoners receive foods and goods.

The focus on marginalization in this chapter is intended to accentuate the dynamic nature of social evolution and to highlight the distinction between a passive, organic-functional model and a political, human agency model in which changes are driven at least in part by opportunism, ambition, and active processes of social negotiation. The agency model appears better equipped to explain social evolution, particularly among complex hunter-gatherers. In all cases, marginalization involves isolating some people from central positions of social and economic influence (decision-making) at the same time that they are moved into increasingly interconnected, dependent socioeconomic circumstances.

This chapter is not intended to serve as a definitive analysis of production, social relations, and marginalization, but rather to begin to operationalize these concepts. A broad survey of cultures is necessary in order to further evaluate the degree to which marginalization is a core process in emergent inequality. One point that should be clear from this discussion is that Marx and other early theorists did not recognize that the potential exists in prestate settings and outside the framework of agricultural society for people to profit from the labor of others. We now see that more can be understood about the expropriation of labor during capitalist development if we explore how ranked, noncapitalist societies such as complex hunter-gatherers controlled and mobilized labor and generated surpluses (see also Paynter 1985). The process of marginalizing others through the increasing control of their labor is among the most powerful agents of social change at many levels of society and appears to have been instrumental in the emergence of socioeconomic hierarchy.

REFERENCES

Ames, K. M., 1991, The Archaeology of the Longue Duree: Temporal and Spatial Scale in the Evolution of Social Complexity on the Southern Northwest Coast, *Antiquity* 95:935–945.
Arnold, D.E., 1985, *Ceramic Theory and Cultural Process*, Cambridge University Press, Cambridge.
Arnold, J. E., 1991, Transformation of a Regional Economy: Sociopolitical Evolution and the Production of Valuables in Southern California, *Antiquity* 65:953–962.
Arnold, J. E., 1992a, *Organizational Transformations in Complex Hunter-Gatherer Evolution*, Paper presented at the Society for American Archaeology annual meeting, Pittsburgh.
Arnold, J. E., 1992b, Complex Hunter-Gatherer-Fishers of Prehistoric California: Chiefs, Specialists, and Maritime Adaptations of the Channel Islands, *American Antiquity* 57:60–84.
Arnold, J. E., 1993, Labor and the Rise of Complex Hunter-Gatherers, *Journal of Anthropological Archaeology* 12:75–119.
Arnold, J. E., 1996, *Transportation Innovation and Social Complexity among Maritime Hunter-Gatherer Societies, American Anthropologist*, in press.
Barnard, A., and J. Woodburn, 1988, Property, Power, and Ideology in Hunting and Gathering Societies: An Introduction, in: *Hunters and Gatherers 2: Property, Power and Ideology* (T. Ingold, D. Riches, and J. Woodburn, eds.), Berg, New York, pp. 4–31.
Binford, L. R., 1983, *In Pursuit of the Past*, Thames and Hudson, New York.
Brumfiel, E. M., 1992, Breaking and Entering the Ecosystem—Gender, Class, and Faction Steal the Show, *American Anthropologist* 94:551–567.
Brumfiel, E. M., 1994, Factional Competition and Political Development in the New World: An Introduction, in: *Factional Competition and Political Development in the New World* (E. M. Brumfiel and J. W. Fox, eds.), Cambridge University Press, Cambridge, pp. 3–13.
Coupland, G., 1985, Restricted Access, Resource Control and the Evolution of Status Inequality among Hunter-Gatherers, in: *Status, Structure and Stratification: Current Archaeological Reconstructions* (M. Thompson, M. T. Garcia, and F. J. Kense, eds.), University of Calgary Archaeological Association, Calgary, pp. 217–226.
Coupland, G., 1988, Prehistoric Economic and Social Change in the Tsimshian Area, in: *Research in Economic Anthropology*, Supp. 3 (B. Isaac, ed.), JAI Press, Greenwich, pp. 211–243.
Cowgill, G., 1981, Comment, *Current Anthropology* 22:203.

102   JEANNE E. ARNOLD

Donald, L., 1985, On the Possibility of Social Class in Societies Based on Extractive Subsistence, in: *Status, Structure and Stratification: Current Archaeological Reconstructions* (M. Thompson, M. T. Garcia, and F. J. Kense, eds.), University of Calgary Archaeological Association, Calgary, pp. 237–243.

Donald, L., 1994, *"Class" Stratification and Political Organization on the Northwest Coast of North America*, Paper presented at Complex Hunter-Gatherers of the World: An International Symposium, UCLA Institute of Archaeology, Los Angeles.

Gilman, A., 1981, The Development of Social Stratification in Bronze Age Europe, *Current Anthropology* 22:1–23.

Gosden, C., 1989, Debt, Production, and Prehistory, *Journal of Anthropological Archaeology* 8:355–387.

Green, S. W., and S. M. Perlman, 1985, Frontiers, Boundaries, and Open Social Systems, in: *The Archaeology of Frontiers and Boundaries* (S. W. Green and S. M. Perlman, eds.), Academic Press, Orlando, pp. 3–13.

Hayden, B., 1993, *The Dynamics of Emergent Inequality*, Paper presented at the Society for American Archaeology annual meeting, St. Louis.

Hayden, B., M. Eldridge, and A. Eldridge, and A. Cannon, 1985, Complex Hunter-Gatherers in Interior British Columbia, in: *Prehistoric Hunter-Gatherers: The Emergence of Cultural Complexity* (T. D. Price and J. A. Brown, eds.), Academic Press, San Diego, pp. 181–199.

Hirth, K. G., 1978, Interregional Trade and the Formation of Prehistoric Gateway Communities, *American Antiquity* 43:35–45.

Hornbeck, D., 1989, Economic Growth and Change at the Missions of Alta California, 1769–1846, in: *Columbian Consequences 1: Archaeological and Historical Perspectives* (D. H. Thomas, ed.), Smithsonian Institution Press, Washington, pp. 423–434.

Hurtado, A. L., 1988, *Indian Survival on the California Frontier*, Yale University Press, New Haven.

Kelly, R., 1991, Sedentism, Sociopolitical Inequality, and Resource Fluctuations, in: *Between Bands and States* (S. A. Gregg, ed.), Southern Illinois University Center for Archaeological Investigations, Occasional Paper no. 9, Carbondale, pp. 135–158.

Marquardt, W. H., 1988, Politics and Production among the Calusa of South Florida, in: *Hunters and Gatherers 1: History, Evolution, and Social Change* (T. Ingold, D. Riches, and J. Woodburn, eds.), Berg, Oxford, pp. 161–188.

Meillassoux, C., 1981, *Maidens, Meal and Money*, Cambridge University Press, Cambridge.

Mitchell, D., 1985, A Demographic Profile of Northwest Coast Slavery, in: *Status, Structure and Stratification: Current Archaeological Reconstructions* (M. Thompson, M. T. Garcia, and F. J. Kense, eds.), University of Calgary Archaeological Association, Calgary, pp. 227–236.

Park, R., 1969, Human Migration and the Marginal Man, in: *Classic Essays on the Culture of Cities* (R. Sennett, ed.), Prentice-Hall, Englewood Cliffs, New Jersey, pp. 131–142.

Paynter, R., 1985, Surplus Flow between Frontiers and Homelands, in: *The Archaeology of Frontiers and Boundaries* (S. W. Green and S. M. Perlman, eds.), Academic Press, Orlando, pp. 163–211.

Price, T. D., and J. A. Brown (eds.), 1985, *Prehistoric Hunter-Gatherers: The Emergence of Cultural Complexity*, Academic Press, San Diego.

Roscoe, P. B., 1993, Practice and Political Centralisation: A New Approach to Political Evolution, *Current Anthropology* 34:111–140.

Ruyle, E. E., 1973, Slavery, Surplus, and Stratification on the Northwest Coast: The Ethnoenergetics of an Incipient Stratification System, *Current Anthropology* 14:603–631.

Sahlins, M., 1958, *Social Stratification in Polynesia*, University of Washington Press, Seattle.

Sahlins, M. D., 1974, *Stone Age Economics*, Tavistock, London.

Stein, J., and S. B. Flexner (eds.), 1984, *The Random House Thesaurus College Edition,* Random House, New York.

Veblen, T., 1953, *The Theory of the Leisure Class,* New American Library, New York.

Wallerstein, I., 1984, Household Structures and Labor-Force Formation in the Capitalist World-Economy, in: *Households and the World-Economy* (J. Smith, I. Wallerstein, and H. Evers, eds.), Sage Publications, Beverly Hills.

Chapter 4

The Cultural Foundations of Inequality in Households

RICHARD E. BLANTON

INTRODUCTION

In this chapter I follow up on a frequently expressed argument that an elaboration of culture, especially in the realms of symbolic systems and ritual behavior, is a process central to the establishment and institutionalization of social inequality. For example, Bloch (1977:289) argues that ritual communication creates a "mystified nature" in which an order of inequality "takes on the appearance of an inevitable part of an ordered system" (cf. Bourdieu's [1978–79] concept of "symbolic power"). I propose a hypothesis relating culture to inequality within a specific social context: the household. I then evaluate the hypothesis by analyzing a category of data commonly available to archaeologists, namely, the form of the house. Because the analysis required me to contextualize the formal properties of houses with reference to the social and cultural behavior of their residents, the data I use were coded from ethnographically described cases, and the method I use is cross-cultural.

I believe my venture into cross-cultural research has produced results of considerable relevance for archaeologists interested in the foundations of social inequality. First, my formal evaluation of a hypothesis relating cultural expression and inequality should go further to convince archaeologists of the

RICHARD E. BLANTON • Department of Sociology and Anthropology, Purdue University, West Lafayette, Indiana 47907.

Foundations of Social Inequality, edited by T. Douglas Price and Gary M. Feinman. Plenum Press, New York, 1995.

importance of the interactions among these variables than the untested assertions of cultural anthropologists like Bloch. Second, my method relating house form to degree of cultural elaboration should be a source of ideas for archaeologists attempting to operationalize variables related to symbolic expression. Last, the theoretical framework I preliminarily developed while doing the cross-cultural study will, I think, further enrich archaeological discussion of household inequality and its causes. As I conducted the cross-cultural study, I found that an exclusively materialist approach (e.g., see Hayden's Chapter 2, where the sources of power are considered to reside exclusively in the control of material resources and labor) would wrongly ignore the many nonmaterial dimensions of behavior underlying inequality. Specifically, what I found as I coded the cross-cultural data is that an analysis couched in terms of "mode of production" (see below) would be inadequate in light of the complex nature of household inequality. In the following paragraphs, I develop a broader concept that I call "household social reproductive strategy."

Mode of Production and Household Social Reproductive Strategy

In current discussions of "middle-range" societies, it has become commonplace for anthropologists to explain surplus production for prestige-giving feasting (as well as other kinds of distributions, payments, and exchanges, as discussed by Hayden, Chapter 2, this volume) by reference to the mobilization of labor based on kinship relations (e.g., Arnold 1993; Leacock 1972; Meillassoux 1972, 1981:41–49; Moore 1991), although as Arnold (Chapter 3, this volume) points out, Meillassoux's argument pertaining to agricultural communities will have to be extended to include complex hunter-gatherers as well. This is Wolf's (1982:92–94) "kin-ordered mode of production." To begin my discussion of social reproductive strategies, I modify Wolf's conceptualization, and those like it, by noting that from the analytical perspective utilized here, kin-ordered social formations are only misleadingly regarded either as entirely kin-ordered or as representing a mode of production, strictly speaking. While economic mobilization in middle-range societies is largely predicated on kin relations (i.e., rights and obligations vested in culturally constituted relations of gender and generation [e.g., Siskind 1978:864]), other categories of social relations are also potential contexts for surplus appropriation, including slavery (as discussed by Kenneth Ames, Chapter 6, this volume). Additionally, in some cases, the domestic social formations of the type I will discuss below are not entirely kin-ordered in the sense that their memberships may include unrelated persons, for example, individuals who by choice join the successful households of important Big Men in New Guinea (e.g., Brown and Brookfield 1967:120; Pospisil 1963:38; Strathern 1982:47). Thus the phrase "kin-ordered mode of production" is misleading, and should be regarded only as a shorthand way to refer to situations where kin-ordered relationships are often the primary, but not the only, basis for economic mobilization or other dimensions of household inequality.

I also wish to amend the "mode of production" aspect of Wolf's and Siskind's Marxist-inspired concepts by pointing to the fact that mobilization of labor, especially control of junior members' production by elders, represents only one dimension of a more encompassing pattern of centralized control found in households. But much social science theorizing seems to focus on this one element. Bell's (1986–87) discussion of inequality in households, although couched in a neoclassical economic framework, is like a mode of production analysis in that it also emphasizes the primacy of social relations as production relations (he uses the phrase "social technology" [p. 108] rather than mode of production). In contrast with both the Marxist and neoclassical viewpoints, I start my analysis by pointing out that individuals, whether acting alone or in groups, strive to attain, and maintain, some acceptable level of social status (or social approval) in society; that is, they strive socially to reproduce themselves at what they regard as an acceptable level of social approval. The strategies brought to bear to achieve social reproductive goals are highly variable, and while they will often entail the mobilization of the labor of others, social reproductive strategies include many possible elements in addition to labor mobilization, including the control of children's marriages for political or status purposes (e.g., Bourdieu 1976; Goody 1990:261–265). In some cases, not just control of labor and wealth, but an ideal of exemplary behavior—for example, the maintenance of appropriate separation of the sexes—is an important determinant of household status (e.g., Dumont 1980:56).

An approach developed from the perspective of household social reproduction does not bring with it the assumption that social actors attempt to maximize social status at all times (contra Lindenberg 1989:190), since only some individuals will strive for maximum possible status (as Hayden points out in his Chapter 2), and then, probably, only during certain life stages. Whether or not a person or group strives for maximum status is irrelevant to the arguments presented below, although, as Hayden (1990, see also Chapter 2, this volume) points out, the actions of those who actively engage in social striving may be instrumental in precipitating processes of sociocultural and technological change (cf. Blanton and Taylor 1995). The key feature of the approach I draw from is not that it assumes social striving in all cases, but, instead, that it investigates the sociocultural outcomes of the varying social reproductive strategies deployed to attain and maintain desired levels of social status in society.

SOCIAL REPRODUCTIVE STRATEGIES AND HOUSEHOLDS

In this chapter, I discuss the outcomes of social reproductive strategies in the context of household behavior. I should point out that many of the characteristic features of the kin-ordered forms of social control associated with middle-range societies are deployed in households in more complex societies as well, for example, in the Chinese households mentioned below. I will leave it to Marxists to decide whether or not the kin-ordered partial social structures of households like these constitute a "mode of production," given that the households in question are imbedded within complex societies exhibiting other forms of social relations in addition to the kin-ordered forms. My goal is not to analyze a particular mode of production or "social technology" as a stage in the evolution of society. It is, instead, to investigate the processes of social reproduction in households in general, with the goal of throwing light on the origins of inequality in domestic settings.

Cross-culturally, the household is typically the most important domain for social reproductive behavior in middle-range societies, as it is in more complex societies, although alternate venues may be equally important in some historical or regional contexts (see discussions in Blanton [1994:chap. 3; cf. Bell 1986–87:97], Netting et al. [1984], and Sahlins [1972:76] regarding the significance of household behavior). By households I mean "task-oriented residence units" (Netting et al. 1984:xx; cf. Blanton 1994:5). What may be involved in household "tasks" is a cross-cultural and temporal variable (Netting et al. 1984:xxv). Here I emphasize the task of achieving and maintaining desired social status. The question of whose status is established and reproduced through household behavior is always relevant. The relevant entity may be the household itself taken as a collective unit (e.g., Morgan 1979:12), but in situations of greater inequality, discussed below, senior members may socially reproduce themselves (i.e., achieve and maintain desired levels of social status) in part through their control over junior members (e.g., Harris 1977:86–88; Selby et al. 1990:56) (or men through their control over women), potentially leading to intrahousehold conflicts of interest.

Many household behavioral domains may be manipulated to achieve desired social reproductive outcomes. Centralized control of production is often central to household strategies in this regard. Other behaviors are involved, including those related to decisions about time allocation, reproduction, and human capital. Blanton (1994), Douglas and Isherwood (1979), and McCracken (1988) emphasize the social reproductive aspects of consumer behavior (cf. Orlove and Rutz 1989). Goody (1990) emphasizes the intergenerational devolution of property in the "passing on" of household status in the preindustrial societies of Eurasia. Bourdieu's (1976) discussion revolves around the control of children's marriages. In what follows, I emphasize the interrelationships between postmarital residence, economic mobilization, and control of marriage in my discussion of inequality within households. Before I analyze variation in these behaviors in relation to the symbolism of houses, I first discuss the basis for household inequality.

VARIATION IN HOUSEHOLD INCORPORATION AND CENTRALIZATION

Wilk (1991) poses a question that can be paraphrased as: How do households go about changing themselves in light of altered circumstances? This is not easily answered because the circumstances to which households adapt are so varied, and because household structure and function are so varied. A central dimension of household behavior that helps us approach a solution to Wilk's question relates to variation in the degree of cooperative behavior that is found. In the purest instance of cooperative behavior, household emergence, maintenance, and change are entirely outcomes of a congruence of individual member interests; that is, the household truly is a "knot of individual interests" (Laslett 1984). This is the process of incorporation as discussed by Barth (1981:63–75; cf. Hechter et al. 1990:5), or, in Bell's (1986–87:107) terminology, "voluntary collectivization."

The process of incorporation cannot be the entire basis of household formation; for example, it would obviously not apply in the case of a child born into a household, but would apply to that child's later postmarital residence decision, among other decisions relevant to his or her later participation in, and contribution to, the household. In my following characterization of the decision-making basis of the cooperative household, I paraphrase the arguments made in Bell (1986–87, 1991: especially p. 253), but I restate his text to account for the household social reproductive perspective I employ in this discussion. In the cooperative household, the household's strategy is a group strategy where each participant is satisfied that his or her desired social status is best realized through continued participation in the activities of the current household as it is constituted; if not, the form of the household may change, or participation will cease. This need not imply a complete equality of rewards and costs to each household participant, since differences in generation and gender might bring with them differences in costs and benefits. But the cooperative group remains intact insofar as (1) each person evaluates his or her relationship to the collectivity, and prefers to maintain that relationship rather than do without it; and (2) each party has objectively evaluated a number of alternative group memberships and perceives that there is no preferred feasible alternative.

I point to the incorporation process not to promote the idea that all households at all times can be assumed to maximize "joint utility," to use the economists' terminology, or that household decision-making will be cooperative (assumptions that are sometimes made; e.g., Becker 1976, 1981; cf. Folbre 1988; Hart 1992; Wilk 1993:194–195). The degree of incorporation, while found to some degree in all households, is, instead, variable in space and time (e.g., Netting et al. 1984:xviii). My purpose in presenting the incorporation model is to establish the conceptual foundation for an analytical approach that can assess the degree to which incorporation is or is not the basis of household formation and maintenance in any particular instance. From this point of view, any household, or household type (see below), can be placed along a continuum of degree of incorporative process. Those household formations more closely approximating the incorporation ideal are regarded as displaying a greater degree of egalitarian structure, since the group's existence and activities are based to a greater degree on the unconstrained choices of its constituent members.

Households, even complex ones (i.e., consisting of more than one married couple), that illustrate a pronounced component of voluntary collectivization are known, for example, the aptly named "tacit communities" (or "family communities") of the European Middle Ages described in Segalen (1986:14–18). As she puts it, "In troubled times, during wars, epidemics and calamities of all kinds, people formed groups for mutual help and support and to work together." In these weakly hierarchical households, behaviors ranging from food sharing to marriage arrangements had as their goal the strengthening of communal solidarity and the protection of corporate resources. Tacitly based households declined in importance when "the need grew less as collective insecurity decreased" (Segalen 1986:17), an expected outcome of the incorporative process.

The behaviors evident in the assembly and maintenance of a Big Man's household in Highland New Guinea also illustrate features of incorporative processes, although in these relatively egalitarian cases, local cultural practices include elements of gender-based power inequality that imply a less than perfect degree to which household members can exercise unconstrained choices related to household participation (households are frequently referred to as "factions" in this literature, owing to their often variable composition, sometimes including nonrelatives). Incorporation is evident in the Big Man systems in the sense that, as stated by Strathern (1982:47), the "possibility of switching group affiliation is explicitly recognized, and it is a built-in feature of flexibility." Success in gaining renown through public prestations of food and valuables requires the concerted productive efforts of a Big Man's household members, although, alternatively, these items can be obtained from extra household sources through what Strathern (1969) calls finance transactions. Even when these external sources are employed, however, the Big Man strategy is strongly predicated on intensified household production (e.g., in the situation interestingly described by Boyd 1985:119–120).

The comparative predominance of incorporative processes among Highland New Guinea households forces the Big Man to walk a fine line, balancing his desire for individual acclaim against the sacrifices required of faction members. Excessive demands may result in accusations of exploitation (Strathern 1985:106). Overly extractive Big Men cause factions to destabilize (Sahlins 1963:292–293; Strathern 1971:223). Strathern's (1984) account of the Melpa Big Man Ndamba illustrates the difficulties inherent in assembling a voluntary following of wives and sons willing and able to produce at levels sufficient to support the Big Man prestations of their husband/father. In this situation, as Strathern (1984:207) puts it, "succession to big-manship is a hazardous and contingent matter," but the faction finally resulting from Ndamba's efforts was made up of members committed to the values of the Big Man competition.

Part of the Big Man's strategy is to assemble a faction willing to support his social ambitions. In Strathern's (1984) account, household members not willing to participate abandon the enterprise. But we all know of households where there is a considerably greater institutionalized degree of centralized control based on gender and age difference, and where household members face few choices other than continued residence in, and participation in, the parent's household (e.g., Collomp 1984:151; or in Strathern's [1982:46–47] comparison of the New Guinea Guro, where eldership is an ascribed category, versus the Hagen Big Man system, where Big Men have to attract a following). Segalen (1986:18–20), for example, contrasts the tacit communities mentioned above, which illustrate incorporative process, with the "stem family," a multigenerational entity in which the eldest child traditionally inherited the estate and household authority. Other offspring were excluded from succession; those who stayed in the house unmarried had a status "somewhere between that of servant and kinsman" (Segalen 1986:19). These are not the constructed factions of New Guinea Big Men, which illustrate to some degree a playing-out of incorporative processes, but, rather, are institutionally structured households characterized by a measured inequality among members, based on distinctions of gender and age, which is maintained across generations. These centralized households occupy a position opposite those manifesting a greater degree of incorporation when placed along a variable axis distinguishing degrees of incorporation and centralization (although no household known to me illustrates complete incorporation or complete centralization). The foundations of household inequality are to be found in the evolution of the centralized households. Under centralization, the household persists only when marginalized members' choices are constrained in some way, given the lack of a complete community of interests and a greatly increased potential for intrahousehold conflict (e.g., Hart 1992). How does this happen?

INEQUALITY AND THE EVOLUTION OF HOUSEHOLD CULTURE

When faced with the necessity to explain inequality in households, Bell (1986–87:97) simply pulls "ideology" out of his bag of potent concepts (but so does Siskind [1978:868]; cf. Vernier 1984:36). In Bell's presentation (1986–87:97), "ideology . . . demonstrates the rightness and appropriateness of its particular system of inequality." His argument points also to the importance of physical coercion in enforcing the demanding requirements of differential privilege. In fact, he sees a relation between ideology and force: "Without physical force the ethical principles would be ignored and without those principles physical force would be prohibitively costly" (1986–87:97). But it is not clear to me to what degree, empirically, physical force has been a widespread basis for social control in the evolution of household inequality. Here I expand on the ideology aspect of his formulation.

To go back to Wilk's question, we could ask: How would household heads go about changing the structure of their households in the direction of a greater degree of institutionalized inequality? Anthropologists have identified a number of strategies that have been employed to construct such households. The most important dimension of these changes, in my view, is to be found, as Bell suggests, in an ideology upheld, I suggest, through household ritual and habitus (household culture), to which I turn in the next paragraph. But analysts have also made note of various other strategies of domestic centralization. Although often stated in terms of lineage or community centralization, rather than in households per se, one dimension of emergent inequality resides in the monopolistic control, by elders, of prestige goods required for the social reproduction of junior household members, for example, items required for bridewealth payments (e.g., Meillassoux 1978:138–141; see also Hayden, Chapter 2, this volume). This same monopolizing strategy may extend to the senior-generation control of knowledge (Meillassoux 1978:138). The consumer behavioral process of "curatorial consumption" may also play a role in constraining the household decisions of junior members (Blanton 1994:112–114; the phrase is from McCracken 1988:chap. 3). In this process, for the senior generation to invest in an elaborate house is to assure that the reproduction of acceptable social status by children can be maintained only through their continued residence in the parental dwelling, because they lack the resources to build a comparable residence. Thus their postmarital residence choice is constrained.

The promulgation of ideology is found in conjunction with materialist strategies like prestige-goods systems and curatorial consumption in the evolution of household inequality. Viewed broadly, the sources of such ideologies are varied. Structural inequalities in the households of the seventeenth and eighteenth centuries in Haute-Province, described by Collomp (1984), resulted in endemic conflicts that were played out against the backdrop of the French civil code of the period. In the middle-range societies in which comparable institutions of state jurisprudence are lacking, the household itself must become a kind of primitive government to sustain an order of inequality, although it is likely that to some degree all centralized households, even those in societies with civil codes, are dependent on household government. The degree to which state adjudicative institutions substitute for household-centered political systems in the evolution of complex societies is an empirical question not yet addressed in anthropological inquiry. In my comparative study of peasant households (Blanton 1994), I found ample evidence of household-based social controls.

Bell's appeal to ideology as the underlying control mechanism of inequality is a useful starting point for understanding how household government would work, but is too simple as he stated it. Why would ideology be binding, and not subject to a myriad of interpretations? Siskind's (1978:868) suggestion adds a symbolic dimension to the ideology theory. According to her: "Ideology provides motive power for both men and women to share their products, embroidering necessity with mystery, relating human production to nature, spirits, and sex." This is like the "insistent significations" of Wolf's (1984:396) "value culture." The arguments of Wolf and Siskind imply that ideology is composed of symbols and that motivation would be predicated on a shared understanding of the meaning of symbols among household members. But I submit that shared meaning itself explains little. Shared meaning is only the outcome of household political processes that are comprehended at a deeper level by reference to the behavioral and material dimension of symbolic expression. Symbols, in Bloch's (1974, 1977, 1980) argument, are significant because they occur in "ritualized, that is, formalized, communication" (1980:93; cf. Rappaport 1979:199). I include as formalized contexts for symbolic expression both household ritual and habitus, the latter referring to a formalization of everyday activities, described below.

It is precisely in ritual and habitus that an order of household inequality is made to appear powerful and holy. Messages so conveyed and accepted as valid constrain the ability of household members to make objective choices, thus limiting the playing-out of incorporative processes in centralized household formations (cf. Rappaport 1979:196–197). I preliminarily evaluate this proposal empirically in the next section, at least insofar as it applies to the role of habitus, after I lay out the nature of this kind of argument. Many anthropologists have pointed to a relation between ritual and the establishment and maintenance of social orders of inequality (e.g., Aldenderfer 1993; Bloch 1974, 1977, 1980; Douglas 1973:81; Firth 1951:238–242; Rappaport 1971:72, 1979:197; J. Turner 1992; Wallace 1966:126–127). Habitus, in Bourdieu's (1977) useful conceptualization, makes an analogous argument by showing how everyday behaviors in the house legitimate an arbitrarily constructed domestic social order (cf. Bailey 1990:26; Ostrow 1981; Sewell 1992:14). As Bourdieu (1977:89) puts it:

> In a social formation in which the absence of the symbolic-product-conserving techniques associated with literacy retards the objectification of symbolic and particularly cultural capital, inhabited space—and above all the house—is the principal locus for the objectification of the generative schemes; and, through the intermediary of the divisions and hierarchies it sets up between things, persons, and practices, this tangible classifying system continuously inculcates and reinforces the taxonomic principles underlying all the arbitrary provisions of this culture.

I relate habitus to what I refer to, following Rappaport (1979:179), as the canonical communication of the house (Blanton 1994:8–13, chap. 3). This involves the communication of invariant and durable messages through various material media in the house, including symbolically structured spatial organization, shrines, gender-specific space uses, and so on, described in the next section (cf. Douglas 1972; Rapoport 1982:43–48).

Although further research will be required to fully elucidate how ritual and habitus are processually related (e.g., J. Turner 1992:294), I propose that both are mechanisms through which a certification of arbitrary social conventions is achieved by sanctifying them (cf. Rappaport 1971, 1979). Sanctified conventions are inculcated and reinforced through their incorporation into ritual and the ritualized behavior of the habitus, both of which involve a stereotypy of behavior (or formalization of behavior in Bloch's [1974] sense, routines in Gidden's [1984:60] terminology) (cf. Rappaport 1979; J. Turner 1992). Habitus is thus analogous to ritual, but works more continuously, resulting in a ritualization of everyday household behavior (to modify a phrase from Davis 1981). Following from Rappaport's (1971, 1979) arguments, I suggest that, whether as a result of ritual or ritualized everyday behaviors, sanctification of a cultural code comes about from the establishment of an affective response to domestic symbols. This affect, or sentiment, is established and reinforced through the fixity or formality of action in both ritual and ritualized daily domestic contexts of the habitus (cf. Foster 1980:382; Lewis 1980; Ornter 1973:1341–1342). As described by J. Turner (1992:292), for example, in Matailabau, Fiji,

> ritual is a medium for the expression of hierarchy, but it also involves a patterning of behavior and an embodiment of attitude and meaning that carry over to non-

ritual contexts. . . . I will argue that this is a consequence of the sheer repetitiveness of Fijian ritual. Moreover, the conceptual distinctions that structure placement and interactions in rituals like *yagona* drinking are also operative in nonritual contexts (e.g., daily meals). In such a cultural milieu ritual is everyday practice, and everyday practice becomes ritualized. The hierarchy, sacralized through ritual, is continuously reproduced in everyday practice, and the power of those who occupy superior positions (e.g., men vis à vis women) is sustained in the process.

In addition to daily meals, mentioned by Turner for Fiji, other potential contexts for the ritualization of everyday behavior in houses include hierarchically arranged sleeping spaces, the structured placement of food preparation areas by references to ideas of purity and danger, and gender-restricted space uses, among many other possibilities (Blanton 1994:chap. 3).

Thus, sanctification, not ideology alone, is proposed here as the basis for the primitive government of the centralized household systems, through its ability, as expressed by Kelly and Rappaport (1975:33), to certify "messages that might otherwise strike receivers as dubious." Sanctification constrains the choices of marginalized members of the household by obscuring the inequality inherent in its social hierarchy, and thus is a counter to the more egalitarian process of incorporation. According to the argument made here, the importance of symbolism to household structure and function is not so much to be found in the fact of shared meaning, but in the sentiment that is attached to symbols through the behavioral process of sanctification as it is established through ritual and habitus.

AN EVALUATION OF THE HYPOTHESIS RELATING HOUSEHOLD CENTRALIZATION TO THE ELABORATION OF HABITUS

Many anthropologists have described and interpreted the symbolism of houses in particular ethnographic settings, but no theory has been proposed to explain cross-cultural, temporal, or within-group variation in the symbolic elaboration of houses, so I set about attempting to build such a theory. Initially, my work was guided by the idea that material culture, including the house, is discursive; that is, habitus both reflects social structure and reproduces it, as Bourdieu (1977:89) suggests, through the divisions and hierarchies it instills (cf. Bailey 1990; Giddens 1984:1–40). Theoretically, in the presentations of both Bourdieu and Giddens, discursive theory can account for variation and change in social structure, because habitus only results in behavioral propensities; it is not completely determinative. Social actors may reject or alter customary behaviors and habitus, but why such change might occur is not adequately discussed in discursive theory (Jenkins 1982). Based on Miller (1987:104), Jenkins (1982), and Sewell (1992), among other sources, I was led to formulate a behavioral theory that could account for variation more effectively than the structural theories of Giddens and Bourdieu (Blanton 1994:19–20). My behavioral approach focuses on habitus as part of a household strategy of social reproduction, rather than on habitus serving in the reproduction of social structure in society as a whole. In this view, to paraphrase Miller (1987:104), habitus does not simply reproduce rules of social structure in general, but is an expression of strategy carried out by household members. From this theoretical formulation we can derive the hypothesis that symbolic differences in the domestic built environment reflect differing degrees to which the processes of incorporation versus centralization are operative in household political economy.

   This hypothesis relating household centralization to the ritualization of household behavior can be evaluated through one of its test implications, namely, that households with more centralized political structure should manifest a domestic built environment with more evidence for the ritualization of everyday behaviors, that is, with more evidence of what I earlier referred to as canonical communication of the habitus. Ideally, given the goal of this volume to throw light on the origins of inequality in middle-range societies, this test would make use of comparative data from societies of this type. But I can preliminarily evaluate the hypothesis using data from my comparative study of peasant houses and households in 26 communities described ethnographically (Blanton 1994), based on the assumption that the evolution of household culture is a process found in a wide range of geographic settings and in societies of varying degrees of social complexity.

   In my comparative study of houses and households, I coded houses for degree of canonical communicative content using a method described below. Based on the community ethnographic data, I was also able to estimate the degree to which households are comparatively centralized or more egalitarian. While there are a number of dimensions of household centralization found in my diverse sample (which included communities in Japan, Java, Thailand, China, Taiwan, Nepal, India, Pakistan, Iran, Iraq, Syria, Turkey, and Mexico), I found it feasible to code for a major recurring feature of household social reproductive strategy related to children's postmarital residence (Blanton 1994:6–7, chap. 3). In what I call the "household continuity strategy," the goal of parents is to maintain the multigenerational continuity of the complex household, in which married offspring are expected to reside in the parental house or house compound until the death of the senior generation, or even beyond. In the "neolocal strategy," parents' main goal is to position their married offspring in separate, viable households, either at marriage, or as soon as possible thereafter. The neolocal strategy, as described for India by Shah (1974:149), is one in which there is "a greater tendency on the part of sons to establish separate households during the lifetime of their father." While, typically, married offspring might reside in the parental house for a short period after marriage, this is regarded as a temporary situation.

The distinction between household continuity strategy and neolocal strategy can be used as a proxy measure of the degree of household inequality. I infer that the neolocal strategy is a better reflection of incorporative process, that is, egalitarian household structure, because in these cases there is a greater degree to which the postmarital residence decision reflects a choice made by the newly married couple, especially surrounding the affordability of separation from the parental household (e.g., Beals 1946:192). The neolocal strategy should embody less inherent conflict among household members, since married children are encouraged to establish themselves as independent householders when feasible rather than continuing to contribute to the communal household economy of husband's or wife's parents.

I also infer a greater degree of centralization and enhanced potential for conflict within those households making use of the household continuity strategy. While there exists a large literature describing the advantages of complex households in certain situations (e.g., Pasternak et al. 1976; Reyna 1976; Wilk 1984:240; Wilk and Rathje 1982), it is also clear that there may be costs (e.g., Freedman 1958:27; Sung-hsing 1985), especially to younger household members who must sacrifice their own and their nuclear family's autonomy for the benefit of the larger domestic enterprise controlled by the senior generation. Hsu (1949:109) describes the central elements of what he calls the "big family ideal" in West Town, China:

> In West Town the socially upheld usage is the big-family ideal, which emphasizes unity in the household, not primogeniture. Unity is promoted by parent-arranged marriages . . . preferential mating, early betrothal—not romantic attachment. This unity is to be arrived at not so much by better adjustment of the many personalities involved as by a gradual inculcation in the individual of his or her place in the kinship hierarchy. This unity is . . . promoted by a common family home as well as by a graveyard which will be adequate for many generations. It is further buttressed by worship of the same ancestors and by unity in the clan.

In this description, the big-family ideal requires an inculcation of individuals, and is dependent on promotion and buttressing. Evidently, complex households of this type could not persist on the basis of a rational calculation of costs and benefits by its junior members. The sources cited above (Freedman 1958:27; Sung-hsing 1985) describe the conflicts that can result from the pooling of resources in the communal household economy (cf. Cohen [1976:73], in his discussion of households in Yen-liao, Taiwan). In the household continuity strategy, women in particular are often at a disadvantage, married through arrangements made by their parents into households in which there is more importance attached to agnatic solidarity and the communal economy than to the nuclear family and affinal ties, and this, too, is described as a source of conflict in Chinese households as elsewhere (Hsu 1985:25; Sung-hsing 1985; cf. Goody 1990:261–265 on north India). In Kaihsienkung, China, a newly married woman grudgingly accepts her marginal position, "facilitated by religious beliefs" (Fei 1939:46).

The Elements of Household Social Reproductive Strategy

I suggested previously that household social reproduction involves more than mode of production, and thus is best analyzed by considering more than economic mobilization. A number of social reproductive strategies may be utilized to achieve social status goals. I illustrate this by statistically associating several aspects of household behavior relating to social reproduction that I coded from my comparative study of 26 communities, but this should not be regarded as a complete study of all possible dimensions of household social reproduction. This analysis is meant only to indicate the validity of using type of postmarital residence strategy as a proxy for degree of household centralization. Tables 1 and 2 show the statistical associations between my main household social reproduction variable, which distinguishes household continuity from neolocal strategy, and other aspects of behavior that have social reproductive outcomes, although this list could be expanded. I coded these variables as follows (coded values for the 26 cases are in Blanton 1994: appendix 7):

Postmarital residence strategy. Although ethnographic sources do not always describe the aims of postmarital residence strategies in sufficient detail for precise coding, it was possible to place most of the coded communities roughly along a continuum ranging from neolocal strategy (to which was given the value 0 in the code), to the extreme forms of the household continuity strategy (to which was given the value of 2). I included in the latter those cases in which continuity is based on the extended family (i.e., where collateral relatives live together as adults, as is described above in the quote from Hsu describing West Town), as well as lineal households where continuity is vested primarily in one son or daughter (e.g., Niiike, Japan [Beardsley et al. 1959:chap. 9]). I coded a value of 1 for cases where the ideal social reproductive strategy was less clearly either neolocal or of the continuity form.

Arranged marriage. This simply codes for the degree to which parents arrange children's marriages. A 0 in the code implies that children have considerable freedom in identifying and arranging their own marriages. A coded value of 1 indicates children have some, but not total, freedom in marriage arrangements, and a value of 2 implies strong parental control over the choice of mate and other aspects of the marriage arrangement.

Close or distant marriage. A value of 1 for this variable implies a predominance of community endogamy. The values 2 and 3 indicate progressively greater likelihood of a distant marriage; a 2 implies local and distant marriages are roughly equally likely, while 3 implies most marriages are distant (i.e., community exogamy). I included this variable based on comments like those in Goody (1990:261–265) that show that distant marriages are less desirable from the point of view of the bride, who is thus removed from her natal community. Distant marriage is at the same time more consistent with the idea that marriages of offspring are arranged strategically to achieve economic or political goals of the household heads (Goody 1990:261–265).

Pooling of household resources. This variable codes for the presence or absence of a centrally controlled economy in complex households (i.e., households consisting of more than one nuclear family, whether or not social reproductive strategy was neolocal or household continuity). This was difficult to code because the actual decision-making within households is rarely described in any detail in ethnographic sources, so the code indicates the practice regarded by informants as normal or usual in each community.

Tables 1 and 2 show the results of chi-square and regression analyses carried out with the coded variables. Table 1 shows the significance values of chi-squares calculated from the cross-tabulation of the values of postmarital residence strategy by each other variable. Since the variables' values range from lower (0 or 1), indicating more egalitarian structure, to higher (2 or 3), indicating more centralization, the strength of the associations can also be assessed through a measure of the steepness of the slope of the regression line (Table 2).

While this kind of analysis could be considerably expanded to investigate the interrelationships between other domains of social reproductive strategies found in my study's households, these results support the suggestion that social reproduction involves more than economic mobilization. The latter variable is, however, important. Pooling of resources (i.e., centralized control

Table 1. Values of Chi-Square, Degrees of Freedom, and Significance Levels (for Total Chi-Square), Postmarital Residence Strategy by Arranged Marriages, Close or Distant Marriage (Marr), and Centralized Control of Household Resources (Pooling)

	Chi-square	*d.f.*	*p*
Arranged marriage	8.4	4	.08
Marr	5.4	4	.25
Pooling	15.8	2	.0004

Table 2. Table of Significance Values of the *t* Test for the Beta
Coefficient (for the Slope of the Regression Line), Postmarital
Residence Strategy by Arranged Marriages, Close or Distant Marriage
(Marr), and Centralized Control of Household Resources (Pooling)

	R-squared	Slope	*p*
Arranged marriages	.272	.424	.02
Marr	.207	.42	.04
Pooling	.68	.486	.0001

of resources) is strongly statistically associated with the household continuity strategy. But arranged marriage is also statistically significantly associated with household continuity, as is distant marriage, although the latter shows a weaker relationship. I take these results to indicate that a social reproductive strategy aimed at household continuity across multiple generations has associated with it limitations on the degree of choice of younger family members, particularly related to economic mobilization and marriage, along with postmarital residence.

An Evaluation of the Hypothesis Linking Household Centralization to the Ritualization of Behavior in the Habitus

Household social reproductive strategies limiting choices of marginalized members should be statistically associated with formal aspects of houses that would indicate an emphasis on the canonical communication of habitus. Specifically, households with more emphasis on household continuity, centralized economy, and control of children's marriages should have more evidence for the structured ritualization of everyday practice. Two variables were coded that measure the degree of canonical communication of the house (a more detailed accounting is found in Blanton 1994:chap. 3):

Gender-specific space use. This simply coded for the presence or absence of gender restrictions on space use or other sex-specific space uses (e.g., separate sleeping quarters for females) within the house. This simple presence–absence coding says nothing about the ideational bases underlying gender separation (which often are not described), but is used as an indicator of the presence of some kind of gender-based restriction on space use in the house (cf. Bourdieu 1977:89–94).

Canonicality. This coding draws from descriptions of actual houses in each community, but the coded value is the highest value of canonical communication of the houses described in each community (the data were not

Table 3. Values of Chi-Square, Degrees of Freedom, and
Significance Levels (for Total Chi-Square), Postmarital Residence
Strategy by Gender-Specific Space Use and Canonical
Communication of the House

	Chi-square	d.f.	p
Gender-specific space use	6.4	2	.04
Canonicality	19.8	10	.03

available to derive a more representative average value). To arrive at a representative value of canonicality for each community, I created a scale variable by summing the values of presence or absence of the following features: (1) physical evidence of lineage ideology in the house; (2) physical evidence of liminal spaces such as shrines; (3) preferential orientation of the house based on cosmological principles; (4) cosmological principles that govern the layout of the house; and (5) location of the house dictated by cosmological principles.

Tables 3 and 4 show the results of this analysis. These results are consistent with the idea that the layout, shrines, gender-specific space uses, and other symbolic features of the house reinforce generational and gender-based ranking within households. Where there is less potential for intrahousehold conflict, in the more egalitarian neolocal social reproductive strategy, with its accompanying features of relatively decentralized production relations and marriage arrangements, the ritualization of everyday behaviors of the habitus is comparatively weakly developed.

CONCLUSIONS

The results of this study suggest the important role played by symbolic behavior and its expression in the ritualized everyday behaviors of the habitus

Table 4. Table of Significance Values of the *t* Test for the Beta
Coefficient (for the Slope of the Regression Line), Postmarital
Residence Strategy by Gender-Specific Space Use and Canonicality

	R-squared	Slope	p
Gender-specific space use	.263	.316	.01
Canonicality	.414	1.35	.0005

in the development and maintenance of household inequality. It follows that archaeologists should directly address the role of symbolic communication as they pursue questions related to the evolution of inequality (e.g., Shanks and Tilley 1982:132–134). But it is important to note that the behavioral approach I propose here, although centered around the expression of symbolism, does not take a position like that represented by Geertz (e.g., 1973:5) or other interpretational anthropologists, who argue that the cultural analysis of symbols should aim at clarifying meaning. I reject the interpretationalist approach because the results of interpretive inquiry have little potential for an evaluation of either validity or reliability. As Lewis (1980:221) puts it:

> Here the main stresses in my argument on understanding and interpretation are, first, that the anthropologist is not free to speculate according to his fancies on the meaning of the rites, for then he may tell about himself and his preoccupations rather than those of the people he would wish to understand, and secondly, since "meaning" is a word of such easy virtue . . . we would do well to be wary of its temptations (cf. J. Turner 1992:292–293).

Rather than interpret, Lewis (1980:221) proposes a behavioral approach to ritual that recognizes how "people respond to the events of ritual with feelings of enjoyment, excitement, puzzlement, pain, etc., and that the rites may be designed to produce such feelings" (cf. Douglass 1992:2, 3, 17–21; Goodsell 1988:211, fn. 3; V. Turner 1978:575).

Rather than attempting to interpret meaning, in Lewis's view the anthropologists' response to ritual should be: "This is odd. This is ritual. Why do they do it like that?" (1980:9). I had a similar response to the variation I began to perceive in the degree of symbolic expression in house form as I conducted my cross-cultural project. In some of the cases in my sample habitus is elaborately developed, while in other cases there is little in the way of ritualization of ordinary behavior or the expression of symbols through the form of the house. Not that I found a complete absence of elements of habitus in these latter cases, or a complete absence of emotional attachment to domestic values, but, by comparison, in these houses there was more flexibility in the use of space by gender and age that would militate against assigning symbolic or hierarchical significance to particular spaces, rooms, or activities. In these cases, counter to Bourdieu's (1977:89) argument, the house does not "set up divisions and hierarchies between things, persons, and practices." Bourdieu's discussion of habitus is inadequate because his theory is unable to account for situations like these where habitus is weakly developed. A more complete theory will permit an understanding of variation in household social reproductive strategies and their outcomes in ritualized behavior and symbolism.

Many possible economic and political changes in the social environment of households, as well as those taking place within households, could alter the nature of household social reproductive strategy and hence the form of expression of habitus. For example, a process of intensification or elaboration in feasting or other distributive events that establish household status will bring with it a necessity to increase household production. Under these circumstances, changes in the direction of centralized household political economy and its associated system of habitus should result. Similarly, any change making it more likely that junior couples can more easily establish independent households (e.g., a decline in warfare, or increased economic opportunities) may bring in its wake changes in household social reproductive behavior as senior couples find new ways to maintain the vitality of the multigenerational household. These are topics requiring further development of theory and more case studies (I test several similar hypotheses in Blanton [1994]). Besides change in the external social environment of households bringing about change in social reproductive behavior, internal factors may also transform the character of habitus. For example, marginalized household members may themselves devise new symbolic systems in reaction to the oppressiveness of their social roles, such as those rituals of Moroccan women that provide relief from male domination (Maher 1984). To quote Dahrendorf (1968:227): "Power produces conflict, and conflict between antagonistic interests gives lasting expression to the fundamental uncertainty of human existence, by ever giving rise to new solutions and ever casting doubt on them as soon as they take form."

My goal in these few concluding comments is not to develop a theory of household social reproductive behavior, but to emphasize that symbolic systems are products of human behavior in the context of political economy (e.g., Medick and Sabean 1984:11). As archaeologists develop and evaluate theories of social change, including explanations for the foundation of social inequality, they need to effectively incorporate, as testable hypotheses, variables related to symbolic behavior in domestic life.

REFERENCES

Aldenderfer, M., 1993, Ritual, Hierarchy, and Change in Foraging Societies, *Journal of Anthropological Archaeology* 12:1–40.

Arnold, J. E., 1993, Labor and the Rise of Complex Hunter-Gatherers, *Journal of Anthropological Archaeology* 12:75–119.

Bailey, D. W., 1990, The Living House: Signifying Continuity, in: *The Social Archaeology of Houses* (R. Samson, ed.), Edinburgh University Press, Edinburgh, pp. 19–48.

Barth, F., 1981, *Process and Form in Social Life*, Routledge and Kegan Paul, London.

Beals, R. L., 1946, *Chéran: A Sierra Tarascan Village*, Institute of Social Anthropology, Publication 2, Washington, Smithsonian Institution, DC.

Beardsley, R. K., J. W. Hall, and R. E. Ward, 1959, *Village Japan*, University of Chicago Press, Chicago.

Becker, G. S., 1976, A theory of the allocation of time, in: *The Economic Approach to Human Behavior* (G. S. Becker, ed.), University of Chicago Press, Chicago, pp. 89–114.

Becker, G. S., 1981, *A Treatise on the Family,* Harvard University Press, Cambridge.

Bell, D., 1986–87, Production and Distribution within Hierarchically Structured Cooperative Groups, *Journal of the Steward Anthropological Society* 16 (1 and 2):96–124.

Bell, D., 1991, Reciprocity as a Generating Process in Social Relations, *Journal of Quantitative Anthropology* 3:251–260.

Blanton, R. E., 1994, *Houses and Households: A Comparative Study,* Plenum Press, New York.

Blanton, R. E., and J. Taylor, 1995, Patterns of Exchange and the Social Production of Pigs in Highland New Guinea: Their Relevance to Questions about the Origins and Evolution of Agriculture, *Journal of Archaeological Research.*

Bloch, M., 1974, Symbols, Song, Dance and Features of Articulation: Is Religion an Extreme Form of Traditional Authority? *European Journal of Sociology* 15:55–81.

Bloch, M., 1977, The Past and the Present in the Present, *Man* (n.s.) 12:279–292.

Bloch, M., 1980, Ritual Symbolism and the Nonrepresentation of Society, in: *Symbol as Sense: New Approaches to the Analysis of Meaning* (M. L. Foster and S. H. Brandes, eds.), Academic Press, New York, pp. 93–102.

Bourdieu, P., 1976, Marriage Strategies as Strategies of Social Reproduction, in: *Family and Society* (R. Forster and O. Ranum, eds.), Johns Hopkins University Press, Baltimore, pp. 117–144.

Bourdieu, P., 1977, *Outline of a Theory of Practice,* Cambridge University Press, Cambridge.

Bourdieu, P., 1978–79, Symbolic Power, *Telos* 38:77–85.

Boyd, D. J., 1985, We Must Follow the Fore: Pig Husbandry, Intensification and Ritual Diffusion among the Irakia Awa, Papua New Guinea, *American Ethnologist* 12:119–136.

Brown, P., and H. C. Brookfield, 1967, Chimbu Settlement and Residence: A Study of Patterns, Trends, and Idiosyncracy, *Pacific Viewpoint* 8:119–151.

Cohen, M. L., 1976, *House United, House Divided: The Chinese Family in Taiwan,* Columbia University Press, New York.

Collomp, A., 1984, Tensions, Dissensions, and Ruptures Inside the Family in Seventeenth- and Eighteenth-Century Haute Provence, in: *Interest and Emotion: Essays on the Study of Family and Kinship* (H. Medick and D. W. Sabean, eds.), Cambridge University Press, Cambridge, pp. 145–170.

Dahrendorf, R., 1968, *Essays on the Theory of Society,* Stanford University Press, Stanford.

Davis, R., 1981, The Ritualization of Behavior, *Mankind* 13:103–112.

Donham, D. L., 1981, Beyond the Domestic Mode of Production, *Man* (n.s.) 16:515–541.

Douglas, M., 1972, Symbolic Orders in the Use of Domestic Space, in: *Man, Settlement, and Urbanism* (P. Ucko, R. Tringham, and G. Dimbleby, eds.), Duckworth, London, pp. 513–522.

Douglas, M., 1973, *Natural Symbols,* Vintage Books, New York.

Douglas, M., and B. Isherwood, 1979, *The World of Goods: Towards an Anthropology of Consumption,* W. W. Norton, New York.

Douglass, L., 1992, *The Power of Sentiment: Love, Hierarchy, and the Jamaican Family Elite,* Westview Press, Boulder.

Dumont, L., 1980, *Homo Hierarchicus: The Caste System and Its Implications,* University of Chicago Press, Chicago.

Fei, H., 1939, *Peasant Life in China: A Field Study of Country Life in the Yangtze Valley,* Routledge and Kegan Paul, London.

Firth, R., 1951, *Elements of Social Organization,* Philosophical Library, New York.

Folbre, N., 1988, The Black Four of Hearts: Toward A New Paradigm of Household Economics, in: *A Home Divided: Women and Income in the Third World* (D. Dwyer and J. Bruce, eds.), Stanford University Press, Stanford, pp. 248–262.

Foster, M. L., 1980, The Growth of Symbolism in Culture, in: *Symbol as Sense: New Approaches to the Analysis of Meaning* (M. L. Foster and S. H. Brandes, eds.), Academic Press, New York, pp. 371–397.

Freedman, M., 1958, *Lineage Organization in Southeastern China,* Athlone, London.

Geertz, C., 1973, *The Interpretation of Cultures,* Basic Books, New York.

Giddens, A., 1984, *The Constitution of Society: Outline of the Theory of Structuration,* University of California Press, Berkeley.

Goodsell, C., 1988, *The Social Meaning of Civic Space: Studying Political Authority through Architecture,* University of Kansas Press, Lawrence.

Goody, J., 1990, *The Oriental, the Ancient, and the Primitive: Systems of Marriage and the Family in the Pre-Industrial Societies of Eurasia,* Cambridge University Press, Cambridge.

Harris, C. C., 1977, Changing Conceptions of the Relation between Family and Societal Form in Western Society, in: *Industrial Society: Class, Cleavage, and Control* (R. Scase, ed.), St. Martin's Press, New York, pp. 74–89.

Hart, G., 1992, Imagined Unities: Constructions of "The Household" in Economic Theory, in: *Understanding Economic Process* (S. Ortiz and S. Lees, eds.), University Press of America, Lanham, Maryland, pp. 111–129.

Hayden, B., 1990, Nimrods, Piscators, Pluckers, and Planters: The Emergence of Food Production, *Journal of Anthropological Archaeology* 9:31–69.

Hechter, M., K.-D. Opp, and R. Wippler, 1990, Introduction, in: *Social Institutions: Their Emergence, Maintenance, and Effects* (M. Hechter, K.-D. Opp, and R. Wippler, eds.), Aldine de Gruyter, New York, pp. 1–9.

Hsu, F. L. K., 1949, *Under the Ancestor's Shadow: Chinese Culture and Personality,* Routledge and Kegan Paul, London.

Hsu, F. L. K., 1985, Field Work, Cultural Differences, and Interpretation, in: *The Chinese Family and Its Ritual Behavior* (H. Jih-Chang and C. Ying-Chang, eds.), Academica Sinica, Institute of Ethnology, Taipei, pp. 19–29.

Jenkins, R., 1982, Pierre Bourdieu and the Reproduction of Determinism, *Sociology* 16:270–281.

Kelly, R., and R. Rappaport, 1975, Function, Generality, and Explanatory Power: A Commentary and Response to Bergmann's Arguments, *Michigan Discussions in Anthropology* 1:24–44.

Laslett, P., 1984, The Family as a Knot of Individual Interests, in: *Households: Comparative and Historical Studies of the Domestic Group* (R. M. Netting, R. R. Wilk, and E. J. Arnould, eds.), University of California Press, Berkeley, pp. 353–379.

Leacock, E. B., 1972, Introduction, in: *The Origin of the Family, Private Property and the State* (F. Engels, ed.), International Publishers, New York, pp. 7–67.

Lewis, G., 1980, *Day of Shining Red: An Essay on Understanding Ritual,* Cambridge University Press, Cambridge.

Lindenberg, S., 1989, Choice and Culture: The Behavioral Basis of Cultural Impact on Transactions, in: *Social Structure and Culture* (H. Haferkamp, ed.), Walter de Gruyter, Berlin, pp. 175–200.

Maher, V., 1984, Possession and Dispossession: Maternity and Mortality in Morocco, in: *Interest and Emotion: Essays on the Study of Family and Kinship* (H. Medick and D. W. Sabean, eds.), Cambridge University Press, Cambridge, pp. 103–128.

McCracken, G., 1988, *Culture and Consumption: New Approaches to the Symbolic Character of Consumer Goods and Activities,* Indiana University Press, Bloomington.

Medick, H., and D. W. Sabean, 1984, Interest and Emotion in Family and Kinship Studies: A Critique of Social History and Anthropology, in: *Interest and Emotion: Essays on the Study of Family and Kinship* (H. Medick and D. W. Sabean, eds.), Cambridge University Press, Cambridge, pp. 9–27.

126 **RICHARD E. BLANTON**

Meillassoux, C., 1972, From Reproduction to Production: A Marxist Approach to Economic Anthropology, *Economy and Society* 1:93–105.

Meillassoux, C., 1978, "The Economy" in Agricultural Self-Sustaining Societies: A Preliminary Analysis, in: *Relations of Production: Marxist Approaches to Economic Anthropology* (D. Seddon, ed.), Frank Case, London, pp. 127–157.

Meillassoux, C., 1981, *Maidens, Meal, and Money: Capitalism and the Domestic Economy,* Cambridge University Press, Cambridge.

Miller, D., 1987, *Material Culture and Mass Consumption,* Basil Blackwell, Oxford.

Moore, J. H., 1991, Kinship and Division of Labor in Cheyenne Society, in: *Marxist Approaches in Economic Anthropology* (A. Littlefield and H. Gates, eds.), University Press of America, Lanham, Maryland, pp. 135–158.

Morgan, H. J., 1979, New Directions in Family Research and Theory, in: *The Sociology of the Family: New Directions for Britain* (C. Harris, M. Anderson, R. Chester, D. H. J. Morgan, and D. Leonard, eds.), Sociological Review Monographs 28, pp. 3–18.

Netting, R., McC., R. R. Wilk, and E. J. Arnould, 1984, Introduction, in: *Households: Comparative and Historical Studies of the Domestic Group* (R. M. Netting, R. R. Wilk, and E. J. Arnould, eds.), University of California Press, Berkeley, pp. xiii–xxxviii.

Orlove, B. S., and H. J. Rutz, 1989, Thinking about Consumption: A Social Economy Approach, in: *The Social Economy of Consumption* (H. J. Rutz and B. S. Orlove, eds.), University Press of America, Lanham, Maryland, pp. 1–57.

Ortner, S. B., 1973, On Key Symbols, *American Anthropologist* 75:1338–1346.

Ostrow, J. M., 1981, Culture as a Fundamental Dimension of Experience: A Discussion of Pierre Bourdieu's Theory of Human Habitus, *Human Studies* 4:279–297.

Pasternak, B., C. R. Ember, and M. Ember, 1976, On the Conditions Favoring Extended Family Households, *Journal of Anthropological Research* 32:109–123.

Pospisil, L., 1963, *Kapauku Papuan Economy,* Yale University, Department of Anthropology, Publications in Anthropology 67, New Haven.

Rapoport, A., 1982, *The Meaning of the Built Environment: A Nonverbal Communication Approach,* Sage, Beverly Hills.

Rappaport, R. A., 1971, Ritual, Sanctity, and Cybernetics, *American Anthropologist* 73:59–76.

Rappaport, R. A., 1979, The Obvious Aspects of Ritual, in *Ecology, Meaning, and Religion* (R. Rappaport, ed.), North Atlantic Books, Richmond, California, pp. 173–221.

Reyna, S. P., 1976, The Extending Strategy: Regulation of the Household Dependency Ratio, *Journal of Anthropological Research* 32:182–198.

Sahlins, M., 1963, Poor Man, Rich Man, Chief: Political Types in Melanesia and Polynesia, *Comparative Studies in Society and History* 5:285–303.

Sahlins, M., 1972, *Stone Age Economics,* Aldine-Atherton, Chicago.

Segalen, M., 1986, *Historical Anthropology of the Family,* Cambridge University Press, Cambridge.

Selby, H. A., A. D. Murphy, and S. A. Lorenzen, 1990, *The Mexican Urban Household: Organizing for Self-Defense,* University of Texas Press, Austin.

Sewell, W. H., Jr., 1992, A Theory of Structure: Duality, Agency, and Transformation, *American Journal of Sociology* 98:1–29.

Shah, A. M., 1974, *The Household Dimension of the Family in India: A Field Study in a Gujarat Village and a Review of Other Studies,* University of California Press, Berkeley.

Shanks, M., and C. Tilley, 1982, Ideology, Symbolic Power, and Ritual Communication: A Reinterpretation of Neolithic Mortuary Practices, in: *Symbolic and Structural Archaeology* (I. Hodder, ed.), Cambridge University Press, Cambridge, pp. 129–154.

Siskind, J., 1978, Kinship and Mode of Production, *American Anthropologist* 80:860–872.

Strathern, A., 1969, Finance and Production: Two Strategies in New Guinea Highlands Exchange Systems, *Oceania* 15:42–67.

Strathern, A., 1971, *The Rope of Moka: Big-Men and Ceremonial Exchange in Mount Hagen New Guinea,* Cambridge University Press, Cambridge.

Strathern, A., 1982, Two Waves of African Models in the New Guinea Highlands, in: *Inequality in New Guinea Highlands Societies* (A. Strathern, ed.), Cambridge University Press, Cambridge, pp. 35–49.

Strathern, A., 1984, "A Brother Is a Creative Thing": Change and Conflict in a Melpa Family (Papua New Guinea), in: *Interest and Emotion: Essays on the Study of Family and Kinship* (H. Medick and D. W. Sabean eds.), Cambridge University Press, Cambridge, pp. 187–209.

Strathern, A., 1985, Lineages and Big-Men: Comments on an Ancient Paradox, *Mankind* 15:102–111.

Sung-hsing, W., 1985, On the Household and Family in Chinese Society, in: *The Chinese Family and Its Ritual Behavior* (H. Jih-Chang and C. Ying-Chang, eds.), Academica Sinica, Institute of Ethnology, Taipei, pp. 50–58.

Turner, J. W., 1992, Ritual, Habitus, and Hierarchy in Fiji, *Ethnology* 31:291–302.

Turner, V., 1978, Encounter with Freud: The Making of a Comparative Symbologist, in: *The Making of Psychological Anthropology* (G. Spindler, ed.), University of California Press, Berkely, pp. 558–583.

Vernier, B., 1984, Putting Kin and Kinship to Good Use: The Circulation of Goods, Labour, and Names on Karpathis (Greece), in: *Interest and Emotion: Essays on the Study of Family and Kinship* (H. Medick and D. W. Sabean, eds.), Cambridge University Press, Cambridge, pp. 28–76.

Wallace, A. F. C., 1966, *Religion: An Anthropological View,* Random House, New York.

Wilk, R. R., 1984, Households in Process: Agricultural Change and Domestic Transformation among the Kekchi Maya of Belize, in: *Households: Comparative and Historical Studies of the Domestic Group* (R. M. Netting, R. R. Wilk, and E. J. Arnould, eds.), University of California Press, Berkeley, pp. 217–244.

Wilk, R. R., 1991, The Household in Anthropology: Panacea or Problem? *Reviews in Anthropology* 20:1–12.

Wilk, R. R., 1993, Altruism and Self-Interest: Towards an Anthropoligical Theory of Decision Making, in: *Research in Economic Anthropology* (B. Isaac, ed.), JAI Press, Greenwich, Connecticut, pp. 191–212.

Wilk, R. R., and W. Rathje, 1982, Household Archaeology, *American Behavioral Scientist* 25:617–639.

Wolf, E. R., 1982, *Europe and the People without History,* University of California Press, Berkeley.

Wolf, E. R., 1984, Culture: Panacea or Problem? *American Antiquity* 49:393–400.

Chapter *5*

Social Inequality at the Origins of Agriculture

T. DOUGLAS PRICE

Technology and demography have been given too much importance in the explanation of agricultural origins; social structure too little. (Bender 1978:204)

The development of sedentism and status inequalities may both be necessary prerequisites for the development of agriculture. (Matson 1985:245)

INTRODUCTION

The emergence of social inequality is an intriguing and important issue. There is a very large body of literature, in a number of disciplines, on the subject. Philosophers, social theorists, and others have considered the topic in great detail since the Renaissance. Cultural anthropologists have dealt with the subject for many years (e.g., Collier and Rosaldo 1981; Fried 1967; Kelly 1993; Leach 1965; Sahlins 1958; Service 1978; Terray 1972). In archaeology, a variety of ideas have developed on what social inequality is and how and why it began (e.g., Aldenderfer 1992; Feinman and Neitzel 1984; Flannery 1972; Johnson and Earle 1987; Kelly 1991; McGuire and Paynter 1991; Paynter 1989; Upham 1990).

The focus in archaeology on inequality has shifted through a variety of

---

T. DOUGLAS PRICE • Department of Anthropology, University of Wisconsin–Madison, Madison, Wisconsin 53706-1393.

Foundations of Social Inequality, edited by T. Douglas Price and Gary M. Feinman. Plenum Press, New York, 1995.

time periods, places, and levels of sociocultural complexity. This shifting focus reflects a great deal of confusion and uncertainty about the beginnings of status differentiation and the context in which it took place. I would suggest that this confusion stems from a misdirected search; we have been looking in the wrong time and place for the emergence of inequality. It is my intent in this chapter to discuss both the context and the impetus for basically egalitarian societies to invest control and decision-making in a small subset of their numbers—a rather momentous decision. I discuss the emergence of institutionalized social inequality in the context of the transition to agriculture. I will argue that these two phenomena are closely linked. My basic premise is that the initial indications of status differentiation are associated with the beginnings of farming. This is in many ways a reiteration of the stimulating argument made by Barbara Bender in 1978. Matson elaborated on this point in 1985 in an examination of the relationship between sedentism and social differentiation among hunter-gatherers. The idea, then, is not new, but rather restated and emphasized once again.

There are several important premises to this argument. It is clear that egalitarian and nonegalitarian relations are present in all societies, along dimensions of sex, age, ability, health, and the like (Cashdan 1980; Collier and Rosaldo 1981; Flanagan 1989). Such differences are also apparent in primate and other animal societies. Thus, the emergence of status differentiation in and of itself is not an issue. What is of interest, and of great import for the rise of hierarchical societies, is the institutionalization of inequality, that is, the formalization of status differentiation along dimensions of kin or class. This formalization is represented by the pivotal distinction between achieved and ascribed status, denoted in anthropology by inheritance. Status is ascribed and institutionalized when one's status and position is determined at birth in relation to other members of the society.

While there are alternative pathways to social inequality, such as those discussed by Hayden (Chapter 2, this volume), it is my contention that hereditary inequality is closely related to the intensification of subsistence and more specifically with agriculture. The basis for my argument lies largely in the recognition that there are no known examples among prehistoric hunter-gatherers in which hereditary inequality is unequivocally present. I thus suspect that the institutionalization of inequality arose among agricultural societies in the prehistoric world. The evidence for such differentiation among early farming groups is striking. Social inequality may in fact have played an important role in the spread of agriculture into many parts of the world. The very few ethnographic cases of inequality among hunter-gatherers, as among the Northwest Coast Indians of North America (see Ames, Chapter 6, this volume), certain groups in California, or perhaps the Calusa of southern Florida, are clearly exceptions to this rule and a relatively late phenomenon.

To make my point, I begin my discussion with a specific case study from southern Scandinavia. This area is likely typical of many in which the transition to agriculture took place and it is certainly one of the best known archaeologically. I then move to a more general consideration of complexity among hunter-gatherers. Next I consider the transition to agriculture in light of recent evidence and new ideas. In my conclusions I hope to convince you the reader that in order to understand the beginnings of agriculture we need to look carefully at the emergence of social inequality, and vice versa.

A SPECIFIC CASE: FIRST FARMERS IN SOUTHERN SCANDINAVIA

Prehistoric southern Scandinavia is essentially a laboratory for human prehistory. By 9000 B.C. (calibrated ^{14}C years), following the retreat of terminal Pleistocene ice sheets, a forest landscape had spread into this gradually warming area and the first Mesolithic hunter-gatherers appeared. By 3900 B.C. the ideas and materials of farming communities began to occur in the area, heralding the onset of the Neolithic. Within a period of a few thousand years, then, it is possible to examine one of the major transitions in human prehistory in some detail (Figure 1).

An intensification in food procurement can be traced through the Mesolithic period in southern Scandinavia. The variety of extraction sites, including large fish weirs, and the faunal remains of a wide range of marine fish and mammals, including seals, dolphins, and whales, document the diversity of the subsistence base. Carbon isotope ratios in human bone point to the predominance of marine foods in the diet (Tauber 1981). A coastal focus is pronounced; inland sites are known almost exclusively from small, summer camps.

Significant regional variation in artifact types and styles is documented from the later part of the Ertebølle; distinctive differences between eastern and western Denmark, and between smaller areas within Zealand, have been reported (S. H. Andersen 1981; Vang Petersen 1986). Some form of territoriality can be inferred from the limited, local distributions of certain artifact types in this period (Vang Petersen 1986). Exchange in exotic materials is documented by the presence of foreign objects obtained from early Neolithic farmers to the south. In addition to the crude Ertebølle pottery, bone combs, t-shaped antler axes, and "shoe-last" axes of exotic amphibolite appear in a late Ertebølle context in Denmark (S. H. Andersen 1973; Fischer 1982; Jennbert 1984).

Funnelbeaker (TRB) pottery is the hallmark of the early Neolithic, first appearing around 3900 B.C. The earliest radiocarbon dates for the Neolithic

Stages   Periods

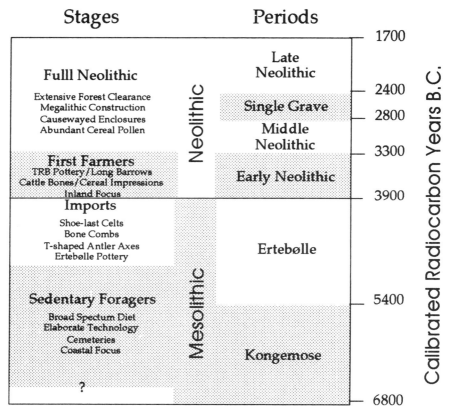

Figure 1. Chronology and periodization of the later Mesolithic and Early Neolithic in southern Scandinavia.

come from large, earthen long barrows with timber burial chambers, bog offerings, and flint mines. The number of known early Neolithic residential sites is quite limited. The first settlement dates are 100 years younger than the earliest dates for the Neolithic, frequently at sites in continuous use from the Mesolithic period. Residential sites are small with a thin cultural layer compared to the Ertebølle, suggesting that coresident groups in the Neolithic were smaller and perhaps more mobile. Sites are more inland than in the Mesolithic, often located at lakes or streams where fresh water was easily obtainable and conditions for grazing were favorable (Madsen 1991, Madsen and Jensen 1982; Nielsen 1985). Evidence for cereals and domesticated animals is found after 3900 B.C. (Andersen and Rasmussen 1993), but hunting, fishing, and gathering still played an important role during the first 800 years of the Neolithic (S. H. Andersen 1991; Skarrup 1973). The shift from a coastal focus is also indicated by carbon isotope ratios in Neolithic skeletons, which indicate a greater dependence on terrestrial resources.

The introduction of farming was accompanied by a number of innovations: thin-walled pottery and new pot shapes, large, polished flint axes for forest clearing and timber work along with a related flint mining industry, weapons like groundstone battle axes and mace heads, flint daggers, grinding stones for processing cereals, copper axes as well as personal ornaments made of amber and copper, and the ard—the first primitive type of plow. Trade in flint, polished axes, and amber was part of an apparently extensive network of exchange.

A residential settlement spanning the transition to agriculture from the latest Mesolithic to the earliest Neolithic has recently been excavated at the site of Bjørnsholm (S. H. Andersen 1991). Bjørnsholm is a large kitchen midden in the central Limfjord area of northern Jutland. The shell midden itself is more than 300 m long and 10–50 m wide along the coast of the fjord, not far from its mouth at the sea. The late Mesolithic layers at Bjørnsholm date from 5050 to 4050 B.C., and the early Neolithic from 3960 to 3530 B.C. Finds from the Early Neolithic include a stone axe blade imitating a central European copper axe and a typical Danubian shaft hole ax.

A number of important observations have been made at this site. The location of residence clearly did not change from the Mesolithic to the Neolithic; in fact, residence continued in virtually the same spot through the transition. The latest Mesolithic occupations are enormous, extending several hundred meters along the coastline of the fjord. The earliest Neolithic settlement is somewhat smaller and a few meters higher above the coastline, perhaps in response to rising sea levels. There is a change from oysters to cockles in the contents of the shell midden at about the time of the transition, which suggests that some changes in the environment may have been taking place. However, the earliest Neolithic pottery was present in the sequence before this shift in the midden occurred. Neolithic subsistence remains were very similar to those from the Mesolithic with the addition of small amounts of wheats, barley, sheep, cattle, and pig. In addition to the settlement remains at Bjørnsholm, the presence of an early Neolithic earthen long barrow documents the introduction of a new burial practice.

From the beginning of the Middle Neolithic period around 3300 B.C., substantial residential sites began to reappear on the coast as well as at inland locations and the number of hunting sites decreased. Territorial demarcation among settlements appears to be fixed by this time, emphasized by the construction of one or more megalithic tombs in relation to settlements (Madsen 1991; Skaarup 1973, 1985). Large-scale forest clearance, together with more evidence for cereal growing and stock rearing, indicates an agricultural expansion at this time (Andersen and Rasmussen 1993). Wheats comprise 96% of the cereals at the beginning of the Middle Neolithic, but barley represents 22% of the cereal remains found at sites from the end of this period (Jørgensen 1977). Cattle were the most important livestock and become more common through the Funnelbeaker period, representing more than 80% of the domestic animals at some later sites.

The transition to agriculture in southern Scandinavia appears to represent a case of local hunters adopting farming from agricultural groups to the south in north-central Europe. Most archaeologists today believe the Early Neolithic developed from the local Mesolithic under greater or lesser influence from various Danubian groups (Fischer 1982; Jennbert 1984; Madsen and Petersen 1984; Nielsen 1985, 1986; Rowley-Conwy 1985). Most recent theories about why Ertebølle foragers opted for agriculture, and about the transition to agriculture in general, involve either stress resulting from changes in population or environment, or demands from increasing social differentiation. The paragraphs below outline this debate in terms of three major issues: population, resource availability, and social change.

Population

One of the major hypotheses concerning the transition to agriculture suggests that population growth resulted in too many people with too little food (e.g., Binford 1968; Cohen 1977). Agriculture then provided increased food yields to feed growing numbers of people.

In southern Scandinavia, there appears to be an intensification in subsistence and settlement through the Mesolithic with sedentary communities present by the middle period. There was a relatively dense population during the late Mesolithic Ertebølle, especially at the coasts. Changes in the landscape increased population density, even if population numbers remained stable. Rising sea levels and increasing forest density operated during the Mesolithic to reduce the amount of land available for the population. Marine transgression was the hallmark of the early Holocene, while at the same time the vegetation was changing from more open birch and pine woodlands to more dense, closed deciduous forest with reduced biomass (Clutton-Brock and Noe-Nygaard 1990).

There is, however, no obvious evidence for population pressure preceding the transition to agriculture. The total number of sites from the Mesolithic is never particularly large. No increase in the total number of settlements is seen in the earliest Neolithic; if anything, a decrease in the number of settlements from the late Mesolithic to the earliest Neolithic may have taken place. The first farmers settled in scattered, small habitations combined with seasonal extraction camps (Madsen and Jensen 1982). Population size does appear to have grown somewhat around 3300 B.C., but there is no indication of increasing population immediately before or during the introduction of agriculture.

The question of population pressure at the time of the transition in southern Scandinavia is best examined in terms of the number and size of sites by time period. The systematic archaeological survey of the Saltbæk Vig area in northwestern Zealand (Price and Gebauer 1992) provides some of this information. To date, the survey has examined approximately 18 km² of the research area and registered more than 350 sites. The survey has revealed a variety of settlements primarily from the Mesolithic and Neolithic periods, including a number of important new sites.

Settlement locations are concentrated on points of land and peninsulas on or very near the former coastlines (Figure 2). The majority of both Mesolithic and Neolithic sites are found on the south shore of the inlet, concentrated toward the mouth. Mesolithic and Neolithic sites generally tend to be in similar locations, suggesting a continuity of occupation. Neolithic sites tend to be richer in terms of artifact density and more diverse in settlement size, whereas some of the Mesolithic sites surpass the larger Neolithic sites in size; settlements in the later Mesolithic were large with linear occupation areas often more than 100 m in length. The number of sites per time period and the relative density of sites per period is presented in Table 1. The average number of sites per year from the time of the late Mesolithic and the transition to agriculture is very similar. There is a threefold increase, however, from the transition to the latter part of the Neolithic. This information does not suggest any dramatic changes in population density during the time of the transition, but rather a delay in population expansion concomitant with a fully agricultural economy.

Resource Availability

Binford (1968) and many others have argued that agriculture is adopted because of growing population and/or declining food resources. Some imbalance between population levels and available resources in southern Scandinavia is implied in a number of papers (S. H. Andersen 1973, 1981; Larsson 1987; Paludan-Müller 1978; Rowley-Conwy 1983, 1984, 1985; Zvelebil and Rowley-Conwy 1984). In Denmark, possible environmental changes that might affect this relationship could have involved climate, sea level, marine resources, usable land area, and/or vegetation. For example, colder air temperatures could reduce or change vegetation, and lower the temperature and level of the sea.

During the early Atlantic period, after 6000 B.C., rising sea levels caused the expansion of the North Sea and turned the western part of the Baltic Sea into a saltwater ocean. These changes in sea level greatly reduced the land

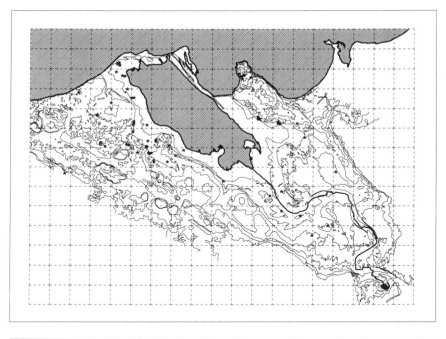

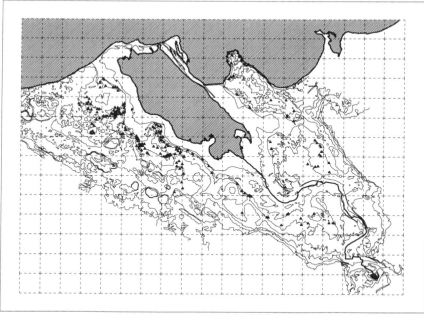

Figure 2. Mesolithic (above) and Neolithic (below) sites recorded during the Saltbæk Vig survey.

Table 1. The Saltbæk Vig Survey

Period	Number of sites	Approximate duration in years	Sites per year
Late Mesolithic	68	1,500	.045
Transition	46	1,000	.046
Neolithic	214	1,600	.134

surface available to human populations in northwestern Europe. The shift from Atlantic to Subboreal conditions occurred ca. 3900 B.C. at the same time as the transition to agriculture. Oscillating transgressions and regressions continued throughout the Atlantic and Subboreal periods, but these later changes in sea levels were less dramatic. The bays, inlets, and estuaries created by rising sea levels were among the richest resource zones for Mesolithic groups. The Subboreal was slightly cooler and drier than the preceding Atlantic. A decrease in the pollen of ivy indicates cooler winters when the fjords and inlets might have been frozen. Even though winter temperatures may have been slightly lower, annual averages remained higher than today. The presence of mistletoe and a certain species of tortoise in the Subboreal, both found only to the south of Denmark today, suggests that environmental conditions after 3900 B.C. were still quite favorable. Thus, the environmental changes associated with the shift from the Atlantic to the Subboreal were not major. The sea continued to be rich in fish and sea mammals, and a considerable game population inhabited the forest.

It is the case that climate was changing frequently and dramatically throughout the entire early Holocene period in northwestern Europe. It is, therefore, difficult to argue for one specific moment of environmental change having more impact on human populations than another. Given current evidence, it is not possible to envision a significant ecological crisis at the time of the adoption of farming.

The physical anthropology of the inhabitants of the late Mesolithic and the early Neolithic also reveals no significant change in resource availability. There is no evidence for nutritional stress among the known populations of the Mesolithic (Meiklejohn and Zvelebil 1991). Bennike (1993), in fact, reports a slight decrease in stature of approximately 1 cm for both males and females from the late Mesolithic to the early Neolithic. Such a decline does not suggest an improvement in subsistence resources immediately following the transition to agriculture. It is difficult to argue that agriculture was adopted in order to obtain more food in the face of environmental degradation.

Social Change

Other scholars have suggested that the transition to agriculture was caused not by population excess or environmental constraint, but rather by factors involving social conditions and the emergence of inequality (e.g., Bender 1978, 1990; Hayden 1990, 1992; Jennbert 1984; Price and Gebauer 1992). Hypotheses invoking social causes for the transition suggest that leaders or higher-status individuals may have encouraged others to adopt agriculture as a means for producing food surpluses and for increasing wealth and exchange. In southern Scandinavia, Fischer (1982) and Jennbert (1984, 1985) have argued for close connections between farmers of north-central Europe and the foragers of Denmark, pointing to a number of "borrowed" artifacts and ideas, including ceramics and certain stone and antler axes in the late Mesolithic. They suggest that these successful foragers did not require additional sources of food and that the only obvious reason for farming was to generate surplus. Jennbert argues that certain leaders were likely responsible for encouraging the accumulation of wealth through cultivation and herding. Competition between higher-status individuals for prestige then might explain why successful foragers adopted farming.

It is clearly the case that changes in social, economic, and religious spheres in the earliest Neolithic are more pronounced than are changes in subsistence. It is important to recall here the three categories of sites that have the earliest radiocarbon dates from the Neolithic: long barrows, bog sacrifices, and the flint mines. Clear evidence for emerging social differentiation comes from the earthen long barrows, the earliest dated manifestations of the Neolithic. Early Neolithic long barrows with wooden funeral structures were first recognized in Denmark in the early 1970s. Almost 40 nonmegalithic barrows are known today, predominantly from Jutland in western Denmark. The barrows are low (1–2 m in height), and vary in length from 50 to 150 m (Madsen 1979). Only one grave, or a very few, have been found in each of these mounds.

The appearance of the barrows at the onset of the Neolithic suggests substantial changes in social organization. Nothing like these elite, mound-covered burials are known from the Mesolithic period; Mesolithic cemeteries reveal a distinction in grave goods based on criteria of age and sex, but there is no indication of status differentiation beyond these criteria. Obviously, a limited segment of the Neolithic population was entitled to monumental burial. Clear communal involvement and participation in the construction, maintenance, and enlargement of these monuments suggests that the barrows represent more than just places for the disposal of the dead. The earthen long barrows likely formed local ceremonial centers, some of which maintained their significance for several centuries. Subsequent megalithic burial constructions were a continuing elaboration of this earlier tradition.

Ceremonial sites in the bogs (Becker 1948; Bennike and Ebbesen 1986; E. K. Nielsen 1983) and sacrificial deposits of flint axes, amber beads, and copper ornaments and axes (Becker 1948; P. Nielsen 1977; Randsborg 1975; Rech 1979) are further evidence of religious activity and exchange at this time. Both earthen long barrows and bog sacrifices represent communal involvement and participation, and both types of sites helped define a ceremonial landscape. Both types of sites involved the consumption of labor, either through monumental construction and a range of funeral activities or through feasting and sacrifices of pots with food, cattle, and occasionally people. Consumption of labor is also evident in the withdrawal of luxury items from circulation with the deposition of flint axes, amber beads, and copper items in votive hoards from the Early Neolithic into the Middle Neolithic period. The expenditure of labor in the Early Neolithic represents a considerable increase in surplus production invested in activities beyond basic subsistence.

Another category of the earliest Neolithic sites is represented by the flint mines. One of the most archaeologically visible remains of the Neolithic are the tens of thousands of polished flint axes scattered across the landscape of southern Scandinavia. Much of the tabular flint for the manufacture of these axes came from mines and quarries in the chalk belts across northern Denmark and southern Sweden (Becker 1973, 1980, 1993; P. Nielsen 1977; Vang Petersen 1993). These flint mines and the polished axes are the remaining evidence for an extensive network that involved the trade of amber and other materials, as well as axes. Flint axes of Danish origin are known from the Neolithic in the Netherlands and Germany (Rech 1979). Far-reaching connections to south-central Europe are reflected in the import of copper ornaments and jewelry, axe blades, and the battle axe, a model for the Scandinavian axes (Randsborg 1979). Metallurgical analyses indicate that the copper artifacts have the very low arsenic content common to copper from southeastern Europe, perhaps from sources in western Austria (Madsen and Petersen 1984). The materials traded from Scandinavia in return are unknown. A number of organic products such as fur, feathers, lamp oil from seals, and honey likely were included among the exports.

There are several conclusions to be drawn with regard to the evidence for the transition to agriculture in southern Scandinavia. This transition was a long-term process, delayed for a substantial period by the presence of resident hunter-gatherers in the area. There was no sudden shift from foraging to farming, but rather a very gradual process involving the adoption of specific imported tools and weapons and ideas prior to the incorporation of domestic plants and animals. Contact with farmers preceded actual cultivation and herding by at least 500 years and perhaps as much as 1,500 years. Agriculture became the primary subsistence regime only 1,000 years later following a period of experimentation and changes in technology and settlement. It is particularly striking that the first evidence of the Neolithic, confirmed by radiocarbon dates and the presence of TRB pottery, comes from objects and activities that are more clearly associated with status differentiation, exchange, and exotic materials, rather than changes in subsistence and settlement.

This evidence suggests that the search for causality should focus in the realm of internal decisions within Mesolithic society, rather than external changes in climate, environment, or population. Human groups at the onset of the Neolithic participated in a larger sphere of trade and formalized the higher status of certain individuals through burial and other practices. It seems most reasonable to suggest a scenario in which interaction through exchange networks among foragers and farmers fostered the rise of an elite component in late Mesolithic societies. The Neolithic ushered in the surplus production available with domestication and the establishment of extensive, long-distance trade.

COMPLEXITY AND HUNTER-GATHERERS

Consideration now turns to the nature of complexity among prehistoric hunter-gatherers. For too long, anthropologists uncritically have adopted a very simplistic model of foraging society. More than 50 years ago in 1940, Fortes and Evans-Pritchard described such groups as economically homogeneous, egalitarian, and segmentary. This frame became the reference for anthropologists and archaeologists in spite of a variety of warnings to the contrary. For example, in 1958, Sahlins pointed out that egalitarian societies did not truly exist and that minimal stratification was present based on age, sex, and personal characteristics.

Today, however, the pendulum seems to be swinging in the opposite direction (e.g., Koyama and Thomas 1981; Price and Brown 1985). Many archaeologists are seeking and finding complexity among prehistoric hunter-gatherers. It more generally seems to be the case that many groups of prehistoric foragers, at least during the last part of the Pleistocene and the early Holocene, were more complex than formerly realized. It is essential to examine the nature of complexity among hunter-gatherers in detail in order to understand the beginnings of inequality.

What does this concept of complexity mean? There seem to be as many definitions of complexity as there are archaeologists interested in the subject. I personally prefer the dictionary definition of complexity—things complex have more parts and more connections between parts. McGuire (1983) has distinguished heterogeneity and inequality as major aspects of complexity. These concepts are quite similar to the more parts and better integration noted above. Heterogeneity means more, different parts; integration is often achieved through hierarchy and inequality—more connections.

It is also important to recognize the characteristics that document complexity for archaeologists. Some of the hallmarks of complexity among foragers are thought to include things like higher population and population density, sedentism, territoriality, storage, elaborate technologies, intensive subsistence practices, long-distance trade, a medium for exchange, among others (e.g., Keeley 1988; Koyama and Thomas 1981; Price and Brown 1985; see Marquardt 1986 for an extensive list for the Calusa of South Florida).

Status differentiation and social inequality are also frequently attributed to more complex foragers. This certainly appears to be the case among a few ethnographically or historically known groups of hunter-gatherers, especially for various groups along the western coast of North America, among the Inuit whale hunters of northern Alaska (e.g., Sheehan 1985), and perhaps the Calusa on the southern coast of Florida (Marquardt 1986, 1988; Widmer 1988).

But, in fact, the number of ethnographically known groups of hunter-gatherers exhibiting hereditary social inequality is strikingly small and limited in both recent time and geographic space. It is also clear that most ethnographically known groups of hunter-gatherers lack such hierarchical organization and can be said to be egalitarian.

More importantly, there is very little or no evidence for hereditary inequality among prehistoric hunter-gatherers anywhere outside the western coast of North America (e.g., Ames 1985, Chapter 6, this volume; Arnold 1992; King 1971; Maschner 1991). Elite residence or burial has been suggested to have been present among the Jomon of Japan, but incipient agriculture is highly likely in this context (e.g., Crawford 1987, 1992). O'Shea and Zvelebil (1984) argued for status differentiation in a large Mesolithic cemetery in Karelia in northwestern Russia, but a number of lines of evidence make this interpretation dubious (Jacobs 1988; Price and Jacobs 1990). King (1978) suggests that hereditary rank and a hierarchical authority structure is evidenced in the cemeteries of prehistoric groups in central California between A.D. 200 and 800. This inference was based largely on the type of interment (cremation, body position flexed or extended) and abundance of grave goods. At the same time, however, he also notes that the evidence is equivocal; such variation could be explained by chronology or other dimensions of variability. Wright's (1978) analysis of Natufian burials suggests that status differentiation is present in the terminal Pleistocene Near East on the basis of mode of interment and presence of grave goods, primarily dentalium shell. More recent evidence and reanalysis of the data, however, have indicated an absence of social inequality in the Natufian period and suggested that differences in

Natufian burials are largely a function of chronology (Bar-Yosef and Belfer-Cohen 1989).

There are, in fact, remarkably few prehistoric or ethnographic studies of hunter-gatherers where hereditary social inequality is clearly revealed. In most areas that we know about, with the exceptions noted above, the first evidence for institutionalized social inequality comes no earlier than the first agriculturalists. This evidence takes the form of a major shift in the quantities of exotic and rare materials, the appearance of significant differences in house sizes and storage facilities, a marked elaboration of burial structures and grave goods, an increase in the expenditure of energy in the form of labor and surplus in the form of storage, and/or an intensification of ritual as seen in facilities and paraphernalia.

Given this inference that inherited status differentiation is closely involved with the transition to agriculture, it is now useful to reexamine complex hunter-gatherers and the question of social inequality. Evidence from prehistoric Holocene foragers in many areas clearly documents a pattern of intensification in technology, subsistence, exchange, territoriality, and art (see, e.g., Cohen 1977). On the other hand, it is among early farming populations that evidence is first found signaling dramatic changes in settlement size, trade, ritual, and status. This dichotomy emphasizes two important components of cultural complexity. One component has to do with elaboration of existing structures—the creation or acquisition of more parts (i.e., in technology, subsistence, storage, settlement type, art, and other categories). Most of the groups we recognize prehistorically as complex foragers in fact exhibit this kind of horizontal intensification. The other aspect of complexity has to do with vertical intensification and integration between parts. This component of complexity pertains more to internal social and economic relations and the emergence of inequality. It is, in fact, the development of hierarchy that permits a qualitative increase in cultural complexity, operating as a means to integrate, to connect, the increasing number of parts that are present in such societies.

This is very much what Gregory Johnson was saying in his discussion of sequential and simultaneous hierarchy (Johnson 1982). Johnson's focus was on organization and decision-making. He examined the question of scalar stress and hierarchical development in human society. Scalar stress refers to constraints on the growth of a society related to the difficulties of decision-making. According to Carniero (1967:239), "if a society does increase significantly in size, and if at the same time it remains unified and integrated, it must elaborate its organization." Johnson argues that sequential hierarchies are characteristic of egalitarian societies. Sequential organization involves horizontal social organization of groups into nuclear families, extended families, and coresident groups along lines of kinship. Decision-making is done on a sequential, consensus basis within each unit. In addition to such sequential decision-making, ceremony and ritual provide another mechanism for reducing scalar stress.

Simultaneous hierarchies, by contrast, are found in other societies and serve to enhance integration through control and regulation by a small proportion of the population. As Johnson (1978, 1982) noted, status ascription and social ranking may well be associated with the rise of simultaneous hierarchies. He suggests that status differentiation, access to resources, and social integration are closely related in such groups.

To understand the emergence of social inequality, it is essential that we decouple the concept of cultural complexity and distinguish between vertical and horizontal intensification. While a trajectory of horizontal intensification clearly is to be seen through prehistory of fully modern *Homo sapiens sapiens,* the evidence for vertical, hierarchical organization is not evident until the Holocene and, I would argue, is directly associated with the origins and spread of agriculture.

SOCIAL INEQUALITY AND THE TRANSITION TO AGRICULTURE

I find it useful to distinguish four aspects of the transition to agriculture; the mechanism, conditions, consequences, and causes. These distinctions allow us to be more specific and accurate in discussions of the question. "Mechanism" refers to the means for the dissemination of agriculture, either directly through colonization by farming populations or indirectly through adoption by indigenous foraging groups. In most cases, farming appears to have spread through adoption, initially by more complex, sedentary groups in relatively abundant environments (Gebauer and Price 1992). This is true in most areas where we have substantial evidence, including the early example from the Near East (Bar-Yosef and Belfer-Cohen 1989, 1992; Byrd 1992). Recent genetic evidence indicates that the domestication of individual species in the Near East took place at a single location (Hillman and Davies 1990; Zohary 1989). Each domesticate spread from its point source to other areas. It is difficult to envision individual groups of colonists, each carrying one of these six or seven species across the landscape of Southwest Asia. Rather, an active network of trade and exchange likely moved various domesticates along with obsidian, bitumen, carnelian, lapis, and a wide variety of other goods from Egypt to Afghanistan in a relatively brief period (Byrd 1992).

We can also identify some of the conditions necessary for the adoption of agriculture by hunter-gatherers. These include sufficient population, sedentism, some level of social circumscription, and abundant resources (Gebauer and Price 1992). Permanently settled communities of more complex hunter-gatherers appear to be the norm in many areas in the late Pleistocene and early Holocene. Circumscription refers to the limitation of movement by the presence of neighboring groups and geographic barriers. Evidence for group conflict is present in a number of areas where agriculture was adopted. In every area where the adoption of agriculture is well documented there appears to have been a variety and abundance of foods available to the inhabitants (Gebauer and Price 1992; Hayden 1990). Farming was not adopted under conditions of nutritional stress; populations at risk are reluctant to try new strategies for survival (Wills 1992).

We can also identify some of the consequences of the shift to farming: the widespread use of ceramics, the invention of new technologies for cultivation and herding, the continental dispersal of certain domesticated plants and animals, larger communities, more people, and an increased pace along the path to more complex social and political organization. The consequences, of course, are what makes the question of agricultural transitions so important in the first place.

But what *caused* the adoption of agriculture? Population, climatic change, and circumscription are impossible to indict as immediate causes of change. More people per se do not dictate the adoption of agriculture; how are more mouths to feed directly translated into the cropping of hard-grained cereals? The consequences and conditions discussed above in fact suggest that human populations were pulled into the adoption of farming rather than pushed. Answers to such questions about the transition to agriculture clearly have more to do with internal social relations than with external events involving climate and the growth of human population.

How does the emergence of status differentiation relate to the transition to agriculture? Roy Brunton may have provided part of the answer to this question in his 1975 consideration of why the Trobriand Islanders have chiefs. The Trobriand Islanders have neither exceptional population density nor agricultural productivity. Brunton argues that it is a participation in a closed system of exchange that limits the range of people who can effectively compete for leadership. Such a situation results in the emergence of a few Big Men who encourage the creation of surplus.

In a discussion of Northwest Coast ranking, William Elmendorf (1971) notes that status relations were dependent on a network of intervillage relations that involved kinship ties, economic exchange, and ceremonial activities. Rubel and Rosman (1983) describe the relationship between exchange structure and rank among Northwest Coast and Athabaskan Indians in North America. These authors emphasize the importance of internal structural arrangements, rather than differences in the environment, in relation to ranking and status differentiation (in contrast to Riches 1979; Suttles 1962).

In an examination of the origins of agriculture Barbara Bender (1978:206) argued that "the enquiry into agricultural origins is not, therefore, about intensification per se, not about increased productivity, but about increased production and about why increased demands are made on the economy." Bender pointed out that food production was a question of commitment and social relations, about alliance structures and the individuals operating within such structures, not about technology or demography. Bender was among the first to point out that leadership, alliance, and exchange gave rise to a need for surplus production. Bender's seminal paper has needed a number of years to take root and to grow but it is beginning to bear fruit.

In a recent paper (1990) and in this volume, Brian Hayden has elaborated on Bender's argument and suggested that it is specifically the feasting aspects of rivalries between leaders that are the driving force behind food production. Hayden argues that highly competitive individuals, or "accumulators," emerge in resource-rich communities and that these individuals used the competitive feast as a means for developing and enhancing their power and leadership through a series of alliance and debt relationships.

In this volume, Hayden discusses the transition to social inequality in terms of different pathways or stages. In this context he defines specific types of accumulators or aggrandizers as Despots, Reciprocators, and Entrepreneurs. These individuals are the focus of change. These types of leaders respectively define a sequence of intensifying social inequality and institutionalized power. Despot communities witness an increase in warfare along with evidence of feasting. Several strategies are used to increase the power of the leader. Feasting is used to build alliances; compensation payments for injury or death in conflict are made to allies. Equivalent exchange and egalitarian relations are the ideal in these societies and differences in residence and wealth are, archaeologically speaking, not pronounced. The Despot is operative only in one or two realms such as warfare and production and a number of different leaders may be present in the community. The position of Despot is ephemeral and most often achieved.

Reciprocator communities are overtly nonegalitarian and leaders compete within the community. Reciprocators are described as wealthier, with more wives and larger social networks. Several new strategies for creating debts, surplus, and power include bridewealth, more elaborate feasts, and perhaps child growth payments. Hayden suggests that agriculture may have originated a means for more intensive food production among Reciprocator organizations.

Entrepreneur groups are characterized by intensive food production. Loans and investments are the primary strategies that aggrandizers use to obtain wealth and power. Surplus is now used in competitive feasts to create contractual debt involving interest payments. Warfare is less important in such societies as it interferes with the generation of surplus and the exchange of wealth. Marriage also becomes a major conduit of wealth through bride payments. Entrepreneurs also try to consolidate various roles of leadership, including ritual, military, and financial. Entrepreneur communities have distinct patterns of status inheritance and represent clear situations of institutionalized inequality.

Spencer (1993a,b) and Feinman (Chapter 10, this volume) have focused on different modes of leadership in transegalitarian societies. Spencer (1993b) points to the internal and external dimensions of leadership; Feinman distinguishes corporate versus network modes of leadership. Both refer to the work of Werner (1980) in his analysis of uncentralized groups in Brazil. Among the Mekranoti-Kayapó in the state of Pará, those seeking to be leaders build networks with members of other groups. These alliances play an important role in the exchange and movement of exotic items that leaders use as gifts for their followers. In contrast, leaders among the Akwe-Shavante in the state of Mato Grosso in Brazil give less importance to external contacts and much more to internal, corporate ties to one's lineage and affiliates. Spencer (1993a:45) argues that the shift from sequential to simultaneous hierarchies (à la Johnson 1982) requires the establishment of links between both internal and external leadership functions. Aldenderfer (1992) argues that such linkages, leading to the institutionalization of inequality, often take place in the context of ritual activities.

CONCLUSIONS

To return to the Danish data, in this area it seems clear that external factors such as demography, climate, or environment are not responsible for the introduction of agriculture. There is no obvious correlation between these factors and the appearance of elite tombs and domesticated plants and animals. What is remarkable is the almost simultaneous appearance of domesticated plants and elite burial. Such evidence strongly suggests that agriculture and hereditary social inequality may be moving hand in hand across the European continent.

Social change appears to be at the center of the agricultural revolution that quickly became the most successful human subsistence strategy known to date. To understand the transition to agriculture, investigations must be refocused on issues concerned with how and why the rules enforcing egalitarian behaviors were relaxed among prehistoric hunter-gatherers and why elite individuals emerged among these groups toward the end of the Pleistocene, particularly in contexts involving the domestication of plants. How and why did presumably egalitarian bands of hunter-gatherers give up individual rights? Presumably more hierarchically organized groups in contact with these foragers involved them in more complex patterns of networked structures. The very rapid spread of agriculture across both the Old and the New World may be testimony to the efficacy of this new, hierarchical form of social, political, and economic organization. The question of course remains as to where the more hierarchically organized groups originated.

ACKNOWLEDGMENTS

This chapter is dedicated to Barbara Bender for her insight, perseverance, contribution, and especially her "just-so" story. Thanks also to Gary Feinman, Brian Hayden, and Larry Keeley for their ideas, wealth of knowledge, and stimulation.

REFERENCES

Aldenderfer, M., 1992, Ritual, Hierarchy, and Change in Foraging Societies, *Journal of Anthropological Archaeology* 12:1–40.
Ames, K. M., 1985, Hierarchies, Stress, and Logistical Strategies among Hunter-Gatherers in Northwestern North America, in: *Prehistoric Hunter-Gatherers* (T. D. Price and J. A. Brown, eds.), Academic Press, Orlando, pp. 155–180.
Andersen, S. H., 1973, Overgangen fra 230ldre til yngre stenalder i Sydskandinavien set fra en mesolitisk synsvinkel, in: *Bonde*—veidemann. Bofast—ikke bofast i Nordisk forhistorie (P. Simonsen and G. Stamsø Munch, eds.), Universitetsforlaget, Tromsø, pp. 26–44.
Andersen, S. H., 1981, Ertebøllekunts. Nye østjyske fund af mønstrede Ertebølleoldsager, *Kuml* 7–62.
Andersen, S. H., 1991, Bjørnsholm, a Stratified Køkkenmødding on the Central Limfjord, North Jutland, *Journal of Danish Archaeology* 10:59–96.
Andersen, S. T., and P. Rasmussen, 1993, *Geobotanishe undersøgelse af Kulturlandskabet Histories,* DGU, Miljøministeret, Copenhagen.
Arnold, J. E., 1992, Complex Hunter-Gatherer-Fishers of Prehistoric California: Chiefs, Specialists, and Maritime Adaptations of the Channel Islands, *American Antiquity* 57:60–84.
Bar-Yosef, O., and A. Belfer-Cohen, 1989, The Origins of Sedentism and Farming Communities in the Levant, *Journal of World Prehistory* 3:447–498.
Bar-Yosef, O., and A. Belfer-Cohen, 1992, From Foraging to Farming in the Mediterranean Levant, in: *Transitions to Agriculture in Prehistory* (A. B. Gebauer and T. D. Price, eds.), Prehistory Press, Madison, pp. 21–48.
Becker, C. J., 1948, Mosefundne Lerkar fra Yngre Stenalder. *Aarbøger for Nordisk Oldkyndighed og Historie,* 1947.
Becker, C. J., 1973, Studien zu neolitischen Flintbeilen, *Acta Archaeologica* 44:125–186.
Becker, C. J., 1980, Katalog der Feuerstein/Hortnstein/Bergwerke, Dänemark, in: *5000 jahre feuersteinbergbau* (G. Weisgerber, ed.), Dentschen Bergbau-Museum, Bochum, pp. 456–470.
Becker, C. J., 1993, Flintminer og flintdistribution ved Limfjorden, in: Kort- og råstofstudier omkring Limfjorden, *Limfjordsprojektet Rapport* 6.

Bender, B., 1978, From Gatherer-Hunter to Farmer: A Social Perspective, *World Archaeology* 10:204–222.

Bender, B., 1990, The Dynamics of Nonhierarchical Societies, in: *The Evolution of Political Systems* (S. Upham, ed.), Cambridge University Press, Cambridge, pp. 62–86.

Bennike, P., 1985, *Palaeopathology of Danish Skeletons. A Comparative Study of Demography, Disease and Injury,* Køobenhavn, Akademisk Forlag.

Bennike, P., 1993, The People. in: *Digging into the Past. 25 Years of Danish Archaeology* (S. Hvass and B. Storgaard, eds.), Universitetsforlag, Aarhus, pp. 34–39.

Bennike, P., and K. Ebbesen, 1986, The Bog Find from Sigersdal. *Journal of Danish Archaeology* 5:85–115.

Binford, L. R., 1968, Post Pleistocene Adaptations, in: *Ner Perspectives in Archaeology* (S. R. Binford and L. R. Binford, eds.), Aldine, Chicago, pp. 313–341.

Brunton, R., 1975, Why Do the Trobriands Have Chiefs? *Man* 10:544–558.

Byrd, B., 1992, The Dispersal of Food Production across the Levant, in: *Transitions to Agriculture in Prehistory* (A. B. Gebauer and T. D. Price, eds.), Prehistory Press, Madison, pp. 49–62.

Carniero, R. L., 1967, On the Relationship between Size of Population and Complexity of Social Organization, *Southwestern Journal of Archaeology* 23:234–243.

Cashdan, E., 1980, Egalitarianism among Hunters and Gatherers, *American Anthropologist* 82:116–120.

Cohen, M., 1977, *The Food Crisis in Prehistory,* Yale University Press, New Haven.

Collier, J. F., and M. Z. Rosaldo, 1981, Politics and Gender in Simple Societies, in: *Sexual Meanings: The Cultural Construction of Gender and Sexuality* (S. B. Ortner and H. Whitehead, eds.), Cambridge University Press, Cambridge, pp. 275–329.

Clutton-Brock, J., and N. Noe-Nygaard, 1990, New Osteological and C-Isotope Evidence on Mesolithic Dogs: Companions of Hunters and Fishers at Star Carr, Seamer Carr and Kongemose, *Journal of Archaeological Science* 17:643–653.

Crawford, G. W., 1987, Ainu Ancestors and Prehistoric Asian Agriculture, *Journal of Archaeological Science* 14:201–213.

Crawford, G. W., 1992, The Transitions to Agriculture in Japan, in: *Transitions to Agriculture in Prehistory* (A. B. Gebauer and T. D. Price, eds.), Prehistory Press, Madison, Wisconsin, pp. 117–132.

Elmendorf, W. W., 1971, Coast Salish Status Ranking and Intergroup Ties, *Southwestern Journal of Anthropology* 27:353–380.

Feinman, G., and J. Neitzel, 1984, Too Many Types: An Overview of Sedentary Prestate Societies in the Americas, *Advances in Archaeological Method and Theory* 7:39–102.

Fischer, A., 1982, Trade in Danubian Shaft-Hole Axes and the Introduction of Neolithic Economy in Denmark, *Journal of Danish Archaeology* 1:7–12.

Flanagan, J. G., 1989, Hierarchy in Simple "Egalitarian" Societies, *Annual Review of Anthropology* 18:245–266.

Flannery, K. V., 1972, The Cultural Evolution of Civilization, *Annual Review of Ecology and Systematics* 3:399–426.

Fried, M., 1967, *The Evolution of Political Society,* Random House, New York.

Gardner, P. M., 1991, Foragers' Pursuit of Individual Autonomy, *Current Anthropology* 32:543–572.

Gebauer, A. B., and T. D. Price, 1992, Foragers to Farmers: An Introduction, in: *Transitions to Agriculture in Prehistory* (A. B. Gebauer and T. D. Price, eds.), Prehistory Press, Madison, Wisconsin, pp. 1–10.

Hayden, B., 1990, Nimrods, Piscators, Pluckers, and Planters: The Emergence of Food Production, *Journal of Anthropological Archaeology* 9:31–69.

Hayden, B., 1992, Contrasting Expectations in Theories of Domestication, in: *Transitions to Agriculture in Prehistory* (A. B. Gebauer and T. Douglas Price, eds.), Prehistory Press, Madison, Wisconsin, pp. 11–20.

Hillman, G., and M. S. Davies, 1990, Measured Domestication Rates in Wild Wheats and Barley under Primitive Cultivation, and Their Archaeological Implications, *Journal of World Prehistory* 4:157–222.

Jacobs, K., 1988, A Late Mesolithic Cemetery from the Russian Northwest: Oleneostrovski Mogilnik, Abstract, 86th annual meeting, American Anthropological Association.

Jennbert, K., 1984, *Den produktiva gåvan. Tradition och innovation i Sydskandinavian för omkring 5300 år sedan,* Acta Archaeologica Lundensia, Series in 4, No. 16, CWK Gleerup, Lund.

Jennbert, K., 1985, Neolithisation—a Scanian Perspective, *Journal of Danish Archaeology* 4:196–197.

Johnson, A. W., and T. Earle, 1987, *The Evolution of Human Societies from Foraging Groups to Agrarian States,* Stanford University Press, Stanford.

Johnson, G. A., 1978, Information Sources and the Development of Decision-Making Organizations, in: *Social Archaeology: Beyond Subsistence and Dating* (C. L. Redman, M. J. Berman, E. V. Curtin, W. T. Langhorne, Jr., N. M. Versaggi, and J. C. Wanser, eds.), Academic Press, New York, pp. 87–112.

Johnson, G. A., 1983, Organizational Structure and Scalar Stress, in: *Theory and Explanation in Archaeology: The Southampton Conference* (C. Renfrew, M. J. Rowlands, and B. A. Seagraves, eds.), Academic Press, New York, pp. 389–421.

Jørgensen, G., 1977, Et kornfund fra Sarup. Bidrag til Belynsning af Tragtb230gerkulturens Agerbrug. *Kuml* 1976:47–64.

Keeley, L. H., 1988, Hunter-Gatherer Economic Complexity and "Population Pressure": A Cross-Cultural Analysis, *Journal of Anthropological Archaeology* 7:373–411.

Kelly, R. C., 1993, *Constructing Inequality,* University of Michigan Press, Ann Arbor.

Kelly, R. L., 1991, Sedentism, Sociopolitical Inequality, and Resource Fluctuations, in: *Between Bands and States* (S. A. Gregg, ed.), Center for Archaeological Investigations, Carbondale, Illinois, pp. 135–158.

King, C. D., 1971, Chumash Intervillage Economic Exchange, *Indian Historian* 4:1.

King, T. F., 1978, Don't That Beat the Band? Non-egalitarian Political Organization in Prehistoric Central California, in: *Social Archaeology* (C. L. Redman, ed.), Academic Press, New York, pp. 225–248.

Koyama, S., and D. H. Thomas, 1981, *Affluent Foragers,* University Press, Kyoto.

Larsson, M., 1987, Neolithization in Scania—A Funnel Beaker Perspective, *Journal of Danish Archaeology* 5:244–247.

Leach, E., 1965, *Political Systems of Highland Burma,* Beacon, Boston.

Madsen, T., 1979, Earthen Long Barrows and Timber Structures: Aspects of the Early Neolithic Mortuary Practice in Denmark, *Proceedings of the Prehistoric Society* 45:301–320.

Madsen, T., 1991, The Social Structure of Early Neolithic Society in South Scandinavia, in: *Die Kupferzeit als historische Epoche* (J. Lichardus, ed.), Saarbrücken Beiträge zuer Altertumskunde, Bonn, pp. 489–496.

Madsen, T., and H. J. Jensen, 1982, Settlement and Land Use in Early Neolithic Denmark, *Analecta Praehistorica Leidensia* 15:63–86.

Madsen, T., and J. E. Petersen, 1985, Tidligneolitiske anlæg ved Mosegården. Regionale og kronologiske forskelle i tidligneolitikum, *Kuml* 1982–83:61–120.

Marquardt, W. H., 1986, The Development of Cultural Complexity in Southwest Florida: Elements of a Critique, *Southeastern Archaeology* 5:63–70.

Marquardt, W. H., 1988, Politics and Production among the Calusa of South Florida, in: *Hunters* and Gatherers I: History, Evolution, and Social Change (T. Ingold, D. Riches, and J. Woodburn, eds.), Berg, Oxford, pp. 161–188.

Maschner, H. D. G., 1991, The Emergence of Cultural Complexity on the Northern Northwest Coast, *Antiquity* 65:924–934.

Matson, R. G., 1985, The Relationship between Sedentism and Status Inequalities among Hunters and Gatherers, in: *Status, Structure, and Stratification* (M. Thompson, M. T. Garcia, and F. Kense, eds.), Archaeological Association of the University of Calgary, Calgary, pp. 245–252.

McGuire, R., 1983, Breaking Down Cultural Complexity: Inequality and Heterogeneity, *Advances in Archaeological Method and Theory* 6:91–142.

McGuire, R., and R. Paynter, 1991, *The Archaeology of Inequality*, Blackwell, Oxford, pp. 1–27.

Meiklejohn, C., and M. Zvelebil, 1991, Health Status of European Populations at the Agricultural Transition and the Implications for the Adoption of Farming, in: *Health in Past Societies* (H. Bush and M. Zvelebil, eds.), British Archaeological Reports, Oxford, pp. 129–145.

Nielsen, E. K., 1983, *Tidligneolitiske Keramikfund*, Unpublished dissertation, University of Copenhagen.

Nielsen, P. O., 1977, Die Flintbeile der frühen Trichterbecherkultur in Dänemark, *Acta Archaeologica* 48:61–138.

Nielsen, P. O., 1985, De første bønder. Nye fund fra den tidligste Tragtbægerkultur ved Sigersted, *Aarbøger for Nordisk Oldkyndighed og Historie* 1984:96–126.

Nielsen, P. O., 1986, The Beginning of the Neolithic—Assimilation or Complex Change? *Journal of Danish Archaeology* 5:240–243.

O'Shea, J., and M. Zvelebil, 1984, Oleneostrovski Mogilnik: Reconstructing the Social and Economic Organization of Prehistoric Foragers in Northern Russia, *Journal of Anthropological Archaeology* 3:1–40.

Paludan-Müller, C., 1978, High Atlantic Food Gathering in Northwest Zealand, Ecological Conditions and Spatial Representation, in: *New Directions in Scandinavian Archaeology* 1:120–157.

Paynter, R., 1989, The Archaeology of Equality and Inequality, *Annual Review of Anthropology* 18:369–399.

Price, T. D., and J. A. Brown (eds.), 1985, *Prehistoric Hunter-Gatherers. The Emergence of Cultural Complexity*, Academic Press, Orlando.

Price, T. D., and A. B. Gebauer, 1992, The Final Frontier: First Farmers in Northern Europe, in: *Transitions to Agriculture in Prehistory* (A. B. Gebauer and T. D. Price, eds.), Prehistory Press, Madison, pp. 97–116.

Price, T. D., and K. Jacobs, 1990, Olenii Ostrov: First Radiocarbon Dates from a Major Mesolithic Cemetery in Karelia, *Antiquity* 64:849–853.

Randsborg, K., 1975, Social Dimensions of Early Neolithic Denmark, *Proceedings of the Prehistoric Society* 41:105–118.

Randsborg, K., 1979, Resource Distribution and the Function of Copper in Early Neolithic Denmark, in: *The Origins of Metallurgy in Atlantic Europe* (M. Ryan, ed.), Proceedings of the Fifth Atlantic Colloquium, Stationary Office, Dublin, pp. 303–318.

Rech, M., 1979, Studien zu Depotfunden der Trichterbecher- und Einzelgrabkultur des Nordens, *Offa-Bücher 39*, Neumünster.

Riches, D., 1979, Ecological Variation in the Northwest Coast: Models for the Generation of Cognatic and Matrilineal Descent, in: *Social and Ecological Systems* (P. Burnham and R. F. Ellen, eds.), Academic Press, New York, pp. 145–166.

Rowly-Conwy, P., 1983, Sedentary Hunters: The Ertebølle Example, in: *Hunter-Gatherer Economy* (G. Bailey, ed.), Cambridge University Press, Cambridge, pp. 111–126.

Rowley-Conwy, P., 1984, The Laziness of the Short-Distance Hunter: The Origin of Agriculture in Western Denmark, *Journal of Anthropological Archaeology* 3:300–324.

Rowley-Conwy, P., 1985, The Origin of Agriculture in Denmark: A Review of Some Theories, *Journal of Danish Archaeology* 4:188–195.

Rubel, P. G., and A. Rosman, 1983, The Evolution of Exchange Structures and Ranking: Some Northwest Coast and Athabaskan Examples, *Journal of Anthropological Research* 39:1–25.

Sahlins, M., 1958, *Social Stratification in Polynesia.* AES Monograph 25, University of Washington Press, Seattle.

Service, E. R., 1978, *Profiles in Ethnology,* Harper and Row, New York.

Sheehan, G. W., 1985, Whaling as an Organizing Focus in Northwestern Alaskan Eskimo Society, in: *Prehistoric Hunter-Gatherers* (T. D. Price and J. A. Brown, eds.), Academic Press, Orlando, pp. 123–154.

Skaarup, J., 1973, *Hesselø-Sølager. Jagdstationen der südskandinavischer Trichterbecherkultur,* Arkæologiske Studier 1, Akademisk Forlag, Copenhagen.

Skaarup, J., 1985, *Yngre stenalder på øerne syd for Fyn.* Langelands Museum, Rudkøbing.

Spencer, C. S., 1993a, Human Agency, Biased Transmission, and the Cultural Evolution of Chiefly Authority, *Journal of Anthropological Archaeology* 12:41–74.

Spencer, C., 1993b, Factional Ascendance, Dimensions of Leadership, and the Development of Centralized Authority, in: *Factional Competition and Political Development in the New World* (E. Brumfiel and J. Fox, eds.), Cambridge University Press, Cambridge.

Suttles, W., 1962, Variation in Habitat and Culture on the Northwest Coast, in: *Proceedings of the 34th International Congress of Americanists,* Verlag Ferdinand Berger, Vienna, pp. 522–537.

Tauber, H., 1983, $\delta^{13}C$ Evidence for Dietary Habits of Prehistoric Man in Denmark, *Nature* 292:332–333.

Terray, E., 1972, *Marxism and Primitive Society,* Monthly Review Press, New York.

Upham, S., 1990, *The Evolution of Political Systems,* Cambridge University Press, Cambridge.

Vang Petersen, P., 1986, Chronological and Regional Variation in the Late Mesolithic of Eastern Denmark, *Journal of Danish Archaeology* 3:7–18.

Vang Petersen, P., 1993, *Flint fra Danmarks oldtid,* Høst & Son, Copenhagen.

Werner, D., 1980, *The Making of a Mekranoti Chief: The Psychological and Social Determinants of Leadership in a Native South American Society,* Ph.D. dissertation, University of Michigan, Ann Arbor.

Widmer, R. J., 1988, *The Evolution of the Calusa: A Nonagricultural Chiefdom on the Southwest Florida Coast,* University of Alabama Press, Tuscaloosa.

Wills, W. H., 1992, Plant Cultivation and the Evolution of Risk-prone Economies in the Prehistoric American Southwest, in: *Transitions to Agriculture in Prehistory* (A. B. Gebauer and T. D. Price, eds.), Prehistory Press, Madison, Wisconsin, pp. 153–176.

Wright, G. A., 1978, Social Differentiation in the Early Natufian, in: *Social Archaeology* (C. L. Redman, ed.), Academic Press, New York, pp. 201–223.

Zohary, D., 1989, Domestication of the Southwest Asian Neolithic Crop Assemblage of Cereals, Pulses, and Flax: The Evidence from the Living Plants, in: *Foraging and Farming: The Evolution of Plant Exploitation* (D. R. Harris and G. C. Hillman, eds.), Unwin Hyman, London, pp. 358–373.

Zvelebil, M., and P. Rowley-Conwy, 1984, The Transition to Farming in Northern Europe: A Hunter-Gatherer Perspective, *Norwegian Archaeological Review* 17:104–128.

Part III

Studies in Emerging Social Inequality

The chapters in this section of the volume reflect more specifically empirical studies of the nature of social inequality as it appears in the archaeological record. These studies range in time from the historical record of Northwest Coast foragers, the prehistoric southwestern U.S., prehispanic Colombia during the first millennium A.D., to the rise of chiefdoms in medieval Europe. Several important variables in the equation of social inequality are examined here, including household production, labor, agricultural resources, social organization, and competition.

Kenneth Ames has for a long time been interested in the emergence of complexity among hunter-gatherers in North America. As a logical extension of these interests, he writes here regarding the rise of inequality or chiefly power and economic production on the Northwest Coast. Ames examines the circumstances under which inequality becomes institutionalized and persists irrespective of production levels and other social and economic changes. Ames examines the relationship between production, consumption, and power and concludes that power is basically a difference in the wealth of households.

Stephen Plog has worked in the southwestern United States for a number of years, investigating the evolution of prehistoric society. Plog examines a number of variables here—using data from across the American Southwest—to argue that social inequality emerges in this area in the context of staple agricultural production, sedentism, exchange, and lineage formation. Plog points out that both egalitarian and hierarchical relationships existed in many places of the prehistoric Southwest after subsistence became dependent on agriculture.

Robert Drennan is interested in the rise of chiefdoms in both Mesoamerica and South America. His recent work in Colombia with Dale Quattrin provides the context for the study presented here. Drennan and Quattrin examine the relationship between social inequality and agricultural resources using information on the location of prime agricultural land and settlement distribution in the Valle de la Plata during the first millennium A.D. Their conclusion, which emphasizes the importance of social and political mechanisms over environmental causes, is extremely important.

Antonio Gilman has worked in Spain for a number of years on questions concerned with the rise of hierarchical society. As a Marxist, his perspective is reflected in the questions he seeks to answer and the variables on which he focuses. Gilman—using data collected from the Copper and Bronze Ages in La Mancha—examines the emergence of class stratification, concluding that these inequalities emerge from the competition over areas suitable for intensive farming.

Chapter 6

Chiefly Power and Household Production on the Northwest Coast

Kenneth M. Ames

INTRODUCTION

Inequalities may have always existed in human societies, at least at the level of relationships between individuals (e.g., Bender 1989; Olszewski 1991), relationships that are fluid—depending upon the interplay between individual character, age, and gender—since they are structured by social organization, culture, and economy, among other factors (including our biological heritage as terrestrial primates). Why and how do permanent elites grow from this seedbed? There are two broad classes of materialist answers: elite-as-managers and elite-as-thugs (cf. Gilman 1981). The first category includes Haas's (1982) integrationist school and the second his conflict school.

The elite-as-manager approach sees elites arising from the needs of complex divisions of labor for coordination of tasks, task groups, and information flow. In Service's (1975) classic formulation, emerging elites manage regional specialization in production through redistribution—leading to the formation of chiefdoms. It is clear now that chiefs may do little or no redistribution. The

KENNETH M. AMES • Department of Anthropology, Portland State University, Portland, Oregon 97207.

Foundations of Social Inequality, edited by T. Douglas Price and Gary M. Feinman. Plenum Press, New York, 1995.

absence of any elite-as-manager models in this collection is an indicator of the present status of this approach.

Elites-as-thugs models presently dominate the literature. In these models, some interest group within a society gains control of production, ultimately over labor (Arnold 1991, 1991, 1993, Chapter 3, this volume; Webster 1991) since labor is the ultimate limit on production in nonindustrial economies. This control may be overt and direct, or indirect. The core idea is that elites gain control and reproduce themselves out of their own self-interest. They do not arise from any societal need to coordinate anything—they may do that, but that is not how they come to exist.

Hayden (Chapter 2, this volume) describes societies in which control over production is indirect and fluid, based ultimately on the ability of individuals to manipulate the production of others through debt and contract. In his model, these situations arise, ultimately, where rich environments or highly productive economies permit. The central question becomes, What are the circumstances in which inequality of the kind he and others describe becomes institutionalized and persists irrespective of production levels and of other social and economic changes?

Societies along the Northwest Coast of North America had some form of status distinctions for more than 4,000 years, and elites for at least 3,000 years. The elite developed in concert with significant social and economic changes. Explanations for this evolution easily fall into the managerial or thug categories. Schalk (1977) and Ames (1981, 1985) argue that the complex task organization required for taking and preserving large quantities of salmon, coupled with the need to perform other subsistence tasks simultaneously, required economic management leading to the evolution of an elite. Matson (1983, 1985, 1989, 1992) and Coupland (1988) argue that the Northwest Coast's elite developed from the control of resources, either as a consequence of resource ownership itself (Matson) or out of conflict over their control (Coupland) (Ames 1994 reviews these matters and the relevant evidence in detail). To the south, in California, Arnold (1991, 1992) holds that chiefs arose among the Channel Island Chumash through their control of specialized production.

The Northwest Coast case is crucial to understanding the evolution of inequality since the coast's eighteenth- and nineteenth-century societies are the world's best examples of complex hunter-gatherers and of hereditary class distinctions among hunter-gatherers. As such, many considerations of the evolution of inequality are directly and indirectly informed by Northwest Coast ethnography. A review of the nature of the Northwest Coast's hereditary elite is essential to continued theory building about the development of elites. In addition to being hunter-gatherers, the societies of the Northwest Coast are examples of stratification in the absence of large polities. As we will see, the household was the polity; there were none beyond the household.

At its heart, this chapter argues that the evolution of social class on the Northwest Coast cannot be understood apart from the evolution of the household economy of the coast's societies (Ames 1985, 1994a; Coupland 1985, 1988). The coast's elites were financed by households. My own recent research has focused on the Northwest Coast household as an instrument of production (Ames i.p.), and some results of that work are incorporated below. However, the elite played out their roles at the village, town, and regional scales. This chapter examines the relationships between production, consumption, and the power of the Northwest Coast's elite class by exploring their roles in production—in controlling it, managing it, and as producers themselves. It considers the power exercised by that elite, and its spatial scale. I agree with Kristiansen (1991) that cultural evolution is as much a *spatial* process as it is a temporal process (see also Ames 1989, 1991). Finally, this chapter investigates the limits of chiefly power on the coast, asking why coastal societies were not more stratified, why they did not have paramount chiefs similar to those, for example, of Hawaii.

Power

Central to this chapter is the nature of the power wielded by Northwest Coast chiefs and their kin. Particularly useful here is the distinction between *power to,* and *power over.* Cobb (1993:51) defines *power to*:

> Individuals or interest groups may not have the secular means to enforce demands on others in terms of outright wresting surplus from them, but some individuals may wield considerable sway by virtue of holding informal offices, belonging to higher status lineages or clans, falling within esteemed age grades, or being male or female.

Power over implies the capacity to "coerce subordinates, including the ability to implement demands through the institutionalization of negative sanctions, ranging from the use of force to jural rights" (Cobb 1993:50). Power over usually comes with power to, but the reverse does not always follow. Hastorff (1990) refines these terms to "power to organize and *power over organization.*" I will argue below, that in the main, Northwest Coast chiefs had power to organize, but not power over organization.

Wolf's scale of power is fundamental to my understanding of power and it is a framework for understanding the power of the coastal elite in the household and beyond the household. He (Wolf 1990:586) describes four modes of power. The first "is power as an attribute of a person"; the second is the capacity of an individual to impose his will upon another; the third is tactical or organizational power in which an actor has the ability to circumscribe or control the acts of others in determinate settings. The fourth mode, structural power, is power that structures the political economy; it is power "to deploy and allocate social labor . . . [s]tructural power shapes the social field of action as to render some kinds of behavior possible, while making others less possible, or impossible" (Wolf 1990:587).

Embedded Specialists

Classifications of specialists generally place them into "blue-collar" relationships with elites. Earle's influential model of specialists is an example. He sees specialization as a continuum between "attached" specialists and independent specialists. Attached specialists "produce goods or provide services to a patron, typically either a social elite or a governing institution. Attached specialists are *contractually bound* to the patrons for whom they work" (Brumfiel and Earle 1987:5; emphasis mine). Independent specialists "produce goods or services for an unspecified demand crowd that varies according to economic, social and political conditions" (Brumfiel and Earle 1987:5). Costin (1991) presents a more complex typology of specialists, with many more parameters than Earle's, but artisans remain in the lower rungs of society. Neither Earle's continuum nor Costin's typology are conceptually adequate to address specialization on the Northwest Coast. Northwest Coast elite individuals may have both contributed to production and controlled production as specialists in the making of important objects such as masks and houses. Earle's continuum requires at least one more pole (changing it from a continuum to a field): "embedded specialists."

Embedded specialists are full- or part-time specialists whose vocation is a part of the household or local economy, and the specialist's activity is integral to the functioning of that economy. Performance is part of the individual's social role defined not on a purely economic or class basis, but on a kinship basis. Embedded specialists are neither contractually bound nor do they produce for a "demand crowd." Embedded specialists may be members of the elite, and making particular elite goods is part of their "power to" and "power over."

THE NORTHWEST COAST

The Northwest Coast extends from southeast Alaska to northern California (Suttles 1990). Its societies shared a number of features, including stratification, but also differed regionally in how those traits were expressed. For the purposes of this chapter, that diversity will be condensed into two broad regions: the northern Northwest Coast (northern Vancouver Island and the adjacent British Columbia mainland north to include southeast Alaska) and the southern Northwest Coast (south to northern California) (Figure 1).

The Northwest Coast Mode of Production

Small, autonomous, village-based "local groups" were the basic territorial unit. Most, but not all, of these groups had populations large enough to be biologically self-sufficient, that is, from 180 to 500 individuals (Wobst 1974, 1976). The household or coresidential corporate group (Hayden and Cannon 1982) was the basic unit of both consumption and production. Households were organized into villages and towns. The means of household recruitment and reproduction varied along the coast. There was a fairly strong, gender-based division of labor, which Norton (1985:248) describes as "independent cooperative behavior by both genders" directed to a common end. Moss (1993), however, suggests that the strength (rigidity) of the sexual division of labor has been exaggerated. Slave labor was important. There was what Mitchell and Donald (1988) call a "fair amount of specialization" for hunter-gatherers.

Salmon (*Onchorynchus* spp.) were the key resource, because they were storable and occurred abundantly in predictable places, but their importance cannot be taken for granted in every case. Secondary resources were quite significant, as was local resource variation. Though local groups were generally sedentary or semisedentary, on a regional level, patterns of mobility associated with the annual round were quite complex. Resources and resource patches were owned, but ownership patterns varied along the coast (Richardson 1981). A great many resources were stored; preservation and storage were crucial. The relatively short shelf life of stored salmon (ca. six months) was an important limiting factor affecting spring subsistence practices. Creation of wealth was ultimately dependent upon producing food surpluses, though wealth took forms other than food. Redistribution through the potlatch and other means was important. There was a strong ethos against hoarding. Regional systems of exchange and trade were probably important. (The foregoing is based primarily on Mitchell and Donald's [1988] definitive description of the Northwest Coast's mode of production in the eighteenth and nineteenth centuries; see also Ames 1994.)

Households occupied one or more of the large, cedar plank houses that were the primary form of dwelling. Households were generally big, ranging in size from 80 to 150 or more individuals. They owned estates of corporeal and noncorporeal property. In this chapter, these estate-holding households are termed Houses, with a capital H. Corporeal property included resource localities, the ground upon which the House's dwellings were built, the dwell-

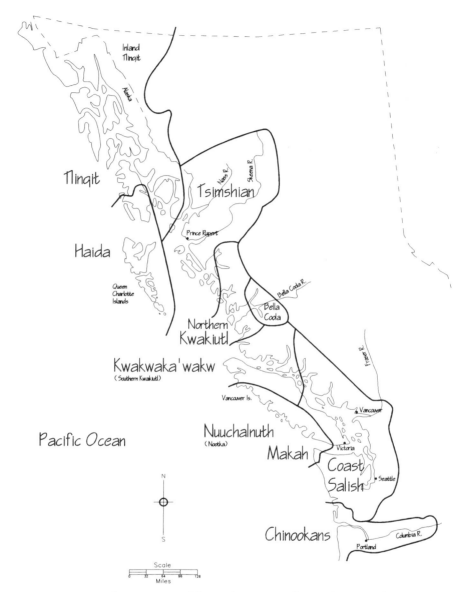

Figure 1. Map of the Northwest Coast showing locations of
ethnic/tribal groups mentioned in the text.

ings themselves, and the processed food and wealth produced by the household; noncorporeal property included the rights to resource localities, to songs and ritual performances, and to particular animal helpers and spirit beings. Noncorporeal property is commonly termed "privileges" in the ethnographic literature. Households had genealogical depth and maintained oral household histories. In theory, at least, household members had equal access to the household's property.

Rectangular surface structures—probably plank houses—appear in the archaeological record of this region between 3200 and 2800 b.p. The earliest occur at the two ends of the coast, in Oregon (Connelly 1992) and northern British Columbia (Coupland 1985).

Social Stratification on the Coast

Nineteenth-century Northwest Coast societies were stratified. For example, Coast Tsimshian society was divided into two social strata: free and slave. Free people were divided into three classes: *smkikét* (real people), *li`qakikét* (other people), *wa?á?ayin* (unhealed people), and slaves (*túnkit*). Real people include the chiefly families that held the largest number of titles and crests, while other people were titleholders, but holding fewer titles than the *smkikét* (Halpin and Seguin 1990). Unhealed people held no titles, but were free. The Coast Tsimshian social strata are paralleled among other groups (Kan 1989), and carry implications of a continuum of ritual purity, from chiefs who were pure, through commoners, who were maximally impure. Distinctions between these classes were maintained by marriage within classes and a rule that children of a marriage inherited "rank no higher than that of the lower-ranked parent" (Halpin and Seguin 1990:275). While details varied, this form of social stratification existed all along the Northwest Coast. The elite formed a distinct class because of marriage rules that required a woman to marry a man of equal status, just as slavery was perpetuated because the children of a slave were slaves.

Scale is important here. At the House level, distinctions between the elite and other free members of the household were not always clear cut; free individuals were ranked rather than sharply stratified. The elite become more evident at the level of village or region. Northwest Coast societies also varied in the strength of the rules against marriages and liaisons that crossed class boundaries, and their oral traditions are rich in stories of lovers from the wrong social class.

These distinctions crosscut kin groups, households, towns, regions, even species. In fact, in Northwest Coast oral narratives, chiefs among the salmon-people and bear-people, as well as other animals, were much more powerful than human chiefs. All Northwest Coast societies, despite differences, had some form of this basic set of social strata. Societies varied in how chiefs became chiefs and how sharp were the distinctions between the highest-ranking elite families and those elite individuals below them. But the very highest ranking families, those from whom chiefs were drawn, usually formed a clearly recognized and distinct group.

Below the highest-ranked individuals were what Drucker (1951) describes as the middle class or, in Coast Tsimshian terms, the other people. These families held fewer titles and were usually collateral relatives of the chiefly family, who were direct descendants of the household's founder. These lesser titleholders frequently included many of the household's specialists.

Commoners were members of the household by birth, marriage, or choice, but were clearly not titleholders. Many, perhaps all, were clients of the House chief (Adams 1981). These were poor people who had no House. The terms used for such individuals by the native people themselves include "dirty" and "lazy." Commoners could shift their allegiances and join other Houses. People were not bound to their household or local group. Low-status people were not serfs in the sense that they were part of a House's estate, though some were hangers-on, rather than members.

The success, wealth, prestige, and long-term strength of a House depended on the productivity of its estate and on the number of members it possessed. The prestige of a House (and therefore of its chief) and its size were directly tied to the ecological productivity of the household's estate, particularly of its salmon resources (Donald and Mitchell 1975). Houses had a certain minimum population size, below which they did not have enough members to perform the basic tasks necessary to reproduce the House (Adams 1973, 1981; Drucker 1951). Commoners and titleholders could be attracted to and join Houses that were wealthier than their own. Adams (1973, 1981) has argued that if the potlatch redistributed anything, it redistributed population, since potlatches were a measure of the success, health, and wealth of a household group. Chiefs had to work to attract and hold household members.

Northwest Coast societies were stratified rather than ranked societies (as defined by Fried 1967) because of the existence of slaves on the Northwest Coast (Donald 1983, 1985). Donald (1985:242) describes Northwest Coast societies as "class-divided" societies: "class is present and important but does not dominate or determine all social relationships." He distinguished class-divided societies from incipient class societies, where class structure is rudimentary, and from class societies in which class dominates and determines all social relationships. Donald (1985:241) defines class so:

> Class is present in a society when significant segments of that society have relatively permanent differential access to resources and/or power. In addition, a class must

be capable of reproducing itself biologically. This precludes gender or age categories from being regarded as classes.

Among the two free classes on the coast, kin group affiliation, rather than class, was the source of primary social identity.

Slaves were both labor and wealth (Mitchell 1984). Their labor could be used to produce wealth, but they could also be traded directly for other wealth items. Mitchell describes slave raiding as a means of creating wealth for the raiders. His description is stark: "[T]he free populations of the coast can be seen as analogous to uncaught salmon and uncut trees. And just as the fisherman turned the salmon into food and the woodworker trees into shelter, the predatory warrior converted freeman into wealth" (Mitchell 1984:46).

A History of Northwest Coast Status Distinctions

It is possible to broadly outline changing status distinctions on the coast over the past few millennia based primarily on evidence from burials. Between ca. 5000 and 1500 b.p., burial practices included inhumation in residential sites, as well as in other occupation sites. This custom ended sometime between 1500 and 1000 b.p. virtually everywhere on the coast. The principle lines of evidence available relating to status currently include grave goods, and the wearing of labrets, or lip plugs. Labrets were worn by high-status women on the North Coast during the contact period; it is clear that labret wear was restricted to a limited number of people for at least 4,000 years on the coast. The archaeological data suggest that gender and region of origin are two major dimensions structuring status on the coast. Definitions of status appear to have undergone at least two major changes during the past five millennia. The data on burial practices are drawn primarily from southern Northwest Coast sites in the Gulf of Georgia region, and from Prince Rupert Harbor in the northern coast (Figure 2) (see Ames 1944b; Beattie 1981; Burley and Knusel 1989; Cybulski 1993).

Labrets

Stone labrets are important evidence for status differences on the coast because wearing them leaves indelible evidence on the teeth (Figure 3) (Cybulski 1993; Murray 1981). Labret wear therefore directly reflects attributes of the living individual rather than postmortem ritual (Figure 4). Labrets only sometimes occur as grave goods. Calculating the frequency of labret wear is made difficult by tooth loss during life and after death, sometimes making it impossible to determine if an individual wore a labret. Cybulski (1993) believes that some of this tooth loss is probably the result of labret wear, but cannot prove it. Matson (1989) speculates that the presence of labrets as grave

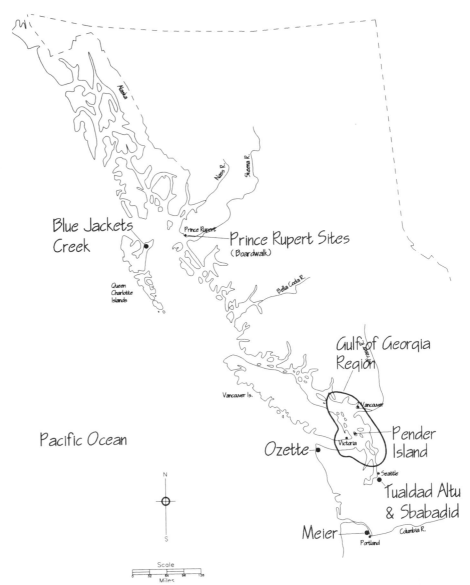

Figure 2. Map of the Northwest Coast showing locations of archaeological regions and sites discussed in the text.

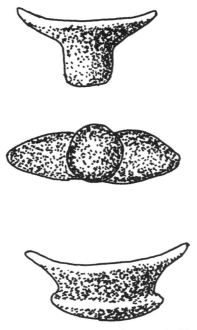

Figure 3. Two types of labrets. The upper is a side view of a labret style sometimes called a "hat-shaped" labret. The middle drawing is a front view of a hat-shaped labret. The lower drawing is a side view of a large "button" labret. The flanges rested against the teeth and the labret body extended through an incision in the lower lip.

goods marks achieved status, and their absence (tooth wear present, no labret) reflects ascribed status, suggesting that with ascribed status, labrets were heirlooms and passed on to the living. This is difficult to demonstrate; labrets occur in a variety of nonmortuary archaeological contexts, curiously enough, often broken.[1]

Labret wear is found on individuals at two sites predating 3500 b.p.: Pender Island on the southern coast and Blue Jackets Creek on the northern coast. Labret wear appears to have been quite restricted at this time in terms of how many people wore them, but available to both men and women in relatively equal proportions. The wide geographic separation of these two sites suggests this practice was widespread on the coast at this time.

Patterns of labret wear began to diverge markedly between the northern

[1]Curiously, since it is difficult to imagine how labrets could be broken in the normal course of wearing. It seems likely they were being broken before they were discarded, perhaps to maintain the value of labrets as a status marker.

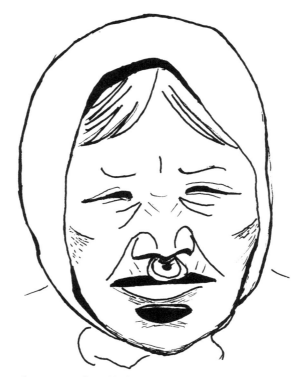

Figure 4. Drawing of an elderly Haida woman ("Queen Johnny of Masset")
in 1884, wearing a labret in her lower lip.

and southern coasts after 3500 b.p. On the northern coast between ca. 3500
and 1500 b.p., labret wear was more common than previously, but they were
worn almost exclusively by males. After 1500 b.p., labrets were worn exclusively by females. In contrast, on the southern coast, labret wear appears to
have been more common between 3500 and ca. 2000 b.p. then earlier, but
worn equally by females and males. After 2000 b.p. or so, the custom ends,
being replaced by cranial deformation for both males and females (Beattie
1981; Cybulski 1993). Cranial deformation for high status and free individuals
continued on the southern coast until the contact period.

Labret wear is a permanent and highly visible modification of the face,
and is an unambiguous status marker—one wears a labret or one does not
(Ames 1989). Cranial deformation is only somewhat less unambiguous. The
evidence suggests that for the last 4,000 years on the coast it was important
to distinguish certain individuals in as clear-cut a fashion as possible. It has also

been important to indicate from what region of the coast they originated and to mark gender.

Grave Goods

Pre-3500 b.p. burials primarily contain items of daily use (Ames 1994b; Burley and Knusel 1989; Severs 1974). Three individuals at Blue Jackets Creek were ochre-stained. Pender Island contains dramatic grave goods. Carlson (1991) recovered 10 horn spoons, several with handles carved in Northwest Coast–style zoomorphic motifs. Some of these spoons rested on or near the jaws of individuals, as though they had been laid across their mouths. Carlson believes this represents a ritual feeding of the dead. The earliest appear to predate 4000 b.p.

Grave goods become relatively widespread and rich after 2500 b.p. along the entire coast. Grave goods include shell-bead necklaces, chipped stone burial blades, copper beads, copper sheets, bone blades, and so on. While the data from the south coast do not suggest site hierarchies, the burial patterns in Prince Rupert Harbor raise the possibility of a site hierarchy (Ames 1994b) there. The richest burials and occupational debris occur at the Boardwalk site in the harbor. Other, contemporary sites are generally similar to Boardwalk, but lack copper and other exotic items.

The mortuary patterns are actually more complex than this summary suggests, because differences between burials extend to the presence or absence of boxes (as coffins), stone cairns, the use of sea otter teeth as decorative studs on boxes, dog burials, human trophy skulls, and so forth. It is quite clear, however, that during this period there are significant differences between graves in terms of the wealth of the accompanying grave goods.

Gender is a major dimension structuring burial practices, particularly in the north. In the south during this period (3500 to 1500 b.p.), there does not appear to be a significant gender bias in the distribution of grave goods, nor in the numbers of males and females recovered. There is a strong male bias in the north, in the number of interments with grave goods, in the kinds of grave goods, and in the sex ratios of the interred. Males significantly out-number females (1.86 males:1 female). This particular bias may extend throughout the prehistoric burial record of the northern coast.

After ca. 1500 b.p. interments in residential sites virtually cease in both regions. The most recent such burial complex on the coast is the Greenville burial ground on the northern coast, dating between 1600 and 500 b.p., though most burials predate 1000 b.p. (Cybulski 1993). With the exception of burial boxes, some dog remains, and elderberry,[2] the Greenville graves lack grave goods of the kind so common earlier.

---

[2]In Tsimshian oral tradition, elderberries are linked to human mortality.

Slavery

The evidence for the antiquity of slavery is ambiguous. Cybulski suggests that the sex ratios (1.87 males:1 female) for the Prince Rupert Harbor burials may indicate slavery. Historically, slaves' corpses were disposed of casually, even thrown into the surf. If a significant portion of Prince Rupert Harbor's ancient population were female slaves and their bodies were similarly treated, the skewed sex ratio would result. This reasoning would suggest that slavery existed on the Queen Charlotte Islands around 4000 b.p., given the sex ratio for the Blue Jackets Creek burials.[3] One must also conclude that in the south slavery played a minor role at this time, and was more likely to involve males (given the generally higher numbers of females in southern coast burial populations, which have an overall sex ratio of 1.08 males:1 female), an interesting possibility. A south coast sample of 34 burials predating 2500 b.p. does have a sex ratio of 1.44 males:1 female, a ratio that after 2500 falls to .98:1 (data from Cybulski 1993). This would imply an early reliance on female slaves. This argument also implies that at least a quarter of the Prince Rupert Harbor's free female population had been enslaved and taken elsewhere. I do not think that Cybulski's hypothesis can sustain all this inferential weight without additional supporting evidence.

The evidence is clear for raiding in Prince Rupert Harbor at this time. Several individuals appear to have been found and decapitated. Middle-aged females are the most common victims (Cybulski 1979). Other individuals were found in what Cybulski (1979) calls "unconventional" burial postures. Most burials are flexed; these unconventional ones are quite loosely extended (most of these predate 3500 b.p.). These data could be read in two ways as evidence for slavery. The bound individuals were killed in the course of raids as not being worth enslaving, or, alternatively, they were slaves who were killed as part of ritual disposition of wealth. These inferences remain speculative, however. On the southern coast, the skeletons of scalped females predating 2200 b.p. have been recovered, suggesting the existence of slavery to the investigators (ARCAS 1991).

Contemporary Events

The widespread presence of wealthy graves by 2500 b.p. is somewhat later than evidence for several major shifts on the coast: (1) the development

---

[3]The Blue Jackets Creek material was originally examined by Murray (1973), whose results differ from Cybulski's. Murray identified 8 males and 9 females for a sex ratio of .9:1. Cybulski identified 13 males and 6 females for a ratio of 2.6:1. Cybulski cannot account for the different results. Blue Jackets' small sample size precludes placing much inferential weight on these patterns.

of heavy reliance on stored salmon (Ames 1991, 1994 and citations therein; Matson 1992 and citations), (2) the appearance of plank house villages (Ames 1991, 1994), and (3) warfare in the north (Cybulski 1975); Mitchell (1988) suggests that the elaboration of burials in the south was also due to increased levels of warfare, but he has no direct evidence.

The second change in how status was marked on the coast occurred between ca. 2000 and 1000 b.p. This change seems to be part of the broader shift in funerary ritual marked by the end of subsurface interments. In the north, these changes may be related to evidence of an expansion in warfare (Maschner 1991; Moss and Erlandson 1992) and shifting tribal distributions (Wooley and Haggarty 1989). A number of investigators have independently argued that during this period the large chiefly houses of the historic period appear, as well as multi-House villages (Acheson 1991; Coupland i.p.; Maschner 1991, 1992), though this is as yet unproven. The evidence for the south is in some ways more subtle but, in addition to the changing burial customs, includes an apparent change in the production of art and in subsistence technology, and an increase in warfare (Fladmark 1982). It may also be accompanied by the appearance of houses of enormous size (Ames 1991), though that remains to be demonstrated (Ames i.p.).

The Power and Functions of Northwest Coast Chiefs

Household chief was the basic, elite office everywhere on the coast. All chiefs were House chiefs, regardless of what other chiefly offices they might hold. House chiefs were usually drawn from the highest-ranking family in the House though, in practice, rules of succession were flexible. Individuals, including commoners, could found new Houses. Levels of chief above the House chief existed on the central and northern coast, but not on the southern coast among the Coast Salish. Among the Coast and Southern Tsimshian, the chief of the highest-ranked House (matrilineage) in a town was town chief. There are four Tsimshian matriclans and a clan's highest-ranked lineage chief was clan chief, and the tribal chief was the highest-ranked clan chief. A Haida town chief was the chief of the House or lineage segment that owned the town site itself. Among the Nuuchalnulth, whose local groups were tied together into confederacies, the highest-ranked town chief was confederacy chief.

There were also Great Chiefs, chiefs of remarkable social stature who could organize large raiding expeditions, command tribute, or have influence over several villages. Great Chief was not a formally recognized status; the term has been invented by anthropologists. Generally, Northwest Coast people did not rank chiefs linguistically, usually having only one term (e.g., Drucker 1951). For de Laguna (1983), Great Chiefs were a result of the fur trade that began in the late eighteenth century, but Stearns (1984) and

Garfield (1939) think they predate contact among the Haida and Tsimshian. Stearns suggests they existed among the Haida at first contact with Europeans and represent a precontact phenomenon, while Garfield suggests the office (which she terms tribal chief) developed among the Coast Tsimshian only a century or so before European contact and as a consequence of changes in Coast Tsimshian settlement patterns. The most famous Great Chiefs include Maquinna among the Nuuchalnulth, and Legax among the Coast Tsimshian. Maquinna may have "controlled" some 10,000 people (Penthick 1979), and both chiefs dominated trade in their respective regions.

House chiefs managed their House's estates. Stearns (1984) distinguishes between *instrumental* power and *expressive* power exercised by Haida chiefs. Chiefs exercised instrumental power over the House's physical resources, and expressive power over the House's noncorporeal estate. An important aspect of instrumental power lay in the chief granting permission to non-House individuals to hunt, fish, or gather at resource localities that were owned by the House. Permission was always, or almost always, granted. Not asking, however, was a deep affront that could lead to a blood feud. Nuuchalnulth chiefs were given tribute in return for this permission (Drucker 1951). Chiefs declared major resource seasons open, and decided the timing of seasonal residential moves. They organized raids and wars.

There was either variation along the coast in the power chiefs held with regard to their household's resources and territories, or in how various observers have interpreted and described that power. On the one hand, many (e.g., Stearns 1984) describe the chief as managing the House's estates, but the estates (including rights and privileges) belonging ultimately to the House. Theoretically, a House's estate belonged to all members of the house, but chiefs usually treated the House's noncorporeal property as though it were their own. Drucker (1951), on the other hand, describes the estates as belonging to the Nuuchalnulth chiefs: all the titleholders of a household group owned rights to some resources, territory, and the like, and these rights were theirs, not household property. Richardson (1981), reviewing evidence for resource ownership on the coast, concludes that Nuuchalnulth chiefs held rights to resources in trust for their house, and did not own them. He suggests that only Coast Tsimshian chiefs held rights to resources apart from their House's estate; however, I am not sure I agree with his reading of the appropriate passages in Garfield (1939). Caution is necessary in making inferences about resource ownership based on normative descriptions of Northwest Coast practices. Riches (1979:151) states that individuals among the Coast Salish and Chinookans owned resources. Suttles (1968) places individual ownership among central Coast Salish in this context in quotation marks. Richardson shows that among the southern Coast Salish and Chinookans a few key resources were controlled by the community, not by individuals or families, while among the more northerly central Coast Salish crucial resources were controlled by extended families. There was considerable variation around the theme of resource ownership.

Further, what was owned varied. In some cases, everything within an owned patch was controlled; in other instances ownership actually included only rights to exploit a particular resource and all other resources in the patch were part of the commons. The owned resources were not inevitably essential to group survival (e.g., Suttles 1951).

Expressive powers involved displays of crests and performances of songs, dances, and narratives, and of spirit powers. Chiefs could be shamans, but not necessarily. In the north, their spirit powers were related to, but different than, shamanic power (e.g., Guedon 1984). Organizing and participating in the public rituals in which the House's privileges were shown was a central part of the chief's job. The continued stature and prestige of the House depended on his taking part in potlatches and/or other public rituals. The activities of chiefs "above" Haida House chiefs were primarily expressive or ceremonial. Coast Tsimshian tribal chiefs, in contrast, could call on all the young men of their group to do their bidding and could field war parties against opposition (Garfield 1939). Nuuchalnulth chiefs above the household also wielded considerable instrumental power.

In spite of their power, chiefs everywhere on the coast had to seek advice from councils, whatever their stature. Stearns notes that the power of Haida town chiefs was dependent on the power and support of the town's House chiefs. House chiefs also had councils.

It is evident from the ethnographies that while chiefs enjoyed considerable authority and prestige, they had little direct power over free individuals. The Tlingit paid little attention to their chiefs (Emmons 1991). Mitchell (1983), in his all-too-brief study of the power of Legax, the early nineteenth-century Tsimshian Great Chief, concludes that Legax had little or no direct power over other Coast Tsimshian individuals or groups within his tribe (in sharp contrast to Garfield's conclusions). The powers of Northwest Coast chiefs present a conundrum: they appear powerful, but what power did they actually exercise?

While a Legax could muster the resources of the chiefs below him (clan and lineage) for a potlatch, he had no control over their House's estates; he could neither tell another Tsimshian what to do nor could he coerce him. House chiefs had the *power to* wage war, to conduct trade, to permit outsiders to use resources belonging to the House's estate, to declare the fishing or hunting seasons open, and to display the House's privileges. There seems little evidence that they had *power over* the estate or their fellow House members. I can find only one case where chiefs appear to have exercised power over House members and resources. Chinookan chiefs and elite individuals may have had the power to seize the food of lower-status individuals, apparently causing occasional famines (Ray 1938). Chinookan chiefs could apparently take anything they wanted; Ray (1938) noted that they were more powerful than chiefs elsewhere on the coast.

Many early European voyagers observed, for example, that while chiefs attempted to formally control trade between the ships and their people, everyone traded. Their powers were circumscribed by the existences of councils, by rivals for their status, by the ability of members of their House to join other Houses, or even to establish new ones, and by their strong need, therefore, to hold their followers. They did have wealth. They also had power over slaves. Before turning to slaves there is one other important element of chiefs' power to discuss, and that is its spatial scale.

The instrumental base of chiefs' power was their House's estate. Powerful Houses and chiefs were so because, ultimately, their estates had rich, productive resources that attracted people to join the House (Adams 1973, 1981; Ames 1981; Donald and Mitchell 1975). In Haida towns, sometimes the town chief (whose lineage owned the townsite as part of its estate) was weaker than a House chief whose House had a richer resource base and more people. However, chiefs operated on a larger spatial scale than their household's territorial estate or the town in which they resided. The village or town was the basic stage for political activities (Stearns 1984), but Houses, and therefore their chiefs, were linked through potlatch and marriage ties to several towns or households scattered over fairly large areas. Adams (1981) asserts that at this regional scale, chiefs formed a ruling oligarchy. Extensive potlatching linkages created a kind of international politics (in Adams's terms), so that the field of political behavior extended well beyond the village (Adams 1981). The northern and southern coasts, as regions, probably represent the maximum size of these linkages, as each was probably an interaction sphere (Ames 1989; Suttles 1990). However, it is doubtful that these regional networks or interaction spheres can be construed as polities, anymore than can towns or villages. The House was the political unit on the coast. In this context, it is worth noting that slaves were drawn from an enormous territory.

Chiefs owned their slaves, and could do as they desired with them, including killing them as part of potlatches and other important events. The wealth of chiefs, the resources they accumulated and gave away through potlatching, depended on slave labor (Donald 1983, 1985). Since slaves did not exist socially, they were not subject to any strictures imposed by the division of labor (Donald 1985). Having no gender—socially—they could do any tasks, no matter their biological sex. Slaves were people who, by their capture (most slaves were war captives, though chiefs traded for them as well), had been stripped of whatever social personae they possessed and lived in a state of social nakedness.

In sum, chiefs were firmly rooted in their households or territories, and all chiefs were first of all household chiefs. A House's prestige, and therefore that of its chief, rested on the productivity of the household's estate, and on the ability of the household's chief to operate in the larger arena in which the prestige of individual chiefs was measured. Typically chiefs could only command the production of their own household. Chiefs had extensive power to use the resources of their House's estate, but there seems little evidence to suggest that, as a class, chiefs had direct power over free individuals. They had tremendous authority and, with the right personality, might become autocrats (Boas 1916). On the other hand, people frequently paid no attention to them. Chiefly power was limited by the existence of councils and the need to gain councilors' support. It was also limited by the possibility that other members of the House could establish their own House (Stearns 1984). Chiefs owned slaves, and may have depended on them to procure the resources they needed to participate in the regional systems of potlatching and ritual. Slaves and their labor were the only resource over which chiefs exercised clear unambiguous power. Otherwise, coastal chiefs had a great deal of *power to*, but had rather limited *power over.*

Chiefs, Household Production, and Embedded Specialists

Chiefly Labor

Chiefs appear to have been directly involved in production, but it is not clear to what extent or in what ways. The ethnographic data on the role of House chiefs and elite individuals in daily subsistence production are mixed, making it difficult to establish the extent to which chiefs and their immediate families (as opposed to all high-ranking individuals) actually hunted, fished, gathered shell fish, and the like. According to Oberg (1973), Tlingit chiefs were not supposed to perform tasks of this kind. Drucker's (1951) account of Nuuchalnulth chiefs is similar—they did not do daily tasks. However, Huelsbeck (1989) argues that whaling and sea mammal hunting by Nuuchalnulth chiefs was economically important to their households. Boas (1916) states that Tsimshian chiefs were supposed to be expert in all activities and Princes were expected to be excellent hunters. Barnett (1955) suggests that the participation of Coast Salish chiefs in daily subsistence activities was a matter of their own choice. Apparently, however, chiefs did receive food from their House members whether they hunted or fished or not. It is unlikely—given the population of most Houses, and the rather large numbers of all title-holders in any house—that elite individuals who were not members of the current chief's family could avoid daily tasks. In any case, it may be in the areas of slave raiding and specialized production that the labor of the elite was crucial to household reproduction.

Slavery

Slave labor was the only labor directly controlled by Northwest Coast chiefs. The products of their labor contributed to the general pool, but could be appropriated by the chief who owned them. Mitchell's (1985) estimates of the number of slaves present in the different societies along the coast range from 2% and 3% to almost 30% of some groups. Since they were acquired through warfare or trade by chiefs, slaves were a major contribution by chiefs to the House's economy. In addition to standing outside the sexual division of labor so their labor could be employed for any task, slaves also may have provided a means of solving short-term labor bottlenecks (Bogucki 1993). Labor bottlenecks would arise when complex simultaneous tasks (Wilk and Rathje 1982) required many hands, but only a few were available. Slaves could be acquired, used, and disposed of or traded all in short order.

Specialists

In Northwest Coast Houses, embedded specialists did things necessary for the economic and social reproduction of the household. They appear to have been members of their House by birth, their specialization an inherited trade; they may or may not have been members of the chiefly elite, though they held titles (Drucker's middle class). Such specialists could also be hired by other Houses, usually by chiefs. The crucial point here is that when they were part of the elite, they produced elite goods, not as dependents of an elite class, but as part of their *roles* as elite individuals.

It is difficult to establish how many tasks were performed by specialists. Most ethnographies mention wood-carvers and painters who sometimes supported their families on commissions from the elite. Canoe making may have been another embedded specialty. Boas (1916) implies it was associated with high status. He also indicates that there was village-level specialization in production of food and prestige objects among the Coast Tsimshian (Allaire 1984). Specialization appears to have been inherited and widespread for both women and men. There is no evidence suggesting that chiefs could coerce the production of specialists.

For the Northwest Coast, woodworking and wood carving provide the clearest examples of embedded specialization. The most famous woodworking specialists on the Northwest Coast are carvers, but there were a number of other specialists in wood. On the southern coast, embedded specialists included plank makers who made the wide, cedar planks with which houses were walled (Mauger 1978). Wood carving, however, appears to have been primarily a high-status or elite specialty (though anyone could carve, including slaves). There are a number of lines of evidence to support this.

Among the Coast Tsimshian, some carvers were members of the *gitsonkt* (Shane 1984). The word *gitsonkt* is from the Coast Tsimshian word *gidson* meaning "inner or secret room." The *gitsonkt* carved masks and made mechanical devices used in *naxnoq* performances by members of the Coast Tsimshian elite, particularly chiefs. These performances related to important spirit powers possessed by chiefs as part of their expressive powers (Guedon 1984). The institution was not limited to the Tsimshian, existing among at least the Northern Kwakiutl. In addition to carving, the *gitsonkt* were a secret council of advisors to their chiefs, hence their name. Their methods for carving and making the devices were secret, and the punishment for discovering or revealing these secrets was death. Thus, production and use of certain critical privileges was tightly controlled and restricted.

Many of these individuals were of high or chiefly status; before contact the *gitsonkt* may have always had high status (Shane 1984). High-status individuals also carved other objects related to the prestige and crest systems. One of the most famous of these is the "rain screen" that stood at the back of the Whale House in the Yakutat Tlingit town of Klukwan. The screen was carved either by two commissioned Tsimshian carvers, or by two Tlingit House chiefs: Kate-su, who built the Whale House during the 1830s and carved the screen, and his later successor, Skeet-lah-ka, who painted it (Emmons 1991:64).

Before the introduction of iron and steel, stone adze blades of nephrite were the primary hard, sharp, wood-carving tool. Nephrite is rare on the coast and the adze blades were widely traded. Archaeologically, these items are often reworked and resharpened down to exhaustion. Nephrite adzes were worth one or two slaves among the Tlingit (Emmons 1991). Thus only slave holders—elite individuals—could purchase them.

Good carvers and painters were commonly hired. They and their families lived in the house of the chief who commissioned them for the project's duration. In this case, the relationship between carver and client approximates Earle's concept of attached specialists. However, the contractual relationship lasted only for the life of the project, after which the carver moved on. Further, if the carver was of high status, then the relationship was not one between patron and dependent, but between social equals. Famous carvers appear to have called their own tune.

The possibility that elite individuals functioned as embedded specialists is not limited to the Northwest Coast. Recent evidence from Copan and other late Classic Maya sites suggests that scribes and sculptors (who made the stelae) were members of the elite, not of the upper levels from which Kings were drawn, but elite nonetheless (Hammond 1991).

Gender

Both men and women held high rank; both men and women could wield chiefly power and influence. Norton (1985) reviews the debate over how commonly women formally and informally exercised such power. Women's production was central to the house for both household consumption and exchange and trade. Norton (1985) argues that during the colonial period at least, women's products set coastal standards of value. The archaeological data clearly indicate that gender was a central dimension of high status for the last 2,500 years. The interplay between gender and burial ritual was much more subtle than indicated above (Ames 1994b), but a full discussion is beyond the scope of this chapter.

The Role of Chiefs/Elites in Household Production in the Archaeological Record

Household Production

There are four sets of excavated structures with sufficient exposures to be useful here. All are in the southern subarea: Tualdad Altu near Seattle, Washington; Sbabadid, also near Seattle (Chatters 1989); Meier, near Portland, Oregon (Ames et al. 1992); and the famous Ozette site, on Washington's Olympic Peninsula (Huelsbeck 1989, Samuels 1989). Sbabadid was a plank house dating between A.D. 1790 and 1825 (Chatters 1989). Artifact distributions within the house indicate the presence of a harpooner; debris distributions suggest specialization in working copper, bone, and lithics.

At Ozette, a Makah (culturally related to Nuuchalnulth) village on the northwest tip of Washington's Olympic Peninsula dating to ca. 250 b.p., one high-status and two lower-status houses were sampled (Samuels 1989). Within the high-status house (House 1), the evidence suggests that chiefly status families (1) may have worked less at daily tasks than other residents, (2) hosted feasts, (3) participated in whaling as harpooners, and (4) controlled access to valuables. Contrasts between houses indicate that the high-status household had access to high-status foods, such as whales and preferred shellfish beds. As noted above, Huelsbeck (1988) argues that sea mammal hunting by high-status individuals was an important contribution to the household economy.

The Meier site was occupied between ca. A.D. 1400 and ca. 1830 and is located within historic Middle Chinookan territory. The excavations exposed a single, large house 14 m wide and 28 m to 32 m long, representing some 44,000 to 75,000 board feet of lumber (the equivalent of four to seven modern, North American single-family dwellings). The house was used and rebuilt over 400 years, requiring something on the order of 400,000 to 1,100,000 board feet (figures are based on Ames et al. [1992], Ames [i.p.]), or between 40 and 110 modern houses—a large housing tract. The precontact permanent population of Middle Chinookan territory was at least between 3,000 and 6,000 people (Boyd 1985). If the Meier house was home to perhaps 80 individuals, one can easily calculate the total requirements for wood for structures alone. The house itself was a major focus for household labor. The household's elite lived in its northern end, as indicated by the distribution of wealth and prestige markers. Bulk food processing (butchering, roasting) occurred in the south end. Interestingly, shellfish may have been processed in the high-status end. In addition to prestige markers, a range of valuable equipment (nets, guns, metal-tipped arrows and spears, and heavy stone tools such as mauls) was cached or stored in the north, or high-status end. In general, tools with high labor costs are concentrated in the north end. Three stone adzes (two of nephrite) were associated with the same hearth in the northern third of the house (in contrast to antler-splitting wedges, which are ubiquitous in the deposits). Ethnohistoric evidence suggests that members of the same extended family shared a common hearth within these large structures. The evidence from Meier indicates elite control of some aspects of the means of production, including guns, nets, and metal tools, and over access to prized trade goods, including elite markers (European uniforms) and tools (iron projectile points). The evidence may also indicate direct involvement of elite family members in subsistence production. Freshwater mussel processing features are concentrated in the house's north end, for example, and the presence of nets suggests the people at the north end may have done the fishing. Elite individuals may also have been woodworkers or carvers (recall the construction requirements for wood).

Tualdad Altu is the oldest of these excavated south coast structures; its uppermost deposits date to A.D. 400 to 500. Chatters (1989) found sharp differences between the west and east ends of the structure in subsistence and fabricating tools and in some classes of mammal and fish remains, suggesting some specialization in hunting large terrestrial predators and sea mammals, and in net making.

Specialization

Copper objects recovered from graves in Prince Rupert Harbor, dating as early as 2300 b.p., may be the earliest evidence of production specialization on the coast (Coutre 1975; Ames 1994b). Coutre (1975) suggests that the work-manship required some level of specialization and perhaps mass production. An anthropomorphic handle is the earliest wood-carving tool from the coast; it dates between 3800 and 4200 b.p. (Matson 1976). The zoomorphic spoon handles recovered from Pender Island are contemporary and older than the handle, are well executed, and display basic features of the Northwest Coast art style. Traditional Northwest Coast woodworking skills existed by 3500 b.p., indicated by the presence of stone adzes of many sizes, and wooden burial boxes (Cybulski 1993). It is possible that large freight canoes existed by this time as well, but they certainly existed by 2200 b.p. (Ames 1994a,b). There is evidence from Prince Rupert Harbor for a possible specialized woodworking site (Ames 1994b) dating between 3500 and 1500 b.p.

SUMMARY AND CONCLUSIONS

Nineteenth-century Northwest Coast chiefs had considerable power to organize production, public ceremonial, and ritual. They had the power—and obligation—to accumulate and display the wealth employed for potlatching. This power is balanced by their lack of power over free individuals and the limits imposed on their power by councils, and by the ability of household members to vote with their feet by leaving the household, or even to establish a new House.

This does not mean, however, that chiefs did not exercise tactical power over production and over the organization of production at the household scale or larger. The Meier site data indicate that elite members of that house-hold may have controlled access to crucial tackle and equipment, including nets and guns. At Ozette, elite individuals appear to have been harpooners, perhaps controlling the production of crucial offshore resources. Equivalent evidence unfortunately does not yet exist for other portions of the coast. High-status individuals at Ozette may not have been otherwise involved in daily economic activities. Chiefs also affected production through slaves and as embedded specialists.

Nineteenth-century Nuuchalnulth chiefs, and, by implication, all North-west Coast chiefs, depended on slave labor to produce the wealth required for potlatching (Donald 1983, 1985). But slaves also contributed labor to the House itself as extra hands, particularly during periods of labor bottlenecks. Of course, slaving could have created or exacerbated those bottlenecks when raiders carried off household members. Chiefs also had houseless commoners as clients who, though free, were at the very bottom of the social ladder (slaves were not on the ladder). Their labor could also be commanded. Interestingly, there are no accounts of chiefs diverting slave labor into overtly "thug" directions—no slave bodyguards to enforce a chief's will, for example. But, if a chief did behave in that way, the rest of the household could leave. The antiquity of slavery on the coast is difficult to establish. It could have begun as early as ca. 3000 to 2500 b.p., at about the same time that plank houses, villages, and elaborate social distinctions appear in the record.

Titleholders may have also exercised tactical control over production as embedded specialists. This control may have been exercised in two ways. In the first, titleholders themselves may have produced many of the masks and other objects crucial to the display of household privileges as part of their *power to,* and if, as among the *gitsonkt,* they were the only ones who could make the object, as part of their *power over* the noncorporeal portion of the household's estate. Titleholders also commissioned carvings. They appear to have been the only House members with the wealth to acquire crucial equipment, such as nephrite adzes and, during the colonial period, steel. Finally, as both producers and consumers of carvings, elite specialists could set the standards against which the work of other, lower-ranked, or even slave, artisans could be measured.

The second form of tactical control involves the House itself and other major tools, such as canoes. The House was a major focus of labor and skill, and the household's primary instrument of production (Ames i.p.; Suttles 1968). The household owned its House, even in areas where ownership of resources was diffuse (Suttles 1968). Northwest Coast houses may have had use-lives of up to several hundred years. The family or line that controlled or owned such a house could exert enormous influence over the rest of the household, without that influence necessarily having to be overt on a daily basis. On the northern coast, the name borne by a House chief was also the name of the House and of its house, clearly showing the tie between chiefly status, the physical dwelling, and the corporate human group. The archaeological data from the Meier site suggest woodworking was associated with high status. Boas (1916) indicates that canoe making was a skill associated with princes—young members of elite families. It is possible then that Northwest Coast chiefly and higher-status families monopolized certain crucial skills that were central to household economic production, to its ritual and ceremonial functions, and to the construction and maintenance of the House's house.

The control exercised by chiefs over natural resources apparently varied along the coast, as did the importance of the resources so controlled. In only one case (the Chinookans) is there evidence of elite individuals taking food from the mouths of lower-status people.

It is not clear that Northwest Coast chiefs had strategic power as defined by Wolf (1990:586). The power of Great Chiefs seems decidedly slippery; they had wealth, and great power to organize. It may have been their power to organize at a regional scale that represents their strategic power. Otherwise, strategic power may have rested more with the chiefly oligarchy than with any individual, but that is hard to determine.

    Northwest Coast chiefs had their feet planted firmly on both sides of a major contradiction. On the one hand their position depended on their place within the household, on their ability to "manage" the House's estate, on their control—both quite indirect and direct—of certain key aspects of production, perhaps including fundamental craft skills, and their continued ability to cajole, manipulate, and wheedle their household into doing what they, the chiefs, wanted them to do. On the other hand, their position depended on a steady supply of slave labor, stolen from outside the House. It is this contradiction that produces the competing views of Northwest Coast chiefs as managers or thugs.

    All chiefs were ultimately House chiefs even though they functioned at the town and regional level. This is a second contradiction at the heart of Northwest Coast chiefship. I can find no evidence that any chief ever completely transcended his House and expanded his power base to include several houses or even one village, to the extent that a chief could be said to have exercised the same kind of power over an entire community, as he did over his House, such as, for example, a Hawaiian paramount chief could. Great Chiefs had great wealth and the ability to *influence* events in many Houses, perhaps even many villages, but no power over them.

    There is archaeological evidence for elites on the Northwest Coast for at least the last 2500 to 3000 years. It is unimaginable to me that some elite individuals did not attempt to extend their reach beyond their House. The tantalizing hints of site hierarchies noted above may be archaeological evidence of such experiments in polity building. Why did they fail? Or never occur?

    It was not because these people were hunter-gatherers or had low population densities. Tremendous wealth was available as a result of their economy. Ethnographically it was dispersed among many Houses, but if one individual, or small number of individuals, had control of all of the wealth of, for example, the Coast Tsimshian, they could have lived in extraordinary splendor, certainly rivaling any other North American elites. Populations in some areas were sufficient for a small, well-stratified polity. The Coast Tsimshian who wintered in Prince Rupert Harbor, a small, circumscribed area, numbered some 6,000 people. The Chinookans on the south coast may have numbered over 20,000 people (Boyd 1985).

    In some cases, populations were very spatially circumscribed. On the lower Columbia River, near present-day Portland, Oregon, dense human populations were tightly constrained to a small floodplain. In other instances, particular groups controlled resources or resource localities crucial to the subsistence of entire regions that could easily have been used as leverage to gain economic power over adjacent groups.

The question becomes not why did hierarchical inequality exist on the Northwest Coast at all, but why was there not more of it? Why did not a few Great Chiefs exercise *power over* many households. Part of the answer I think is scale. The regional and demographic scales at which Northwest Coast chiefs operated were vast. One interaction sphere (the Northern coast [Ames 1989; Suttles 1990]) minimally included Southeast Alaska, the British Columbia mainland coast, and the Queen Charlotte Islands, with a population in the early nineteenth century of some 45,000 people.[4] Estimating 100 people per House,[5] there were 450 Houses in the region and 450 House chiefs. This number is probably too low but the actual figure is not important. What is crucial here is that the simple number of chiefs who interacted, and the distances across which they interacted, probably made it impossible for any individual or group to dominate even some portion of the interaction sphere for very long, let alone the entire region.

The origins of the Northwest Coast elite certainly lie in the formation of large, permanent extended households around 3,000 to 3,500 years ago. I believe the original elite were the genealogical core of those early house-holds—the people directly descended from the founder who gave the house-hold its cross-generational continuity. Households controlled resources and competed for members. The household core originally controlled household production by controlling the House itself, and the House, as I have shown, could stand for several hundred years, but required considerable labor and skill to maintain. The household core may also have controlled some of the skills crucial to reproducing the House. This proto-elite either were labret wearers or appropriated labret wear as a marker of their emerging status. Differences in wealth and status were and remained at base differences in the wealth of households.

The use of slaves may have evolved as the chiefs' inability to exercise power over household production conflicted with their desire to reproduce themselves as an elite. From the standpoint of chiefs, the loss of household members they could not control to slave raiders was balanced by the acquisition of slaves they could control. I note above the possibility that large Houses appeared on the coast ca. 1500 b.p. The increase in mean House size after 1500 b.p. on the Northwest Coast is just the increase required to accommodate a few slaves per household (Ames i.p.). The burial record in-

[4]This figure is based on Boyd's (1985) estimates for the Tlingit, Haida. Tsimshian (including Coast Tsimshian, Nishga, Gitksan, and Southern Tsimshian), and Haisla. Boyd's figures are minimum estimates for the precontract populations.
[5]House membership could range from 20 or 30 to well over a hundred individuals. I assume 100 people here to produce a reasonable minimum estimate.

dicates that gender and region of origin were significant dimensions of elite status. Historically, woman's labor was important in production for household consumption and for trade (Norton 1985)—the regional aspect of the Northwest Coast's household economy. Adams (1973) describes chiefs as forming a regional oligarchy, and the archaeological and ethnographic records indicate rather far-flung interaction spheres (Ames 1989).

The evolution of inequality on the Northwest Coast can only be understood at several interacting scales. The scale of the household is fundamental, but so too are the regional scales of social, political, and economic interaction. The Northwest Coast lacked stratified polities. The development of polities on the coast (and by extension anywhere else in the world) would have required a simultaneous reorganization of household and regional social and political economies by a preexisting or emerging elite. Such changes would probably have occurred swiftly, rather than over long-term transitions. A materialist approach to the evolution of inequality must account for why such transitions occur, and why they succeed or fail.

ACKNOWLEDGMENTS

I would like to thank Doug Price and Gary Feinman for the invitation to participate in the stimulating symposium on which this volume is based. Their editing significantly improved this chapter. I also want to thank Madonna Moss for her extensive comments on an earlier draft. Any errors of course are mine.

REFERENCES

Acheson, S. R., 1991, *In the Wake of the ya'åats'xaatgáay* [Iron People]: *S Study of Changing Settlement Strategies among the Kunghit Haida,* Unpublished Ph.D. dissertation, University of Oxford.

Adams, J. W., 1973, *The Gitksan Potlatch, Population Flux, Resource Ownership and Reciprocity,* Holt, Rinehart & Winston, Toronto.

Adams, J. W., 1981, Recent Ethnology of the Northwest Coast, *Annual Review of Anthropology* 10:361–392.

Allaire, L., 1984, A Native Mental Map of Coast Tsimshian Villages, in: *The Tsimshian: Images of the Past, Views of the Present* (M. Seguin, ed.), University of British Columbia Press, Vancouver, pp. 82–98.

Ames, K. M., 1981, The Evolution of Social Ranking on the Northwest Coast of North America, *American Antiquity* 46:789–805.

Ames, K. M., 1985, Hierarchies, Stress and Logistical Strategies among Hunter-Gatherers in Northwestern North America, in: *Prehistoric Hunter Gatherers, the Emergence of Cultural Complexity* (T. D. Price and J. Brown, eds.), Academic Press, New York, pp. 155–180.

Ames, K. M., 1989, Art and Regional Interaction among Affluent Foragers on the North Pacific Rim, in: Preprint Proceedings: Circumpacific Prehistory Conference, Seattle, Vol. III, Part 2, unpaginated.

Ames, K. M., 1991, The Archaeology of the *Longue Durée*: Temporal and Spatial Scale in the Evolution of Social Complexity on the Southern Northwest Coast, *Antiquity* 65:935–945.

Ames, K. M., 1994a, The Northwest Coast: Complex Hunter-Gatherers, Ecology, and Social Evolution, *Annual Review of Anthropology* 23:209–229.

Ames, K. M., 1994b, The Archaeology of the Northern Northwest Coast: The North Coast Prehistory Project Excavations in Prince Rupert Harbour, British Columbia, Report on file, Archaeological Survey of Canada, Ottata.

Ames, K. M., i.p., Life in the Big House, Household Labor and Dwelling Size on the Northwest Coast, in: *People Who Live in Large Houses* (G. Coupland, ed.), Prehistory Press, Madison.

Ames, K. M., D. F. Raetz, S. Hamilton, and C. McAfee, 1992, Household Archaeology of a Southern Northwest Coast Plank House, *Journal of Field Archaeology* 19:275–290.

ARCAS (ARCAS Consulting Archaeologists, Ltd.), 1991, *Archaeological Investigations at Tsawwassen B.C.*, Report on file, B.C. Heritage Branch, Victoria.

Arnold, J. E., 1991, Transformation of a Regional Economy: Sociopolitical Evolution and the Production of Valuables in Southern California, *Antiquity* 65:953–962.

Arnold, J. E., 1992, Complex Hunter-Gatherer-Fishers of Prehistoric California: Chiefs, Specialists, and Maritime Adaptations of the Channel Islands, *American Antiquity* 57:60–84.

Arnold, J. E., 1993, Labor and the Rise of Complex Hunter-Gatherers, *Journal of Anthropological Archaeology* 12:75–119.

Barnett, H. G., 1955, *The Coast Salish of British Columbia*, The University Press, University of Oregon, Eugene.

Beattie, O. B., 1981, *An Analysis of Prehistoric Human Skeletal Material from the Gulf of Georgia Region of British Columbia*, Unpublished Ph.D. dissertation, Simon Fraser University, Burnaby.

Bender, B., 1989, The Roots of Inequality, in: *Domination and Resistance* (D. Miller, M. Rowlands, and C. Tilley, eds.), Unwin Hyman, London, pp. 83–92.

Boas, F., 1916, Tsimshian Mythology, *Thirty-First Annual Report of the Bureau of American Ethnology 1909–1910*, Government Printing Office, Washington, D.C., pp. 27–1037.

Bogucki, P., 1993, Animal Traction and Households in Neolithic Europe, *Antiquity* 67:492–503.

Boyd, R. T., 1985, *The Introduction of Infectious Diseases among the Indians of the Pacific Northwest, 1774–1874*, Unpublished Ph.D. dissertation, University of Washington, Seattle.

Brumfiel, E. M., and Earle, T. K., 1987, Specialization, Exchange, and Complex Societies: An Introduction, in: *Specialization, Exchange and Complex Societies* (E. Brumfiel and T. K. Earle, eds.), Cambridge University Press, Cambridge, pp. 1–9.

Burley, D., and Knusel, C., 1989, Burial Patterns and Archaeological Interpretation: Problems in the Recognition of Ranked Society in the Coast Salish Region, in: Preprint Proceedings: Circumpacific Prehistory Conference, Seattle, Vol. III, Part 2, unpaginated.

Carlson, R. L., 1991, The Northwest Coast before A.D. 1600, in: *Proceedings of the Great Ocean Conferences, Volume One the North Pacific to 1600*, The Oregon Historical Society, Portland, pp. 109–137.

Chatters, J. C., 1989, The Antiquity of Economic Differentiation within Households in the Puget Sound Region, Northwest Coast, in: *Households and Communities* (S. MacEachern, D. J. W. Archer, and R. D. Garvin, eds.), Archaeological Association of the University of Calgary, Calgary, pp. 168–178.

Cobb, C. R., 1993, Archaeological Approaches to the Political Economy of Nonstratified Societies, in: *Archaeological Method and Theory, Volume 5* (M. B. Schiffer, ed.), University of Arizona Press, Tucson, pp. 43–100.

Connelly, T. J., 1992, Human Responses to Change in Coastal Geomorphology and Fauna on the Southern Northwest Coast: Archaeological Investigations at Seaside, Oregon, *University of*

Oregon Anthropological Papers 45, Department of Anthropology and Oregon State Museum of Anthropology, University of Oregon, Eugene.

Costin, C. L., 1991, Craft Specialization: Issues in Defining, Documenting and Explaining the Organization of Production, in: *Archaeological Method and Theory, Volume 3* (M. B. Schiffer, ed.), University of Arizona Press, Tucson, pp. 1–56.

Coupland, G., 1985, Household Variability and Status Differentiation at Kitselas Canyon, *Canadian Journal of Archaeology* 9:39–56.

Coupland, G., 1988, Prehistoric Economic and Social Change in the Tsimshian Area, in: *Research in Economic Anthropology*, Supp. 3 (B. Issac, ed.), JAI Press, Greenwich, pp. 211–245.

Coupland, G., i.p., The Evolution of Multi-Family Households on the Northwest Coast of North America, in: *People Who Live in Large Houses* (G. Coupland, ed.), Prehistory Press, Madison.

Coutre, A., 1975, Indian Copper Artifacts from Prince Rupert, *Physical Metallurgical Laboratories Report MRP/PMRL-75-3(IR)*, Canada Centre for Mineral and Energy Technology, Energy and Mines Resources Canada, Ottawa, Archaeological Survey of Canada Archives Ms. No. 1079.

Cybulski, J. S., 1975, Skeletal Variation in British Columbia Coastal Populations: A Descriptive and Comparative Assessment of Cranial Morphology, *National Museum of Canada Mercury Series, Archaeological Survey of Canada Paper No. 30*, Ottawa.

Cybulski, J. S., 1979, *Conventional and Unconventional Burial Positions at Prince Rupert Harbour, British Columbia*, Archaeological Survey of Canada Archive Manuscript No. 1486.

Cybulski, J. S., 1993, *A Greenville Burial Ground: Human Remains in British Columbia Coast Prehistory*, Archaeological Survey of Canada, Canadian Museum of Civilization, Ottawa.

de Laguna, F., 1983, Aboriginal Tlingit Political Organization, in: *The Development of Political Organization in Native North America* (E. Tooker, ed.), Proceedings of the American Ethnological Society, Washington, D.C., pp. 71–85.

Donald, L., 1983, Was Nuu-chah-nulth-aht (Nootka) Society Based on Slave Labor? in: *The Development of Political Organization in Native North America* (E. Tooker, ed.), Proceedings of the American Ethnological Society, Washington, D.C., pp. 108–119.

Donald, L., 1985, On the Possibility of Social Class in Societies based on Extractive Subsistence, in: *Status, Structure and Stratification: Current Archaeological Reconstructions* (M. Thompson, M. T. Garcia, and F. J. Kense, eds.), Archaeological Association of the University of Calgary, Calgary, pp. 237–243.

Donald, L., and D. H. Mitchell, 1975, Some Correlates of Local Group Rank among the Southern Kwakiutl, *Ethnology* 14:325–346.

Drucker, P., 1951, The Northern and Central Nootkan tribes, *Bureau of American Ethnology*, Bulletin 144, Smithsonian Institution, Washington, D.C.

Emmons, G. T., 1991, *The Tlingit Indians* (F. de Laguna, ed.), University of Washington Press, Seattle.

Fladmark, K. R., 1982, An Introduction to the Prehistory of British Columbia, *Canadian Journal of Archaeology* 3:131–144.

Fried, M., 1967, *The Evolution of Political Society*, Random House, New York.

Garfield, V., 1939, Tsimshian Clan and Society, *University of Washington Publications in Anthropology* 7:169–340.

Gilman, A., 1981, The Development of Social Stratification in Bronze Age Europe, *Current Anthropology* 22:1–23.

Guedon, M.-F., 1984, An Introduction to Tsimshian World View and Its Practitioners, in: *The Tsimshian: Images of the Past; Views for the Present* (M. Seguin, ed.), University of British Columbia Press, Vancouver, pp. 137–159.

Haas, J., 1982, *The Evolution of the Prehistoric State*, Columbia University Press, New York.

Halpin, M., and M. Seguin, 1990, Tsimshian Peoples: Southern Tsimshian, Coast Tsimshian, Nisga, and Gitksan, in: *Handbook of North American Indians, Volume 7, Northwest Coast* (W. Suttles, ed.), Smithsonian Institution, Washington, D.C., pp. 267–284.

Hammond, N., 1991, Inside the Black Box: Defining Maya Polity, in: *Classic Maya Political History* (T. P. Culbert, ed.), Cambridge University Press, Cambridge, pp. 253–284.

Hayden, B., and A. Cannon, 1982, The Corporate Group as an Archaeological Unit, *Journal of Anthropological Archaeology* 1:132–158.

Hastorff, C. A., 1990, One Path to the Heights: Negotiating Political Inequality in the Sausa of Peru, in: *The Evolution of Political Systems; Sociopolitics in Small-Scale Sedentary Societies* (S. Upham, ed.), Cambridge University Press, Cambridge, pp. 146–176.

Huelsbeck, D. R., 1989, Food Consumption, Resource Exploitation and Relationships with and between Households at Ozette, in: *Households and Communities* (S. MacEachern, D. J. W. Archer, and R. D. Garvin, eds.), Archaeological Association of the University of Calgary, Calgary, pp. 157–166.

Kan, S., 1989, Why the Aristocrats Were "Heavy" or How Ethnopsychology Legitimized Inequality among the Tlingit, *Dialectical Anthropology* 14:81–94.

Kristiansen, K., 1991, Chiefdoms, States, and Systems of Social Evolution, in: *Chiefdoms, Power, Economy, and Ideology* (T. Earle, ed.), Cambridge University Press, Cambridge, pp. 16–43.

Maschner, H. D. G., 1991, The Emergence of Cultural Complexity on the Northern Northwest Coast, *Antiquity* 65:924–934.

Maschner, H. D. G., 1992, *The Origins of Hunter-Gatherer Sedentism and Political Complexity: A Case Study from the Northern Northwest Coast,* Unpublished Ph.D. dissertation, University of California, Santa Barbara.

Matson, R. G., 1976, The Glenrose Cannery Site, *Archaeological Survey of Canada Paper, Mercury Series No. 52,* Ottawa.

Matson, R. G., 1983, Intensification and the Development of Cultural Complexity: The Northwest versus the Northeast Coast, in: The Evolution of Maritime Cultures on the Northeast and Northwest Coasts of America (R. J. Nash, ed.), *Department of Archaeology Publication No. 11,* Simon Fraser University, pp. 124–148.

Matson, R. G., 1985, The Relationship between Sedentism and Status Inequalities among Hunter-Gatherers, in: *Status, Structure and Stratification: Current Archaeological Reconstructions* (M. Thompson, M. T. Garcia, and F. J. Kense, eds.), Archaeological Association of the University of Calgary, Calgary, pp. 245–252.

Matson, R.G., 1989, The Locarno Beach Phase and the Origins of the Northwest Coast Ethnographic Pattern, in: Preprint Proceedings: Circumpacific Prehistory Conference, Seattle, Vol. III, Part 2, unpaginated.

Matson, R. G., 1992, The Evolution of Northwest Coast Subsistence, in: Long-Term Subsistence Change in Prehistoric North America (D. E. Croes, R. A. Hawkins, and B. L. Isaac, eds.), *Research in Economic Anthropology, Supp. 6,* JAI Press, Greenwich, pp. 367–430.

Mauger, J. E., 1978, Shed Roof Houses at the Ozette Archaeological Site: A Protohistoric Architectural System, *Project Report Number 73,* Washington Archaeological Research Center, Washington State University, Pullman.

Mitchell, D., 1983, Sebassa's Men, in: *The World as Sharp as a Knife: An Anthology in Honour of Wilson Duff* (D. N. Abbott, ed.), British Columbia Provincial Museum, Victoria.

Mitchell, D., 1984, Predatory Warfare, Social Status and the North Pacific Slave Trade, *Ethnology* 23:39–48.

Mitchell, D., 1985, A Demographic Profile of Northwest Coast Slavery, in: *Status, Structure and Stratification: Current Archaeological Reconstructions* (M. Thompson, M. T. Garcia, and F. J. Kense, eds.), Archaeological Association of the University of Calgary, Calgary, pp. 227–236.

Mitchell, D., 1988, Changing Patterns of Resources Use in the Prehistory of Queen Charlotte Strait,

British Columbia, in: *Prehistoric Economies of the Northwest Coast, Research in Economic Anthropology, Supp. 3* (B. Issac, ed.), JAI Press, Greenwich, Connecticut, pp. 245–292.

Mitchell, D., and L. Donald, 1988, Archaeology and the Study of Northwest Coast Economies, *Prehistoric Economies of the Northwest Coast, Researchin Economic Anthropology, Supp. 3* (B. Issac, ed.), JAI Press, Greenwich, Connecticut, pp. 293–351.

Moss, M. L., 1993, Shellfish, Gender and Status on the Northwest Coast: Reconciling Archaeological, Ethnographic, and Ethnohistoric Records of the Tlingit, *American Anthropologist* 95:631–652.

Moss, M. L., and J. M. Erlandson, 1992, Forts, Refuge Rocks, and Defensive Sites: The Antiquity of Warfare along the North Pacific Coast of North America, *Arctic Anthropology* 29:73–90.

Murray, J. S., 1981, Prehistoric Skeletons from Blue Jackets Creek (FIUa 4), Queen Charlotte Islands, British Columbia, in: Contributions to Physical Anthropology, 1979–1980, (J. S. Cybulski, ed.), *National Museum of Man Mercury Series, Archaeological Survey of Canada Paper 106,* National Museums of Canada, Ottawa, pp. 127–168.

Norton, H. H., 1985, *Women and Resources on the Northwest Coast: Documentation from the Eighteenth and Nineteenth Centuries,* Unpublished Ph.D. dissertation, University of Washington, Seattle.

Oberg, K., 1973, *The Social Economy of the Tlingit Indians,* University of Washington Press, Seattle.

Olszewski, D. I., 1991, Social Complexity in the Natufian? Assessing the Relationship of Ideas and Data, in: *Perspectives on the Past, Theoretical Biases in Mediterranean Hunter-Gatherer Research* (G. A. Clark, ed.), University of Pennsylvania Press, Philadelphia, pp. 322–340.

Penthick, D., 1976, *First Approaches to the Northwest Coast,* J. J. Douglas Ltd., Vancouver.

Ray, V., 1938, Lower Chinook Ethnographic Notes, *The University of Washington Publications in Anthropology* 7(2):29–165.

Richardson, A., 1981, The Control of Productive Resources on the Northwest Coast of North America, in: *Resource Managers: North American and Australian Hunter-Gatherers* (N. Williams and E. S. Hunn, eds.), AAAS Selected Symposium No. 67.

Riches, D., 1979, Ecological Variation on the Northwest Coast: Models for the Generation of Cognatic and Matrilineal Descent, in: *Social and Ecological Systems* (P. Burnham and R. F. Ellen, eds.), Academic Press, New York, pp. 145–166.

Samuels, St.R., 1989, Spatial Patterns in Ozette Longhouse Middens, in: *Households and Communities* (S. MacEachern, D. J. W. Archer, and R. D. Garvin, eds.), Archaeological Association of the University of Calgary, Calgary, pp. 143–156.

Schalk, R. F., 1977, The Structure of an Anadromous Fish Resource, in: *For Theory Building in Archaeology* (L. R. Binford, ed.), Academic Press, Orlando, pp. 207–249.

Service, E. R., 1975, *Origins of the State and Civilization, The Process of Cultural Evolution,* W. W. Norton, New York.

Severs, P., 1974, Recent Archaeological Research at Blue Jackets Creek, FIUa 4, The Queen Charlotte Islands, *The Midden* 6(2):22–24.

Shane, A. P. M., 1984, Power in Their Hands: The Gitsonkt, in: *The Tsimshian: Images of the Past; Views for the Present* (M. Seguin, ed.), University of British Columbia Press, Vancouver, pp. 160–174.

Stearns, M. L., 1984, Succession to Chiefship in Haida Society, in: *The Tsimshian and Their Neighbors of the North Pacific Coast* (J. Miller and C. M. Eastman, eds.), University of Washington Press, Seattle, pp. 190–219.

Suttles, W., 1951, Economic Life of the Coast Salish of Haro and Rosario Straits, Unpublished Ph.D. dissertation, University of Washington, Seattle.

Suttles, W., 1968, Coping with Abundance: Subsistence on the Northwest Coast, in: *Man the Hunter* (R. B. Lee and I. Devore, eds.), Aldine, Chicago, pp. 56–67.

Suttles, W. (ed.), 1990, *Handbook of North American Indians, Volume 7, Northwest Coast,* Smithsonian Institution, Washington, D.C.

Webster, G. S., 1991, Labor Control and Emergent Stratification in Prehistoric Europe, *Current Anthropology* 31:337–366.

Wilk, R. R., and W. L. Rathje, 1982, Household Archaeology, *American Behavioral Scientist* 25:631–640.

Wobst, H. M., 1974, Boundary Conditions for Paleolithic Social Systems: A Simulation Approach, *American Antiquity* 31:147–179.

Wobst, H. M., 1976, Locational Relationships in Paleolithic Society, *Journal of Human Evolution* 5:49–58.

Wolf, E. R., 1990, Distinguished Lecture: Facing Power—Old Insights, New Questions, *American Anthropologist* 92:586–596.

Wooley, C. B., and J. C. Haggarty, 1989, Tlingit-Tsimshian Interaction in the Southern Alexander Archipelago, Paper presented to the 16th annual meeting of the Alaska Anthropological Association, Anchorage.

Chapter 7

Equality and Hierarchy
Holistic Approaches to Understanding
Social Dynamics in the Pueblo Southwest

STEPHEN PLOG

The issue of social differentiation in the prehistoric American Southwest is not one that has stimulated a long history of research. Most studies conducted prior to the late 1970s simply ignored the topic (particularly in the Pueblo area), making it exceedingly difficult to cite more than a handful of efforts that raise the question explicitly (and even these are comparatively recent [e.g. Grebinger 1973]). In the last two decades, however, more scholars have raised questions about the nature and degree of social differentiation and some have advanced the view that there was a significant degree of social inequality during at least some time periods (e.g., Upham 1982). The subsequent debate over the latter proposal has become one of the more contentious discussions in the Southwestern literature.

This dialectic suggests that scholars are devoting some much needed attention to the social dynamics of prehistoric Southwestern societies and indeed that is the case. Nevertheless, it is clear that most studies of what would be, in most regions, such related topics as aggregation and complexity still avoid the issue completely (e.g., Leonard and Reed 1993). In a region with many extant villages inhabited by individuals descended from the prehistoric peoples and with such a long and rich history of both archaeological and

STEPHEN PLOG • Department of Anthropology, University of Virginia, Charlottesville, Virginia 22903.

Foundations of Social Inequality, edited by T. Douglas Price and Gary M. Feinman. Plenum Press, New York, 1995.

ethnographic research, how has this come to be? Why has so little emphasis been given to the nature and degree of social differentiation and other aspects of social dynamics? The simplest and most common answer to these questions revolves around issues of ethnographic analogy, but the problem is really more complex and deserves to be addressed in greater depth. It is thus worth reviewing the range of contributing factors, beginning with our understanding of the ethnohistoric and historic periods.

THE ETHNOGRAPHIC RECORD: EGALITARIAN OR HIERARCHICAL?

Southwestern archaeologists have commonly highlighted the egalitarian ideology of historic Pueblo societies as one reason to infer that there was little social differentiation in the past. This type of argument raises questions about the use of analogy and the degree of cultural continuity from the past to the present that others have already discussed in some detail (Cordell and F. Plog 1979; Reff 1991; Upham 1982). Here I will be concerned only with the nature of social relations as documented historically.

The egalitarian dimension of Pueblo social relationships is difficult to dispute as there is convincing support provided by classic ethnographies such as those by Titiev (1944) and Eggan (1950). Yet having recognized this egalitarian dimension, it also is clear that there are other aspects of Pueblo society that are hierarchical. Many have highlighted the differential knowledge of ritual and the significance of that knowledge (e.g., Ortiz 1969; Upham 1982), while others (e.g., Levy 1993; see also Titiev 1944:61–62) have focused on control of scarce resources, particularly prime agricultural land. Dozier (1970:154) has concluded that "despotic rule by the religious-political hierarchy did take place in virtually all the pueblos and across the years some Indians lost houses, property and land, and were evicted from their pueblos." Rather than trying to characterize Pueblo social relations using a single label, it seems more accurate to conclude that there are *both* egalitarian and hierarchical aspects of Pueblo societies, a point that has tended to be underemphasized, if not overlooked, during much of the previous discussion in the archaeological literature. As Feinman (1992:179) has argued, "we ought not to conflate egalitarian ideologies with egalitarian social or economic behaviors."

Acknowledging both egalitarian and hierarchical dimensions in Pueblo social organization potentially leads to a somewhat different view of internal social dynamics. Pueblo ethnographers (e.g., Eggan 1950:104; Kroeber 1917:183; Titiev 1944:99) typically stress the role of sodalities in crosscutting kinship units and providing a type of social glue:

> Four or five different planes of systematization crosscut each other and thus preserve for the whole society an integrity that would speedily be lost if the planes merged and therefore inclined to encourage segregation and fission. . . . By countering each other they cause segmentations which produce an almost marvelous complexity, but can never break the national entity apart. (Kroeber 1917:183)

Such analyses thus stress cohesiveness and integration.

Alternative emphases are suggested, however, when we acknowledge the coexistence of both egalitarian and hierarchical dimensions. Crocker (1969:50) has noted that many Native American societies are comparable to the Pueblo in that they are characterized by "two principles of organisation: the inequality of like items related asymmetrically and the equality of unlike items related symmetrically." Crocker's own analysis focused on the Bororo, a society far removed geographically from the Southwest, but similar in terms of many basic cultural principles. For example, compare his statement (1969:44) that "the relations of lineages within the same clan are organised according to hierarchic principles but other, opposed principles underlie relationships between lineages of different clans" with Levy's (1993) analysis of the Hopi village of Oraibi. The similarities are striking. Crocker nevertheless describes the overall structure of Bororo society somewhat differently than the classic summaries of Pueblo social relations such as Kroeber's:

> Bororo society is held together by a series of counterposed *antagonisms and conflicts,* so that units joined in one context and by a single principle are opposed under another . . . persons or units ordered asymmetrically in terms of a pre-existing hierarchy must compete to restrict differences in status. But groups related symmetrically, as equals, exchange to establish contrasting ranks which will secure their complementarity and restrict the grounds of opposition. (Crocker 1969:56; emphasis mine)

Although Crocker, like Kroeber, acknowledges that the multiplicity of relations promotes cohesion in some ways, the difference in emphasis is significant. Whereas discussions of the Pueblo often highlight crosscutting social ties and integration, Crocker accents the tensions and conflicts that also are part of the social matrix.

Some of the most intense conflicts in Bororo villages involve members of different clans in the same moieties. The Bororo "often contrast these clans in terms of the prestige and general behavior of their members and by the amounts and values of their traditional rights" (Crocker 1969:56). Similarly, the well-known schism of the Hopi village of Oraibi centered on two clans, the Bear and the Spider, who are members of the same phratry (Titiev 1944:75). There were many dimensions to this dispute (Whiteley 1983; Levy 1993), but Titiev (1944:75) notes that the Spider people regarded themselves as peers of the Bears because the two clans were "partners" in the same phratry, yet the highest office in the village was held only by the Bear clan and the Spiders were not eligible to be Village chiefs.

Although there may be integration along some planes in Pueblo villages, hierarchical relations create conflicts and tension along others that have been strong enough to tear those villages apart.

The Implications

From this perspective, the internal social relations of prehistoric societies were more dynamic and complex than most of our models allows. Both egalitarian and hierarchical relations probably existed in many areas and during most periods after groups began to depend on agriculture. When we view patterns of culture change over not just decades, but centuries, it should not be surprising if at some points hierarchical dimensions were more dominant and at others egalitarian characteristics were more pronounced. It is therefore critical that we develop more realistic and more holistic models of social dynamics that admit the possibility of hierarchical dimensions and allow for variation in the extent to which hierarchy is apparent. Our current discussions are too often hindered by questionable, *a priori* assumptions about when hierarchy is likely to have developed or when it would not have (Fish 1989:50). We also must recognize the tension and conflicts that coexisted with the integrative ties that traditional interpretations have stressed.

To develop and evaluate more comprehensive and realistic models of prehistoric cultural dynamics we will need to expand upon our typical analyses in order to detect the full complexity of social relations. Assessments of the relative strength of egalitarian and hierarchical dimensions, for example, will require the examination of a variety of different artifact classes (McGuire 1992:3). Put simply, the traditional emphasis on mortuary data will not suffice. Sebastian's (1991:115; emphasis in original) argument that to examine sociopolitical change we must search "not for evidence of leaders, but for evidence of *leadership*" is particularly cogent for a region where an egalitarian ideology has at times been so strong. Southwestern archaeologists have too often stressed the presence or absence of high-status burials in their discussions of social differentiation, while ignoring the imposing public architecture that loomed over their shoulders. And when we examine these multiple classes of data, we also must pose the right questions. It certainly is valuable to estimate the number of hours it took to build a Pueblo Bonito (Figure 1) or a Chaco road and to ask how many households participated in such efforts. But, to paraphrase John Stein (1989:14), households do not independently choose to build roads. Once we estimate the size of the labor pool, the pivotal question becomes how that labor was mobilized.

Figure 1. Pueblo Bonito, Chaco Culture National Historical Park, northwestern New Mexico.

ECONOMY OR POLITICS OR ENVIRONMENT OR . . . ?

There are many possible answers to questions about labor mobilization or other dimensions of social power and inequality. A comprehensive evaluation of those alternatives must acknowledge that economy, politics, ritual, and social relations are not separate, discrete components of human behavior, but are arbitrarily defined aspects of social dynamics that we identify to aid discourse and analysis. As such, it is erroneous to view one aspect as independent of the others. Thus, Titiev (1944:59) stresses that at Oraibi "the sacred and the civil are inextricably commingled in the political structure, for pueblo officials are invariably leaders in one ceremony or another, and all have mythological sanctions for their positions" (see also Dozier 1970:68). Let me quickly add, however, that by interrelated I do not mean "integrated" or "in equilibrium." As the above discussions suggests, some relationships may indeed be integrative, but others may be divisive.

In the models we have developed to explain culture change in the prehistoric Southwest, we too often fail to acknowledge this interconnection and as a result produce overly simplistic formulations in which ritual or social differentiation receives little or no attention and environment and economy are overemphasized. Thus, the tendency for Southwestern archaeologists to place an egalitarian emphasis on prehistoric societies is often reinforced and justified by the view that agricultural production is solely determined by environmental fluctuations. Because both precipitation and the length of the growing season are often marginal for successful farming over much of the region, it is common to stress the risky nature of agricultural production. Some have therefore argued that the potential surplus per capita was low, a significant conclusion if one believes that "ancient complex societies . . . were built on surplus" (Johnson 1989:373–374).

Arguments for little or no surplus production hinge on an incomplete understanding of production, however, since they disregard the impact of social relations. In their study of aggregation, for example, Leonard and Reed (1993:653) argue that "total agricultural production is a function of the amount of available land . . . the amount of available moisture, and the amount of labor." From their point of view, aggregation in Chaco Canyon and at Zuni was simply an effort to increase the amount of labor in response to deteriorating climatic conditions (Leonard and Reed 1993). None of the important questions about internal social dynamics are addressed in their study. How were groups induced to cooperate? Who provided the leadership? Why were villages not fragmented by the internal conflicts inevitable when larger numbers of people live together? Yet as Sahlins (1972:91, 135) has shown, "no compulsion to surplus output is built into the" domestic mode of production, but rather "the political life is a stimulus to production." No estimation of Southwest agricultural production is therefore possible without an understanding of contingent social relations. Nor can we simply assume that when climatic change reduced production, groups always reacted to this stimulus by aggregating.

Certainly some Southwestern evidence already exists to support the impact of social dynamics on production. For example, by recognizing the impact of organization on production in both native societies and early American settlement, Lightfoot (1987) has shown that some Southwestern societies were very capable of producing surpluses. Reff's (1991:278) discussion supports this conclusion by showing that as Southwestern societies were transformed by European colonization, Spanish priests often filled the role of native chiefs—"supervising the distribution of lands, the production and redistribution of surpluses, the conduct of long-distance exchange, and mediating disputes." Similar studies are unfortunately rare, however.

If we ever hope to move beyond the environmentally deterministic perspectives that seem to pervade the Southwestern literature, we must construct more holistic models in which we reconnect the relations that most existing models either have severed or do not even acknowledge. Not too long ago, Southwestern archaeologists neglected the many types of economic, social, ritual, and political ties between local communities as they incorrectly and inappropriately extended the concept of the "amorphous Hopi state" with village autonomy (e.g., Titiev 1944:59–68) into the past. We have made significant strides toward rectifying that problem by developing models of intraregional networks of interaction and by initiating studies of exchange relationships, marriage networks, and shared ritual patterns (Adams 1991; Braun and Plog 1982; Crown 1994; Crown and Judge 1991; Ericson and Baugh 1993; Hegmon 1990; F. Plog 1983; S. Plog 1986; Upham 1982; Upham et al. 1989; Wilcox and Sternberg 1983). We must now continue these types of studies while also focusing greater attention on the many dimensions of social dynamics at two different spatial scales.

One necessary scale involves intensive analyses of individual communities to examine evidence for differential emphasis on equality and hierarchy. The northern Southwest is an optimal area for such studies given the excellent preservation of artifactual and architectural data, the relatively short occupation spans of sites, and the chronological precision that tree-ring dating provides. Unfortunately, the rejection of conclusions reached in some of the examinations of community dynamics conducted early in the era of the new archaeology seems to have inhibited subsequent efforts. Although we may need to ask different questions and use alternative methods, the types of community studies that Longacre (1970) and Hill (1970) pioneered are still necessary. Several recent studies suggest that a greater focus on aspects of architectural patterns may be one productive avenue of study (Lipe and Hegmon 1989; McGuire 1992; Metcalf 1992, 1993).

Additional studies also must examine exchange and interaction beyond the local social network. Despite ethnohistoric evidence for far-flung exchange (Reff 1991; Riley 1987; Spielmann 1991), our models for most prehistoric periods tend to exclude such relationships. Yet these ties may have been a source of labor (Reff 1991), status symbols, or materials necessary to perform rituals. McGuire (1986) is one of the few who has grappled with the potential impact of the fluctuations in these interregional ties (see also Wilcox 1991) without, in turn, placing the Southwest under the domination of Mesoamerican groups.

The lively debate over the degree of prehistoric social inequality in the region that has developed in the last 10 to 15 years is a healthy sign that new questions are being asked. The answers to those questions are sometimes inconsistent with conventional views. There also appears to be a growing acceptance of the idea that some social inequality did exist in the prehistoric Southwest and that we will only hinder our understanding of prehistory by forcing the organizational variation into the long-accepted egalitarian model of Southwestern societies. To better understand culture change in the prehistoric Southwest we must now embed our traditional interests in production and economy within a more complex and more expansive social context.

THE CURRENT EVIDENCE

Although it is valuable to consider how future studies should be structured, it also is important to review what we know at present about the evolution of social inequality in the Southwest. The evidence I discuss in the remainder of this chapter will largely come from the northern Southwest, particularly the Chaco Canyon area of northwestern New Mexico where the first evidence of significant social differentiation appeared in the Pueblo region. Because of limitations of space and expertise, I will add only brief notes on the Phoenix and Tucson basins in southern Arizona and the Paquimé region of northern Mexico. Although there is certainly evidence of social differentiation in other parts of the Southwest, these three regions are perhaps the only ones in which most Southwestern scholars would agree that significant social inequality evolved and was sustained for more than a few decades.

One of central questions posed (e.g., Earle 1991) about the evolution of social inequality is the basis of differences in power, or how social inequality is financed. Both wealth and staple production have been emphasized as alternative answers to that question. These possibilities contrast the "mobilization and disbursement of food and technological goods" (Earle 1991:3) with the mobilization and disbursement of items of symbolic value as the basis of chiefly power. Let me begin to address the question of the basis of power in Southwestern societies by noting a simple but nevertheless important point: there is little evidence of significant social inequality in the Southwest before the evolution of relatively sedentary groups with a largely agricultural economy. Natural plant and animal productivity is low enough through most of the region that mobile, low-density populations generally characterized the pre-agricultural period. Agriculture provided the productivity and locational predictability that allowed sedentism. More importantly, I believe that successful agriculture necessitated modifications of social relationships that substantially altered subsequent patterns of social change (S. Plog 1990).

Many discussions of the organization of prehistoric Southwestern farming communities have emphasized the benefits of sharing, particularly as a means of risk reduction (e.g., Braun and Plog 1982; Tainter 1988:183–186). Three sets of evidence indicate that if the exchange of agricultural products did occur, it most likely was restricted sharing. First, both ethnographic and simulation studies (Hegmon 1991) suggest that Southwestern groups dependent on agriculture had to retain all of their harvest in some years in order to survive. That is, unrestricted sharing has serious long-term liabilities for both individual households and groups as a whole. Second, changes in the nature of village organization and architecture generally show a transition in the nature of storage before and after significant dependence on agriculture. The initial pattern is communal storage in open, visible spaces (Wills and Windes 1989). The subsequent configuration is a tight association between individual residences and storage rooms such that storage areas can be entered only from within the habitation rooms (S. Plog 1990; Wills and Windes 1989). Third, rather than the negative correlation between the intensity of intervillage exchange and annual precipitation that would be expected from widespread sharing as exclusively a risk-reduction strategy, exchange intensity is positively correlated with paleoclimatic conditions that would have minimized agricultural risk (Plog and Hantman 1990; Sebastian 1992). Thus, exchange intensity increased when conditions for agriculture were better and surpluses were more likely; exchange activity then declined when agricultural conditions deteriorated. This pattern suggests that groups opted to limit their obligations when productive risks increased.

Any restrictions on such obligations, however, likely required a transformation of the ethic that characterizes most mobile hunting and gathering groups inhabiting low productivity environments (e.g., Hitchcock 1982:250–251; Leacock and Lee 1982:8–9), an ethic that obligates families to share most, if not all, surplus. At the same time, as mobility declined and individual control of resources increased, the potential for social conflict within and between villages grew in the absence of other changes (Hitchcock 1982:250). These two processes undoubtedly resulted in a transformation of the nature and structure of early farming villages.

The development of alternative rules of social behavior that allowed the accumulation of resources by individual households likely led to, and was initially reinforced by, the smaller villages characteristic of some areas of the Southwest after the transition to agriculture (F. Plog 1974:120–121). Equally important may have been the evolution of lineage organizations that, in comparison to the bilateral kinship patterns typical of many hunting and gathering groups in the western United States, cut potential obligations in half by emphasizing kinship relationships along one line of descent. Restricted sharing arrangements within lineage-size groups produces an expected village pattern that closely parallels the Prudden units or unit pueblos—2–10 masonry storage and habitation rooms and a single subterranean ceremonial structure—long considered typical of the early agricultural period in the northern Southwest. Departures from this pattern did occur, however, and not surprisingly these larger villages were associated with evidence of greatly expanded ritual activity and alternative social arrangements (Wilshusen 1991).

The agricultural diet and the more direct relationship between family size and productivity provided the potential basis and incentive for population growth (S. Plog 1986), and that growth potential appears to have realized just prior to and during the periods when social inequality developed. The density of both people and villages increased and procurement territories decreased in size, a potentially important process if labor mobilization is an important component of the evolution of social elites, whether for agricultural intensification, the construction of public architecture, or in the context of conflicts (Johnson 1989:375; Sebastian 1992). All of these dimensions of the transition to sedentary agricultural communities established a foundation for the subsequent trends toward social differentiation that we observe in some regions. In this sense, staple production undoubtedly was important.

Agricultural Intensification, Surplus, and Labor

Patterns of culture change in Chaco Canyon, the Gila–Salt basin, and the Paquimé region indicate that while simple agriculture and staple production were a necessary foundation for social inequality, they were certainly not a sufficient condition. Although the timing and nature of patterns of change varied significantly among the three areas noted above, agricultural intensification does appear to have been associated with increasing social differentiation in all three regions. In Chaco Canyon, Vivian (1974, 1984) and others have documented what is currently the earliest example of sizable water control systems in the northern Southwest. These systems were based not on water carried by the highly ephemeral Chaco Wash, but on runoff from the bedrock outcrops that primarily occur along the northern rim of the canyon. Runoff was collected and distributed to gridded field areas using diversion dams and small canals. These systems are not well dated, but Vivian (1984:249) believes that simple water collection and diversion features probably were in use in the early tenth century. At the maximum extent of the field systems, virtually all of the land on the north side of the canyon that could be farmed in this manner was utilized (Vivian 1974:109). Vivian (1984:249) suggests that "the placement of early Chacoan towns or 'central places' at drainage confluences seems more important for collecting and controlling water for fields" to increase yields per hectare than as a means of controlling villages within the nearby watershed.

Much more extensive irrigation systems utilizing water from the more perennial Salt and Gila river drainages were a principal component of Hohokam subsistence efforts. In contrast to the very short canals in Chaco, the Hohokam canal networks ultimately included hundreds of kilometers of main canals and branches (Nicholas and Feinman 1989). In more upland areas, away from primary drainages, extensive complexes of agricultural features have been documented, including rock piles, low terraces, and check dams (Fish 1989:40). Similarly, Di Peso (1984:264–268) has described an extensive system of linear borders, terraces, check dams, and irrigation canals around Paquimé in northern Mexico.

Many discussions of these agricultural systems have focused on the greater need for managerial control (Nicholas and Feinman 1989; Vivian 1984) as they grew in complexity, thus creating pressures that may have selected for leadership development. Another dimension of intensified production that has received less attention in the Southwest is the ability of emerging leaders to use surplus from these systems to recruit followers. Although unrestricted sharing is unlikely to be successful in the long run because of the potential for highly variable production in the Southwest, in the short run that same variation undoubtedly attracted those with insufficient resources to those with surpluses. Thus, Sebastian (1992:115) recently has argued that social differentiation evolved in Chaco Canyon as individuals "or the leadership of a corporate group engendered obligations among his/their neighbors through generosity and built a power base by intensifying labor input and thus production on what was already some of the most productive land in the canyon." These two perspectives—managerial control versus surplus production and recruitment—on the sociopolitical ramifications of intensive agriculture are not mutually exclusive, however, as recruitment of followers may have allowed more intensified production, thus increasing both managerial requirements and the surplus that could be used by managers for recruitment.

It is likely that the impressive public architecture in the three areas— Chaco, the Gila–Salt, and Paquimé—is one simple indication of the success of that recruitment. Although Chacoan architecture and, in some cases, the entire Chacoan development seem to be increasingly viewed as primarily a ritual phenomenon by some (e.g., Judge 1989:238; Fowler and Stein 1992), it is important to remember the ethnographic testimonies that ritual and politics are intimately intertwined in the historic Pueblos. We must integrate ritual, politics, or social organization in our models of the past, not separate them. For example, we should entertain the possibility that archaeological evidence of moiety organization in Chaco and ethnographic evidence for similar organization among the Pima are results of efforts to integrate the small lineage labor pools that appear to have been typical of the early agricultural period (Dozier [1970:132, 153] and Adams [1991:187–188] make a similar argument for more recent time periods, but propose the medicine associations and the katsina cult as the integrative mechanism).

Exchange: Subsistence and Prestige

If recruitment did produce surplus production, there is nevertheless no evidence for widespread redistribution of goods as a source of power, a hypothesis that has received considerable attention, particularly in the Chaco region (e.g., Tainter 1988). Rather, local Chacoan exchange seems to be either reciprocal in nature or unidirectional, with materials moving only to the centers, not outward as would be expected in a redistribution economy

(Sebastian 1991:121–124). In all of the areas, however, there appears to be a correlation between political developments and the intensity of regional and interregional exchange of such exotics as shell, copper, macaws, and turquoise, suggesting that nonlocal goods were important in the evolution and maintenance of political authority (McGuire 1986; Steponaitis 1991:212). Lightfoot and Feinman (1982) have noted a similar pattern in the northern Southwest during earlier periods when the first hints of social differentiation emerge.

As Feinman (1992; see also Weigand 1992) argues, it is important to examine exchange and other relationships at multiple scales. Evidence of redistribution within the San Juan Basin may be sparse and connections between Mesoamerica and the Southwest weak (Mathien 1986), but these conclusions do not eliminate Chaco as an (perhaps *the*) important node in northern Southwest exchange networks. Southwestern scholars have tended to neglect the types of interregional exchanges that were so pervasive during the historic period, exchange that involved such items as turquoise, cotton, ceramics, and bison (Riley 1987). Turquoise was a ubiquitous status and ritual symbol in the Southwest and northern Mexico (Weigand 1992); control over "the trafficking of rare, exotic, or valued products was a common mechanism for aggrandizers or emergent leaders to attract followers and prestige in the ancient Americas" (Feinman 1992:180).

When we allow the possibility for these types and scales of exchange, they suggest new possibilities that allow existing evidence to be seen in a new light. Space limitations allow only two possibilities to be outlined. First, we tend to assume that increased corn production was the primary object of intensified agriculture. Recent excavations suggest other alternatives in at least some instances, revealing abundant cotton in flotation samples from the Homol'ovis (Miksicek 1991:98) and cotton pollen in samples from cobbled fields in the northern Rio Grande Valley. Cotton seeds are certainly edible and are not clearly a nonsubsistence resource, but cotton and cotton garments were leading products in the early historic period exchange relationships and were indispensable for people living in a region with such cold winters (Riley 1987:210). We also know that textiles were important commodities in elite exchange ties in numerous areas of the world (Wiener and Schneider 1989). Was agriculture intensification in the Southwest purely an effort to improve subsistence resources or might it also have been associated with the growth of interregional exchange networks and status differentiation?

Second, it seems possible that proximity to trade routes played a significant role in political development. Both historic and ethnohistoric evidence suggest that river drainages were important, but certainly not exclusive, avenues or nodes of communication and exchange in the Southwest

(Brand 1938), and there is an association between those types of locations and some large population centers (e.g., Riley 1987:7, 251). Such a setting seems less applicable to Chaco Canyon, which is typically described as sitting in the center of the arid San Juan Basin, a significant distance from any of the major river drainages (Figure 2). However, the dense, canyon great house distribution actually lies at the southern reaches of that basin, within a small and unique area where the headwaters of the Rio Grande, Little Colorado, and San Juan drainages converge, thus providing access routes to most sections of the northern and eastern Southwest. Moreover, the primary Chacoan roads provide connections between these three important drainage networks. It may be no accident that Chaco is not that distant from Cibola-Zuni, "the key western distribution center for the Pueblo area" during the early historic era (Riley 1987:192) and that both Chaco and Cibola-Zuni seem to have been involved in turquoise trade (Riley 1987:190; Weigand 1992; Windes 1992). The presence of significant numbers of people in the northern Southwest in the eleventh and twelfth centuries and their absence in the sixteenth and seventeenth centuries could explain the more northerly location of Chaco relative to Zuni. Viewing Chaco from such an interregional perspective may explain

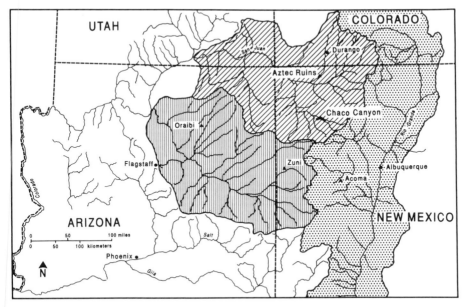

Figure 2. The location of Chaco Canyon in relation to the three major drainage systems in the northern Southwest.

aspects of its development that currently seem anomalous when it is viewed as simply a center for the San Juan Basin or as a transhipment point for commodities heading to Mesoamerica.

Social Conflict

Early models of social change in the Southwest often emphasized conflict between Pueblo groups and outsiders (Kidder 1924:335; Steward 1937), but once studies revealed that the non-Pueblo groups thought to have created the hostilities did not enter the Southwest as early as initially predicted, the possible existence of antagonistic relationships was rarely alluded to for several decades. That omission has now been corrected by the development of new models and by the collection of new data that highlight the likelihood of significant conflict by the late twelfth century (Haas and Creamer 1993; Solometo 1993; Wilcox and Haas 1994), if not even earlier during the Chaco era (Wilcox and Weigand 1993). Recent studies (Haas and Creamer 1993; LeBlanc 1989; Solometo 1993; Wilcox and Haas 1994) discuss a wide range of evidence suggesting that social conflict played significant roles in the evolution of Puebloan groups by at least the thirteenth century. Even such classic "integrative mechanisms" as the katsina cult may have been associated with conflict as much as they were tied to weather control or intergroup cooperation (Plog and Solometo 1994; Solometo 1993). Although we need more thorough testing of these proposals, the evidence from the thirteenth century, in particular, is persuasive and demands that future work devote more attention to this issue. There is still minimal consideration of intravillage tensions or conflicts, however, and this remains an important topic for future studies.

CONCLUSIONS

Prestige exchange, agricultural intensification, conflict, and other changes in social relationships associated with the transition to agriculture and sedentism all appear to have been significant components of the trend toward greater social differentiation in the Southwest. Existing models of culture change too often are overly simplistic and separate aspects of social relations that almost certainly were tightly interconnected. As a result we know less about these issues that we should. With the increasing attention that Southwestern archaeologists are devoting to issues of social dynamics, however, the prospect of a better understanding of such processes of culture change is considerably brighter than it was only a decade ago.

REFERENCES

Adams, E. C., 1991, *The Origin and Development of the Pueblo Katsina Cult,* University of Arizona Press, Tucson.

Brand, D. D., 1938, Aboriginal Trade Routes for Sea Shells in the Southwest, *Yearbook of the Association of Pacific Coast Geographers* 4:3–10.

Braun, D. P., and S. Plog, 1982, Evolution of "Tribal" Social Networks: Theory and Prehistoric North American Evidence, *American Antiquity* 47:504–525.

Cordell, L. S., and F. Plog, 1979, Escaping the Confines of Normative Thought, *American Antiquity* 44:405–429.

Crocker, J. C., 1969, Reciprocity and Hierarchy among the Eastern Bororo, *Man* 4:44–58.

Crown, P. L., 1994, *Ceramics and Ideology: Salado Polychrome Pottery,* University of New Mexico Press, Albuquerque.

Crown, P. L., and W. J. Judge (eds.), 1991, *Chaco & Hohokam,* School of American Research Press, Santa Fe.

Di Peso, C., 1984, The Structure of the 11th Century Casas Grandes Agricultural System, in: *Prehistoric Agricultural Strategies in the Southwest* (S. K. Fish and P. R. Fish, eds.), Arizona State University Anthropological Research Papers, Tempe, pp. 261–269.

Dozier, E. P., 1979, *The Pueblo Indians of North America,* Holt, Rinehart & Winston, New York.

Earle, T. K., 1991, The Evolution of Chiefdoms, in: *Chiefdoms: Power, Economy, and Ideology* (T. K. Earle, ed.), Cambridge University Press, Cambridge, pp. 1–15.

Eggan, F., 1950, *Social Organization of the Western Pueblos,* University of Chicago Press, Chicago.

Ericson, J. E., and T. G. Baugh (eds.), 1993, *The American Southwest and Mesoamerica: Systems of Prehistoric Exchange,* Plenum, New York.

Feinman, G. M., 1992, An Outside Perspective on Chaco Canyon, in: *Anasazi Regional Organization and the Chaco System* (D. E. Doyel, ed.), Maxwell Museum of Anthropology Anthropological Papers 5, Albuquerque, pp. 177–182.

Fish, P. R., 1989, The Hohokam: 1,000 Years of Prehistory in the Sonoran Desert, in: *Dynamics of Southwestern Prehistory* (L. S. Cordell and G. J. Gumerman, eds.), Smithsonian Institution Press, Washington, D.C., pp. 19–63.

Fowler, A. P., and J. P. Stein, 1992, The Anasazi Great House in Space, Time, and Paradigm, in: *Anasazi Regional Organization and the Chaco System* (D. E. Doyel, ed.), Maxwell Museum of Anthropology Anthropological Papers 5, pp. 101–122.

Grebinger, P., 1973, Prehistoric Social Organization in Chaco Canyon, New Mexico: An Alternative Reconstruction, *The Kiva* 39:3–23.

Haas, J., and W. Creamer, 1993, *Stress and Warfare among the Kayenta Anasazi of the Thirteenth Century* A.D., Fieldiana Anthropology 21, Chicago.

Hegmon, M., 1990, *Style as Social Strategy: Dimensions of Ceramic Stylistic Variation in the Ninth-Century Northern Southwest,* Ph.D. dissertation, University of Michigan, University Microfilms, Ann Arbor.

Hegmon, M., 1991, The Risks of Sharing and Sharing as Risk Reduction: Interhousehold Food Sharing in Egalitarian Societies, in: *Between Bands and States,* Center for Archaeological Investigations Occasional Paper 9 (S. A. Gregg, ed.), Carbondale, Illinois, pp. 309–329.

Hill, J. N., 1970, *Broken K Pueblo: Prehistoric Social Organization in the American Southwest,* Anthropological Papers of the University of Arizona 18, Tucson.

Hitchcock, R. K., 1982, Patterns of Sedentism among the Basarwa of Eastern Botswana, in: *Politics and History in Band Societies* (E. Leacock and R. Lee, eds.), Cambridge University Press, Cambridge, pp. 223–267.

Johnson, G. A., 1989, Dynamics of Southwestern Prehistory: Far Outside—Looking In, in: *Dynamics of Southwest Prehistory* (L. S. Cordell and G. J. Gumerman, eds.), Smithsonian Institution Press, Washington, D.C., pp. 371–389.

Judge, W. J., 1989, Chaco Canyon—San Juan Basin, in: *Dynamics of Southwest Prehistory* (L. S. Cordell and G. J. Gumerman, eds.), Smithsonian Institution Press, Washington, D.C., pp. 209–261.

Kidder, A. V., 1924, *An Introduction to the Study of Southwestern Archaeology,* Yale University Press, New Haven.

Kroeber, A. L., 1917, *Zuni Kin and Clan,* Anthropological Papers of the American Museum of Natural History, Vol. 18, Part II, New York.

Leacock, E., and R. Lee, 1982, Introduction, in: *Politics and History in Band Societies* (E. Leacock and R. Lee, eds.), Cambridge University Press, Cambridge.

LeBlanc, S. A., 1989, Cibola: Shifting Cultural Boundaries, in: *Dynamics of Southwest Prehistory* (L. S. Cordell and G. J. Gumerman, eds.), Smithsonian Institution Press, Washington, D.C., pp. 337–369.

Leonard, R. D., and H. E. Reed, 1993, Population Aggregation in the Prehistoric American Southwest: A Selectionist Model, *American Antiquity* 58:648–661.

Levy, J., 1993, *Orayvi Revisited,* University of Arixona Press, Tucson.

Lightfoot, K. G., 1987, A Consideration of Complex Prehistoric Societies in the U.S. Southwest, in: *Chiefdoms in the Americas* (R. D. Drennan and C. A. Uribe, eds.), University Press of America, Lanham, Maryland, pp. 43–56.

Lightfoot, K. G., and G. M. Feinman, 1982, Social Differentiation and Leadership Development in the Early Pithouse Villages in the Mogollon Region of the American Southwest, *American Antiquity* 47:64–86.

Lipe, W. D., and M. Hegmon (eds.), 1989, *The Architecture of Social Integration in Prehistoric Pueblos,* Occasional Papers of the Crow Canyon Archaeological Center 1, Cortez.

Longacre, W. A., 1970, *Archaeology as Anthropology: A Case Study,* Anthropological Papers of the University of Arizona 17, Tucson.

Mathien, F. J., 1986, External Contacts and the Chaco Anasazi, in: *Ripples in the Chichimec Sea* (F. J. Mathien and R. H. McGuire, eds.), Southern Illinois University Press, Carbondale, pp. 220–242.

McGuire, R. H., 1986, Economies and Modes of Production in the Prehistoric Southwestern Periphery, in: *Ripples in the Chichimec Sea* (F. J. Mathien and R. H. McGuire, eds.), Southern Illinois University Press, Carbondale, pp. 243–269.

McGuire, R. H., 1992, *Death, Society, and Ideology in a Hohokam Community,* Westview Press, Boulder, Colorado.

Metcalf, M., 1992, *Patterns of Architectural Change in the Northern Southwest* A.D. *1000–1300,* Paper presented at the 57th annual meeting of the Society for American Archaeology, Pittsburgh.

Metcalf, M., 1993, *Politics and Architecture: Patterns of Labor Investment in the Northern Southwest,* Paper presented at the 58th annual meeting of the Society for American Archaeology, St. Louis.

Miksicek, C. H., 1991, Paleoethnobotany, in: *Homol'ovi II: Archaeology of an Ancestral Hopi Village, Arizona* (E. C. Adams and K. A. Hays, eds.), Anthropological Papers of the University of Arizona 55, Tucson, pp. 88–102.

Nicholas, L. M., and G. M. Feinman, 1989, A Regional Perspective on Hohokam Irrigation in the Lower Salt River Valley, Arizona, in: *The Sociopolitical Structure of Southwestern Societies* (S. Upham, K. G. Lightfoot, and R. A. Jewett, eds.), Westview Press, Boulder, Colorado, pp. 199–235.

Ortiz, A., 1969, *The Tewa World,* University of Chicago Press, Chicago.

Plog, F., 1974, *The Study of Prehistoric Change*, Academic Press, New York.

Plog, F., 1983, Political and Economic Alliances on the Colorado Plateau, A.D. 600 to 1450, *Advances in World Archaeology* 2:289–330.

Plog, S., 1986, Understanding Culture Change in the Northern Southwest, in: *Spatial Organization and Exchange* (S. Plog, ed.), Southern Illinois University Press, Carbondale, pp. 310–318.

Plog, S., 1990, Agriculture, Sedentism, and Environment in the Evolution of Political Systems, in: *The Evolution of Polotical Systems* (S. Upham, ed.), Cambridge University Press, Cambridge, pp. 177–199.

Plog, S., and J. L. Hantman, 1990, Chronology Construction and the Study of Prehistoric Culture Change, *Journal of Field Archaeology* 17:439–456.

Plog, S., and J. Solometo, 1994, Alternative Pathways in the Evolution of Western Pueblo Ritual, *Proceedings of the Twenty-Sixth Annual Chacmool Conference*, Calgary, in press.

Reff, D. T., 1991, *Disease, Depopulation, and Culture Change in Northwestern New Spain, 1518–1764*, University of Utah Press, Salt Lake City.

Riley, C. L., 1987, *The Frontier People*, University of New Mexico Press, Albuquerque.

Sahlins, M., 1972, *Stone-Age Economics*, Aldine-Atherton, Chicago.

Sebastian, L., 1991, Sociopolitical Complexity and the Chaco System, in: *Chaco & Hohokam* (P. L. Crown and W. J. Judge, eds.), School of American Research Press, Santa Fe, pp. 109–134.

Sebastian, L., 1992, *The Chaco Anasazi*, Cambridge University Press, Cambridge.

Solometo, J., 1993, *Conflict and the Early Katsina Cult*, Unpublished honors thesis, Department of Anthropology, University of Virginia.

Spielmann, K. A., (ed.), 1991, *Farmers, Hunters, and Colonists*, University of Arizona Press, Tucson.

Stein, J. R., 1989, The Chaco Roads—Clues to an Ancient Riddle? *El Palacio* 94(3):4–16.

Steponaitis, V., 1991, Contrasting Patterns of Mississippian Development, in: *Chiefdoms: Power, Economy, and Ideology* (T. K. Earle, ed.), Cambridge University Press, Cambridge, pp. 193–228.

Steward, J. H., 1937, Ecological Aspects of Southwestern Society, *Anthropos* 32:87–104.

Tainter, J. A., 1988, *The Collapse of Complex Societies*, Cambridge University Press, Cambridge.

Titiev, M., 1944, *Old Oraibi*, Papers of the Peabody Museum of American Archaeology and Ethnology, Harvard University, 22(2), Cambridge.

Upham, S., 1982, *Polities and Power*, Academic Press, New York.

Upham, S., K. G. Lightfoot, and R. A. Jewett (eds.), 1989, *The Sociopolitical Structure of Southwestern Societies*, Westview Press, Boulder, Colorado.

Vivian, R. G., 1974, Conservation and Diversion: Water-Control Systems in the Anasazi Southwest, in: *Irrigation's Impact on Society* (T. E. Downing and M. Gibson, eds.), Anthropological Papers of the University of Arixona 25, Tucson, pp. 95–112.

Vivian, R. G., 1984, Agricultural and Social Adjustments to Changing Environments in the Chaco Basin, in: *Prehistoric Agricultural Strategies in the Southwest* (S. K. and P. R. Fish, eds.), Arizona State University Anthropological Research Papers 33, Tempe, pp. 243–257.

Weigand, P. C., 1992, The Macroeconomic Role of Turquoise within the Chaco Canyon System, in: *Anasazi Regional Organization and the Chaco System*, (D. E. Doyel, ed.), Maxwell Museum of Anthropology Anthropological Papers 5, Albuquerque, pp. 169–173.

Whiteley, P., 1983, *Deliberate Acts*, University of Arizona Press, Tucson.

Wiener, A. B., and J. Schneider (eds.), 1989, *Cloth and Human Experience*, Smithsonian Institution Press, Washington, D.C.

Wilcox, D. R., 1991, The Mesoamerican Ballgame in the American Southwest, in: *The Mesoamerican Ballgame* (V. L. Scarborough and D. R. Wilcox, eds.), University of Arizona Press, Tucson, pp. 101–125.

Wilcox, D. R., and J. Haas, 1994, The Scream of the Butterfly: Competition and Conflict in the Prehistoric Southwest, in: *Themes in Southwestern Prehistory* (G. Gumerman, ed.), School of American Research Press, Santa Fe, pp. 211–238.

Wilcox, D. R., and C. Sternberg, 1983, *Hohokam Ballcourts and Their Distribution*, Arizona State Museum Archaeological Series 160, Arizona State Museum, Tucson.

Wilcox, D. R., and P. C. Weigand, 1993, *Chacoan Capitals: Centers of Competing Polities*, Paper presented at the 58th annual meeting of the Society for American Archaeology, St. Louis.

Wills, W. H., and T. C. Windes, 1989, Evidence for Population Aggregation and Dispersal during the Basketmaker III Period in Chaco Canyon, New Mexico, *American Antiquity* 54:347–369.

Wilshusen, R. H., 1991, *Early Villages in the American Southwest: Cross-Cultural and Archaeological Perspectives*, Ph.D. dissertation, University of Colorado, University Microfilms, Ann Arbor.

Windes, T. C., 1992, Blue Notes: The Chacoan Turquoise Industry in the San Juan Basin, in: *Anasazi Regional Organization and the Chaco System* (D. E. Doyel, ed.), Maxwell Museum of Anthropology Anthropological Papers 5, Albuquerque, pp. 159–168.

Chapter 8

Social Inequality and Agricultural Resources in the Valle de la Plata, Colombia

ROBERT D. DRENNAN AND DALE W. QUATTRIN

INTRODUCTION

The absence of substantial economic inequality or restricted control of basic resources was a distinguishing feature of chiefdoms or ranked societies in the cultural evolutionary literature of the 1960s (e.g., Fried 1967; Service 1962). The social hierarchies of these relatively simple complex societies were thought to have their basis in something other than accumulation of wealth or the elite's economic control of the means of production. The social hierarchy was sometimes conceived as a vehicle through which members of the elite could provide effective management.

Although this view continues to be accepted by many, it has been challenged by a growing chorus of voices presenting new evidence and new interpretations of old evidence to suggest that much of the empirical support

ROBERT D. DRENNAN and DALE W. QUATTRIN • Department of Anthropology, University of Pittsburgh, Pittsburgh, Pennsylvania 15260.

Foundations of Social Inequality, edited by T. Douglas Price and Gary M. Feinman. Plenum Press, New York, 1995.

for such a stance is weak. Earle (1977, 1978), for example, has argued that the classic accounts of redistributional economies in Hawaiian chiefdoms understate the extent of economic power in the hands of the chiefs and the extent to which these economic systems served to mobilize resources that were then at the disposal of the chiefs. Gilman (1981, 1991:146–149) provides an especially explicit statement of the proposition that even the simplest social hierarchies must be understood in terms of the means of economic control at the disposal of those at the more desirable end of the hierarchy. And Earle (1991b:98), while recognizing the contributions of varied factors to social hierarchy, sees economic control as an essential ingredient as a matter of general principle. This continues to be a subject of vigorous debate, as summarized, for example, by Earle (1991a:5–10).

Our aim here is to delineate and evaluate the importance of some of the ways in which elites in one sequence of prehistoric chiefdom development might either have managed economic affairs or have mobilized resources for their own purposes. Our concentration is on that most fundamental sector of the economy: primary agricultural production. We rely on information from an archaeological study of chiefdom development in the Valle de la Plata, a part of Colombia's Alto Magdalena region. This is the region where the so-called San Agustín Culture flourished for several centuries soon after the time of Christ. Definition of this archaeological culture has emphasized the elaborate stone slab tombs accompanied by large stone statues that it produced (Cubillos 1980; Duque Gómez 1964; Duque Gómez and Cubillos 1979, 1983, 1988; Gamboa Hinestrosa 1982; Hernández de Alba 1979; Pérez de Barradas 1943; Preuss 1931; Reichel-Dolmatoff 1972; Sotomayor and Uribe 1987).

These tombs and statues provide conspicuous archaeological evidence of prehispanic social inequality (Drennan 1994), but until recently the regional settlement context of these tombs and statues has been unknown. Within recent years, however, results of excavations at several residential sites have been published (e.g., Duque Gómez and Cubillos 1981; Llanos 1988, 1990; Llanos and Durán 1983; Moreno 1991; Sánchez 1991), and settlement pattern research has been carried out at a regional scale in the Valle de la Plata (Drennan 1985; Drennan, Jaramillo et al. 1989, 1991; Drennan et al. 1993; Herrera et al. 1989). We present here a summary of the results of one facet of the analysis of regional settlement data from the Valle de la Plata. These data are the product of a systematic archaeological survey of an area totaling nearly 600 km². The archaeological survey has been accompanied by study of modern and paleoenvironments aimed especially at characterizing the region's agricultural potential throughout the prehispanic sequence of sedentary occupation.

VALLE DE LA PLATA ENVIRONMENT

The soils and general environmental parameters of the Valle de la Plata have been described by Botero et al. (1989), and the summary given here is based on their work. At its eastern end the Valle de la Plata (Figure 1) reaches as low as 700 m above sea level. Here the Río Páez is deeply incised in a series of broad natural terraces. The lowest form the current floodplain, while higher ones provide extensive level land. This land today is rotated primarily between extensive cattle grazing and rice cultivation. At these equatorial latitudes, climate at such low elevations is quite warm, with correspondingly high rates of evapotranspiration and, consequently, dry conditions (Rangel and Espejo 1989). Irrigation water is available in abundance in the Río Páez, but the river is so deeply incised that gravity-flow canal irrigation systems require very long feeder canals. Modern rice cultivation depends on raising irrigation water substantial distances from the river at electrically powered pumping stations. Small-scale mixed farming depends on natural precipitation in the rainier months.

Farther upstream, above about 1,000 m (in the north-central section of the map in Figure 1), the valley narrows, and colluvial deposits at the base of the steep slopes on either side reach the river's edge. Since temperatures and, consequently, evapotranspiration rates are lower at these higher elevations, conditions are not as dry, but the steepness of the slopes and the thinness and fragility of their soils constrain agricultural pursuits to the relatively narrow colluvial valley floor. Still farther upstream (to the west), the river and its major tributaries are confined to narrow canyons with very little usable land in their bottoms.

Above 1,500 m, well-watered fertile soils on gentle slopes occur with some frequency, although always dissected by deeply incised streams. This zone (in the south-central section of Figure 1) is today one of mixed cultivation. Corn, beans, and manioc predominate among subsistence crops. Coffee has been the principal cash crop, although recent declines in its profitability have made illegal poppy cultivation an increasingly attractive alternative. Substantially lower rates of evapotranspiration make water shortage a much less severe problem for agriculture than it is at lower elevations, and so one of the principal risks to agricultural production is much attenuated in this sector of the Valle de la Plata.

Conditions become both colder and wetter above 2,000 m (farther west in Figure 1), and agricultural practices begin to include sporadic potato cultivation until low temperatures, very cloudy conditions, and increasingly waterlogged soils bring cultivation to a halt at around 2,400 m. At these elevations today, the landscape consists of cattle pasture of relatively poor quality and

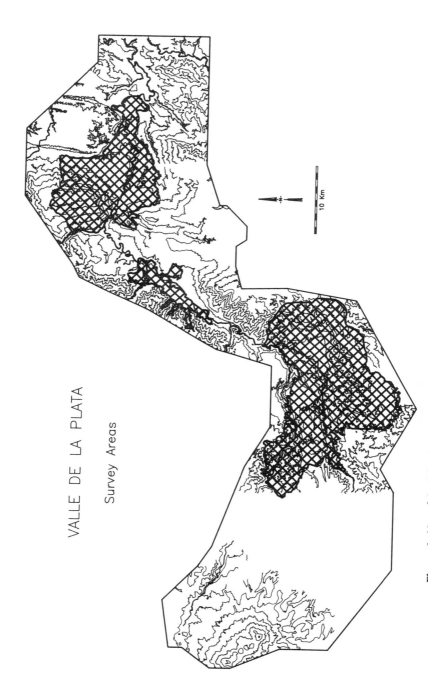

Figure 1. Map of the Valle de la Plata, showing the locations of the three survey zones (cross-hatched).

forest. At 2,800 m, the forest begins to give way to the marshy conditions of the open páramo, capped by permanently snow-covered volcanoes reaching over 4,600 m (at the extreme west in Figure 1).

CHRONOLOGY AND ENVIRONMENTAL CHANGE

The ceramic chronology on which the archaeological settlement pattern analysis is based is illustrated in Figure 2. The general environmental picture

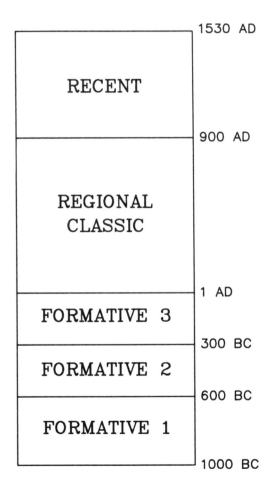

Figure 2. Ceramic chronology for the Valle de la Plata (Drennan 1993:99).

just presented holds true over these 3,000 years or so, although there have been some fluctuations in temperature and precipitation (Drennan, Herrera, and Piñeros 1989). The Formative was a period of somewhat colder and wetter conditions than those obtaining today, with the result that the boundaries between the zones just described occurred at somewhat lower elevations. In general, the lowest elevations would have been at less of a disadvantage in regard to availability of water for agriculture, and the higher elevations would have been more strongly affected by cold, wet conditions.

The Regional Classic period was warmer and, initially, drier. By around A.D. 500, temperatures were higher than they are today. Generally speaking, this represented an improvement in climatic conditions as far as agricultural productivity is concerned—especially at the higher elevations of the Valle de la Plata. Warmer temperatures meant faster plant growth, and, combined with drier conditions, made elevations over 2,000 m more attractive for farming than they had been before. Drier conditions might have meant somewhat greater agricultural risk in the middle elevations, and certainly restricted the possibilities for rainfall agriculture in the lower elevations at the eastern end of the valley. After A.D. 500, temperatures remained high, and precipitation increased substantially as well. Under this regime conditions for agriculture would have been at their optimum for the time period under consideration. The Recent period was one of gradual decline in precipitation and temperature toward modern levels.

REGIONAL SCALE ENVIRONMENTAL DIVERSITY AND PRODUCTIVE SPECIALIZATION

The entire Valle de la Plata study area is less than 100 km long (Figure 1), and the cold and very humid conditions above 2,000 m are in some places found as close as 6 km to the extensive, hot, dry river terraces at 700 to 800 m. Calling broadly upon notions of vertical economy popular among students of prehispanic complex societies in the Andes, it has been suggested that complementary specialized exploitation of the resources of these widely different but closely spaced environmental zones was fundamental to the development of the chiefdoms of the Alto Magdalena (Duque Gómez 1967:296; Reichel-Dolmatoff 1972:14, 1982:70–71, 73–74). Such suggestions have seldom dwelled on the precise mechanisms involved—whether centralized redistribution within a single polity, interpolity or interethnic exchange, management and coordination of production and distribution, mobilization and exploitation by elites who controlled distribution, or other possibilities. By whatever mechanism, however, the varying productive possibilities of this set of closely spaced, vertically differentiated environments have been thought to lead to large-scale economic specialization that encouraged or underwrote the development of social inequality.

Systematic regional settlement pattern survey in the Valle de la Plata spans this full environmental range (Figure 1). The easternmost survey zone covers broad river terraces at low elevation; the central survey zone, the point where those terraces give way to a much more constricted colluvial valley bottom; and the western survey zone, the elevations above 1,400 m. If, at any point in the prehispanic sequence, specialized production in these different zones and interchange of the resulting diversity of products were an important dynamic of the regional economy, we would expect to see substantial occupation of the full range of environments to permit the exploitation of their resources. While the spacing of these zones is sometimes quite close, full realization of such a system of specialized production would entail considerable investment of energy across a patch of landscape too large to be effectively exploited from settlements in only one part of the region. At least semipermanent occupations in other sectors would be required, and these would leave traces detectable in systematic regional survey.

The results of regional survey provide little encouragement to those who would make some species of vertical economy at this scale fundamental to social inequality in the Valle de la Plata. The easternmost zone at the lowest elevations was almost entirely unoccupied during the Formative, although environmental conditions then were probably more favorable for farmers than at any other time. Some occupation did occur during the Regional Classic and Recent, but it was always extremely sparse.

Despite serving as the basis for considerable wealth accumulation in the twentieth century, the soils of these low natural terraces are not very fertile; to be productive most of them require extensive irrigation that would be quite difficult without electric pumps, and their hardness makes them almost impossible to cultivate without heavy machinery. The real contrast between the agricultural resources of this zone and those of higher elevations would appear to be not complementary differences in productive possibilities, but rather drastically limited productive possibilities that made this zone extremely unattractive for prehispanic agricultural exploitation, even under somewhat more favorable climatic conditions than those existing today.

The central survey zone above 1,000 m where the valley narrows sharply, was also almost entirely unoccupied during Formative 1 and 2. Its occupation is considerably denser than that of the easternmost zone during Formative 3 and the Regional Classic, but the total amount of territory of this kind is simply so small that it never carried much demographic weight—not even during the Regional Classic when its occupation was densest. The bulk of the population of the Valle de la Plata in all prehispanic periods lived between 1,500 and 2,200 m (i.e., in the western survey zone). Clearly, the prehispanic inhabitants of the Valle de la Plata did not spread themselves across the full range of environmental zones for varied complementary specializations, but chose instead to focus their settlement very heavily on and around the region's prime agricultural resources—at least when analysis is at the scale of the entire region.

CONTROL OF PRIME AGRICULTURAL RESOURCES AND ANALYSIS AT A SMALLER SCALE

The negative results of investigating complementary productive specialization lead us to ponder the possible importance in the development of social inequality of control over prime agricultural resources. This approach, however, also fails to fit comfortably with the settlement evidence from the Valle de la Plata on the scale it has been discussed thus far. That is, the social inequality to be observed in the Valle de la Plata was not between those in control of the better agricultural resources of the higher western zone and those relegated to the less attractive lower eastern zone, because, even during periods of highest population, the lower eastern zone contained such a tiny fraction of the region's population as to be inconsequential in whatever was the formula of social inequality. The regional patterns of Valle de la Plata society simply seem to be of smaller scale than all three survey zones taken together.

Focusing on only the densely populated western survey zone reveals interesting patterns at a smaller scale. This zone totals 317 km², and Figure 3 shows the distribution of occupation in it during the Regional Classic period. This is the period that produced the famous stone slab tombs and statues of the Alto Magdalena. These occurred at several Regional Classic period sites in the western survey zone of the Valle de la Plata. Although all of these sites have been badly damaged by looting, each of them apparently had between one and four earthen barrows covering tomb chambers made of flat stone slabs. Incorporated into the barrows or standing in the level areas around them were stone statues up to 2 m high. Most of these have been removed from the sites where they were originally located, and many have disappeared entirely, but it is still possible to locate the sites from which statues came, and there may have once been as many as a dozen such statues at some of these sites in the Valle de la Plata. Larger numbers of statues and barrows occurred at other sites in the Alto Magdalena, especially to the south of the Valle de la Plata, in the general vicinity of the modern town of San Agustín. These complexes of funerary monuments provide conspicuous evidence of substantial social inequality, at least in the form of prestige differentiation, in the Regional Classic period.

Looking at the occupation during the Regional Classic in just the western

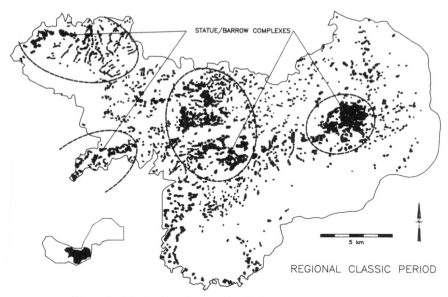

Figure 3. Distribution of occupation in the western survey zone during the Regional Classic period.

survey zone, it is clear that its distribution is far from homogeneous. In Figure 3, ellipses have been subjectively drawn around several areas of particularly concentrated occupation. Noticing these settlement concentrations during the earliest stages of settlement pattern analysis, we began to think of them as prehistoric communities or possibly polities—an impression reinforced when it became apparent that each of the four concentrations contained a single site with a complex of stone slab tombs covered with earthen barrows and accompanied by stone statues.

Despite these concentrations of occupation, settlement in the western survey zone is still very dispersed. The concentrations are not compact, nucleated communities, but rather sizable zones where dispersed households are put more closely together than they are in the intervening areas. Considerable open, presumably farmed, space existed even in the densest parts of the concentrations. Such a dispersed settlement pattern makes it likely that farmers lived quite close to the land that they farmed. Consequently, settlement distribution is likely to be a good indicator of which agricultural resources were most exploited. Farmers might naturally settle in larger numbers in the most productive areas, and this raises the possibility that the concentrations of settlement represent nothing more than concentrations of particularly productive land.

We evaluated this possibility with a study of soils, topography, and climate, resulting in a division of the western survey zone into 20 different soilscapes, each of which was rated for agricultural productivity on the basis of nutrient content and availability, physical characteristics and depth of soil, water retention, and the like (Figure 4). Summary descriptions of these divisions have been provided by Botero et al. (1989), and detailed discussion of their subdivisions and the basis for rating their agricultural productivity will appear in forthcoming reports on the settlement study. These 20 soilscapes range from very attractive to extremely limited in potential for simple agriculture. Geographic Information Systems (GIS) analysis, however, reveals no overall relation between density of Regional Classic period occupation and agricultural productivity ($r_s = -0.108, p > .50$). While the densest occupation is found in relatively productive zones, it is quite clear that density of occupation is not simply a reflection of agricultural productivity—at least not as measured by this approach. The rank-order correlation between density of occupation and agricultural productivity is not improved by increasing the productivity ratings for those zones that would have been more productive under the climatic regime of the Regional Classic period.

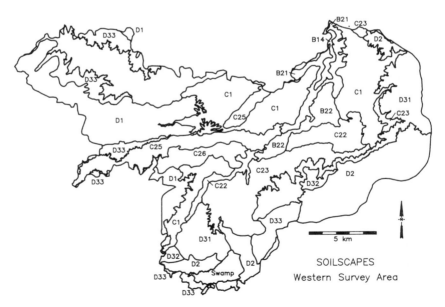

Figure 4. Distribution of soilscapes in the western survey zone (Botero et al. 1989). The analysis discussed in the text was based on subdivisions of these soilscapes into 20 different categories altogether.

There is always the risk that such an absence of correlation between occupation and agricultural productivity may be simply the result of an inadequate characterization of agricultural productivity (or one not directly applicable to the nature of prehispanic agricultural systems). For this reason, we incorporated into the GIS analysis another, entirely different, indicator of agricultural potential—actual current land use in seven broad categories that correspond well to the values placed on the land by farmers today (Figure 5). The source of this information was a study conducted for purposes of planning agricultural development (Unidad Regional de Planificación Agropecuaria 1992).

The most productive land in the western survey zone is today regularly planted in mixed subsistence crops and/or coffee. Less productive land is in grass for extensive cattle grazing. Much of the least productive land is now abandoned cattle pasture and covered with brush. A great deal of primary and secondary forest is left uncleared today because the land is not considered of high enough potential to justify the effort of clearing, although other factors (such as proximity to the network of rudimentary roads in the region) intervene. This approach also fails to reveal any clear relationship between density of Regional Classic occupation and agricultural productivity. Although there is

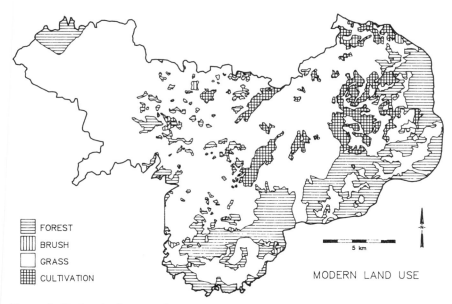

Figure 5. Modern land use in the western survey zone (Unidad Regional de Planificación Agropecuaria 1992). The analysis discussed in the text was based on seven categories altogether.

a weak positive rank-order correlation between the two, its significance level is extremely low ($r_s = .321, p = .48$).

These two approaches to delineating the distribution of agricultural resources of differing productivity levels in the western survey zone were based on different and, for the most part, independent assumptions. It is, nevertheless, impossible to say just how precise either means of assessing productivity is, or to be absolutely certain that either is truly applicable to prehispanic agricultural systems. We thus made yet one more effort to understand the evident settlement concentrations of the Regional Classic as reflections of the distribution of agricultural resources—this time making no assumptions at all about productivity.

This analysis was based on a grid of quadrats 500 m by 500 m covering the entire western survey zone. First, the total area of Regional Classic period occupation was measured for each quadrat individually. Viewed in this way (Figure 6), the settlement concentrations appear as clusters of quadrats with unusually large areas of occupation during the Regional Classic. It is possible that these quadrats might have such dense occupation simply because of some combination of environmental circumstances particularly attractive to Regional Classic farmers. We might not understand the nature of this attrac-

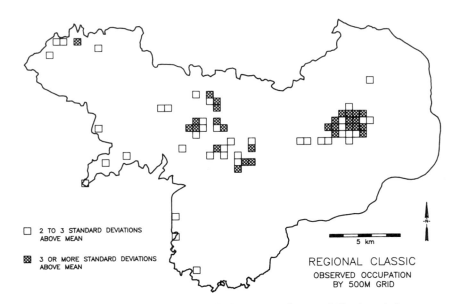

Figure 6. Quadrats with unusually large areas of Regional Classic period occupation in the western survey zone.

tiveness, but if a certain set of conditions was attractive to Regional Classic farmers and that set of conditions happened to be concentrated in these quadrats, then the settlement concentrations might be nothing more than a direct reflection of the concentration of favorable environmental conditions.

We thus extended the GIS analysis to consider all possible combinations of the 20 different soilscapes, 5 different categories for steepness of slope, and 28 different categories for elevation (in increments of 50 m). We calculated the total area in the western survey zone for each of the 2,800 possible combinations of these categories (20 x 5 x 28). We also calculated the total area of Regional Classic period occupation in each of these 2,800 areas. By dividing the total area of Regional Classic occupation by the total area, we arrived at the percentage of total area occupied during the Regional Classic. This percentage of total area occupied was calculated separately and independently for each of the 2,800 combinations of environmental characteristics. This gave us an average or "expected" percentage of area occupied for each of the 2,800 combinations. Given the environmental characteristics of a particular patch of territory, then, we could say what percentage of that patch of territory we would "expect" to show Regional Classic occupation.

Within each of the quadrats in the western survey zone, we calculated the area belonging to each of the 2,800 combinations of environmental conditions. We multiplied this area by the expected occupation percentage for that combination to arrive at the expected occupied area in hectares for that combination in each quadrat. We summed these expected areas for each of the 2,800 combinations to arrive at a total expected Regional Classic occupied area. When this had been accomplished for each of the 500- by 500-m quadrats, we could say how large an occupied area we expected for the Regional Classic in each quadrat, *given the specific environmental characteristics of that quadrat.* The expected occupied area was then subtracted from the occupied area actually observed for each quadrat. This procedure made no assumptions at all about why any particular combination of environmental circumstances may have been considered favorable in the Regional Classic. If, on the one hand, settlement distribution were attributable entirely to the distribution of particularly favorable environmental circumstances, then the difference between the observed and expected occupied areas in each quadrat should be zero. If, on the other hand, the concentrations we had already noted were not attributable to the distribution of particular environmental conditions, then quadrats with unusually high values for observed minus expected occupied area would still appear in the same general locations as for the map of observed occupied area (Figure 6).

As it turns out, some quadrats do have much more Regional Classic occupation than expected, while others have less. Most important, the quadrats with much more occupation than expected are concentrated in precisely

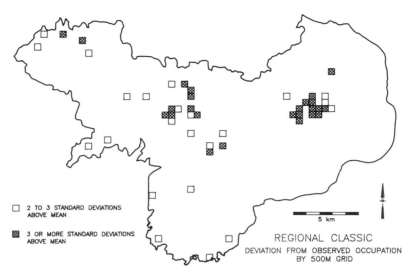

Figure 7. Observed minus expected Regional Classic occupied area
by quadrat in the western survey zone.

the positions already identified as settlement concentrations (Figure 7). This effort to eliminate the contribution of basic environmental conditions to the formation of settlement concentrations, then, failed to make the concentrations disappear or even to attenuate them noticeably. The pattern of observed minus expected occupation by quadrat can be viewed as a topographic surface where elevation represents deviation from expected occupation, and the concentrations stand out even more clearly (Figure 8).

Taking three different approaches to characterizing the distribution of environmental characteristics as related to agricultural productivity, then, we repeatedly failed to find a consistent relationship between density of Regional Classic occupation and either agricultural productivity or any specific environmental conditions. It is not the case that population tended to concentrate in certain areas simply following the uneven spatial distribution of agricultural productivity. This, of course, is not to say that the settlement concentrations existed and were located with no reference whatever to environmental parameters, but rather that they appear to owe their existence more to social and/or political factors than to strictly environmental ones.

Given the existence of such sociopolitical factors, the locations where concentrations of occupation developed consistently had relatively productive soils (although not necessarily the most productive soils of the region) and usually relatively gentle slopes (although again not necessarily the gent-

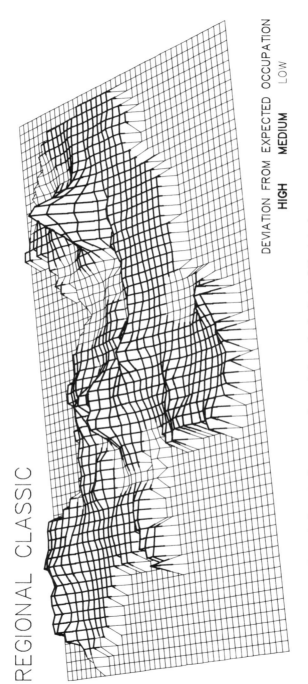

REGIONAL CLASSIC

DEVIATION FROM EXPECTED OCCUPATION

HIGH **MEDIUM** LOW

Figure 8. Deviation from expected occupied area for the Regional Classic in the western survey zone.

lest slopes of the region). Perhaps most distinctive of the locations where concentrations of occupation developed is that they comprised fairly sizable patches of relatively productive soil on relatively gentle slopes. Small, scattered patches of territory of similar or greater productivity on even gentler slopes occurred throughout the region, but they were not occupied nearly as densely as when such conditions occurred in considerable quantity and close proximity.

The GIS analysis at this scale, then, strongly reinforces our original inclination to view these concentrations as the spatial manifestations of individual communities or polities (i.e., as social or political entities rather than as simple, direct responses to the distribution of resources in the region). At the same time, it does not suggest that the most densely settled hearts of these concentrations were in unusually productive agricultural situations, as might be expected if control of prime agricultural land underwrote an economic inequality that was the foundation of social hierarchy. That is, we might hypothesize that the concentrations of occupation resulted from a tendency for population to congregate around wealth accumulations resulting from control over the limited supplies of the most productive agricultural land and consequent relationships of dependency. The presence of widely scattered underoccupied patches with highly desirable environmental characteristics, however, is not consistent with this view. Pursuing this approach further, however, requires proceeding to a still smaller scale of analysis—that of the individual community or polity.

ANALYSIS AT THE SCALE OF THE INDIVIDUAL POLITY

If the settlement concentrations do represent separate communities or polities, then the topographic representation of the deviation of observed from expected occupation provides a systematic basis for delineating their territories. Figure 9 presents this topography in the form of a contour map, in which distinct "valleys" of much lower than expected occupation set the "peaks" of concentrated occupation off from one another. The heavy lines along the bottoms of these occupational "valleys" can serve as approximations of territorial boundaries. Of the four or five concentrations seen in the survey zone, all but two appear to extend well outside the area surveyed. The two that are virtually complete in the survey zone, however, provide an opportunity to carry the GIS analysis to a still smaller scale.

When settlement distribution within each of these polities is compared to the distribution of agricultural productivity, we once again fail to find any overall relationships. Rank-order correlations between productivity ratings of the 20 soilscapes and proportions of area occupied in the Regional Classic are

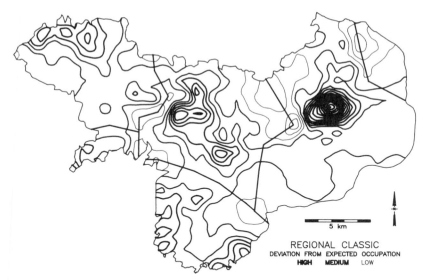

Figure 9. Contour map of deviation from expected occupied area
for the Regional Classic in the western survey zone.

weakly negative and have very little significance for both territories (r_s =
-0.141, $p > .50$ for the eastern territory; $r_s = -0.281$, $p = .24$ for the
north-central territory). Rank-order correlations between productivity ratings
of modern land-use categories and proportions of area occupied in the Regional Classic are moderately positive, but still with low significance levels
($r_s = .667$, $p = .14$ for the eastern territory; $r_s = .464$, $p = .19$ for the
north-central territory).

At the scale of individual polities, then (as at the scale of the western
survey zone and at the scale of the entire Valle de la Plata), we do not find
settlement distribution evidence consistent with the notion that control of
particularly productive agricultural resources formed an economic basis for
social inequality in the Regional Classic period. Failure to find such a pattern,
of course, proves conclusively neither that such control did not exist nor that
it did not lay a foundation for social hierarchy. But it is clear that one of the
simplest and most straightforward indications of such a developmental dynamic that we might expect to find in this case is not present. Clearly, some
parts of the Valle de la Plata did provide sufficient agricultural productivity to
support the concentrations of occupation necessary for the formation of the
communities or polities the settlement study enables us to delineate. If this
condition had not been met, then it would not have been possible for these

polities to take the form that they did in the Regional Classic. This falls far short, however, of saying that the control of prime agricultural land provided an economic basis for social hierarchy. Further expectations derived from this latter view were not borne out by the analysis of the settlement data.

At the scale of individual communities or polities, it is worth considering again the notion of diverse resources, productive specialization, and interchange of basic foodstuffs that we rejected at the regional scale of analysis earlier on. Notions of vertical economies, although they do not seem to apply to the Valle de la Plata as a whole, might work on a much finer scale within the western survey zone. This zone does range from 1,200 to 2,650 m and includes a variety of soils. The different settlement concentrations do occur in somewhat different environmental settings, but especially when the settlement territories delineated here are taken into account (Figure 10), we are not led to think of different polities specializing in different products that would encourage interpolity exchange. The several community cores are located in zones of broadly similar productive possibilities, and each territory includes within its own boundaries a considerable amount of the total diversity available. If this diversity were exploited in a specialized manner, it would seem more likely an intrapolity process than an interpolity one.

Analysis of subsistence remains from recently completed excavations will

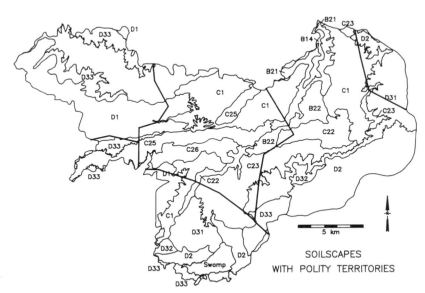

Figure 10. Relation between soilscapes and Regional Classic polity territories as determined in Figure 9.

soon provide complementary information on variation in subsistence practices in different environmental settings in this western survey zone. If such productive specialization seems to have occurred at this scale, then still further investigation can seek to reconstruct the nature of its organization and its relationship to developing social inequality.

THE REGIONAL CLASSIC IN DIACHRONIC CONTEXT

The antecedents of the communities or polities of the Regional Classic period appear in the Formative as well, and their development can be traced for a number of centuries. As early as the Formative 1 (Figure 11), there are tentative indications of settlement concentrations in positions similar to the two Regional Classic ones we have just studied most minutely. These indications become clearer in Formative 2 (Figure 12). There is some shifting of the patterns in Formative 3 (Figure 13). And the concentrations become much more intense in the Regional Classic and for the first time are quite clearly set off from each other by the "valleys" of sparser occupation (Figures 8 and 9). The tendency for settlement to congregate into communities of some kind is recognizable from the earliest sedentary occupation. Like the communities of the Regional Classic, with which they share some of the same locations, the Formative period communities did not consistently locate on the most highly productive agricultural land.

The degree of concentration or centralization of these communities increased dramatically during the Regional Classic. Although it is not reflected in Figures 8 and 11–13 (which show only unevenness of distribution of occupied areas with the effects of environmental variability and of total regional population excluded), regional population size also increased sharply during the Regional Classic period at the same time that settlement concentrated much more tightly into communities or polities. The long-familiar tomb and statue complexes of the Regional Classic suggest that a new degree of social or prestige differentiation accompanied this shift, although it may have much earlier roots. The analysis of settlement distribution in relation to agricultural resources, however, argues against a fundamental role in this process for elite control over prime agricultural resources.

The nature of the Regional Classic tombs and the generally modest offerings included in them have given rise to the suggestion that, whatever social inequality the elaborate tombs of the Regional Classic represented, it had little to do with economic control or wealth accumulation (Drennan 1994). Consistent with the implications of this suggestion, Blick (1993) found almost no evidence of economic differentiation in a small sample of excavated households of the Regional Classic period in the polity located in the eastern

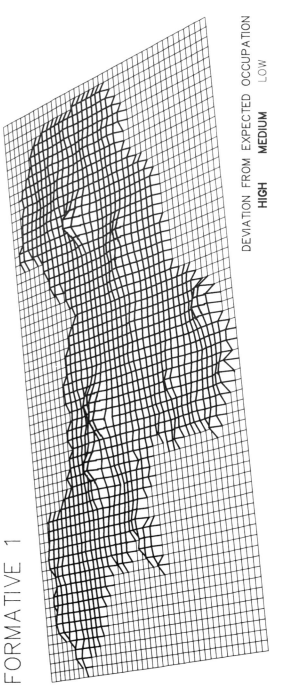

FORMATIVE 1

DEVIATION FROM EXPECTED OCCUPATION

HIGH   MEDIUM   LOW

Figure 11. Observed minus expected occupied area for the Formative 1 in the western survey zone.

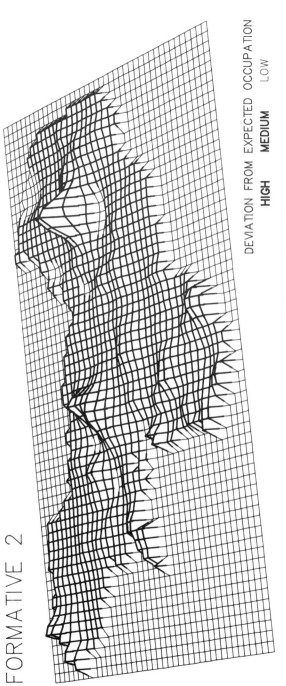

FORMATIVE 2

DEVIATION FROM EXPECTED OCCUPATION
HIGH   MEDIUM   LOW

Figure 12. Observed minus expected occupied area for the Formative 2 in the western survey zone.

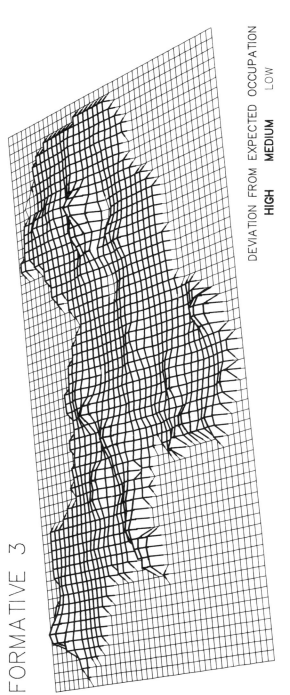

FORMATIVE 3

DEVIATION FROM EXPECTED OCCUPATION

HIGH   MEDIUM   LOW

Figure 13. Observed minus expected occupied area for the Formative 3 in the western survey zone.

section of the western survey zone. Along similar lines, Taft (1993) finds that the patterns of production and distribution of ceramics in the Valle de la Plata indicate that the production of this craft good did not form a basis of economic control or wealth accumulation—at least not during either the Formative or Regional Classic periods. The analysis presented here of settlement distribution and agricultural resources fails to find evidence for yet one more conceivable basis for economic differentiation underlying the social hierarchy of the Valle de la Plata during the Regional Classic.

The evidence available to date, then, leads us to reconstruct a pattern of small-scale, relatively centralized communities or polities in the Valle de la Plata during the Regional Classic period. One of the organizing principles of these polities seems to have been a social hierarchy involving substantial differences in prestige. The beginnings of these patterns are apparent in the Formative, although the Regional Classic marks substantial increase in regional population, much sharper delineation of the separate polities, and much more conspicuous evidence of social differentiation. The economic basis of this social differentiation has proved so elusive in the archaeological record that we must take very seriously the possibility that its primary basis was not economic.

If nonelite segments of the populations of these Regional Classic period polities were not bound to their lower-ranking social positions by economic dependency, then it is worth considering what other factors might have produced such a sharp increase in the centripetal forces of the settlement concentrations in the Regional Classic. Put another way, why would nonelite families have crowded ever closer to the centers where the social hierarchy in which they occupied low positions was most strongly expressed, if they were not obliged to by some economic leverage in the hands of the elites? There are, of course, the potential benefits of a larger-scale more integrated economy. This aspect of Regional Classic polities seems in general to be only weakly developed, although productive specialization based on a range of environmental possibilities within a single polity remains a possibility under investigation. There are also reasons of an ideological nature. The themes of the statues accompanying the burials are often clearly supernatural, and may well have served to legitimate the authority of the leaders of these polities (cf. Drennan 1994). There may also have been competition and even some degree of hostility between polities that encouraged residents of the region to clearly define their membership in one group or another by living in relatively close proximity to its core (although the continued highly dispersed nature of the settlement pattern argues against pervasive warfare or even raiding).

The question can also be reversed: why should families not choose to congregate in central locations? There is surely a social and psychological cost of fully accepting a position of low social rank. There is economic cost in forgoing some possibility of farming more productive land in some other location, although all indications are that populations in even the most crowded portions of the settlement concentrations were still comfortably able to produce an ample supply of food. There is also the economic cost of supporting the social hierarchy, but this would appear to have been fairly low. If elites were prestigious but not wealthy, a very low rate of taxation or its equivalent would have been quite sufficient. The most conspicuous public works related to the social hierarchy that we have evidence of (the funerary monuments), while certainly striking, are on a relatively small scale and would have represented only a tiny fraction of the gross product of one of these polities. Thus the demands elites placed on the lower social echelons were probably minimal. If the costs to nonelites of participation in these social systems were relatively low, then the centripetal forces pulling them together would not have needed to be overwhelmingly strong.

The end of the Regional Classic period represents another set of social changes. It has been suggested elsewhere that the Recent period might represent the emergence of stronger institutionalization of leadership and greater economic differentiation than in the Regional Classic (Drennan 1995). The most conspicuous evidence of social hierarchy (the permanent funerary monuments) ceased to be produced, but this was not a period of decline or dramatic decrease in organizational complexity. Regional population in the Valle de la Plata grew modestly in the Recent period and the settlement concentrations intensified somewhat. Reconstructing the nature of organizational changes between the Regional Classic and the Recent goes beyond the scope of this chapter. We do want to point out in closing, though, that at least some evidence suggests that the Recent period represented neither a continuation nor a reversal of the sequence of progressive intensification of particular patterns that we have described for the Formative and Regional Classic. Instead, there may have been fundamental change in the organizational basis of society with little corresponding alteration in demographic or spatial scale or in degree of regional centralization.

ACKNOWLEDGMENTS

The fieldwork upon which this chapter is based was conducted as part of the Proyecto Arqueológico Valle de la Plata, a collaborative endeavor of the Departments of Anthropology at the University of Pittsburgh and the Universidad de los Andes (Bogotá). Principal funding for the fieldwork was provided by the National Science Foundation (Grant No. BNS-8518290) and the National Endowment for the Humanities (Grant No. RO-21152-86). Further support of various kinds same from the Center for Latin American Studies and the Faculty of Arts and Sciences at the University of Pittsburgh. The GIS analysis was made possible by additional support from the National Science Foundation (Grant No. BNS-9005883).

REFERENCES

Blick, J. P., 1993, *Social Differentiation in the Regional Classic Period (A.D. 1–900) in the Valle de la Plata, Colombia,* Ph.D. dissertation, Department of Anthropology, University of Pittsburgh.

Botero, P. J., J. C. León P., and J. C. Moreno, 1989, Soils and Great Landscapes, in: *Prehispanic Chiefdoms in the Valle de la Plata, Vol. 1: The Environmental Context of Human Habitation* (L. F. Herrera, R. D. Drennan, and C. A. Uribe, eds.), University of Pittsburgh Memoirs in Latin American Archaeology, No. 2, pp. 1–14.

Cubillos, J. C., 1980, *Arqueología de San Agustín: El Estrecho, El Parador, y Mesita C,* Fundación de Investigaciones Arqueológicas Nacionales del Banco de la República, Bogotá.

Drennan, R. D. (ed.), 1985, *Regional Archaeology in the Valle de la Plata, Colombia: A Preliminary Report on the 1984 Season of the Proyecto Arqueológico Valle de la Plata,* Museum of Anthropology, University of Michigan, Technical Reports, No. 16.

Drennan, R. D., 1993, Part One: Ceramic Classification, Stratigraphy, and Chronology, in: *Prehispanic Chiefdoms in the Valle de la Plata, Vol. 2: Ceramics—Chronology and Craft Production* (R. D. Drennan, M. M. Taft, and C. A. Uribe, eds.), University of Pittsburgh Memoirs in Latin American Archaeology, No. 5, pp. 1–102.

Drennan, R. D., 1995, Mortuary Practices in the Alto Magdalena: The Social Context of the "San Agustín Culture," in: *Tombs for the Living: Andean Mortuary Practices* (Tom Dillehay, ed.), Dumbarton Oaks, Washington, D.C., pp. 79–110.

Drennan, R. D., L. F. Herrera, and F. Piñeros S., 1989, Environment and Human Occupation, in: *Prehispanic Chiefdoms in the Valle de la Plata, Vol. 1: The Environmental Context of Human Habitation* (L. F. Herrera, R. D. Drennan, and C. A. Uribe, eds.), University of Pittsburgh Memoirs in Latin American Archaeology, No. 2, pp. 225–233.

Drennan, R. D., L. G. Jaramillo, E. Ramos, C. A. Sánchez, M. A. Ramírez, and C. A. Uribe, 1989, Reconocimiento Arquelógico en las Alturas Medias del Valle de la Plata, in: *V Congreso Nacional de Antropología: Memorias del Simposio de Arqueología y Antropología Física* (S. Mora C., F. Cárdenas A., and M. A. Roldán, eds.), Instituto Colombiano de Antropología and Universidad de los Andes, Bogotá, pp. 117–157.

Drennan, R. D., L. G. Jaramillo, E. Ramos, C. A. Sánchez, M. A. Ramírez, and C. A. Uribe, 1991, Regional Dynamics of Chiefdoms in the Valle de la Plata, Colombia, *Journal of Field Archaeology* 18:297–317.

Drennan, R. D., M. M. Taft, and C. A. Uribe (eds.), 1993, *Prehispanic Chiefdoms in the Valle de la Plata, Vol. 2: Ceramics—Chronology and Craft Production,* University of Pittsburgh Memoirs in Latin American Archaeology, No. 5.

Duque Gómez, L., 1964, *Exploraciones Arqueológicas en San Agustín,* Revista Colombiana de Antropología, Suplemento No. 1, Imprenta Nacional, Bogotá.

Duque Gómez, L., 1967, *Historia Extensa de Colombia, Vol. 1: Prehistoria, Tomo 2, Tribus Indígenas y Sitios Arqueológicos,* Ediciones Lerner and Academia Colombiana de Historia, Bogotá.

Duque Gómez, L., and J. C. Cubillos, 1979, *Arqueología de San Agustín: Alto de los Idolos, Montículos y Tumbas,* Fundación de Investigaciones Arqueológicas Nacionales del Banco de la República, Bogotá.

Duque Gómez, L., and J. C. Cubillos, 1981, *Arqueología de San Agustín: La Estación,* Fundación de Investigaciones Arqueológicas Nacionales del Banco de la República, Bogotá.

Duque Gómez, L., and J. C. Cubillos, 1983, *Arqueología de San Agustín: Exploraciones y Trabajos de Reconstrucción en las Mesitas A y B,* Fundación de Investigaciones Arqueológicas Nacionales del Banco de la República, Bogotá.

Duque Gómez, L., and J. C. Cubillos, 1988, *Arqueología de San Agustín: Alto de Lavapatas,* Fundación de Investigaciones Arqueológicas Nacionales del Banco de la República, Bogotá.

Earle, T. K., 1977, A Reappraisal of Redistribution: Complex Hawaiian Chiefdoms, in: *Exchange Systems in Prehistory* (T. K. Earle and J. E. Ericson, eds.), Academic Press, New York, pp. 213–229.

Earle, T. K., 1978, *Economic and Social Organization of a Complex Chiefdom: The Halelea District, Kaua'i, Hawaii,* Anthropological Papers, Museum of Anthropology, University of Michigan, No. 63.

Earle, T. K., 1991a, The Evolution of Chiefdoms, in: *Chiefdoms: Power, Economy, and Ideology* (T. Earle, ed.), Cambridge University Press, Cambridge, pp. 1–15.

Earle, T. K., 1991b, Property Rights and the Evolution of Chiefdoms, in: *Chiefdoms: Power, Economy, and Ideology* (T. Earle, ed.), Cambridge University Press, Cambridge, pp. 71–99.

Fried, M. H., 1967, *The Evolution of Political Society,* Random House, New York.

Gamboa Hinestrosa, P., 1982, *La Escultura en la Sociedad Agustiniana,* Ediciones Centro de Investigación y Educación Cooperativas (Universidad Nacional de Colombia), Bogotá.

Gilman, A., 1981, The Development of Social Stratification in Bronze Age Europe, *Current Anthropology* 22:1–24.

Gilman, A., 1991, Trajectories towards Social Complexity in the Later Prehistory of the Mediterranean, in: *Chiefdoms: Power, Economy, and Ideology* (T. Earle, ed.), Cambridge University Press, Cambridge, pp. 146–168.

Hernández de Alba, G., 1979, *La Cultura Arqueológica de San Agustín,* Carlos Valencia Editores, Bogotá.

Herrera, L. F., R. D. Drennan, and C. A. Uribe (eds.), 1989, *Prehispanic Chiefdoms in the Valle de la Plata, Vol. 1: The Environmental Context of Human Habitation,* University of Pittsburgh Memoirs in Latin American Archaeology, No. 2.

Llanos Vargas, H., 1988, *Arqueología de San Agustín: Pautas de Asentamiento en el Cañon del Río Granates—Saladoblanco,* Fundación de Investigaciones Arqueológicas Nacionales del Banco de la República, Bogotá.

Llanos Vargas, H., 1990, *Proceso Histórico Prehispánico de San Agustín en el Valle de Laboyos (Pitalito—Huila),* Fundación de Investigaciones Arqueológicas Nacionales del Banco de la República, Bogotá.

Llanos Vargas, H., and A. Durán de Gómez, 1983, *Asentamientos Prehispánicos de Quinchana, San Agustín,* Fundación de Investigaciones Arqueológicas Nacionales del Banco de la República, Bogotá.

Moreno González, L., 1991, *Pautas de Asentamiento Agustinianas en el Noroccidente de Saladoblanco (Huila),* Fundación de Investigaciones Arqueológicas Nacionales del Banco de la República, Bogotá.

Pérez de Barradas, J., 1943, *Arqueología Agustiniana: Excavaciones Arqueológicas Realizadas de Marzo a Diciembre 1937.* Imprenta Nacional, Bogotá.

Preuss, K. T., 1931, *Arte Monumental Prehistórico: Excavaciones Hechas en el Alto Magdalena y San Agustín (Colombia). Comparación Arqueológica con las Manifestaciones Artísticas de las Demás Civilizaciones Americanas,* Escuelas Salesianas de Tipografía y Fotograbado, Bogotá.

Rangel Ch., J. O., and N. E. Espejo B., 1989, Climate, in: *Prehispanic Chiefdoms in the Valle de la Plata, Vol. 1: The Environmental Context of Human Habitation* (L. F. Herrera, R. D. Drennan, and C. A. Uribe, eds.), University of Pittsburgh Memoirs in Latin American Archaeology, No. 2.

Reichel-Dolmatoff, G., 1972, *San Agustín: A Culture of Colombia,* Praeger, New York.

Reichel-Dolmatoff, G., 1982, Colombia Indígena: Período Prehispánico, in: *Manual de Historia de Colombia,* Vol. 1, Instituto Colombiano de Cultura, Bogotá.

Sánchez, C. A., 1991, *Arqueología del Valle de Timaná (Huila),* Fundación de Investigaciones Arqueológicas Nacionales del Banco de la República, Bogotá.

Service, E. R., 1962, *Primitive Social Organization: An Evolutionary Perspective,* Random House, New York.

Sotomayor, M. L., and M. V. Uribe, 1987, *Estatuaria del Macizo Colombiano,* Instituto Colombiano de Antropología, Bogotá.

Taft, M. M., 1993, Part Two: Patterns of Ceramic Production and Distribution, in: *Prehispanic Chiefdoms in the Valle de la Plata, Vol. 2: Ceramics—Chronology and Craft Production* (R. D. Drennan, M. M. Taft, and C. A. Uribe, eds.), University of Pittsburgh Memoirs in Latin American Archaeology, No. 5, pp. 103–185.

Unidad Regional de Planificación Agropecuaria, 1992, *Anuario Estadístico Agropecuario, Departamento del Huila, 1990,* Ministerio de Agricultura, Gobernación del Huila, Neiva, Huila, Colombia.

Chapter *9*

Prehistoric European Chiefdoms
Rethinking "Germanic" Societies

ANTONIO GILMAN

INTRODUCTION

Inequality is a somewhat slippery concept. As Price and Hayden stress in their contributions to this volume, any society is liable to contain potential aggrandizers; and the constraints that suppress these ambitious individuals altogether are imposed only by relatively few societies, all of them (in the ethnographic record, at least) operating in extremely harsh environments, where risk pooling is imperative, and individual accumulation is counterproductive. As a result, one can find some foreshadowing of the characteristics of fully developed "complexity" in almost any simple society. Within the household, as Blanton indicates in his contribution, inequality is pervasive, and households are the charters for society. "Marginalization," the dimension of inequality emphasized in Arnold's contribution, likewise occurs at all social scales: within households as well as between them, within settlements and between them, within polities and between them, and so on. The whole thrust of Boasian relativism was to stress these continuities in the social evolutionary

ANTONIO GILMAN • Department of Anthropology, California State University, Northridge, California 91330-8244.

Foundations of Social Inequality, edited by T. Douglas Price and Gary M. Feinman. Plenum Press, New York, 1995.

scale: the similarities to be found in societies of vastly different scales suggested their essential parity as historical outcomes.

When evolutionists emphasize these similarities, it is not in the service of relativism, of course, but of functionalism and science: the parallels demonstrate the underlying similarity of the causal processes that generated them. As Feinman's contribution argues, aggrandizers at whatever point of the social evolutionary scale can mobilize the resources they require either internally (using a "corporate" strategy) or externally (using a "network" strategy): use by leaders of one or another strategy is attested in tribes, in chiefdoms, and in states. (In the latter, the internal and external strategies would correspond to the distinction between staple and wealth finance drawn by D'Altroy and Earle [1985].) Most processualist models are adaptationist ones, in which chiefs, as Sahlins (1972:140) put it, "institute a public economy greater than the sum of its household parts." Leaders organize, and that organization benefits themselves and their adherents. Inequality arises because of the distribution of these benefits.

All of this is very well, of course, in societies that are, to use Hayden's terms, "transegalitarian," but in "hierarchically stratified" ones, the inequalities that originally were based on the greater initiative of aggrandizers become largely ascribed: inequalities become institutionalized, and those who are more equal than others may fail to organize investments, coordinate long-distance exchange, lead war parties, or sponsor feasts, and still remain powerful. This is a critical turning point in social evolution, and not just in conceptual terms: just as farmers rarely go back to foraging, stratified societies rarely return to being transegalitarian. The elite, once it becomes entrenched, has means of coercion with which to defend itself, and can only be displaced by rival coercers, who can in turn entrench themselves. Inequality, to the extent that it is hereditary, is based on exploitation, and must be explained differently than inequality that is the result of individual initiative and ambition.

MODELS OF SOCIAL INEQUALITY

The later prehistoric record in Europe clearly exhibits the progressive development of social complexity. Until the late 1960s, the development of prehistoric European societies was understood in terms of a pervasive, lasting center–periphery relation to the Near East. For a variety of reasons, the *ex Oriente lux* account of European prehistoric development has been replaced by an evolutionist one, which stresses the autochthonous character of that development. What is odd, however, is that one form of Orientalism has been replaced by another. For Childe (1958) the divergent trajectories of European and Near Eastern culture history were the result of different degrees of

political and economic centralization. The weakness of state power and consequent economic acephaly of Europe would lead to social evolution beyond
the constraints imposed by Asiatic political economies. In recent years, however, the preferred models for the development of social complexity in Europe have stressed the importance of centralized economic systems in which
elites would have gained their privileges thanks to their managerial positions.
Europe becomes populated with, as it were, diminutive *Tempelwirtschaften*,
smaller only in scale to the larger managerial centers of the Orient. Halstead
and O'Shea's (1982) notion that the ruler of a Bronze Age palace in the Aegean
was "a friend in need [who was] a friend indeed" is typical of the integratio-
nism that has constituted the mainstream of the "new" archaeological reinterpretation of European prehistory.

Although adaptationist models of the origins of class-stratified societies
are still universal in introductory anthropology textbooks, they seem to have
lost ground among researchers over the course of the past decade or so (cf.
Earle 1991). As a result, perhaps, of the vigorous criticism directed at adapt-
ationism, we no longer are presented with straightforward scenarios showing
off ruling elites in the active voice as munificent squires and managers of the
common wealth. Instead, adaptationists put forward their views in carefully
impersonal language. Halstead and O'Shea, for example, have more recently
characterized the role of elites as insurers of last resort against peasant subsistence failures as follows:

> The most powerful [risk-buffering] mechanisms, and the most costly, are those
> that cope with problems of unusual severity or exceptional scale. Although prone
> to falling into disuse because of the infrequency with which they are activated,
> these high-level coping mechanisms may serve a critical function in cases of ex-
> treme shortage. As a result there is strong selective pressure for them to become
> increasingly embedded within more regular cultural practices and so, potentially,
> to develop widespread ramifications throughout the social system. In this way, the
> critical energy or information required for the operation of the risk-buffering
> mechanism is maintained, but often at the cost of considerably reduced efficiency.
> (Halstead and O'Shea 1989:5–6)

Now it seems to me only fair that we demand of theorists of emergent
stratification that they answer Lenin's questions: "Who? Whom?" I suppose
that what the above account means to indicate is that peasants would give
landowners a portion of their production in good years, that much of this
production would go to support the comparatively high living of the landowners (this would be the "considerably reduced efficiency" that Halstead and
O'Shea mention), but that in the occasional bad years landowners would in
fact give peasants enough assistance ("energy" would no doubt be more
appreciated than "information") to enable the peasants to get by.

The difficulty with this account is that it is not particularly realistic. It is certain that peasants pay landowners rent in good years and that landowners spend most of that rent as best suits them, but it is not equally certain that the peasants will get help from landowners in bad years: sometimes they do, often they don't. An example from the part of the world I am most familiar with may not be out of place. Reher's recent economic and demographic history of sixteenth- to nineteenth-century Cuenca in central Spain makes it clear that "high-level coping mechanisms" were *supposed* to exist:

> In times of famine towns [were better off than rural areas] because those who controlled the greatest amount of wheat in society, such as the bishop or certain nobles, lived in towns and were the first to be called upon to help in times of crisis. . . . Municipal *pósitos* or storage granaries were also key elements in a system designed to control prices and guarantee supplies. (Reher 1990:156–157)

But the high-level coping mechanisms did not work. The nonresident poor had to be expelled from towns. Once again, Reher:

> In contemporary documents . . . hoarders were blamed over and over again as the instigators of dearth. Who were they? . . . In Castile [where estates were small] the hoarders were local farmers, while in Andalusia [where estates were large] they were invariably nobles. In all areas, suspicion often fell on local authorities or even on the Church. In other words, locally it was . . . those in power . . . who were involved in hoarding. (1990:157)

In systemic terms, then, the homeostatic regulator was not redistribution, but starvation and pestilence. This may not be what Halstead and O'Shea envision, but it is scarcely an exceptional case. With slight variations, the situation in early modern Spain is documented in all agrarian class societies. In good years, peasants, to the extent that they lack power, pay rent; in bad years, peasants, to the extent that they lack power, have no claim on surplus. Adaptationist accounts of the origins of class societies fail because they ignore the differential distribution of power, the principal feature of such societies that requires explanation.

It testifies to the ideological prestige of adaptationist models that they have been widely adopted even by Europeanist prehistorians. Students of European culture history certainly cannot fail to be familiar with a variety of class-stratified social systems that do not easily fit adaptationist models. The exploitative character of feudalism or of Scottish clans is part of our general historical consciousness, even when those social formations are romanticized. In *Kidnapped,* for example, Robert Louis Stevenson has Alan Breck explain to David Balfour how his kinsman collects tribute after the Jacobite defeat in the '45:

> Now, the tenants of Appin have to pay a rent to King George; but their hearts are staunch, they are true to their chief; and what with love and a bit of pressure, and maybe a threat or two, the poor folk scrape up a second rent for Ardshiel. . . . And

it's wonderful to me how little pressure is needed. But that's the handiwork for my kinsman and my father's friend, James of the Glens, . . . Ardshiel's half-brother. He it is that gets the money in, and does the management. (Stevenson 1959 [orig. 1886]:86–87)

In this sense, at least, "managerial" functions can universally and realistically be attributed to elites: they must apply pressure if they are to obtain tribute.

GERMANIC SOCIAL FORMATIONS

The clans of Highland Scotland were, of course, the last surviving examples of the European barbarian societies whose earliest ethnohistoric documentation is in Tacitus's *Germania,* whence the "Germanic" social formation discussed by Marx (1964 [orig. 1857–1858]:78–83) in the *Formen* and Engels (1972 [orig. 1884]:192–216) in the *Origin of the Family.* With some exceptions (e.g., Thomas 1987), Europeanist prehistorians in the West have not paid the attention to the Germanic social formation that it deserves. This is partly due to the sketchiness of Marx's and Engels's own treatment of the subject, partly to the rather formidable scholastic apparatus of the Marxist tradition (e.g., Bonte 1977) and partly to political considerations. All the same, the central features underlined by Marx and Engels are ones familiar in the social landscapes of later prehistoric and protohistoric Europe. These features are: (1) the autonomy of households in their production ("every individual household contains an entire economy, forming as it does an independent centre of production" [Marx 1964:79]); (2) the coalition of households into tribal assemblies ("the isolated, independent family settlement, guaranteed by means of its association with other such settlements . . . , and their occasional assembly for purposes of war, religion, and settlement of legal disputes, etc., which establishes their mutual surety" [Marx 1964:80]); and (3) the development of hereditary leadership from the military and judicial activities of the assembly ("assembly of the people, council of the chiefs of the gentes, and military leader who is already striving for real monarchic power, . . . [this] was the model constitution of the upper stage of barbarism [Engels 1972:205]).

Recent studies by Byock (1988), Miller (1990), Durrenberger (1992), and others of medieval Icelandic society during the period of the Free State (the tenth to thirteenth centuries), based on analysis of the saga literature, give us a more complete and coherent picture of the workings of this constitution. Marx and Engels had no basis on which to discuss, for example, the productive base of the political system. In Iceland, production was based on an intensive livestock-raising and fishing complex. This involved the accumulation of chattel, developed land, and so on, which could be the object of profitable disputes between their possessors. (In Iceland, of course, livestock production and fishing predominated, but elsewhere in Europe intensified agricultural activities would have added to the potential for conflicting claims on productive resources.) Households were autonomous production units whose activities at times brought them into conflict with neighboring households over access to pasture, prime salmon runs, and so on. Such disputes might be settled by direct compromise between the claimants or (since there were no state institutions) by violent conflict, feuds in which the disputants sought to obtain the assistance of kinsmen and others to defend their interests. Such disputes were ultimately arbitrated by the local or national judicial assembly (*alþingi*). To obtain justice at such assemblies farmers had in practice to be represented by a chieftain (goði, pl. *goðar*). *Goðar* were experienced, wealthy, and powerful individuals who could act as legal advocates and as enforcers of the assembly's judicial decisions, and whose fees for their services (in land and chattel) were one important source of their greater wealth and power. The larger land holdings of the chieftains provided them, of course, with rent from their tenant clients. *Goðar* could obtain their positions by achievement, but over the course of the Free State's history, it appears that ascription became progressively more important. The chieftains "solidified their political control in the eleventh and twelfth centuries. By the thirteenth century a small group of the more powerful chieftains . . . emerged from the more wealthy and powerful chieftain families" (Byock 1988:11). The turmoil associated with the concentration of power and wealth in the hands of this group led to the end of the Free State in 1262–1264, when the Icelandic assembly agreed to pay tribute to the Norwegian crown.

Here then is a situation in which stratification emerges without any redistributive function being carried out by those who become more equal than others, and it is clear that the Icelandic case has many parallels. The cattle lords of Celtic Ireland (Patterson 1991), the petty aristocratic bandits of the "reiver economy" of the sixteenth-century borderlands between England and Scotland (Fraser 1972) show substantial parallels to the Iceland of the sagas. The tribal interstices of the Mediterranean world exhibit a similar social dynamic (Figure 1). The Aith Waryaghar of the Moroccan Rif studied by Hart (1976, see also Munson 1989) are a well-documented example. In the ethnographic present they were an acephalous society that practiced a standard Mediterranean polyculture involving plow agriculture, irrigation, tree crop cultivation, and small-scale livestock raising. Their dominant political institution was the blood feud between factions (*lfuf,* sing. *liff*), feuds that arose in competition over arable land. A strongly egalitarian ideology dampened the overt recognition of class distinctions, but there certainly existed considerable differences in land holdings, with the larger landowners serving as patrons to their tenant clients. Political leadership was in the hands of the *imgharen* (sing. *amghar*), the councilors at the weekly market council (a judicial as-

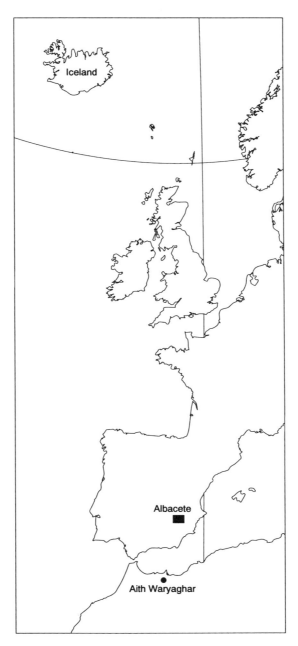

Figure 1. Location of principal areas discussed in this chapter.

sembly analogous in its functions to the local Icelandic *þing*). The power of an *amghar* "was measured in terms of 1) his own physical courage; 2) the number of his agnates, *liff* allies, affines, and other constituents, and the number of guns they could command; and 3) his wealth and personal resources" (Hart 1976:284). As heads of their *lfuf, imgharen* were the leaders in factional quarrels, but at the same time they restrained conflict: they protected outsiders in exchange for a fee, arranged pacts between *lfuf,* and imposed (and guaranteed the collection) of fines for crimes condemned by the judicial assembly. As Hart puts matters:

> Intense egalitarianism; intense competition for council membership (which was what constituted "political office")—rooted, of course, in equally intense competition for land; the principle of self-help carried to its most logical extreme, which is to say, to the bloodfeud; the intense mistrust of one and all by one and all; and the total destitution and banishment of those who murdered their fellow tribesmen on market day, the one decreed day of peace; these were the hallmarks of Aith Waryaghar politics. (1976:292–293)

The Aith Waryaghar case illustrates, then, how an intensified agriculture stimulates rivalries and conflicts of which the beneficiaries are the wealthy purveyors of effective violence. As Hart (1976:445) says, "a successful *amghar* . . . in Waryagharland resembles nothing so much, perhaps, as a successful *capo mafiosi* in La Cosa Nostra."

Similar situations are found in many Mediterranean and Near Eastern enclaves where the power of the state is not fully effective (e.g., Hasluck 1954), and over this range of cases, as Black-Michaud (1975) points out, among sedentary agriculturalists dependent on fixed, relatively scarce sources of land and water, the internecine violence is more uncompromising than among pastoral, nomadic groups. They are also found further afield. For example, Barton's (1922, 1949, 1969 [orig. 1919]) accounts of the Ifugao and Kalinga involve many of these same characteristics, but evolutionists have tended to ignore them. This no doubt is due to their systems-functionalist predilections, but the "Germanic" model has also been the victim of an early case of ethnographic revisionism.

Certainly many of the particular characteristics of the Germanic social formations documented from the history and ethnography of regions such as north-west Europe and the Mediterranean are colored by the fact they are found in societies that are peripheral to established states. Certainly, this would appear to be the case of the strongly egalitarian ideologies prevalent in the Mediterranean cases. As Black-Michaud (1975:148) points out,

> where local office holders acting on behalf of a central government are unsupported by effective coercive force, feud will function as an instrument of "democratization" to maintain a tradition of equality in the face of efforts from above to impose a pyramid of executive authority.

Among the Aith Waryaghar, for example, "dominant *imgharen* competed to be the official representative (and tax collector)" for the Moroccan *makhzen* (Munson 1989:396), and the intense competition to become dominant would have prevented incumbents from becoming too comfortably entrenched in their positions. The eventual failure of Icelandic commoners to restrain the ambitions of their *goðar* led to the end of the Free State. One of the reasons for which the Germanic model may have been ignored is the relative frailty of the contexts in which it is documented ethnohistorically and ethnographically.

THE BRONZE AGE OF IBERIA

Here, then, archaeological evidence may have something to contribute. In later prehistoric Europe there were no states, and the conditions for the development of Germanic institutions would have occurred entirely beyond the reach of their contaminating influences, independent of any dialectic with established centers of power. To explore such scenarios, over the past several years, my colleagues, Manuel Fernández-Miranda (of the Complutense University, Madrid), María Dolores Fernández-Posse and Concepción Martín (both of the Ministry of Culture, Madrid), and I have been engaged in an archaeological settlement-pattern and land-use survey of the Bronze Age in northern Albacete province, Spain, part of La Mancha. Study of Bronze Age settlement patterns in La Mancha provides a clear opportunity for establishing whether the distinctive, uncentralized character of complex European polities goes back, as Childe thought, to the root of their development. The massive and well-preserved character of the period's fortified settlements and the relative stability of the landscape in which they are situated permit systematic documentation of how the centers of political control were located with respect to productive resources and to each other.

The Bronze Age archaeology of the Mancha (Martín et al. 1993) is an archaeology of settlements. Excavations, all dating to the past 15 years, have concentrated primarily on the resolution of the complex vertical problems presented by deeply stratified sites with complex histories of defensive construction. This work makes clear the following:

1. The Mancha Bronze Age is a regional variant of the "classic" Bronze Age of the southeastern quadrant of the Iberian Peninsula. The El Argar culture of Murcia and eastern Andalusia, the Bronce Valenciano culture of the Spanish Levant, and the Mancha Bronze Age are characterized by similar ceramic and metal types (e.g., undecorated carinated pottery and riveted daggers), individualized burial rites, and the fortification or defensive em-

placement of long-term settlements. In calibrated ^{14}C years the time span of the Mancha Bronze Age is about 2250 to 1500 B.C.

2. Known settlements of the Mancha Bronze Age fall into two categories. Some sites are circular forts with ring walls and (sometimes) central towers. These forts may be located either in low-lying river valley bottoms and marshes or on promontories and hilltops. In some cases these forts have settlement areas outside their walls, but more often they seem to be isolated strong points. These forts can be large monuments with a diameter of up to 50 m and walls still standing 7 m high, but many are small, forming mounds of rubble 2 m high and 20 m across. The other principal settlement type consists of occupations on hilltops and terraced hill slopes. Some are fairly large establishments, covering several thousand square meters, with meters of deposits spanning centuries of occupation and with fortifications protecting slopes that provide easier access to the settlement area, but many are small installations, occupying platforms of a few hundred square meters, on top of isolated hills. Recent excavations have concentrated on the larger, more deeply stratified forts and settlements. Radiocarbon dates from these excavations indicate that both site types were long-term, contemporaneous occupations.

3. Detailed evidence on subsistence practices is limited to the analysis of the fauna from the first two sites excavated, but it is apparent that Mancha Bronze Age sites were inhabited by agriculturalists who included the various elements of the "secondary products revolution" in their repertoire. The subsistence base of the Mancha Bronze Age seems to have involved a fairly well-developed system of Mediterranean agriculture.

4. Elsewhere in the Copper and Bronze Ages of Iberia intensified cultivation is associated with emerging social complexity, and the Mancha Bronze Age seems to fit this pattern too. Burial evidence is so far quite limited, but the clear concern for defense implies the importance of wealth differentials, and this tends to be confirmed by evidence for the storage of grain and the production of valuables (metal, ivory) in some of the forts.

Our project has involved a survey to locate and describe fortified Bronze Age sites in the Albacete Mancha and to gauge the relative productivity of those sites' catchment territories, so as to find out whether site hierarchies are a feature of the first stages of emergent social complexity in that region. This work has been informed by the following considerations:

Copper and Bronze Age sequences from various parts of Iberia show a trend toward increased social complexity. Over time one observes increasing defensive preoccupations governing the construction or placement of settlements, a shift from collective to individualizing burial rites, progressively greater wealth differentials in grave goods, the growth of long-distance exchange networks for exotic valuables, and the development of a metallurgical industry. Traditional explanations for this florescence involved, as mentioned earlier, one or another form of diffusion from the eastern Mediterranean, but it is apparent for many reasons that the development toward greater complexity was largely autonomous. Over the past decade numbers of scholars have elaborated contrasting processual explanations for this development. One group has followed the mainstream adaptationist line in explaining this "emerging complexity": either population pressure (Ramos 1981) or the need to stabilize production risks (exacerbated by a dry Mediterranean climate) (Chapman 1990) would lead to long-distance trade and subsistence intensification, the success of which would require leadership. Others have interpreted the development of inequalities as the result of the opportunities for elite exploitation presented by the need for exchange between groups that had become functionally differentiated as metal-working developed (Lull 1983). (This view obviously owes a great deal to Engels's view of the importance of commodity exchange in the origin of the state.) My own position (Gilman and Thornes 1985) has been that intensified farming dampened social fission and created opportunities for leaders to extract tribute from their followers. As one can see, recent debate on the development of social inequalities in later prehistoric Iberia covers most of the theoretical spectrum.

Now, whatever their merits on the available evidence, each of these approaches makes different predictions about settlement patterns. Europeanist prehistorians of the managerial persuasion are agreed that the emergence of complexity, with its centralized, higher-order regulation of economic activity, should be associated with the development of clear settlement hierarchies. Following Brumfiel (1976), this means that administrative centers, partly inhabited by managers and other persons not directly engaged in food production, should be larger than places inhabited by farmers—agricultural resources in their vicinity being equal. Similarly, the commodity exchange approach suggests that settlements whose inhabitants are engaged in specialized production (miners and smiths, for example) should be larger than would be expected from the agricultural resources in their catchment territories, since subsistence goods would be imported from settlements inhabited by farmers. However, the notion that capital intensification of subsistence facilitates exploitation makes no assumptions about settlement hierarchies; the primary producers will inhabit the landscape in densities proportionate to its agricultural productivity, and the tribute collectors will live among the primary producers in proportion to their productivity.

Efforts to demonstrate rigorously the existence of settlement hierarchies in the early stages of emerging complexity face significant difficulties in prehistoric Europe. First, the time periods in question are remote (at least by the standards of the New World archaeology that pioneered such studies). Natural erosion and the intensive exploitation of the landscape over the thousands of years that separate us from the late Neolithic or early Bronze Age can have led to differential loss of sites. Second, differences in the sizes of sites may reflect differences not just in the number of their inhabitants, but also in the density of their residential packing or in the length of their collective stays. Third, these difficulties are compounded by the large chronological blocks, defined mostly by radiocarbon dating, into which sequences are divided. A single period in a particular region (lasting several centuries perhaps) will combine numbers of larger and smaller sites that were not occupied contemporaneously. Finally, assessing relative catchment productivity (a logical necessity often omitted by proponents of settlement hierarchies) can be difficult in time periods that are so distant. These difficulties compound one another. They make it difficult to persuade skeptics of, and easy for believers to maintain their faith in, such hierarchies.

The nature of the landscape of La Mancha and the character of its Bronze Age archaeology make it possible to address, with some confidence of success, whether or not settlement hierarchies exist. First, the massive size of the fortifications of the Mancha Bronze Age sites has facilitated their survival. Second, the sizes of the defensive constructions are a direct reflection of the critical variable to be measured in studies of site hierarchies. The size of the labor force available for fortifying centers of political control should be a reasonable measure of the availability of tribute to those centers. The relative size of the Bronze Age forts on the Mancha will be a more reliable comparative measure of the concentration of power than the size of population aggregations inferred from the site areas. Third, that these sites were in long use (and thus partially contemporaneous) reduces the problem of disentangling chronological palimpsests. Finally, La Mancha has a relatively stable and uniform landscape, and this makes comparative assessment of site catchment productivity relatively straightforward in comparison to other parts of Europe.

To test the various scenarios outlined above, we have conducted a systematic, extensive air photographic survey of some 10,000 km². This has brought the number of Bronze Age localities known within the study area up from about 90 to some 270 sites. On the basis of a supplementary, intensive, field-walking survey of selected areas, we believe that we have located virtually all the larger (over 0.1 ha), fortified Bronze Age settlement sites in the study region (see Figure 2).

What our work makes clear is that the range of site sizes is quite restricted. Thus, larger sites (the putative administrative centers) are on the order of 0.25 to 1 ha in size, while smaller sites (their satellites) may measure less than 0.05 ha. In the absence of evidence for qualitative differences in the functions of larger and smaller sites, these size differences can easily be explained by nonhierarchical factors. Thus, the occasional fission of small social groups from larger ones would be seen in the archaeological record as a settlement "hierarchy," but the differences in site size would not be a reflection of the social power of their inhabitants. In other words, when isolated farmsteads exist at the same time as villages, the settlement hierarchy is not a social hierarchy. It is the presence of towns, functionally differentiated from villages, that implies social differentiation, and in La Mancha towns do not develop until long after the Bronze Age. I do not think that our results will support the managerial view of incipient stratification.

The commodity exchange approach may fare better, but not if the commodity in question is metal. The production of metal in the Iberian earlier Bronze Age in general (cf. Montero 1993), and in La Mancha more than elsewhere in Iberia, is relatively simple technologically and extremely limited in its scale. There is little to suggest that metal was produced by specialists, that it was produced at a mercantile scale, or that its importance to non-metallurgists was such that they would accept exploitation as a lesser cost in order to obtain it. A better candidate for a commodity that might induce dependency is salt: it is a necessity that is limited in its availability and thus amenable to control. La Mancha has a number of saline lagoons, some within our survey area, and our work makes it possible to assess whether such sources attracted larger numbers of sites to their vicinity. The concentration of sites near the saline lagoon at Pétrola is unusual and suggestive, but it is not replicated at other salt-producing localities, so the issue remains unresolved.

I believe, however, that the evidence we are gathering in our survey will tend to support the view of incipient social complexity that I have espoused for some time: that inequalities emerge in the competition over areas suitable for intensified farming. The larger fortified sites in Albacete appear to be located either along watercourses or in areas with permanent pastures. These resources would be worth fighting over, and the investment involved in their development would permit the establishment of rudimentary forms of exploitation.

The pattern observed in La Mancha is particularly well preserved, but it is not unique. Similar archaeological manifestations are characteristic of the Bronze Age of the Iberian Peninsula over the entire area between the Ebro and the Guadalquivir valleys (cf. Chapman 1990). The available evidence suggests that intensive Mediterranean polyculture began to be developed as early as the preceding Copper Age (the third millennium B.C.) and was fully established by the Bronze Age (in the second millennium), long before the first documented contacts with Eastern Mediterranean states. Production throughout this area was household based (as Montero [1993] shows, metallurgy was apparently integrated into household production even in areas with more developed industries than La Mancha's). Settlements were uniformly small

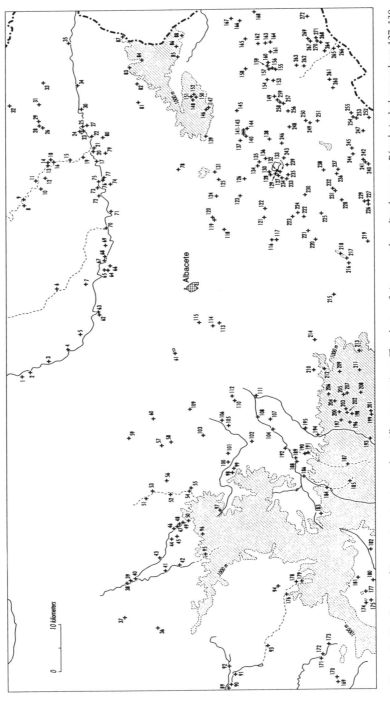

Figure 2. Distribution of Bronze Age sites in northern Albacete province. The cluster of sites near the saline lagoon at Pétrola includes numbers 127–130, 132, 134–136, 233–235, 239, and 243. Only two sites (numbers 94 and 176) are found near the saline lagoon of Pinilla, however.

and their placement was strongly influenced by defensive considerations, suggesting a high level of internecine strife. There was some incipient degree of social stratification, reflected in the differential distribution of metal and other wealth in mortuary contexts. (Wealth differences appear to be larger in areas where increased aridity would require more intensive agricultural production, and where competition over productive land would be exacerbated.) That the rich were buried with their weapons suggests that their part in that strife helped them obtain their relatively privileged positions. We lack, of course, any archaeological evidence of judicial assemblies and cannot say for sure to what extent the positions of the elite depended on their combining large land holdings with the mediation of violence, but the fit with the Germanic social formation is good as far as the evidence goes.

CONCLUSIONS

The principal characteristic of the incipiently stratified societies in much of later prehistoric Europe is the relatively small scale of their inequalities. Leaders could control a limited surplus based on the internal coercion permitted by intensified food production, but they found it difficult to use that surplus to reinforce their power. External, "network" strategies of accumulation were of limited importance, and the possibilities for internal, "corporate" reinvestment likewise were restricted by a variety of technological, ecological, and social factors. Wolf (1981) suggests that "feudal" and "Asiatic" societies are two extremes of a range of "tributary" modes of production. The Germanic societies of Europe—both those of the later prehistoric period and of the early modern periphery—would be even further on the small-scale end of the tributary range than their "feudal" successors and contemporaries. They constitute an important alternative to the functionally hierarchical, redistributive chiefdoms that have dominated anthropological discussions of incipient social complexity. Models in which the redistributive roles of chieftains are secondary to their coercive ones deserve greater consideration in a wide variety of societies at the threshold of social complexity.

ACKNOWLEDGMENTS

The research reported on in this chapter has been funded by the National Geographic Society, by Spain's Ministry of Science and Technology, by the Albacete provincial government, by the Program for Cultural Cooperation between Spain's Ministry of Culture and United States Universities, and by the Fulbright commission.

REFERENCES

Barton, R. F., 1922, Ifugao Economics, *University of California Publications in American Archaeology and Ethnology* 15(5).

Barton, R. F., 1949, *The Kalingas,* University of Chicago Press, Chicago.

Barton, R. F., 1969 [orig. 1919], *Ifugao Law,* University of California Press, Chicago.

Black-Michaud, J., 1975, *Cohesive Force: Feud in the Mediterranean and the Middle East,* Basil Blackwell, Oxford.

Bonte, P., 1977, Non-stratified Social Formations among Pastoral Nomads, in: *The Evolution of Social Systems* (J. Friedman and M. J. Rowlands, eds.), Duckworth, London, pp. 173–200.

Brumfiel, E., 1976, Regional Growth in the Eastern Valley of Mexico: A Test of the "Population Pressure" Hypothesis, in: *The Early Mesoamerican Village* (K. V. Flannery, ed.), Academic Press, New York, pp. 234–249.

Byock, J. L., 1988, *Medieval Iceland: Society, Sagas, and Power,* University of California Press, Berkeley.

Chapman, R., 1990, *Emerging Complexity: The Later Prehistory of South-East Spain, Iberia and the West Mediterranean,* Cambridge University Press, Cambridge.

Childe, V. G., 1958, *The Prehistory of European Society,* Penguin, Harmondsworth.

D'Altroy, T., and T. Earle, 1985, Staple Finance, Wealth Finance, and Storage in the Inka Political Economy, *Current Anthropology* 26:187–206.

Durrenberger, E. P., 1992, *The Dynamics of Medieval Iceland: Political Economy and Literature,* University of Iowa Press, Iowa City.

Earle, T. (ed.), 1991, *Chiefdoms: Power, Economy, and Ideology,* Cambridge University Press, Cambridge.

Engels, F., 1972 [orig. 1884], *The Origin of the Family, Private Property and the State,* International Publishers, New York.

Fraser, G. M., 1972, *The Steel Bonnets,* Alfred A. Knopf, New York.

Gilman, A., and J. B. Thornes, 1985, *Land Use and Prehistory in South-East Spain,* George Allen & Unwin, London.

Halstead, P., and J. O'Shea, 1982, A Friend in Need Is a Friend Indeed: Social Storage and the Origins of Ranking, in: *Ranking, Resource and Exchange: Aspects of the Archaeology of Early European Society* (C. Renfrew and S. J. Shennan, eds.), Cambridge University Press, Cambridge, pp. 92–99.

Halstead, P., and J. O'Shea, 1989, Introduction: Cultural Responses to Risk and Uncertainty, in: *Bad Year Economics: Cultural Responses to Risk and Uncertainty* (P. Halstead and J. O'Shea, eds.), Cambridge University Press, Cambridge, pp. 1–7.

Hart, D. M., 1976, *The Aith Waryaghar of the Moroccan Rif: An Ethnography and History,* University of Arizona Press, Tucson.

Hasluck, M., 1954, *The Unwritten Law in Albania,* Cambridge University Press, Cambridge.

Lull, V., 1983, *La "Cultura" de El Argar,* Akal Editor, Madrid.

Martín, C., M. Fernández-Miranda, M. D. Fernández-Posse, and A. Gilman, 1993, The Bronze Age of La Mancha, *Antiquity* 67:23–45.

Marx, K., 1964 [orig. 1857–1858], *Pre-Capitalist Economic Formations,* International Publishers, New York.

Miller, W. I., 1990, *Bloodtaking and Peacemaking: Feud, Law, and Society in Saga Iceland,* University of Chicago Press, Chicago.

Montero Ruiz, I., 1993, Bronze Age Metallurgy in Southeast Spain, *Antiquity* 67:46–57.

Munson, H., Jr., 1989, On the Irrelevance of the Segmentary Lineage Model in the Moroccan Rif, *American Anthropologist* 91:386–400.

Patterson, N. T., 1991, *Cattle Lords and Clansmen: Kinship and Rank in Early Ireland,* Garland, New York.

Ramos Millán, A., 1981, Interpretaciones Secuenciales y Culturales de la Edad del Cobre en la Zona Meridional de la Península Ibérica: La Alternativa del Materialismo Cultural, *Cuadernos de Prehistoria de la Universidad de Granada* 6:242–256.

Reher, D. S., 1990, *Town and Country in Pre-industrial Spain: Cuenca, 1550–1870,* Cambridge University Press, Cambridge.

Sahlins, M., 1972, *Stone Age Economics,* Aldine, Chicago.

Stevenson, R. L., 1959 [orig. 1886], *Kidnapped,* New American Library, New York.

Thomas, J., 1987, Relations of Production and Social Change in the Neolithic of North-West Europe, *Man* 22:405–430.

Wolf, E. R., 1981, The Mills of Inequality: A Marxian Approach, in: *Social Inequality: Comparative and Developmental Approaches* (G. D. Berreman, ed.), Academic Press, New York, pp. 41–57.

Part IV

Conclusion

Chapter 10

The Emergence of Inequality

A Focus on Strategies and Processes

GARY M. FEINMAN

What I am saying in effect, is that archaeologists still do not know what causes complex societies, what brings them into being. (Binford 1983:231)

Relatively little progress, however, has been made in explaining inequality. (Kelly 1991:136)

INTRODUCTION

In the history of the human species, there is no more significant transition than the emergence and institutionalization of inequality. Yet strangely, until recently, this critical issue has received less direct concern in archaeological discussions of social change than two other important evolutionary questions, the origins of agriculture and the rise of the state. In part, this lack of focused attention accounts for the pessimism cited above, especially when the enormity of this general issue is considered. Yet, in part, these comments also may stem from the inability of ecologically oriented scholars, like Binford and Kelly, to define a specific and parsimonious suite of exogenous conditions

GARY M. FEINMAN • Department of Anthropology, University of Wisconsin–Madison, Madison, Wisconsin 53706-1393.

Foundations of Social Inequality, edited by T. Douglas Price and Gary M. Feinman. Plenum Press, New York, 1995.

(e.g., environment, population) that can convincingly explain this key socio-economic transition.

This overview synthesizes recent work on the emergence of inequality. It is argued that a series of important advances, indeed, have been made relevant to this issue over the last decades, although there is still much to be done. Conceptual changes feature the decoupling of agricultural origins from the emergence of inequality (e.g., Price and Brown 1985a; Upham 1990), and the recognition that a degree of inequality (by gender, age, ability, and tempera-ment) exists in even the most egalitarian human social systems (Cashdan 1980; Collier and Rosaldo 1981; Flanagan 1989). These reconceptualizations, along with the more general evolutionary movement away from prime mover and typological frameworks (Sanderson 1990), have basically served to re-frame the question at issue. A final theme of this essay suggests that more than one general strategy or processual pathway toward institutionalized inequality has been followed during human history. This "dual processual" model (Blan-ton et al. in press) endeavors to account for significant variation in middle-range or ranked societies. By summarizing recent perspectives and proposing new directions, this discussion aims to stimulate and foster constructive de-bate.

DECOUPLING AGRICULTURAL ORIGINS FROM THE EMERGENCE OF NONEGALITARIAN SOCIAL SYSTEMS

Since their rebirth during the middle decades of this century, cultural evolutionary approaches in the social sciences have tended to place causal priority on ecological and economic processes in explanations of societal change. On the origins of inequality, the influential writings of Leslie White (1943:343–344) and V. Gordon Childe (1951) were particularly significant in establishing the broadly held view that the advent of agricultural economies more or less mechanically transformed sociopolitical relations away from egalitarian formations. Although a few exceptions were noted (particularly among the native hunter-gatherer-fisher peoples of the North American Pacific Coast), more recent evolutionary theorists still directly couple in-stitutionalized inequality to explanations of agrarian modes of production. For example, "political-economic egalitarianism is another theoretically predict-able structural consequence of the hunter-gatherer infrastructure" (Harris 1979:81). In major evolutionary perspectives outside of anthropology, these views remain widely held (e.g., Lenski and Lenski 1987).

Yet within the discipline, significant reassessment has occurred. Although institutionalized inequality has long been recognized among a few select hunter-gatherer populations (see Price and Brown 1985b), recent edited collections (Koyama and Thomas 1982; Price and Brown 1985a) have documented that such cases were more prevalent than previously realized. These studies have repeatedly illustrated that agricultural production cannot be considered a necessary precondition for unequal or hierarchically organized social formations, since such sociopolitical transitions have been evidenced in a wide array of nonagricultural populations. This reevaluation has led to the recognition of marked societal variation among certain foraging populations. However, more significantly, it has forced most theorists to consider the issue of the emergence of social inequality on its own terms, rather than simply situating the question as an epiphenomenon of explanations for agricultural origins.

RESITUATING CAUSALITY

Although the emergence of institutionalized inequality can no longer be viewed as the simple product of the agricultural mode of production, the necessary theoretical recasting has not quelled the predilection for infrastructural determination. Paradoxically, there are two divergent streams to this theoretical perspective. The first approach roots the emergence of institutionalized inequality in resource abundance and population density, while the second views its foundation in population pressure/resource stress.

The thesis (e.g., Yesner 1980, 1987) that resource abundance (wild or domesticated) promotes sedentism, surplus, higher population densities, and social differentiation follows the same basic causal linkages as the aforementioned interpretations of the Neolithic Revolution (Childe 1951). Yet dense populations and abundant resources in themselves clearly do not engender either the production of large surpluses or the emergence of institutionalized inequality (Brown and Podolefsky 1976). As Pearson (1957) argued several decades ago, the technological ability to achieve a surplus is not tantamount to its actual production. Sahlins (1972:140), in a revision of his own earlier position, argued that:

> Too frequently and mechanically anthropologists attribute the appearance of chieftainship to the production of surplus. In the historic process, however, the relation has been at least mutual, and in the functioning of primitive society it is rather the other way around. Leadership continually generates domestic surplus. The development of rank and chieftainship becomes *pari passu*, development of the productive forces.

Until the "Garden of Eden" perspective (Yesner 1987) can more clearly define the parameters of resource abundance and how such bounties are achieved, this position is difficult to sustain. It is not the mere accumulation of wealth and status that is important, but the transformation and justification of the social contexts in which it happens and the ways that these contexts are reproduced and permitted to persist (Bishop 1987:81; Aldenderfer 1993:10).

The alternative model of strict infrastructural determinism places resource stress at the core of these socioeconomic transitions (Cohen 1981). Unfortunately, attention is rarely devoted in these studies to a careful measurement of "resource stress" or "population pressure," and these concepts become the assumed consequences of any increase in population or change in diet. A more quantitative study within this genre is the recent comparative, cross-cultural analysis of 94 hunting and gathering groups (Keeley 1988). Keeley finds a high statistical correlation between his measures of population pressure and socioeconomic complexity. On the basis of this correlation, he asserts that population pressure is a necessary and sufficient cause of socioeconomic complexity. In the study, socioeconomic complexity is determined as an amalgam of coded data for storage, sedentism, social inequality, and the use of a medium of exchange. Population pressure is basically measured by higher than expected population densities for the specific latitudes at which the particular hunting and gathering groups were situated. Because of the difficulty of recording specific dietary and environmental information for 94 diverse populations, proxies (like latitude) were employed to facilitate estimations of available food supplies.

Unfortunately, Keeley's findings are beset by several analytical problems. As with many comparable studies, he assumes that high correlation coefficients are tantamount to causality and explanation. More damaging is his assessment of the quantities of food available to the hunting and gathering groups with the highest measured population densities. In Keeley's (1988:382–383) data, these relatively complex, high-population cases were almost entirely from the Pacific Coast of North America. These cases consistently were determined to have had populations greater than expected by the productivity of their terrestrial locations alone. Yet, is this observation really surprising or significant when most of their diet came from abundant marine resources? It many cases, these are the same groups whose organizational complexity has been at least in part attributed to resource abundance (e.g., Maschner 1991, 1992; Hayden, Chapter 2, this volume). Despite ample marine resources, Keeley (1988:395) asserts that unidentified terrestrial resources were somehow stressing/constraining the populations of the Northwest Coast and California. But the specific empirical basis for this critical aspect of his argument is only presented anecdotally (see Maschner 1991:65–68 for a useful critique). The questions of which specific terrestrial resources were lacking, and how they were limiting population, are left entirely unaddressed. While Maschner's (1991:65) characterization of Keeley's productivity measures as useless is seemingly too strong, one can have far more confidence in the positive relationships that Keeley (1988:399) observed between demographic and socioeconomic variables (see also Carneiro 1967; Ember 1963; Plog 1990:188) than his measurements of population pressure and the causal primacy that he assigns to this factor.

The point of the above discussion has not been to redirect the debate concerning the emergence of inequality entirely away from empirical studies of resources, diet, and environmental change, but to challenge the long-held assumption that exogenous or infrastructural factors alone can explain such shifts. At least in archaeology, as Plog (1990:196) has recognized, "the role of the environment has been overemphasized and new models of culture change must be developed." Adequate explanations require a focus on the dynamics between internal (societal) and external factors, not an exclusive concentration on either one at the exclusion of the other (Plog and Braun 1984:623; Plog, Chapter 7, this volume). It must be recognized that relationships between culture and nature are complex, and specific types of environmental changes can have different impacts with diverse socioeconomic arrangements. Resource abundance, scarcity, and risk can all create opportunities and stresses. But these factors do not provide a necessary and sufficient explanation for the significant restructurings that characterize the institutionalization of inequality.

CONSIDERING "POPULATION" AS A CATEGORY RATHER THAN AS A VARIABLE

For at least three decades, cross-cultural studies have recognized a generally strong relationship between population size and societal complexity (Carneiro 1967; Ember 1963; Feinman and Neitzel 1984; Johnson 1982; Naroll 1956). Yet no broadly applicable demographic thresholds have been defined for egalitarian versus nonegalitarian societies. Furthermore, the relationship between societal scale and political organization has been shown to diminish when narrower population ranges are examined (Johnson 1982). In social change studies, there continues to be relatively little in the way of a strictly determinate and globally applicable "social physics" (Bernard and Killworth 1979) in which population sizes can be used directly to predict specific social formations (cf. Upham 1987:354–356).

Nevertheless, important suggestions recently have been advanced concerning the role of population in organizational change. Perhaps the most cogent is Drennan's (1987:309) caution that in evolutionary analyses "population" is far too frequently treated like a variable rather than a category. In many studies, one demographic indicator is presumed to correspond with (or used as a proxy for) others. Yet as Drennan (1987) shows cross-culturally, different demographic variables (societal population, maximal community size, demographic density, and the degree of population nucleation) do not necessarily covary in simple or linear fashion (see also Brown and Podolefsky 1976; Feinman and Neitzel 1984).

Group size may have less direct organizational implications than the sizes of more tightly interacting social entities, like communities. For example, Brown and Podolefsky (1976:214) report wide variation in the sizes and densities of 17 New Guinea tribal and linguistic populations. Yet only one of these groups had an organized political grouping larger than 2,500 people. Likewise, none of the 46 single-community societies studied by Carneiro (1967) or the 37 New Guinea groups compared by Forge (1972) included communities larger than 2,000 people. Lekson (1985) studied maximal community size in 45 nonindustrial societies and also reported a sharp cutoff around 2,500. In his sample (Lekson 1985), societies with communities of fewer than 2,500 people had a broad range of organizational forms, while all of the societies with settlements larger than that size had complex sociopolitical formations. In a sample of 21 middle-range societies in the Americas (Feinman and Neitzel 1984), only two populations had maximal community sizes greater than 2,500. Both of these had hierarchical organizational forms. As in Lekson's study, organizational formations were highly variable in the 19 populations with no communities larger than 2,500. The majority of these 21 New World groups had total populations greater than 2,500 people, and the range of variation in the latter variable was by more than an order of magnitude (Feinman and Neitzel 1984).

Collectively, these recent studies refine previously recognized relationships between organizational and demographic variables. Communities (or tightly integrated political groups) larger than 2,500 ± 500 do seem to be associated with significant organizational complexity. Yet more dispersed populations that may be far greater in total population size are not necessarily organized hierarchically. This wide array of cases, from a diverse range of environmental and economic settings, indicates that the nature of the interaction between group members (and the degree/mechanisms of integration involved) has critical implications for the relationship between population size and organization. In other words, for populations of equivalent size, the levels of interaction and cooperation necessary at the community scale are apparently far greater per capita than at the (more dispersed) societal scale. It is perhaps significant that the empirically observed "threshold" of 2,500 ± 500 corresponds with the maximum size of a group where information can still reach everyone (albeit with some time lag) (Bernard and Killworth 1973, 1979). This same "magic number" also corresponds with estimates for long-term human memory capabilities (Kosse 1990:277, 280–282), and may broadly relate to the number of names/social contacts that can be processed by a given individual.

Several useful observations can be gained from the above discussion. Maximal community sizes above 2,500 ± 500 would appear to be better predictors of societal organization than total group population. However, the causal arrow for this relationship still needs to be further examined and explained. It remains to be decided whether certain community sizes necessitate particular social forms, or do specific societal arrangements promote or permit new levels of population nucleation (see Kirch 1984:99). Interestingly, populations with maximal communities smaller than the threshold (2,500 ± 500) have a diverse array of organizational forms (including hierarchical and unequal ones). Consequently, if there is a critical population size and density threshold that is sufficient for (but does not necessitate) socioeconomic complexity, it lies below the magic number of 2,500, and it remains undefined (Kosse 1990). More importantly, even if such a threshold exists, one could not employ it in a predictive manner without knowing the nature and intensity of the social and ideological linkages that interconnected a particular population. For that reason, it is necessary to expand the remainder of this synthesis beyond resources and demography to a consideration of social relations and processes.

REDEFINING THE EGALITARIAN CONCEPT

As reviewed by Flanagan (1989:245–249), the last 25 years have witnessed a dramatic rethinking of the nature of egalitarian societies. Kelly (1993:2) sees this redefinition as a "significant change in the sociology of knowledge." Traditional anthropological perspectives on egalitarianism emphasized those conditions that allowed populations to remain in a "state of nature," with "as many positions of prestige in any given age–sex grade as there are persons capable of filling them" (Fried 1967:52). In contrast, current views highlight differences in gender, age, authority, skills, and prestige in egalitarian (or nonstratified) social forms (see Flanagan 1989; Paynter and McGuire 1991). These contemporary perspectives question the existence of truly egalitarian social formations.

This reconsideration of the nature of nonstratified societies has dramatic implications for modeling the emergence of inequality. Prior to 1970, most interpretations of change endeavored to define specific exogenous conditions that fostered or necessitated the emergence of select individuals to leadership positions from a state of utopian equality. These individuals were generally perceived as managers, who were sustained by the rest of the population because of the adaptive functions that they carried out for the larger social good. Models that deviated from this perspective by attributing importance to internal or social factors frequently were summarily dismissed as vitalistic or tautological.

Yet, alternatively, if the seeds of inequality are recognized to be present in egalitarian human groupings, then the focus of this central research question must be shifted. Rather than endeavoring simply to account for inequality, the emphasis should be expanded. Attention must be placed both on those mechanisms in nonstratified societies that have served to level extant inequities before they become institutionalized, as well as on the internal and/or external conditions that work to negate those leveling strategies and sanctions so that existent inequalities are permitted to become more institutionalized. The institutionalization process cannot occur unless social and ideological conceptions are transformed (Cashdan 1980:119–120; Flannery and Marcus 1993:263).

Personal differences in ambition, charisma, and skills can be argued to exist in all populations (Clark and Blake 1994). These distinctions have been well documented in many societies (e.g., in Melanesia) that are generally acknowledged to be comparatively egalitarian. However, it must also be clearly recognized that variation in these individual qualities does not represent adequate or sufficient cause to explain the emergence of institutionalized forms of inequality. As long as an attempt is not made to attribute the emergence of greater inequality simply to such inner forces or personal characteristics, then the examination and consideration of social and ideological factors in explanations of societal change does not constitute vitalism or psychological reductionism (Clark and Blake 1994; Hayden, Chapter 2, this volume). In other words, as discussed above, viable explanations of change must ultimately unravel the interplay between human strategies and socio-environmental opportunities and stresses. They also must recognize the historical nature of these social transitions.

Along these lines, increasing concern in the examination of inequality has been given to the strategies of "emergent leaders" (Lightfoot and Feinman 1982), "accumulators" (Hayden and Gargett 1990; Hayden, Chapter 2, this volume), or "aggrandizers" (Clark and Blake 1994), as well as to their relationship to "labor" (Arnold 1993) and "factions" (Spencer 1993). Amplifying an earlier discussion (Sahlins 1963:290–293), Spencer (1993) illustrates that the increasing institutionalization of inequalities in economic and political power follows from the successful coordination and articulation of two sets of potentially opposing relations. The first is defined by the ties between a leader and his local faction, while the second represents that individual's links to the extrafactional arena.

Recognition of the importance of these opposing interpersonal relations, what has been termed the "dialectic of control" (Giddens 1984:374), eliminates the necessity to polarize the so-called functionalist (leaders as "system-serving") and political (leaders as "self-serving") models for the development of inequality (e.g., Hayden and Gargett 1990; Paynter 1989). Clearly, it is difficult to envision ascriptive leadership and increasing inequality simply as societal problem-solving mechanisms (see Paynter 1989:373–376), so the latter argument remains central. Individuals generally act with their perceived self-interest in mind. Yet at the same time, what might be thought of as more functional considerations cannot be entirely dismissed as some postprocessual theorists have been wont to argue.

Aspiring leaders who address and resolve the wants and needs of followers (larger societal concerns) simply are more apt to be retained and supported by their factions despite the potentially selfish aims and strategies of those leaders. As Spencer (1993:48) has argued: "in certain . . . situations, the survival of individuals may become dependent on the success of the group, and the latitude for individual actions such as abandoning a leader is consequently constrained." Factions form because followers perceive benefits and rewards (material, political, or spiritual) for their support. Therefore, the functions served by emergent leaders (in warfare, dispute resolution, the aversion of subsistence risk, social reproduction) and the conditions to which they respond cannot be entirely ignored in the consideration of the institutionalization of inequality. In this regard, the demographic relationships reviewed above between community size and organization are both interesting and relevant (see also Johnson 1982). That is, as integration, dispute resolution, and mutual defense become greater concerns, the willingness to endure a self-serving leader also may grow. Likewise, because these issues clearly and simultaneously involve local as well as extraregional relations, anthropologists cannot any longer ignore that "evolution is a spatial as well as a temporal process" (Kristiansen 1991:24).

IDENTIFYING ALTERNATIVE PATHWAYS TOWARD SOCIAL CHANGE

Over the last decades, social change studies have focused increasingly on variation and comparison. A series of problems (e.g., Feinman and Neitzel 1984; Trigger 1989:329–330; Upham 1990; Yoffee 1985) has been raised with the progressivist typological frameworks rooted in the seminal works of Service (1971) and Fried (1967). Nevertheless, even when significant societal variation has been recognized and described, comparative, generalizing perspectives have remained unilinear (Spencer 1990, 1993; Hayden, Chapter 2, this volume; cf. Sanders and Webster 1978). Such stepladder approaches have been accepted as complementary to (or for some [e.g., Hodder 1985], in stark opposition to) the study of individual cultural/historical sequences (Flannery 1983; Sahlins and Service 1960). In recent generalizing perspectives, this predisposition toward a unilinear trajectory has been so predominant that little consideration has been given to repeated observations of patterned cross-cultural variability, which may reflect alternative (yet still rather general) processes or pathways to inequality and organizational complexity.

The remainder of this discussion briefly reviews these prior comparative studies (e.g., Drennan 1991; Johnson 1982; Renfrew 1974; Strathern 1969, 1978). It is argued that two general political-economic strategies or modes (corporate-based and network-based) represent dual pathways toward inequality. These modes, which have been outlined previously by Blanton (Blanton et al. in press), appear to parallel and recur across these earlier comparative syntheses. The corporate-based and network-based strategies are not proposed as mutually exclusive or nonoverlapping. In fact, to a degree, these strategies coexist in the political dynamics of all social arrangements. However, because these modes also are structurally antagonistic (see Strathern 1969:42–47), they are shown to have had different degrees of relative importance cross-culturally. Their relative importance also often varies within a single region over time (Blanton et al. in press). Therefore, one or the other mode often dominates in any particular spatiotemporal setting (Blanton et al. in press; Strathern 1969:42).

The corporate and network modes may have their basis in the aforementioned external and internal components of the dialectics of control (see Spencer 1993). In describing emergent leadership in lowland South America, Spencer (1993:42–45) contrasts the role of aspiring leaders in two nonstratified Brazilian groups, the Mekranoti-Kayapó and the Akwe-Shavante. Mekranoti-Kayapó leaders (*benjadjwyr*) are described as "culture brokers" who cultivate external ties with individuals in other communities. In part, these links are made so that the leaders can obtain exotic wealth items, which are then dispersed as gifts to secure and solidify the allegiance of followers. The prestige and factional support of a Mekranoti-Kayapó *benjadjwyr* hinge in large measure on that person's *network* of external connections. This privileged network of linkages to the external world often appears to be successfully transmitted from a *benjadjwyr* to his offspring (Werner 1981). Given the importance of personal contacts to prestige, individuals attract attention through various means, including elaborate body ornamentation and the production of handicrafts (Werner 1981:365–366).

Among the Akwe-Shavante, leadership also depends on factional support, but long-distance exchange contacts are not stressed, and exotic items do not have a central role in attracting followers (Maybury-Lewis 1974:172, 205–213; Spencer 1993:44). Akwe-Shavante leaders (*he'a*) derive support from a *corporate* group, which primarily includes the members of their patrilineage

(Maybury-Lewis 1974:169). A powerful *he'a* may attract other coresidents of his village as well as clan and lineage members from outside his community. The personal eminence of a *he'a* is therefore based on the support of his lineage and of any other men who are prepared to join his faction (Maybury-Lewis 1974:148). Several crosscutting associations foster the ability of Akwe-Shavante leaders to build factions beyond their lineages. These include age-sets, which comprise community members of a certain age and gender, and a council of senior men that regularly discusses key village matters with the *he'a*. Akwe-Shavante age-sets play a key role in initiation rituals and other ceremonial activities (Maybury-Lewis 1974:147).

He'a lead community hunts and direct horticultural clearing, planting, and harvesting. They often serve a central role in various ceremonial activities (including distributions of food) where they act on behalf of the community (Maybury-Lewis 1974:197–201). A *he'a* derives prestige from his athleticism, oratory skills, hunting abilities, sense of humor, and ceremonial knowledge; however, the size of his corporate faction is the basis of whatever power he may have (Maybury-Lewis 1974:197). The strength of an Akwe-Shavante leader is rather fleeting, and a single community can have more than one *he'a*, each with his own corporate faction. Akwe-Shavante leaders have no insignia of office and few prerogatives, yet they are relatively successful at the manipulation of age-set organization, so that their own sons eventually are positioned to exercise whatever leadership capabilities they possess (Maybury-Lewis 1974:190).

In comparative analyses of nonstratified societies in the New Guinea Highlands, two distinct organizational strategies (home finance and home production) also are outlined (Strathern 1969, 1978). Home finance defines a mode in which the relative importance of Big Men reflects their position in a network of financial arrangements (Strathern 1969:65). Through the external exchange of portable wealth items (e.g., shell valuables, live pigs), obligations and alliances are created (Strathern 1978:75). Big Men are able to solidify their factions through the local distribution of long-distance gifts that are derived from trade partners. As described for the Melpa of Mount Hagen and the Enga, this mode bears striking resemblance to the strategies employed by Mekranoti-Kayapó leaders. The acquisition of wealth through individual, entrepreneurial linkages, and the use of that wealth by these charismatic figures to attract factions, defines the network-based mode.

In home production, a Big Man's prestige depends on the labor force of his own kin group or settlement to raise the goods needed for feasting and exchange (Strathern 1969:42). For household or settlement heads, access to labor and land is critical, and it is derived largely through corporate descent. As described for the Maring and Siane, the eminence of a Big Man is achieved by obtaining more land and labor than others (Strathern 1969:65). Like influential Akwe-Shavante *he'a*, Siane Big Men do not accumulate great personal wealth (Strathern 1969:50). Intergroup ties, portable wealth, and financial maneuverings are far less important with home production than they are with home finance (Strathern 1978:98–99). In Siane communities, corporate groups (like those of the South American Akwe-Shavante) are integrated by initiation rituals that crosscut these descent-based social segments. Such ceremonies are described as less significant among the Enga and the Melpa (Strathern 1969:44). Home production fits comfortably within the corporate-based mode (Blanton et al. in press) with its emphases on food production, land, labor, kinship, societal segments, and the integration of those segments through crosscutting integratory social and ritual mechanisms (e.g., initiation rites).

The network–corporate continuum bears some similarity to the distinction previously drawn between societies having simultaneous (network) and sequential-ritual (corporate) hierarchies (Johnson 1982). Of course, Johnson's (1982) discussion differs in its narrower concern with decision-making, thereby avoiding a direct tie-in with economics. Simultaneous hierarchies are defined as social arrangements in which a few central individuals exercise integration and control over a larger population (Johnson 1982:403), while sequential-ritual hierarchies are described as relatively more consensual and egalitarian formations in which ritual and elaborate ceremonies are often argued to have key roles in the integration of modular social segments (Johnson 1982:405, 1989:378–381). However, in contrast to Johnson's seminal discussion regarding sequential–simultaneous hierarchies, it is argued here that the relative predominance of either corporate or network strategies in specific societal contexts is not restricted to nonstratified social formations. More specifically, this discussion challenges the unilinear proposition (Spencer 1993) that cultural evolution necessarily moves simply and directly from more consensual to simultaneous (individually focused) forms of organization. Rather, the corporate and network strategies are presented as organizational modes that, indeed, crosscut societal variation in the relative degree of hierarchical complexity and stratification.

In an argument that foreshadowed this analysis, Renfrew (1974) contrasted individualizing and group-oriented forms in a comparison of chiefdoms. The described cases were recognized as relatively similar in overall social complexity, yet organized in very different ways (Renfrew 1974:74). For Renfrew (1974:74–79, 83), group-oriented polities de-emphasized differentials in access to personal wealth, while placing great importance on communal activities and group rituals, which link the geographic segments that comprise these populations. Collective labor and monumental public architecture were evidenced, while great stores and individual displays of personal or portable wealth were rarely apparent. Neolithic Malta, the henge-building peoples of the European third millennium B.C., and ethnographic Polynesia were interpreted as examples of these group-oriented chiefly arrangements.

The emphasis was entirely different in Renfrew's individualizing forms, like those of Minoan–Mycenaean Greece (Renfrew 1974:74–79, 84). The egalitarian ethos was overcome as specific individuals were differentiated and privileged. Marked disparity in personal possessions existed, and the residences and tombs of rulers were far grander than those of the bulk of the population. Exotic trade wealth appears to have had a significant role in prestige accumulation. Some of the goods that were exchanged were elaborately crafted by specialists. In contrast to the group-oriented formations, communal ritual and public construction appear to have had lesser roles.

Significantly, in a comparison of prehispanic chiefdoms in the Americas, Drennan (1991:283) found a similar distinction. In two cases (central Panama, and Alta Magdalena) from the Intermediate Area (lower Central America and northern South America), almost all public building was focused on individuals. Status differentiation was conspicuous. In the best documented of these cases (central Panama), tremendous volumes of portable wealth, reflecting elaborate craftswork, were found in select burials (Lothrop 1937, 1942). The items recovered also signal the importance of extraregional exchange links. Many of the burial inclusions evidently were meant for elaborate personal adornment (Linares 1977:40–41). "A large portion of the resources mobilized in the local economies in central Panama and Alta Magdalena went into competition over status dominance, focused heavily on the person of the chief" (Drennan 1991:283). These cases illustrate clear parallels with Renfrew's individualizing chiefdoms and with the more encompassing network strategy.

In contrast, a markedly different organizational mode is evident in two early-middle Formative period Mesoamerican populations (Valley of Oaxaca, Basin of Mexico). In these regions, public works primarily were carried out to construct spaces (plazas and mound groups) for communal ritual. Although inequalities existed (as they did in Renfrew's group-oriented chiefdoms), they were not expressed elaborately in house construction or burials. For example, at this time in the Valley of Oaxaca, all houses were made of comparable materials (earth and cane) and the most elaborate burials were simply lined by stones and contained no more than a few exotic offerings. While craft specialization, long-distance exchange, and status competition were not entirely insignificant in these regions during this period (e.g., Feinman 1991; Marcus 1989), I concur completely with Drennan's (1991:283) perception that these activities consumed a relatively smaller proportion of the "chiefly domestic product" as compared to the aforementioned cases from the Intermediate Area. Thus, these Formative-era Mesoamerican cases illustrate elements of both the network and corporate strategies (see Drennan 1991);

however, considerable emphasis is on the latter mode, particularly when comparisons are made with the Intermediate Area societies.

In this regard, it is significant that Marcus (1989) has illustrated the almost mutually exclusive association of two sets of motifs (each representing distinct supernatural forces) with burials excavated in different Formative period Oaxacan households. These two mythico-religious symbols are found with infant burials (as well as those of children and adults), occur primarily with males, and each cluster spatially by residential ward (Marcus 1989:169). Based on these data (see also Pyne 1976), Marcus (1989:169–174) postulates that these symbols may signal kin group affiliations. If so, the association of the Formative Oaxaca case with the corporate-based mode would be strengthened.

Focused primarily on these archaeological examples from Europe and the ancient Americas, both Renfrew (1974:74, 82–85) and Drennan (1991:284–285) have argued that long-term social change in nonegalitarian chiefdoms has followed two distinct paths, which have involved somewhat different political-economic strategies and processes. Yet the prior discussion of lowland South America and Melanesia indicates that these different (corporate–network) pathways also are evidenced in societal settings with less institutionalized forms of social differentiation and leadership. One might prudently propose that alternative, general pathways and processes toward inequality are indeed followed. The corporate mode (encompassing what Renfrew called group-oriented forms) emphasizes collective ritual (and its potential manipulation), public construction, integrated social segments, the importance of kinship affiliation, and relatively suppressed economic differentiation (more egalitarian access patterns). In contrast, the network mode (encompassing Renfrew's individualizing polities) places greatest significance on individual prestige and wealth accumulation, personal networks, long-distance exchange, exotic wealth exchange, and the specialized manufacture of status-related craft goods (see D'Altroy and Earle 1985 for a narrower economic focus). However, once network- or corporate-based strategies are in place, one should not presume that the specific political-economic strategy will necessarily remain predominant or unchanging throughout a specific culture historical sequence (see Blanton et al. in press for a discussion of such changes in prehispanic Mesoamerica).

ALTERNATIVE PATHWAYS TO EMERGENT INEQUALITY: A FINAL COMPARATIVE EXAMPLE

In this section, a brief final comparison is drawn between middle-range polities in Polynesia and those from the Northwest Coast of North America. In both of these geographic areas, a diverse range of politically autonomous societies has been described. These polities vary markedly in scale, stratification, and political complexity (e.g., Kelly 1991; Kirch 1984; Riches 1979; Sahlins 1958; Ames, Chapter 6, this volume). Anthropologically, both of these geographic regions have had major illustrative roles in the prior construction of general and unilinear models of middle-range organization (e.g., Fried 1967; Sahlins 1963; Service 1971; Hayden, Chapter 2, this volume). Yet, ethnographic descriptions from each area also have posed problems for general theoretical frameworks. Carneiro (1981:48–49) does not consider the Northwest Coast polities to be chiefdoms because their chiefs often only led single, large, extended family households or communities rather than hierarchically arranged settlement systems. Instead, the Northwest Coast groups were placed with other autonomous village groups at a "lower level" of complexity. Yet, by so doing, Carneiro's rather linear scheme virtually ignores the presence of slaves in some Northwest Coast societies, as well as marked degrees of differentiation in personal wealth, inherited rank, and power.

Likewise, a number of recent frameworks that have proposed to account for the development of institutionalized inequality emphasize the disproportionate personal accumulation of prestige, influence, and wealth as a driving universal factor in this transition. Prestige-goods exchange often is given a central role in such models. Yet for the classic Polynesian polities, prestige-goods systems were relatively unimportant (Friedman and Rowlands 1978:215). In this analysis, the variation between Polynesia and the Northwest Coast is not viewed as simply anomalous, nor is it tossed off to inexplicable specific/historical variation. Rather, it is argued that, whereas Northwest Coast chiefs tended to follow network strategies, the organization of Polynesian polities conforms more closely to the corporate mode with the manipulation of kinship relations at the crux of power.

In other words, distinctly different pathways to inequality appear to have been followed in these two regions. No single variable, threshold, formula, or general model would seem to account for the processual changes in each area. But, more importantly, and despite considerable variation in degrees of scale, complexity, and stratification, these capsule discussions are meant to illustrate key core features between Northwest Coast organization and the previously discussed network-based cases, and between the Polynesian polities and the examples presented above for the corporate-based mode. Although complexity and stratification vary for the three cases from each area, the dominant organizational mode does not. Yet, marked contrasts are evident between the two areas, and reference to the corporate- and network-based strategies helps to account for some of the perceived anomalies discussed above. In each region, both organizational strategies are evidenced in the largest, most stratified contexts, yet the most prominent organizational mode remains dominant.

Along the Northwest Coast of North America, a general south-to-north increase in the importance of inherited wealth and status has been recognized (Drucker 1939; Kelly 1991). Yet up and down the coast, the key to a leader's status and prestige has been shown to be the size of his faction and the accumulation of goods (Drucker 1939:61–62; Kelly 1991; Riches 1979:158–159); Ames, Chapter 6, this volume). Across the geographic region, the specific social arrangements and economic items vary; however, the themes of individual marriage and exchange networks, differential access to precious goods, the importance of household labor, elaborate displays of personal wealth, body adornments, and attached craft production recur.

On California's northern coast, at the southern end of the region, leadership roles (among the Tolowa and Yurok) were less formal and varied somewhat by task. Ambitious individuals acquired prestige items through networks of exchange connections (Gould 1966; Kelly 1991). These wealth items were used in part for bridewealth payments. The acquisition of wives and polygyny provided a means to secure the labor of women and thereby increase household production (Gould 1966:74). Debt slavery and other mechanisms also enabled households to expand their labor force through other strategies (Kelly 1991:148). Wealthier men served as marriage brokers and blood feud negotiators for younger men, securing a degree of allegiance from them (Gould 1966:74). To act in these brokering roles required individual access to wealth, and such roles served as a means to build personal factions. Trade and marriage links were not regularized between groups; instead, interpersonal ties revolved around certain focal individuals. Shells, woodpecker scalps, obsidian bifaces, otter pelts, and other exchange items were enhanced and elaborated through labor inputs to increase their trade value. Many of these crafted items also were used in personal adornment.

On the central Pacific Coast, the social and ceremonial relations associated with marriage tended to be more elaborate than in northern California. Differences in rank and wealth were inherited more formally than they were to the south. Yet a critical key to power was still the acquisition of wealth and labor in large part through marriage transactions (Kelly 1991:149; Suttles 1990:4). Among the Nootka and Kwakiutl, access to resources was inherited, but these ties were cognatically traced through both parents back to apical ancestors (Riches 1979:153). The flexibility of resource access has been much noted, and often rich food patches simply were vested with the most powerful man in a coresident group. Relative degrees of power often came down to faction size, so it is not surprising that group ideology maximized the control of manpower (Riches 1979:154). Slavery also contributed to household differences in labor force and wealth.

At the northern end of this Pacific coastal region, group sizes were larger and factions included more people than the extended family groupings found to the south. Matrilineal descent structures existed, but they tended to be fractious over time and had only a limited degree of solidarity (e.g., Oberg 1973:41). As found to the south, trade connections, marriage relations, and the control of labor and wealth remained critical foundations for status and power (Kelly 1991; Riches 1979). Within settlements, descent groups were ranked. But relative rank and position were based on wealth, and access to it varied over time with individually orchestrated flows of people and goods (Oberg 1973:38–64). The manipulation of corporate affiliation played a greater role in generating inequality than it did for groups to the south, but the primary pathway to inequalities in power and access remained network-based personal connections. The near-absence of monumental construction on the Northwest Coast is significant. Architecturally, the emphasis was on elaborate wooden houses that were associated with specific chiefs and their factions. Placement of families was regularized by rank within these structures.

It is instructive to compare the above descriptions with a similar synthesis of Polynesia, where major processes of diachronic change have been outlined (Kirch 1984:13–15). In this prior discussion of dominant trends, there is no mention of extraregional exchange, sumptuary display, the production of wealth items, or craft specialization. Obviously, such practices existed, but they were not judged to be core features. For example, nonagricultural economic specialization occurred only in the more stratified Polynesian societies. When craft specialization did occur, such specialists were numerically rare, and they often tended to make utilitarian goods. Only the largest, latest, most stratified Polynesian polities (e.g., Hawaii) had attached specialists (few in number) who produced wealth items for the elite (Kirch 1984:29). Rather, and in contrast with the Northwest Coast, greatest importance in Polynesia is given to agricultural intensification (food production), storage, the manufacture of utilitarian goods, and the construction of ceremonial or public (nonresidential) architecture (Kirch 1984:13–15). In addition, as argued specifically for highly stratified Hawaii, "everything depends on the strength and spread of solidarity in the kinship system" (Sahlins 1972:123).

These core features, and the lives of all Polynesians across the social spectrum, were further interconnected by food production, distribution, and consumption (Kirch 1984:29). The role of food, deftly described by Firth (1939) for Tikopia, is approximated across the geographic area (Kirch 1984:30).

> Food serves as a most important manifestation of social relationship, and through it kinship ties, political loyalty, indemnity for wrong, and the canons of hospitality are expressed. It also provides a basis for the initiation of other social relations, such as [those involved] in the acquisition of traditional lore. Again, the major

foodstuffs rest in totemic alignment with the major social groups; ritual appeals are made to the gods and ancestors who are regarded as the sources of food (Firth 1939:38).

Although different degrees of flexibility existed in political relations, Polynesian societies shared a strong ideological tendency toward patrilineage and primogeniture (Kirch 1984:34). Kin group membership and residence were the basis of land ownership, which was vested corporately with the senior males of the coresident group (Kirch 1984:31–32). The genealogical interrelations of these small segmentary corporate groups were linked together through the pyramidal geometry of the conical clan. At the apex of that pyramid was the chief, whose relationship to the commoners reproduced the familial bond between father and son. The chief mediated ritually between commoners and the gods to secure rain, fertility, and comestible bounty (Kirch 1984:37). This kinship rhetoric is a key integrative element of the corporate mode (Blanton et al. in press).

On Pukapuka, one of the least stratified Polynesian polities, there were only two status classes (chiefs and nonchiefs). The chief was considered sacred, and represented the people in rituals to the gods. But no elaborate symbols of office distinguished him from commoners, who were his kin. Various community councils regulated interpersonal affairs (Sahlins 1958:94). Chiefs did not exercise stewardship over land (Sahlins 1958:92). General decisions about agricultural production were reached in communal meetings of males (Kirch 1984:35). Reciprocal feasts and exchanges bound families, descent groups, and villages with no mention of food offerings going directly to the chief (Goldman 1970:386–388).

The social organization of Futuna was more hierarchical and stratified. There was a paramount chief as well as lineage chiefs. Symbols of rank were more developed than on Pukapuka, yet they were still rather minimal. Chiefs' houses were larger than average, and they were situated at the center of the community facing the village plaza (Kirch 1984:35). Nevertheless, as on Pukapuka, economic control was in the hands of kinship groups and the heads of households (Sahlins 1958:86–87). However, chiefs could impinge on this control to a degree through the mobilization of food production for feasts, rituals, and crisis events. Nevertheless, community councils, which also could collect and redistribute surplus foods, were at the crux of economic and social life, and chiefs had to work through these councils to obtain their produce.

In more highly stratified Tongan society, the paramount chief held titular control of the land. Districts and smaller parcels of land were managed in hierarchically embedded subdivisions by rank and kinship. Each manager was subordinate to the higher-ranked individual within whose domain he held stewardship (Sahlins 1958:24–25). Agricultural produce and drafts of communal labor were exacted through council edicts, although these generally began as chiefly decrees in regard to annual ritual cycles, life crisis rites, and mobilizations for public work projects (Sahlins 1958:24–25). Thus, chiefs had great powers, and they were set off from the rest of the population in dress, diet, and house construction. Yet, administrative decisions were still transmitted through the framework of hierarchically arranged councils in which different corporate descent segments were represented (Sahlins 1958:24–25, 198). Furthermore despite the scale and hierarchical complexity of Tongan society, real poverty was apparently not known to commoners (Mariner 1827:230).

These comparative observations illustrate that Polynesian chiefly power was rooted in a corporate-based structure. The Polynesian chief, as titular head, linked the branches of corporate descent, while connecting the gods with the earth and sea that yielded produce. As Kirch (1984:40) has noted: "that the chief occupied the central role in the rituals of production seems to be significant to the later evolution of Polynesian polities, for in the ritually sanctioned control of production lay the seeds of a political economy." "Religious activity formed an integral part of Polynesian economic practice, and it was in his control of ritual that the chief exercised significant power of production" (Kirch 1984:165). The marked difference between this more corporate-based organizational mode and that of wealth-based network systems (such as the Northwest Coast) is illustrated by an account of a Tongan chief when he was introduced to the nature of money (Mariner 1827:213–214).

> Certainly money is much handier, and more convenient, but then, as it will not spoil by being kept, people will store it up, instead of sharing it out, as a chief ought to do, and thus become selfish; whereas, if provisions were the principal property of man, and it ought to be, as being both the most useful and the most necessary, he could not store it up, for it would spoil, and so he would be obliged either to exchange it away for something else useful, or share it out to his neighbors, and inferior chiefs and dependents, for nothing.

The two pathways to greater inequality outlined above are not introduced to establish yet another synchronic societal typology. Rather, it is argued that these modes (corporate–network) have significant diachronic implications. If increasing inequality and stratification are to be understood in specific historical contexts, then the nature of interpersonal relations and faction building in that context must be evaluated. Many prior models have presumed that the basis of inequality lies primarily in either kin group relations and the control of land or the expansion of personal networks and the individual accumulation of personal wealth, but neither of these general frameworks has achieved consensus. What if a portion of this difficulty in reaching broad agreement cannot be attributed simply to scholarly intransigence and taste? Perhaps part of the problem lies in the fact that neither of these unilinear scenarios fits all historical cases equally well, simply because rather distinct alternate pathways to inequality and power have been historically followed. If so, the impact of changes in demography, climate, environment, and other stresses would have had markedly different effects on socioeconomic relations depending on the political-economic strategies that were in place in specific spatiotemporal settings. Nevertheless, it should be clear that this discussion is not a simple call for the abandonment of generalizing or comparative approaches to the study of societal change. Rather, while a broadening of such frameworks away from exogenous and unilineal perspectives is endorsed, the field must continue the search for broad parallels and contrasts (such as the corporate and network strategies) that can be recognized across specific historical sequences.

SUMMARY THOUGHTS

This discussion has outlined five recent theoretical breakthroughs that concern the changing manner in which the emergence and institutionalization of inequality is viewed by anthropologists and archaeologists. It has been suggested that this key socioeconomic process should no longer be conceptualized as a simple product of agricultural origins or severe population stress. Likewise, reconceptualizations of the nature of egalitarian social systems and the relationship between demography and socioeconomic complexity have been advanced. A more lengthy final section has challenged strict unilinear perspectives on this process by outlining two modal pathways to unequal distributions of prestige, power, and resources. For each of these topics, the revised perspectives themselves raise a suite of new research questions and issues. For example, what implications does the relationship between community size and inequality have for the role of sedentism in this general process? Are there different scalar limits for societies in which the corporate mode predominates as compared to those in which the network mode prevails? What factors engender change from one predominant mode to the other?

In sum, this effort endeavors to recast our intellectual agenda farther away from the presumption that any deviation from narrow environmental-demographic determinism and unilinear frameworks necessarily dooms our interpretive endeavors to the opposite pole of idiosyncratic particularism. If over the next decades we can concertedly avoid these two intellectual extremes, which have dominated our disciplinary past, then I suspect that the next generation of data and ideas will yield a more marked increase in our understanding of these issues than even has been achieved over the past quarter century.

ACKNOWLEDGMENTS

I wish to thank Richard E. Blanton, Linda M. Nicholas, T. Douglas Price, and Steadman Upham, who generously offered helpful comments and thoughtful editorial advice on earlier drafts of this chapter. Blanton's writings (and subsequent discussions that I have had with him) provided the crux of the distinction between the corporate and network modes.

REFERENCES

Aldenderfer, M., 1993, Ritual, Hierarchy, and Change in Foraging Societies, *Journal of Anthropological Archaeology* 12:1–40.

Arnold, J. E., 1993, Labor and the Rise of Complex Hunter-Gatherers, *Journal of Anthropological Archaeology* 12:75–119.

Bernard, H. R., and P. D. Killworth, 1973, On the Social Structure of an Ocean-Going Research Vessel and Other Important Things, *Social Science Research* 2:145–184.

Bernard, H. R., and P. D. Killworth, 1979, Why Are There No Social Physics? *Journal of the Steward Anthropological Society* 11:33–58.

Binford, L. R., 1983, In Pursuit of the Past: Decoding the Archaeological Record, Thames and Hudson, New York.

Bishop, C. A., 1987, Coast–Interior Exchange: The Origins of Stratification in Northwestern North America, *Arctic Anthropology* 24:72–83.

Blanton, R. E., G. M. Feinman, S. A. Kowalewski, and P. N. Peregrine, in press, A Dual-Processual Theory for the Evolution of Mesoamerican Civilization, *Current Anthropology*.

Brown, P., and A. Podolefsky, 1976, Population Density, Agricultural Intensity, Land Tenure, and Group Size in the New Guinea Highlands, *Ethnology* 15:211–238.

Carneiro. R. L., 1967, On the Relationship between Size of Population and Complexity of Social Organization, *Southwestern Journal of Anthropology* 23:234–243.

Carneiro, R. L., 1981, The Chiefdom: Precursor of the State, in: *The Transition to Statehood in the New World* (G. D. Jones and R. R. Kautz, eds.), Cambridge University Press, Cambridge, pp. 37–79.

Cashdan, E. A., 1980, Egalitarianism among Hunters and Gatherers, *American Anthropologist* 82:116–120.

Childe, V. G., 1951, *Man Makes Himself*, C. A. Watts, London.

Clark, J. E., and M. Blake, 1994, The Power of Prestige: Competitive Generosity and the Emergence of Rank Societies in Lowland Mesoamerica, in: *Factional Competition and Political Development in the New World* (E. M. Brumfiel and J. W. Fox, eds.), Cambridge University Press, Cambridge, pp. 17–30.

Cohen, M. N., 1981, Pacific Coast Foragers: Affluent or Overcrowded? in: *Affluent Foragers* (S. Koyama and D. Thomas, eds.), National Museum of Ethnology, Senri Ethnological Studies 9, Osaka, pp. 275–295.

Collier, J. F., and M. Z. Rosaldo, 1981, Politics and Gender in Simple Societies, in: *Sexual Meanings: The Cultural Construction of Gender and Sexuality* (Sherry B. Ortner and Harriet Whitehead, eds.), Cambridge University Press, Cambridge, pp. 275–329.

D'Altroy, T. N., and T. K. Earle, 1985, Staple Finance, Wealth Finance, and Storage in the Inka Political Economy, *Current Anthropology* 26:187–206.

Drennan, R. D., 1987, Regional Demography in Chiefdoms: in: *Chiefdoms in the Americas* (R. D. Drennan and C. A. Uribe, eds.), University Press of America, Lanham, Maryland, pp. 307–324.

Drennan, R. D., 1991, Pre-Hispanic Chiefdom Trajectories in Mesoamerica, Central America, and Northern South America, in: *Chiefdoms: Power, Economy, and Ideology* (T. Earle, ed.), Cambridge University Press, Cambridge, pp. 263–287.

Drucker, P., 1939, Rank, Wealth, and Kinship in Northwest Coast Society, *American Anthropologist* 41:55–65.

Ember, M., 1963, The Relationship between Economic and Political Development in Nonindustrialized Societies, *Ethnology* 2:228–248.

Feinman, G. M., 1991, Demography, Surplus, and Inequality: Early Political Formations in Highland Mesoamerica, in: *Chiefdoms: Power, Economy, and Ideology* (T. Earle, ed.), Cambridge University Press, Cambridge, pp. 229–262.

Feinman, G. M., and J. Neitzel, 1984, Too Many Types: An Overview of Sedentary Prestate Societies in the Americas, *Advances in Archaeological Method and Theory* 7:39–102.

Firth, R., 1939, *Primitive Polynesian Economy*, George Routledge and Sons, London.

Flanagan, J. G., 1989, Hierarchy in Simple "Egalitarian" Societies, *Annual Review of Anthropology* 18:245–266.

Flannery, K. V., 1983, Divergent Evolution, in: *The Cloud People: Divergent Evolution of the Zapotec and Mixtec Civilizations* (K. V. Flannery and J. Marcus, eds.), Academic Press, New York, pp. 1–4.

Flannery, K. V., and J. Marcus, 1993, Cognitive Archaeology, *Cambridge Archaeological Journal* 3:260–270.

Forge, A., 1972, Normative Factors in the Settlement Size of Neolithic Cultivators (New Guinea), in: *Man, Settlement, and Urbanism* (P. J. Ucko, R. Tringham, and G. W. Dimblebly, eds.), Duckworth, London, pp. 363–376.

Fried, M. H., 1967, *The Evolution of Political Society: An Essay in Political Anthropology*, Random House, New York.

Friedman, J., and M. J. Rowlands, 1978, Notes towards an Epigenetic Model of the Evolution of 'Civilisation,' in: *The Evolution of Social Systems* (J. Friedman and M. J. Rowlands, eds.), University of Pittsburgh Press, Pittsburgh, pp. 201–276.

Giddens, A., 1984, *The Constitution of Society: Outline of the Theory of Structuration*, University of California Press, Berkeley.

Goldman, I., 1970, *Ancient Polynesian Society*, University of Chicago Press, Chicago.

Gould, R. A., 1966, The Wealth Quest among the Tolowa Indians of Northwestern California, *Proceedings of the American Philosophical Society* 110:67–89.

Harris, M., 1979, *Cultural Materialism: The Struggle for a Science of Culture*, Random House, New York.

Hayden, B., and R. Gargett, 1990, Big Man, Big Heart? A Mesoamerican View of the Emergence of Complex Society, *Ancient Mesoamerica* 1:3–20.

Hodder, I., 1985, Postprocessual Archaeology, *Advances in Archaeological Method and Theory* 8:1–26.

Johnson, G. A., 1982, Organizational Structure and Scalar Stress, in: *Theory and Explanation in Archaeology: The Southampton Conference* (C. Renfrew, M. J. Rowlands, and B. A. Segraves, eds.), Academic Press, New York, pp. 389–421.

Johnson, G. A., 1989, Dynamics of Southwestern Prehistory: Far Outside—Looking in, in: *Dynamics of Southwest Prehistory* (L. S. Cordell and G. J. Gumerman, eds.), Smithsonian Institution Press, Washington, D.C., pp. 371–389.

Keeley, L. H., 1988, Hunter-Gatherer Economic Complexity and "Population Pressure": A Cross-Cultural Analysis, *Journal of Anthropological Archaeology* 7:373–411.

Kelly, R. C., 1993, *Constructing Inequality: The Fabrication of a Hierarchy of Virtue among the Etoro*, University of Michigan Press, Ann Arbor.

Kelly, R. L., 1991, Sedentism, Sociopolitical Inequality, and Resource Fluctuations, in: *Between Bands and States* (S. A. Gregg, ed.), Occasional Paper No. 9, Center for Archaeological Investigations, Southern Illinois University, Carbondale, pp. 135–158.

Kirch, P. V., 1984, *The Evolution of the Polynesian Chiefdoms*, Cambridge University Press, Cambridge.

Kosse, K., 1990, Group Size and Societal Complexity: Thresholds in the Long-Term Memory, *Journal of Anthropological Archaeology* 9:275–303.

Koyama, S., and D. H. Thomas (eds.), 1982, *Affluent Foragers*, Senri Ethnological Studies 9, National Museum of Ethnology, Osaka.

Kristiansen, K., 1991, Chiefdoms, States, and Systems of Social Evolution, in: *Chiefdoms, Power, Economy, and Ideology* (T. Earle, ed.), Cambridge University Press, Cambridge, pp. 16–43.

Lekson, S. H., 1985, Largest Settlement Size and the Interpretation of Socio-Political Complexity at Chaco Canyon, New Mexico, *Haliksa'i: UNM Contributions to Anthropology* 4:68–75.

Lenski, G., and J. Lenski, 1987, *Human Societies: An Introduction to Macrosociology*, fifth edition, MacGraw-Hill, New York.

Lightfoot, K. G., and G. M. Feinman, 1982, Social Differentiation and Leadership Development in Early Pithouse Villages in the Mogollon Region of the American Southwest, *American Antiquity* 47:64–86.

Linares, O., 1977, *Ecology and the Arts in Ancient Panama: On the Development of Social Rank and Symbolism in the Central Provinces*, Dumbarton Oaks, Washington, D.C.

Lothrop, S. K., 1937, *Coclé: An Archaeological Study of Central Panama, Part 1,* Memoirs of the Peabody Museum of Archaeology and Ethnology, vol. 7, Harvard University, Cambridge.

Lothrop, S. K., 1942, *Coclé: An Archaeological Study of Central Panama, Part 2,* Memoirs of the Peabody Museum of Archaeology and Ethnology, vol. 7, Harvard University, Cambridge.

Marcus, J., 1989, Zapotec Chiefdoms and the Nature of Formative Religions, in: *Regional Perspectives on the Olmec* (R. J. Sharer and D. C. Grove, eds.), Cambridge University Press, Cambridge, pp. 148–197.

Mariner, W., 1827, *An Account of the Tongan Islands in the South Pacific Ocean* (J. Martin, ed.), 2 vols., third edition, Constable Press, Edinburgh.

Maschner, H. D. G., 1991, The Emergence of Cultural Complexity on the Northern Northwest Coast, *Antiquity* 65:924–934.

Maschner, H. D. G., 1992, *The Origins of Hunter and Gatherer Sedentism and Political Complexity: A Case Study from the Northern Northwest Coast*, Ph.D. dissertation, University of California, Santa Barbara.

Maybury-Lewis, D., 1974, *Akwe-Shavante Society*, Oxford University Press, New York.

Naroll, R., 1956, A Preliminary Index of Social Development, *American Anthropologist* 58:687–715.

Oberg, K., 1973, *The Social Economy of the Tlingit Indians*, University of Washington Press, Seattle.

Paynter, R., 1989, The Archaeology of Equality and Inequality, *Annual Review of Anthropology* 18:369–399.

Paynter, R., and R. H. McGuire, 1991, The Archaeology of Inequality: Material Culture, Domination, and Resistance, in: *The Archaeology of Inequality* (R. H. McGuire and R. Paynter, eds.), Blackwell, Oxford, pp. 1–27.

Pearson, H. W., 1957, The Economy Has No Surplus: Critique of a Theory of Development, in: *Trade and Market in the Early Empires* (K. Polanyi, C. M. Arensberg, and H. W. Pearson, eds.), Henry Regnery, Chicago, pp. 320–341.

Plog, S., 1990, Agriculture, Sedentism, and Environment in the Evolution of Political Systems, in:

The Evolution of Political Systems: Sociopolitics in Small-Scale Sedentary Societies (S. Upham, ed.), Cambridge University Press, Cambridge, pp. 177–199.

Plog, S., and D. P. Braun, 1984, Some Issues in the Archaeology of "Tribal" Social Systems, *American Antiquity* 49:619–625.

Price, T. D., and J. A. Brown (eds.), 1985a, *Prehistoric Hunter-Gatherers: The Emergence of Cultural Complexity,* Academic Press, San Diego.

Price, T. D., and J. A. Brown, 1985b, Aspects of Hunter-Gatherer Complexity, in: *Prehistoric Hunter-Gatherers: The Emergence of Cultural Complexity* (T. D. Price and J. A. Brown, eds.), Academic Press, San Diego, pp. 3–20.

Pyne, N. M., 1976, The Fire-Serpent and Were-Jaguar in Formative Oaxaca: A Contingency Table Analysis, in: *The Early Mesoamerican Village* (K. V. Flannery, ed.), Academic Press, Orlando, pp. 272–282.

Renfrew, C., 1974, Beyond a Subsistence Economy: The Evolution of Social Organization in Prehistoric Europe, in: *Reconstructing Complex Societies* (C. B. Moore, ed.), Supplement to the Bulletin of the American Schools of Oriental Research, No. 20, Cambridge, pp. 69–85.

Riches, D., 1979, Ecological Variation on the Northwest Coast: Models for the Generation of Cognatic and Matrilineal descent, in: *Social and Ecological Systems* (P. C. Burnham and R. F. Ellen, eds.), Academic Press, London, pp. 146–166.

Sahlins, M. D., 1958, *Social Stratification in Polynesia,* University of Washington Press, Seattle.

Sahlins, M. D., 1963, Poor Man, Rich Man, Big-Man, Chief: Political Types in Melanesia and Polynesia, *Comparative Studies in Sociology and History* 5:285–303.

Sahlins, M. D., 1972, *Stone Age Economics,* Aldine, Chicago.

Sahlins, M. D., and E. R. Service (eds.), 1960, *Evolution and Culture,* University of Michigan Press, Ann Arbor.

Sanders, W. T., and D. Webster, 1978, Unilinealism, Multilinealism, and Evolution of Complex Societies, in: *Social Archaeology: Beyond Subsistence and Dating* (C. Redman, M. Berman, E. Curtis, W. Langhorne, N. Versaggi, and J. Wanser, eds.), Academic Press, New York, pp. 249–302.

Sanderson, S. K., 1990, *Social Evolutionism: A Critical History,* Blackwell, Cambridge, Massachusetts.

Service, E. R., 1971, *Primitive Social Organization: An Evolutionary Perspective,* second edition, Random House, New York.

Spencer, C. S., 1990, On the Tempo and Mode of State Formation: Neoevolutionism Revisited, *Journal of Anthropological Archaeology* 9:1–30.

Spencer, C. S., 1993, Human Agency, Biased Transmission, and the Cultural Evolution of Chiefly Authority, *Journal of Anthropological Archaeology* 12:41–74.

Strathern, A., 1969, Finance and Production: Two Strategies in New Guinea Highlands Exchange Systems, *Oceania* 40:42–67.

Strathern, A., 1978, "Finance and Production" Revisited: In Pursuit of a Comparison, *Research in Economic Anthropology* 1:73–104.

Suttles, W., 1990, Introduction, in: *Handbook of North American Indians, vol. 7, Northwest Coast* (W. Suttles, ed.), Smithsonian Institution, Washington, D.C., pp. 1–15.

Trigger, B. G., 1989, *A History of Archaeological Thought,* Cambridge University Press, Cambridge.

Upham, S., 1987, A Theoretical Consideration of Middle Range Societies, in: *Chiefdoms in the Americas* (R. D. Drennan and C. A. Uribe, eds.), University Press of America, Lanham, Maryland, pp. 345–367.

Upham, S., 1990, Decoupling the Processes of Political Evolution, in: *The Evolution of Political Systems: Sociopolitics in Small-Scale Sedentary Societies* (S. Upham, ed.), Cambridge University Press, Cambridge, pp. 1–17.

Werner, D., 1981, Are Some People More Equal than Others? Status Inequality among the Mekranoti Indians of Central Brazil, *Journal of Anthropological Research* 37:360–373.

White, L. A., 1943, Energy and the Evolution of Culture, *American Anthropologist* 45:335–356.

Yesner, D. R., 1980, Maritime Hunter-Gatherers: Ecology and Prehistory, with CA Comment, *Current Anthropology* 21:727–750.

Yesner, D. R., 1987, Life in the "Garden of Eden": Causes and Consequences of the Adoption of Marine Diets by Human Societies, in: *Food and Evolution* (M. Harris and E. Ross, eds.), Temple University Press, Philadelphia, pp. 285–310.

Yoffee, N., 1985, Perspectives on Trends toward Social Complexity in Prehistoric Australia and Papua New Guinea, *Archaeology in Oceania* 20:41–49.

Index